# THE FIRST VIETNAM WAR

PETER M. DUNN

# The First
# Vietnam War

ST. MARTIN'S PRESS, NEW YORK

St. Martin's Press, Inc., 175 Fifth Avenue, New York, NY 10010
Printed in Great Britain
First published in the United States of America in 1985
ISBN 0-312-29314-3

## Library of Congress Cataloging in Publication Data

Dunn, Peter M.
   The first Vietnam War.

   Bibliography: p.
   Includes index.
   1. Indochinese War, 1946–1954.   I. Title.
DS553.1.D86   1985        959.704'1        84–17842
ISBN 0-312-29314-3

# CONTENTS

# PLATES

# MAPS

# PREFACE AND ACKNOWLEDGMENTS

Over the past two decades the name Vietnam has become familiar to people in every part of the world. America found herself heavily engaged there, almost through oversight, in one of the longest, most frustrating and least successful wars in her history. France had earlier fought a scarcely less frustrating and unpopular war there, and encountered even less success. Yet another war, which antedated these two larger conflicts, remains almost unknown beyond the dwindling circle of those directly involved, except to a handful of specialist scholars. From this first struggle, which involved British, Vietnamese, French, Japanese and, less directly, Americans, though localized and short in duration, came the factors which governed the two subsequent wars. For this reason it is of very great historical importance. Without knowledge of what happened in this earlier struggle it is impossible fully to understand the two later wars.

Britain, whose forces under General Douglas Gracey occupied Saigon immediately after the Second World War, became the first Western democracy to clash with a Communist-led revolution in Asia. It is probable that, by frustrating the Viet Minh's desperate seizure of power, Gracey afforded South Vietnam the opportunity of resisting the communist takeover which befell North Vietnam in 1954 and of continuing to defend her freedom for the next three decades.

Some, even before the primary source material had become available for study, rushed to criticize Gracey's action as little more than an imperialist bid to "keep the natives in their place". Recent developments may have given them cause to regret their impetuosity, for, among other things, the natives are today more securely kept in their place than they had ever been before. Whatever the imperfections of her own regimes — compared with those of the communist successor-regime, these appear very minor — South Vietnam survived for three decades, much of the time under intense and unrelenting pressures from a grim totalitarian North Vietnam supported by the resources of the entire communist world and even of some countries of the free world — Sweden, for example. That survival was made possible largely by the achievements of that early British occupation.

For readers in the United States the story contains salutary reminders of the fallibility of some American policymakers, and they may be persuaded to reflect before criticizing the efforts of others in South East

Asia. Unshakeable belief in one's own rightness tends to blind, especially when it is tinged with self-interest. China, North Vietnam, Laos , and later South Vietnam were deemed by the United States to be American responsibilities; all are communist today. Burma, Malaya, Singapore, Thailand, Indonesia, and Northern Borneo were British responsibilities; they are all anti-communist today. This is not an oversimplification.

On wartime Indochina, there are questions that still remain unanswered and may never be answered satisfactorily, of which the following are but a few. Why did the USAAF shoot down two, possibly three, RAF aircraft in bright moonlight? Why did Americans help the common enemy, the Japanese, to keep Allied prisoners locked up in camps after the war was over? Why, during the war, did the United States adamantly oppose the transfer to Indochina of the French force which might have destroyed Ho Chi Minh's communist movement before it could establish itself? Were certain sections of the OSS in Southeast Asia simply as naive and ignorant as now appears, or were they ideologically motivated to act as they did — or both? How did the Viet Minh use the hundreds of millions of piasters which they received from the Japanese? How did the communists manage to convince some historians that they were organized and running an effective government in Saigon?

At times it seemed that in South East Asia the United States was as concerned to oppose her own allies, Britain and France, as she was to fight the Japanese. In Vietnam a later generation of Americans reaped a bitter harvest from the seeds sown during the waning hours of the Second World War. For whatever reason, the United States opposed her own allies while doing all in her power to protect Ho Chi Minh and advance the cause of his Vietnamese communists; for it was these who formed the Viet Minh, and without their control over it the movement would certainly have foundered. This United States opposition to Britain and France might even be viewed as the first in the series of Vietnam wars. Indeed, the clash of policies resulted in loss of life — the destruction of the RAF aircraft, the annihilation of the French groups, and the murder of individual French officers such as Captain Klotz (executed under the complaisant gaze of personnel of the OSS "Raven" mission in Laos, discussed later). US-French relations deteriorated to such a point that, after the war, the United States objected to the transfer of British Mosquito aircraft to France because the propellors were American-made and hence subject to lend-lease regulations.

The initial refusal of strong nearby US forces to intervene to prevent

the Japanese pursuit of retreating or cornered French groups came, ironically, only a few months after Americans had deplored Stalin's refusal
to permit nearby Soviet forces to intervene to prevent the German destruction of the Poles in Warsaw. De Gaulle — and France — never
forgot it. When it was America's turn in Vietnam she found herself
without large-scale support in fighting the monster she had herself
helped to create, and which influential segments of her own society were
still helping to sustain. Many Americans never understood why there
was so little European support for their own Vietnam war.

Saigon in the later part of 1945 was the scene of the most complex
intrigue and action. Four major groups, each with its own sub-groups,
maneuvered in the still elegant city in delicate equilibrium — Vietnamese, French, Japanese and the British/Indian forces. America was
also represented by a small OSS mission, although the sum total of its
achievement was to have itself shot up and its leader killed. Had the
wishes of certain factions of the OSS been satisfied, the terrible happen-
ings in Indochina since 1975 might well have occurred years earlier.

Next some words of explanation concerning the text. Messages and telegrams usually omit understood words such as "the" and "I" so that
messages cited verbatim may be found to read somewhat inelegantly.
But I have considered it preferable to retain the original text rather than
intersperse it with explanations or cosmetic additions; also I have let
much of the original material speak for itself rather than paraphrase it.

I have ascribed all revolutionary and insurrectionist activity in Cochinchina to the Viet Minh. Readers should bear in mind that some of the
fighting described was done by sectarian groups, bandits, and rogue
Japanese who acted on their own. All of these were relatively unsophis-
ticated by comparison with the trained communist cadres, and most
groups operated, at least nominally, under the Viet Minh umbrella.

Most of my background material deals with what I call the "Mountbatten–Wedemeyer dispute" over pre-operational clandestine activity in
Indochina. This may have had a decisive influence on the course of that
region's history. In this regard I draw attention to the Appendix to
Chapter 4 (pp. 113–18). General Wedemeyer has now commented on
his instructions from President Roosevelt regarding Indochina, and this
information was added after the completion of the first draft of the
manuscript.

The translations from French documents, books, and personal correspondence are my own and, while they may possibly contain minor tech-

nical errors, I believe the thrust of the originals is retained. Vietnamese diacritical marks are both difficult and expensive for Western typesetters to reproduce, and for that reason all such marks have been omitted. The book itself is based on the research I conducted for my doctoral dissertation (a much longer work) for the School of Oriental and African Studies, University of London. That research was conducted in three continents. Sources include newly-released archival material in the Public Record Office, London, and the National Archives, Washington (abbreviated throughout as PRO and NA respectively); official and unofficial published material in the British Library, the Imperial War Museum, the French Army's Historical Service in Paris, and papers of senior British officers in the Liddell Hart Centre for Military Archives, King's College (London University). Personal interviews were also conducted with key contemporary British, French, American, and Vietnamese military and civil officials. Of vital importance were the personal papers of the Allied Force Commander in Saigon, the late General Sir Douglas D. Gracey. These papers had never previously been examined, and they shed a great deal of light on events in Saigon in 1945–6; they also refute much of what has been written on this period by a variety of historians.

Pertinent French records of the period remain closed, but interviews with key French officials have answered the most important questions. The Mountbatten papers are not available for scholarly research at this time. The greatest gaps concern the activities of the Viet Minh. Its organization at that time was rudimentary and, since the movement was actively engaged in armed revolution, it possessed no facility for the maintenance of records. Consequently there exist no Viet Minh archives to be consulted, and most of the participants in Viet Minh activity had either died or were inaccessible. This makes the recollections of Nguyen De and other Vietnamese witnesses all the more valuable.

The long years of armed struggle in Vietnam, with repercussions in so many areas, personal, national, and international, make it a most difficult undertaking to write a completely objective history. There are no neutrals on Vietnam.

## Acknowledgments

It is improbable that this work would have been written, at least at this time, without the help and encouragement of Professor P. J. Honey, whose interest in the subject led to my admission to the School of Oriental and African Studies. His unique knowledge of Vietnam, its people, and its language has been invaluable in helping me to understand the background of the events described in this book. My thanks must also go to Professor Michael Howard, now Regius Professor of Modern History, Oxford University, who first directed me towards Professor Honey. I am in the debt of Mr J. T. Bishop, the Registrar, and to the administration of the School of Oriental and African Studies, which made special arrangements for me to enter the school in the middle of the term and so to organize my studies that they would fit in with my status as a serving officer in the US Air Force.

To Lady (Cecil) Gracey goes my deepest gratitude for her generous permission to study the papers of her late husband, General Gracey, around whom this story inevitably revolves. They shed much light on a most capable man of remarkable character who grappled successfully with extraordinarily complex problems.

I very much appreciate the assistance of Mr John Taylor of the US National Archives in Washington, who was of great help in steering me through the masses of War Department and OSS files now available for study.

Yet no quantity of archival material can match in interest a first-hand account of a participant in the event, and these key contemporary military and civilian officials allowed me to bring the story to life and to quote them where needed: Louis Allen, Hugh Astor, P. C. Bastit, Charles Blascheck, Sir Norman Brain, Jean Cédile, Sir Walter Cheshire, Robert Clark, François de Langlade, E. Gibbons, E. Gopsill, Lady Gracey, P. J. Honey, Cyril Jarvis, Michael Kelleher, Sir Brian Kimmins, P. G. Malins, Jacques Massu, M. S. K. Maunsell, Pierre Messmer, Marcel Mingant, E. C. W. Myers, Nguyen De, Richard Ogden, Peter Prentice, Raoul Salan, H. Vallat, A. G. Trevor-Wilson, D. E. Taunton, A. C. Wedemeyer, and E. C. J. Woodford. My sincere thanks go also to a former RAF Squadron Leader, still in government service at the time of this writing, who wished to remain unnamed. Particular thanks go to Lady (Mary) Cheshire and Mrs Ruth Maunsell for giving permission for their husbands' words to be used.

All the personal accounts were enlightening and some fascinating, while a few were of particular interest for what was left unsaid. This was certainly due in part to a desire not to disclose classified information, and to protect individuals, even so long after the events. However, both British and American archives of that period have now been declassified with the exception of small amounts of particularly sensitive material.

I very much regret that three of the principal figures mentioned here have died since they contributed to this work; Brigadier Mark Maunsell, Air Chief Marshal Sir Walter Cheshire and Lieutenant-General Sir Brian Kimmins. Their participation was extremely important, and deeply appreciated.

About ten years ago a Major Stewart in the Ministry of Defence, London, helped me to obtain a 1945 Saigon street plan from the British Army's map depot; this was vital to my fixing locations and events, since all Saigon area coordinates referenced in the British archives were keyed to this grid. Without this map I would have walked the streets of Saigon in vain. I am most grateful for for this bit of help.

Special thanks must go to several senior US Air Force officers from Lieutenant-General to Colonel, who supported my request for unpaid leave to complete my studies at SOAS. Interest in learning more of recent Indochina history and their strong letters of support for this study overcame the lack of interest of the civilians who administer the US Air Force Education Program. This year of leave was the key to the completion of this work. Thanks also to Drs Robert Gregg, H. Fowler, Rosemary Masek, and Banu Churchill for their letters of support.

I gratefully acknowledge the following bodies for the permission to quote from the named material: The Institute of Royal Engineers, *The Royal Engineers Journal*, "Sappers and Miners in Saigon" by Major J. H. Clark; the University of Durham and the Editor, *The Durham University Journal*, "Studies in the Japanese Occupation of South-East Asia 1942–1945 (II)" by Louis Allen; Her Majesty's Stationery Office, *British Military Administration in the Far East, 1943–46* by F. S. V. Donnison; The Royal Society for Asian Affairs, *The Journal of the Royal Central Asian Society*, "General Gracey and the Viet Minh" by Dennis Duncanson and "Aspects of the Present Situation in Indo-China" by Melvin Hall; the Trustees and Librarian of the Liddell Hart Centre for Military Archives, King's College, University of London, for permission to quote from the papers of Generals Ismay, Penney, and Pyman; the Trustees of the Broadlands Archives for permission to reproduce portions of a letter from Lord Mountbatten to General Gracey; Mr Michael Charlton, British Broadcasting Corporation, for permission to draw on his series "Many Reasons Why"; Nguyen Duc Minh, for letting me quote from his unpublished doctoral dissertation at London University, "A Study of the Literature of Political Persuasion in North Vietnam"; the Department of Photographs, Imperial War Museum; and the Historical Office of the late South Vietnamese Joint General Staff for photographs.

My thanks also go to Miss Phan Thi Nhu, who interpreted for me when in 1972 I retraced Gracey's steps in Saigon, and who took photographs of key points for me after I left Indochina. Similarly, Major Le Van Ban, a historian with the South Vietnamese Joint General Staff, showed interest in this research, and on occasion gave my feet a rest by accompanying me throughout Saigon in his Jeep. I hope they all got out.

There were so many documents studied, so many places visited, so much correspondence, and so many people seen during the ten years — on and off — that this project has taken as it competed with extremely demanding military duties that it is likely that I have failed to mention someone who helped me. If so, it was unintentional, and I apologize.

Finally, my thanks and gratitude go to the indispensable half of this team, my wife Jill, who did so much to provide the environment in which the work was done.

The opinions expressed herein are entirely my own and in no way represent those of any military or civilian officials, agencies, or organizations of any part of the US Government.

PETER M. DUNN

# ABBREVIATIONS AND DEFINITIONS

| | |
|---|---|
| ABCD | American British Chinese Dutch |
| ACSEA | Air Commander South East Asia |
| ADM | Administration, Admiralty |
| ALFFIC | Allied Land Forces French Indo China |
| AGAS | Air-Ground Aid Service |
| ALFSEA | Allied Land Forces South East Asia |
| AOC | Air Officer Commanding |
| APWI | Allied Prisoners of War and Internees |
| ARGONAUT | Yalta Conference |
| Bde | Brigade |
| BIBBER | Occupation of Siam |
| BIRDCAGE | Leaflet drops on POW camps, Far East |
| BMA | British Military Administration |
| Bn | Battalion |
| BO | British Officer |
| BOR | British Other Rank (Enlisted Man) |
| BRITCHIN | British Forces China |
| BT | British Troops |
| CA | Civil Affairs |
| CAS | Civil Affairs Service |
| CBI | China–Burma–India Theater (US) |
| CCS | Combined Chiefs of Staff |
| CIGS | Chief of the Imperial General Staff |
| C-in-C | Commander-in-Chief |
| CLI | *Corps Léger d'Intervention* (French Light Intervention Corps) |
| Comd | Commander |
| COS | Chiefs of Staff |
| COSSEA | Chiefs of Staff to South East Asia (message designator) |
| Coy | Company |
| CSDIC | Combined Services Detailed Interrogation Centre |
| CT | China Theater |
| DB | *Division Blindée* (French Armored Division) |
| DGER | *Direction Générale des Etudes et Recherches* |
| DIC | *Division Infanterie Coloniale* |
| Div | Division |

| | |
|---|---|
| FCNL | French Committee of National Liberation |
| FFR | Frontier Force Rifles; Frontier Force Regiment |
| FIC | French Indo China |
| FO | Foreign Office |
| Force 136 | SOE in the Far East |
| GO | Gurkha Officer |
| GOR | Gurkha Other Rank |
| Havildar | Indian Sergeant, Indian Army (of any religion) |
| HMG | His Majesty's Government |
| Hybad | Hyderabad |
| IBT | India Burma Theatre |
| IEME | Indian Electrical and Mechanical Engineers |
| Ind Inf Bde | Indian Infantry Brigade |
| IO | Indian Officer |
| IOR | Indian Other Rank |
| Jemadar | VCO in Indian Army, performing duties of a 2nd Lieutenant (troop or platoon commander) |
| JPS | Joint Planning Staff |
| LAD | Light Aid Detachment |
| LMG | Light Machine-Gun |
| MASTERDOM | Reoccupation of southern French Indochina |
| MG | Machine-Gun |
| MASTIFF | Medical Supply Drops and POW Evacuation, Far East |
| Naik | Indian Corporal, Indian Army |
| NEI | Netherlands East Indies |
| OO | Operation Order |
| OSS | Office of Strategic Services |
| PAO | Principal Administrative Officer |
| PHPS | Post Hostilities Planning Staff |
| PIAT | Projector Infantry Anti-Tank |
| PID | Political Intelligence Department (Foreign Office) |
| Pn, Pl | Platoon |
| POW | Prisoner-of-War |
| PRO | Public Record Office |
| PYTHON | Repatriation of British forces personnel to UK after a defined period of overseas service |
| QUADRANT | First Quebec Conference |
| RA | Royal Artillery |
| RAF | Royal Air Force |
| RAPWI | Repatriation of Allied Prisoners-of-War and Internees |

| REME | Royal Electrical and Mechanical Engineers |
|------|-------------------------------------------|
| RN | Royal Navy |
| RIASC | Royal Indian Army Service Corps |
| RIC | *Régiment d'Infanterie Coloniale* |
| RIEME | Royal Indian Electrical and Mechanical Engineers |
| SA | *Service d'Action* |
| SA(A) | Small Arms (Ammunition) |
| SAC | Supreme Allied Commander |
| SACSEA | Supreme Allied Commander South East Asia |
| SCAP | Supreme Commander Allied Powers (General MacArthur) |
| SD | Special Duty (RAF) |
| SEAC | South East Asia Command |
| SEACOS | South East Asia to Chiefs of Staff (message designator) |
| SEXTANT | Cairo Conference |
| SOE | Special Operations Executive |
| SR | *Services des Renseignements* |
| Subadar | VCO in Indian Army, performing duties of 1st Lieutenant |
| Subadar Major | Battalion Commander's Adviser on Indian matters affecting the battalion; exercised special authority over the VCOs |
| SWPA | South West Pacific Area |
| TIDERACE | Plan for rapid occupation of Singapore |
| TPS | Troops |
| TPT | Transport |
| USAAF | United States Army Air Force |
| USG | United States Government |
| VCO | Viceroy's Commissioned Officer (Jemadars and Subadars, who were granted commissions by the Viceroy of India; 2nd Lieutenants and up were KCOs, or King's Commissioned Officers) |
| VP | Vital/Vulnerable Point |
| ZIPPER | Plan for capture of Port Swettenham and Port Dickson areas |

*Examples of regimental designations*

| 4/10 GR | 4th Battalion, 10th Regiment, Gurkha Rifles |
|---------|---------------------------------------------|
| 4/17 Dogra | 4th Battalion, 17th Dogra Regiment |

# 1

# BACKGROUND:
# THE COMMUNISTS AND
# THE VIET MINH

While our primary focus is on the post-war Allied occupation of Saigon, it is necessary to place the Viet Minh in context as one of the major contenders for power during this crucial period. And since the Viet Minh was a classic example of a Communist umbrella organization, the supreme role played by Indochina's first Communist, Ho Chi Minh, must be examined.

Ho Chi Minh was most widely known as Nguyen Ai Quoc until 1940, 1941 or 1943 (opinions differ on this). For simplicity he will be referred to as Ho Chi Minh throughout this book. It may be that the final challenge to France in Indochina began, ironically, in France just after the First World War. The young Ho Chi Minh was there in the course of extensive travels, which have been well documented. He had left Indochina in 1911 at the age of twenty-one and was not to return for thirty years.

In 1920, after Lenin had published his *Theses on the National and Colonial Questions* for the Second Congress of the Communist International, Ho was in Paris. A friend gave him a copy of Lenin's *Theses*, in which he hoped to find the answer to his question as to which International (the Second or Lenin's Third) sided with the peoples of colonial countries. When Ho had earlier raised the question at a meeting, he was told that it was the Third, and given the *Theses*. He read and re-read the paper, making sure that he clearly understood every line of it. Then, to use his own words, "What emotion, enthusiasm, clear-sightedness, and confidence it instilled in me! I was overjoyed to tears. Though sitting alone in my room I shouted aloud as if addressing large crowds: 'Dead martyrs, compatriots! this is what we need, this is the path to liberation!' After then, I had entire confidence in Lenin, in the Third International."[1]

Here was the fountainhead of his inspiration, of what became a trickle

---

1. Bernard B. Fall (ed.), *Ho Chi Minh on Revolution* (New York: Signet Books, 1968), pp. 23–4.

1

and eventually a torrent which washed the French and then the Americans out of Indochina. The Theses addressed fifteen groups of peoples, from the Polish Jews to the Irish and the American Negroes. One of the fifteen was less specific, a sort of catch-all labelled "Colonies", in which fell places like Indochina.[2]

Lenin warned that the Western bourgeoisie was perpetuating inequality and class differences by "pretending that all men are absolutely equal." The Communist Party must base its national policy on solid principles based on local (economic) situations; the revolutions would overthrow the landowners and holders of wealth. Fifty years later, much of that plan has been fulfilled. Lenin's words are still valid:

All events in world politics are inevitably revolving around one central point, *viz.* the struggle of the world bourgeoisie against the Soviet Russian Republic, around which are inevitably grouping, on the one hand, the movement for Soviets among the advanced workers of all countries, and, on the other, all the national liberation movements in the colonies and among the oppressed nationalities, whom bitter experience is teaching that there can be no salvation for them except in the victory of the Soviet system over world imperialism.

Only the Soviet system could grant real equality to nations, and it was "necessary that all Communist Parties render direct aid to the revolutionary movements among the dependent and subject nations (for example, in Ireland and among the Negroes of America) and in the colonies." This last statement was of prime importance; the Communist Parties *must* assist the revolutionary movements. It set the Third International apart from the Second.

What most impressed the young Ho Chi Minh were the comments directed specifically "to the more backward states and nations, in which feudal or patriarchal and patriarchal-peasant relations predominate". There were six main points. First, all Communist Parties must involve themselves in the liberation movements, which must be led by workers, not peasants. Second and third, to combat the clergy and Pan-Islamism (of growing importance today). Fourth, to support peasant against landlord, to lend the peasant movement "the most revolutionary character", and to set up "Working People's Soviets". Fifth, to enter alliances with anybody, provided the Party kept its own distinct character. And sixth, to remind the toilers that independent states created by the imperialists were really anything but that, being tied to their creators by

2. *Lenin on the National and Colonial Questions* (Peking: Foreign Language Press, 1967), p. 21.

economic or military bonds. There was "no salvation for dependent and weak nations except in a union of Soviet republics".

Lenin particularly stressed the distinction between oppressed and oppressor nations. The emphasis was on the idea that the world was divided into two camps, a small group of imperialist countries being ranged against the Soviet system headed by Russia. Lenin wrote with unambiguous clarity: "If we let this escape us, we shall not be able correctly to pose a single national or colonial question, even if it concerns a most remote corner of the world."

Since peasants make up most of the population in the backward countries, they were to be won over, even though they would not be allowed to lead the revolution. And, very important, it would be possible for backward countries to pass straight over to the Soviet system without going to the capitalist stage. This was an early unilateral twisting of Marxist theory, for even at that early stage its flaws were readily apparent. Such, very briefly, was the teaching which so profoundly affected Ho Chi Minh.

It was thus patriotism which brought Ho to Lenin; after that it was a relationship as of disciple to Messiah. To Ho, only Lenin had the answers to the problems of the oppressed, and Lenin's program would provide the vehicle by which Ho's goals would be realized. At the 18th Congress of the French Socialist Party, held in Tours in December 1920, Ho aligned himself with the Marxists and voted to join the Third International. He thus became not only a founder-member of the French Communist Party, but the first Vietnamese Communist.

In 1923 Ho went to Moscow, where he became deeply and totally wedded to the Party, and where he was schooled in the techniques of revolution at the Eastern Workers' University. In return he wrote for *Pravda* and handled the Comintern's international correspondence.[3] Recognized as a bright and industrious young man, he became head of the Southern Section of the Eastern Department of the Comintern.

In early 1923, also, the Sun-Joffe agreement brought into being Kuomintang-Soviet cooperation. Sun Yat-sen had turned in vain to the West for help in his struggle against the Peking government.[4] Sun permitted Communists to join his revolutionary movement as individuals, but not as an organized party. The early Comintern Congresses had paid scant

---

3. Robert F. Turner, *Vietnamese Communism, Its Origins and Developments* (Stanford, Calif.: Hoover Institution Press, 1975), p. 7.
4. Charles B. McLane, *Soviet Strategies in Southeast Asia* (Princeton University Press, 1966), p. 34.

attention to the problems of peasants in Far Eastern colonial countries, being exercised almost exclusively by the industrialized capitalist countries, but the unrest in China appeared to Russia to offer scope for profitable intervention.

Lenin, the Communist messiah, died in 1924, and within half a century his disciples would have brought half the world's population under Communism, a performance which not even Christ's movement could match. In December of that year, Ho was sent to China in his first major assignment as a Comintern agent. He was offically designated as interpreter to Mikhail Borodin, Comintern adviser to Chiang Kai-shek; his real mission was to organize Southeast Asian movements which would be directed by Moscow. There were scattered and splintered revolutionary groups in existence, and they provided Ho with ready recruits as he began his task of building Communism in South East Asia. The memorable achievement of this period in South China was the formation of the *Viet Nam Thanh Nien Cach Mang Dong Chi Hoi* (Vietnam Association of young Revolutionaries), or *Thanh Nien*, which eventually became the Indochinese Communist Party.

The most promising new Party members were sent to the famous Whampoa Military Academy, which numbered among its distinguished faculty and students such people as Chou En-lai, Chiang Kai-shek, and Pham Van Dong. At this institution Ho lectured on politics. According to Fall, he established between January 1925 and July 1927 200 cadres, who were infiltrated back to Indochina.[5] Those who pursued their own nationalistic courses, rather than the Communist line, were betrayed by the Communists to the French security forces. The money received from the French for these tips was used by Ho Chi Minh to build up his own units.[6] In 1927 Chiang broke with the Communists, and Ho was obliged to leave China. His mysterious and varied travels, and his arrest in 1931 in Hong Kong by the British, have been the subject of considerable interest.[7] In this early period his talent for survival and his unmatched sense of opportunism are amply illustrated.

There were other groups competing for power during this period. The VNQDD (*Viet Nam Quoc Dan Dang* — Vietnam Nationalist Party) was probably the first and best known of these modern nationalist move-

---

5. Bernard B. Fall, *The Two Vietnams* (New York: Praeger, 1967), p. 93; see also Hoang Van Chi, *From Colonialism to Communism* (New York: Praeger 1964), p. 19.
6. Turner, p. 11, and Hoang Van Chi, p. 18.
7. Dennis Duncanson has done much to clear this up in his article "Ho Chi Minh in Hong Kong, 1931–32" (*China Quarterly*, no. 5, Jan.–Mar. 1974, pp. 84–100).

ments. Nguyen Thai Hoc was the force behind the new party, which was based roughly on the Kuomintang in China. The ever-essential publishing house was set up in Hanoi, and this provided cover for an internal clandestine group. Hoang Van Chi stated that by early 1929 the group had already grown to some 1,500 members, organized in 120 cells.[8] However, the murder of a French labor recruiter named Bazin provoked swift response from the French security forces. The murderer was never found, but when the *Sûreté* began systematically apprehending the group's more important members, Nguyen Thai Hoc ordered an armed uprising (already planned for a later date) to start immediately while the VNQDD still possessed the capacity to implement it.

But confused orders for executing the rising resulted in only one garrison revolting, the famous Yen Bay mutiny of 10 February 1930. French reaction was predictable and those who remained of the VNQDD leadership were beheaded or fled to China. They tried to come back in 1945 but were liquidated by the Communists. While the VNQDD was scattered after Yen Bay, the Thanh Nien had built up a solid core of workers. However, there were now two other Communist organizations competing for recognition, the "Indochinese Communist Party" and the "Indochinese Communist League". But although these parties were in competition, their messages were similar and falling on receptive ears. In the late 1920s, factory workers, miners and plantation workers were being organized by the thousands into Red Unions, and strikes were carried out throughout Annam and Tonkin. French Communist agents played important parts in organizing the early Communist movement in the Far East. In 1929 the Thanh Nien became the Annamese Communist Party; the Tonkin branch of the Thanh Nien had coalesced into the Indochinese Communist Party. Each of the three Communist parties claimed recognition by the Comintern, which understandably would not tolerate for long this fragmentation and overlapping.

In 1929 Ho Chi Minh was in Siam, subverting the 30,000 or so Vietnamese émigrés there. In early 1930 the Comintern ordered him to Hong Kong, where he was to make one party out of the three. In February 1930 he imposed the Comintern will on the unification meeting, and the result was the single Vietnam Communist Party. When the documents were sent to Moscow for examination and verification, the Party was directed, through the Southern Bureau in Shanghai, to rename itself the Indochinese Communist Party to embrace

8. Hoang Van Chi, pp. 22–3.

all Indochina and not just Vietnam.[9] The new, unified Party (with a total of 211 Communists) was admitted to the Comintern in April 1931. Although this high-level direction from Moscow was gratifying, central Party interest was not exactly transfixed on Indochina, which was thought to be politically in the stone age ("politically inert").[10] The Vietnamese, of course, were anything but that.

The depression years brought the Party's first major test — the well-known Nghe-Tinh soviets and what is generally called the Red Terror of 1930. The Sixth Comintern Congress had concluded that this capitalist crisis was a good time to rise, but that decisions would have to be taken locally. Thus, along with widespread strike activity, Communist cadres organized the peasants of Nghe An and Ha Tinh to take land from the landlords (the "Land to the Tiller" slogan). A good deal of secondary source material, often based on questionable documentation, has established this scenario. These self-run mini-communes were called "*xo-viet*" (soviets), and some lasted for more than a year before the French security forces, stretched and busy elsewhere, were able to deal with them. For while these *xo-viets* were easily created, Party histories record that no means of self-defense were simultaneously formed. Peasant associations were set up under the hammer and sickle, guided by local cadres, and richer peasants were executed.[11]

The Communists were joined at first by more moderate elements who saw an opportunity to hit the French, but the Communists preferred to operate alone at this time. The alliances came later, when the Party had grown wiser. On 12 September 1930, thousands of peasants were mobilized to march on the provincial capital at Vinh. They were repulsed by a small detachment of French-led Vietnamese troops, and over 170 Vietnamese were killed by the soldiers and a couple of aircraft. The *Sûreté* picked off the leadership, and when the Foreign Legion was brought in, it exacted a hideous and often sadistic revenge, known as the White Terror of 1931. The Communist organizers fled, leaving the poor peasants to bear the brunt of the retaliation in the area. It is estimated that 90 per cent of the ICP was destroyed in the French reaction. According to the Party, the Comintern did not appreciate this effort and admonished the ICP for the poor planning and results which had cost

9. Milton Sacks, "Marxism in Vietnam", in *Marxism in Southeast Asia: a study of Four Countries*, ed. Frank N. Trager (Stanford University Press, 1959), p. 124.
10. McLane, p. 105.
11. William J. Duiker, *The Rise of Nationalism in Vietnam, 1900–1941* (Ithaca, NY: Cornell University Press, 1976), p. 225.

them so dearly. But the experience of the soviets was regarded by the Party as a trial run for the August Revolution of 1945. As the Party's own historians put it, speaking of the Nghe-Tinh soviets: "During and after the Nghe-Tinh soviet movement, although it suffered heavy losses, our Party was steeled and tempered in the fire of revolutionary struggle and accumulated experiences in seizing revolutionary power for the people."[12] Anyway, new cadres were being trained at the Stalin school in Moscow, the University of the Toilers of the East. The training lasted from one to three years and men like Tran Van Giau were soon to be introduced to Indochina (in his case to Cochinchina).[13]

While the Party was recovering, the Trotskyists were building up, primarily in the south. Ironically, as with the Marxist-Communists who were exposed to the new doctrines in France during the First World War, the Trotskyists were motivated early in 1932 by Tha Thu Thau, a university man who had recently returned from France. Although small Trotskyist groups had appeared a few months earlier, Tha Thu Thau became the leader. Rebuilding, like the Stalinists, after *Sûreté* action, they merged with Tran Van Giau's Party in 1933 to work openly through the system.[14] Together they published that most famous of revolutionary papers, *La Lutte* (The Struggle). As a matter of fact, the Communist coalition legally elected three members to the Saigon municipal council in 1937. From then on, the Trotskyists refused to conform to central Stalinist direction from Moscow and took over *La Lutte*. They grew stronger, but the Japanese entry into Indochina changed everything.

Although the ICP was following Comintern instructions to the letter, to form alliances with anybody if it furthered Party plans, Ho enunciated the Stalinist line from afar: with the Trotskyists no compromise, no concession, was possible. All means available was to be used to unmask them as fascist agents, to be politically annihilated.[15] As it turned out, most of the Trotskyists were later physically liquidated, which certainly "politically annihilated" them. During the rebuilding

12. *Thirty Years Struggle of the Party* (Hanoi: Foreign Languages Publishing House, 1960), p. 36.
13. William J. Duiker, "Building the United Front: The Rise of Communism in Vietnam", in *Communism in Indochina*, ed. Joseph J. Zasloff and MacAlister Brown (Lexington, Mass.: Lexington Books, 1975), pp. 8–9.
14. Ellen Hammer, *The Struggle for Indochina, 1940–1955* (Stanford University Press, 1954), p. 89.
15. *An Outline History of the Vietnam Workers' Party 1930–1970* (Hanoi: Foreign Languages Publishing House, 1970), p. 26.

the Party "severely criticized" almost everything: "leftist deviation, such as isolationism, narrow-mindedness, failing to use legal and semi-legal forms to push the movement forward", as well as "rightist devia-tions" such as "legalism, overrejoicing at partial successes. . .lack of vigilance, Trotskyists, and reckless cooperation with them." Not co-operation, but *reckless* cooperation.

The major Communist program of the 1930s was the United Front; even the Trotskyists were for it. As the Nazis consolidated their power in Germany, and Fascism was on the rise in Italy and Japan, the Comin-tern directed a worldwide strategy of anti-Fascist alliances. The pressure on the Communists in Indochina eased somewhat when in 1936 the Popular Front government assumed office in France, supported by the Communists and Socialists, and the French signed a mutual defense pact with Russia. In this new atmosphere the Trotskyists secured 80 per cent of the votes cast in the 1939 elections in Cochinchina.[16] But hopes for changes in the colonies were never realised.

Local Party workers worldwide had a difficult time explaining Russia's complete policy reversals; the pact Stalin signed with Hitler in 1939 surprised cadres everywhere. It should have surprised no one, given Lenin's dictum of signing a pact with the devil if it would further the Party's interests. Even the Party's writers admit to the perplexity of the cadres. The old enemy was now an ally. Following the Soviet-German treaty "a number of our Party members became confused and waver-ing," and to rectify this a book had to be written, the title (and expla-nation) being *The Soviet Union is always Faithful to Peace*.

In 1938 the Popular Front government in Paris fell, eventually result-ing again in increased pressure on the revolutionaries. When the Soviets signed their pact with the Nazis, they and the French were no longer allies and the move was on again to root out the Communists every-where. By now Party slogans emphasizing class struggle were replaced by messages concentrating on the imperialist war and national liberation. The years 1936–9 had given the Party invaluable experience with broad front strategy.

The pre-war years had also given rise to two other groups in Cochin-china which became important because of their rapid growth. These were the Cao Dai and Hoa Hao sects, eclectic religions indigenous to the south, centred around Tay Ninh and Cantho respectively. The Cao Dai were later armed by the Japanese, who also protected from the French

16. Sacks, p. 143.

the Hoa Hao founder, Huynh Phu So, known as the "mad *bonze*" (Buddhist monk). When the Japanese were later disarmed and the Allies confined to key areas around Saigon, the Viet Minh "honor units" killed him and chopped up his body by order of Tran Van Giau, who showed a distinct propensity for solving his problems in this manner.

The Japanese entry into Indochina brought new trials and opportunities for the Party, which suffered further damage from more premature revolts. An uprising accompanied by an assault on the French fort at Bac Son in 1940 was quickly crushed, and when 1,500 native troops in Saigon rebelled on receiving orders to move to the Thai border, the local Party cadres decided to start a revolt. Hanoi forbade the planned uprising, but such few of its emissaries as avoided arrest by the ubiquitous *Sûreté* were ignored, and the insurrection took place on 23 November 1940. By December the revolt had been crushed, for the local native troops had been disarmed earlier. The Party was again badly hurt in the French repression, and Tran Van Giau, who invariably inclined towards violence, was in official disgrace. A smaller uprising in Nghe An was similarly suppressed.

Again, after the failure of the 1940 risings, the Party analyzed the reasons for the failures. As it wrote later, the Party must be more careful about the timing of the revolt. It must organize where the enemy was weak (namely, in the countryside), and then gradually move outwards. And the Party was reinforced in its view that the peasants must be mobilized and led by the workers, but there were precious few workers in Indochina, reflecting the peasant-based economy.

The German attack on Russia in June 1941 caused the Party cadres worldwide once again to accommodate an abrupt reversal in strategy. Earlier, in November 1940, the Seventh Plenum of the Indochinese Communist Party changed the name of the front from the "Indo-Chinese Anti-Imperialist National United Front" (of the Sixth Plenum) to the "National United Front Against the French and Japanese Fascists in Indo-China", to reflect the fact that overnight the fascists (and one imperialist) had again become the main enemy. The Sixth Plenum had already subordinated the main theme of class struggle to that of national liberation. There was no more talk of worker soviets — the slogans were now of a Vietnamese government, a democratic republic. It was a shrewd and powerful appeal, which could hardly fail to attract support from patriotic Vietnamese of all political hues.

Ho's whereabouts during the period are a matter of conjecture, and most "authoritative" sources have been compelled to rely on second-hand information to support their conclusions. For this study, the 1941–5 years are of particular importance.[17] On February 1941, Ho, still better known as the veteran revolutionary Nguyen Ai Quoc, finally went to Indochina. For the first time since 1923 he was acting largely on his own, the Russians being too pre-occupied with their own survival in the West to bother about anything else. To use his own words, his life up till now had been mapped out for him, and he had simply followed orders.

Ho now went to Pac Bo, in Cao Bang province. During 10–19 May 1941, the Eighth Plenum of the Party Central Committee was held. This is of more than passing interest because the Party took a hard look at the political situation and made a decision of profound importance. This was recognized as the start of the Party's most vital period — its chance, as Truong Chinh later wrote, such as appears but once in a thousand years, and which had been made possible by the war.[18] The Party Central Committee — no doubt as the result of intelligence received from Russia — had traced the course and causes of the war and had expected Germany to attack Russia. War would flare up in the Pacific and the imperialists would be hit badly, but the anti-fascist alliance would survive and eventually win. As Party histories noted with hindsight, just as the First World War brought the Soviet Union into being, so the Second World War would see the birth of other Socialist states. It reaffirmed the policy of subordinating the class struggle to the call for independence, as this would produce a wider response from the masses. With Ho personally guiding the Plenum, a more urgent sense of purpose was impressed on the Party members. But the *Sûreté* was still effective, and several Party members were ambushed and captured while returning from the meeting.

The Eighth Plenum was of great historical significance for another reason. The decision was made to form a broad front alliance which would reach more people and be more effective than a purely Communist organization. This was to be the *Viet Nam Doc-Lap Dong-Minh Hoi*, or Viet Minh. This is the Party's version, although other sources say that the Viet Minh was formed at Chingshi, across the border in China. Represented, in any case, were the Communists, the new Viet Nam Party, the Viet Nam Revolutionary Youth League, what was left of the

---

17. See the works of King Chen, Philippe Devillers, and Hoang Van Chi respectively.
18. *History of the August Revolution* (Hanoi: Foreign Languages Publishing House, 1972), pp. 24–8.

Viet Nam Nationalist Party (VNQDD), and a few smaller groups.[19] These made up the Viet Minh.

By now Nguyen Ai Quoc (Nguyen the patriot) was "Ho Chi Minh" (He who enlightens), although again authoritative sources say he took the name when he left prison the following year. His Viet Minh included something for everyone. To organize the masses, a forest of "National Salvation" associations sprang up. There were Workers for National Salvation, Peasants for National Salvation, and National Salvation Associations for Old Folks, Women, Army men, Youth, Buddhist *bonzes*, and more. (There are similar National Salvation groups in conquered Kampuchea [Cambodia] today.) Everything was *National Salvation*, not anti-bourgeois, proletarian, anti-imperialist or anti-capitalist. Everything was aimed at the right time to rise, and the training of cadres took on top priority. Lenin's idea of "less foes, more allies" was being put into practice.

Not only were there associations for everyone, there were slogans and songs for everything. For traditionalists, there was a neat Party twist to the old Confucian ode on ethics:

> To have a solid foundation
> Our association should start with small cells
> Having three to nine members
> Who elect a leader for themselves.
> A group of two, three cells
> Should elect an executive committee,
> Strict discipline must be maintained
> And bi-weekly meetings well attended. . . .[20]

Bernard Fall described this start as a "private political venture (with economic overtones) of the Kuomintang warlord of Kwantung province, General Chang Fa-kwei" Chinese influence was undoubtedly great, but the idea certainly coincided with Ho's thoughts on making alliances. While the Bac Son base area was being built up, Ho went back to China (the Party histories say he went to the Chinese for help). But on 29 August 1942 he was arrested as he crossed the border into Kwangsi province. For months the Party thought he was dead. These events, like almost everything else before about 1945, are open to conjecture, and a

19. Bernard Fall, *The Viet Minh Regime* (New York: Institute or Pacific Relations, 1956), p. 1.
20. Nguyen Duc Minh, "A Study of the Literature of Political Persuasion in North Vietnam" (unpublished Ph. D. dissertation, School of Oriental and African Studies, University of London, 1973), pp. 42–3.

reader's opinions will be formed by what and whom he reads. Ho's whereabouts, the site of the Eighth Plenum and the formation of the Viet Minh, when Nguyen Ai Quoc became Ho Chi Minh, and more — there will be variations and contradictions from one source to the next.

It remains unclear why Ho was arrested in the first place. Certainly his Communist and revolutionary background was fundamental to his arrest — some even say that the reason went back to his old days with Borodin. Whatever the reason, it seems clear that he was in jail, sustained largely by his beliefs and keeping his mind active by writing poetry of questionable quality. His party had suffered greatly at the hands of the French. In 1931 it had about 1,500 members, and at this time the membership was about the same. According to Party sources, Ho was released from prison on 16 September 1943.[21] His release was partly the result of the failure of the Dong Minh Hoi to supersede the Viet Minh. On 4 October 1942, Chang Fa-kwei (military governor of the Fourth War Zone, in Kwangsi) had sponsored a political congress in Liuchow. By 10 October the *Viet Nam Cach Menh Dong Minh Hoi* was formed. It was composed primarily of the old VNQDD, *Phuc Quoc*, and seven other groups, and was to provide information for the Chinese and eventually perhaps assume the form of a government in exile. It could not compete with the Communists, and a network of cells and organization could not be created overnight. After all, the Communists, in assiduously building their Party over a period of fifteen years, had through stern trial and error accumulated a fund of experience with which other groups were largely unable to compete.

Somewhere at this point enter the Americans. The accepted story is that Ho wrote to Chang Fa-kwei from prison, offering the services of his organization in exchange for his release. Bernard Fall cites a source stating that the United States successfully intervened with the Chinese on Ho's behalf, and "the Americans handed the Soviets, as often elsewhere during the war years, another trump card."[22] The most dangerous Communist revolutionary in South East Asia was now freed to do his historic work. According to Chang, the reorganization (which saw Ho's apparatus incorporated into the overall Vietnamese group) had two main objectives: to help the revolutionists gain independence and to

21. *Thirty Years Struggle*, p. 74.
22. Fall, *The Two Vietnams*, p. 99, quoting Wolfgang Appel, *Südostasien im Brennpunkt der Weltpolitik* (Würzburg: Marienburg Verlag, 1960).

help the Chinese military advance to Vietnam at a later date.[23] Ho, biding his time, accepted a lesser role in the group.

In 1943 the Cao Bang base areas had been developed, and intensive work had been carried out in the provinces of Ha Giang, Bac Can and Lang Son. In August 1943, converging "columns" led by Giap and Chu Van Tan met, and what the Party called a "political corridor" was created, which formed the basis of the future "liberated zone" and joined the base areas of Cao Bang and Bac Son. In 1944 a thirst for direct action almost moved the Party into a confrontation with the French, a confrontation for which the Communists were not yet wholly ready. However, Ho was able to stop any premature rising, although he did direct the establishment of an armed force. Thus the forerunner of the North Vietnamese Army (NVA) was created by Giap later in the year, on 22 December 1944: it was called the Vietnam Propaganda and Liberation Unit.

It was not surprising that the ICP was able to build up its base areas in the Bac Son and Lang Son regions. The *hautes régions* of Tonkin, among others, were never fully pacified by the French, and the Viet Minh found ready recruits among the Tho tribesmen. In May 1955, the Commander-in-Chief of the French Forces in Indochina issued a three-volume work which was distributed to a limited number of officials. This summarized the French experiences of the war and sought to provide guidance for similar wars in the future. Volume 2 explained, in part, Giap's success in recruiting in the base areas:

What we have observed in Indochina confirms a fact known in our African possessions: there exists a permanence or continuity in the centers of unrest. History and geography reveal that certain regions are traditional cradles of insurgent movements, and these later serve as preferred areas for the guerrillas.

It is in the Provinces where the population has always shown itself to be proud, bold and independent that the revolt has taken on the most acute and intense forms (the Plain of Reeds, the region of Vinh, the mountains of Langson etc.) It is striking to compare some recent engagements with the history of certain battles which recurred during the conquest. The events were often the same and even happened in the same places. Some of the writings from Tonkinese and Mandarin to our forces were written in the same vein as Viet Minh pamphlets.[24]

23. King Chen, *Vietnam and China, 1938–1954* (Princeton, NJ: Princeton University Press, 1969), p. 71.
24. *Lessons of the War in Indochina*, v.2, transl. Col. V. J. Croizat (Santa Monica, Calif.: Rand Corporation, 1967), p. 33.

In late 1944 a US pilot was shot down and somehow fell into Ho's hands. It was a great chance for a formal introduction to the Americans, and the OSS eventually arranged to set up a liaison unit with the Viet Minh. The OSS are not known to have worked actively with, or trained, any non-Communist groups, even though their main concern was obviously with the established Party network. It is one of the assertions of this work that Ho's recognition of the political immaturity of his OSS colleagues, and the manner in which the Communists were able to manipulate the anti-colonialism of the US officers, was a major factor in their eventual triumph. It was one thing for the Americans to make temporary alliances with the enemy of an enemy, but the real damage was done after the war with Japan had ended, when the OSS, with little political experience and training, were simply not in the same class as the Communists and were unable to look ahead. The OSS, for those crucial post-war weeks in South East Asia, appeared to be acting independently, certainly indulging in what Donald Lancaster calls their "policy-framing proclivities"[25] in contradiction to the changed US policy — and doing it clumsily.

Earlier, although General Chennault had been warned of Ho's Communist background by the KMT and advised not to see him, Ho secured an interview by a trick. Charles Fenn described it as follows:

Then Ho said he had a small favor to ask the General . . . all Ho wanted was the General's photograph. There's nothing Chennault likes more than giving his photograph. So he presses a bell . . . In due course it's another girl who produces a folder of eight-by-ten glossies. "Take your pick," says Chennault. Ho takes one and asks would the General be so kind as to sign it? . . . Chennault writes across the bottom, 'Yours sincerely, Claire L. Chennault.' And out we all troop into Kunming's sparkling air. As we shall see, it was by waving this photograph like a magic wand that Ho was later to produce a magnificent rabbit.[26]

Ho's later meeting with Colonel Helliwell is well documented elsewhere. OSS men were dropped in to Ho, and supplies followed. The small OSS group trained Giap's troops in the use of small arms, grenades and crew-served weapons. One of the American medical corpsmen may even have saved the veteran revolutionary's life when Ho went down with a bad fever.[27]

25. Donald Lancaster, *The Emancipation of French Indochina* (London: Oxford University Press, 1961), p. 143.

26. Charles Fenn, *Ho Chi Minh* (London: Studio Vista, 1973), pp. 78–9.

27. Ho Chi Minh's long and active career as a key Communist revolutionary (he was

All this OSS activity was supposed to produce a force to fight the Japanese. As with their Chinese ideological comrades in Yenan, the Viet Minh were noted for their ability to avoid the Japanese. Bernard Fall could only find a single recorded instance of a Viet Minh attack on the Japanese, when a battalion-sized group of Viet Minh attacked an outpost of forty men, killing eight of them[28] As in China, the OSS were apparently pretty much in the dark as to Communist activity in Tonkin,[29] for Ho had no intention of wasting his troops against the Japanese, who he knew would lose the war and leave anyway. It was heady stuff, but apparently not unduly hazardous, given the studiousness with which the Viet Minh avoided the Japanese.

On 9 March 1945 the sword, which had been hanging over the heads of the French for more than four years, fell. The *coup* by the Japanese will be discussed elsewhere in this work; suffice it to say that it was one of the major reasons for the ultimate success of the Communists. For now the French security forces were completely neutralized, and the Japanese

---

fifty-five now) should have been well known to the OSS, who should also have had at least a nodding acquaintance with Lenin's works, the Party's fundamental program of eternal struggle against non-soviet systems, their treatment of dissidents, the history of bloody purges and group liquidations, the "Gulag Archipelago" of concentration camps, the use of temporary alliances and détentes to further Party goals, and more. If they were ignorant of all this, they had no right to be called an intelligence agency. If they were not, a large question mark must hang over the Southeast Asian branch of the OSS, particularly in regard to the actions of some of their personnel in the weeks immediately following the Japanese surrender.

28. In fact, at the war's end the Viet Minh used as a primary argument in trying to persuade the Japanese to turn over political power to them the fact that "they had inflicted no injury on the Japanese, French or anyone" (NA RG 457, French Indochina [Political Situation], Pacific Strategic Intelligence Section, Chief of Naval Operations, 11 October 1945). P. J. Honey, in an interview on 18 May 1977, recalled a conversation with a former OSS officer who had worked with the Viet Minh. The officer said that the Viet Minh generally would not allow the OSS to observe their attacks on the Japanese. The Viet Minh units would leave in the morning on a "raid", and return in the evening looking none the worse for wear. The suspicion grew that they were not fighting the Japanese, but merely intimidating the population or storing their arms and ammunition. Finally on American insistence the OSS were allowed to observe a raid in which a horde of Viet Minh guerillas, firing wildly, descended on a small Japanese supply column. The Japanese took one look, put the spurs to their mules and departed; no appreciable harm was done to either side, and it was apparent to the OSS man that the Viet Minh had very little experience, if any, at this sort of thing.

29. See Vice-Admiral Milton E. Miles, USN, *A Different Kind of War* (Garden City, NY: Doubleday), pp. 342–3.

generally evinced interest in the Viet Minh only when they threatened their lines of communication. There followed that single known Viet Minh attack on the small Japanese outpost in July, and in August the Japanese laid down their arms. This was the historic moment the Party had been waiting for: the Allies were slow in arriving (due largely to MacArthur's order), the Japanese were neutral, and the French were helpless. The Japanese had earlier declared Vietnam independent, and Tran Trong Kim had formed a government at the request of Emperor Bao Dai. (Although under French rule the Vietnamese emperors had been reduced to figureheads, the current emperor Bao Dai now saw his chance to free the country from its colonial status.)

At about this time the terms of the Potsdam Conference became known. On 13 August 1945 the Indochinese Communist Party held its Second National Congress at Tan Trao village, to discuss strategy and the coming rising. News of Japan's surrender spread rapidly, and the Insurrection Committee[30] issued General Order no. 1, the "Call for a General Insurrection". It proclaimed the surrender of the Japanese Fascists and called for a general uprising. Political and military tasks must be carried out simultaneously, and an ultimatum was sent to the Japanese Army. In the call for general insurrection the ICP could be excused a Freudian slip in forgetting, in the excitement of the moment, the emphasis on nationalism by declaring, "The *Party* expects you to make great sacrifice."[31] On 16 August, to give the uprising a semblance of legitimacy, a Viet Minh People's Congress was convened at Tan Trao, the famous "Lightning Session", so called because by the time the non-Communist element of the Viet Minh heard about the Congress it was over.[32] The Congress rubber-stamped the decisions taken by the Party a few days earlier, and approved the gold-star red flag and the national anthem, *March to the Front*. It endorsed the insurrection and the ten-point domestic and foreign policy statement of the Viet Minh League.[33] It also

30. The National Insurrection Committee was composed of Truong Chinh, Vo Nguyen Giap, Tran Van Don, Le Thanh Nghi, and Chu Van Tan (from "Historic Week Before 1945 August Revolution", *Vietnam Youth*, no. 124, Aug 1976), p. 9.

31. *Documents of the August 1945 Revolution in Vietnam*, trans, C. Kiriloff, ed. Rima Rathausky (Canberra: Australian National University, 1963), p. 54.

32. On 16 August, also, a Liberation Army unit under Vo Nguyen Giap held a departure ceremony under the Tan Trao banyan tree, then proceeded to seize its first objective, Thai Nguyen; some sources say that Giap was accompanied by an OSS section. ("Historic Week", *Vietnam Youth*, August 1976, p. 10.)

33. Ho's ten-point program may have been the most effective handbill ever produced in Vietnam. According to Nguyen Duc Minh, "The brief platform answered the

adopted the National Liberation Committee, which became the Provisional Government under President Ho Chi Minh; this made its first appearance on 17 August.

The tremendous urgency and instant bursts of activity of the Viet Minh may be imagined when one considers that on 17 August the Viet Minh, with carefully planned tactics, infiltrated and took over a mass rally in Hanoi. The Viet Minh flag replaced the imperial flag of the Bao Dai government, and on the next day the Japanese permitted the Viet Minh to seize the arms of the *Garde Indochinoise*.[34] On 18 August the Revolutionary Military Committee (Uprising Committee of the Party Committee in Hanoi) moved its office from a village in the suburbs to inside Hanoi.

On 19 August a huge demonstration in Hanoi, orchestrated by the Viet Minh, sealed the Front's ascendancy. A mass meeting was called for 1100 hours at the Municipal Theatre Square. A military contingent fired a salvo, the new national flag was displayed, and the anthem was played. A member of the Revolutionary Military Committee repeated the call for general insurection, and the Viet Minh cadres fanned out to seize the organs of the government. The same thing happened at the provincial capitals Yen Bay, Thai Binh, Phuc Yen, Thanh Hoa, and others. On 20 August it was the turn of Bac Ninh, Thai Nguyen, Ninh Binh, and on 21 August, Cao Bang, Tuyen Quang, Son Tay, Kien An, Nghe An, Ninh Thuan, and so on, as the cadres went flying out from the capital.

---

perennial popular complaint against heavy taxation, touched on the sensitive issues of religion and political restriction, considered the needs of all groups, professions, and walks of life, and promised to fulfil them.'' (Nguyen Duc Minh, p. 51.)

The Ten-Point Domestic Policy of the Viet Minh government was as follows:

1. Abolition of all tax, which was required by the imperialists; new taxation very light and just. Freedom of belief and freedom of assembly.
2. Every peasant will have rice fields to cultivate and sufficient help to be prosperous in agriculture.
3. Eight-hour day for workers with sufficient salary for their families.
4. Obligatory schooling; state aid for all children.
5. Free commerce for all citizens, abolition of miscellaneous taxes like sea tax, streetside tax, market tax, and so forth.
6. Civil servants will receive worthy remuneration according to their talents.
7. Women are equal to men in every field; political, economic as well as cultural; equal pay for equal work.
8. Soldiers will be highly esteemed for the defense of the fatherland.
9. The old and the sick will be given help.
10. Infants will receive care, aid and protection from the state.

(Nguyen Duc Minh, p. 53.)

34. Lancaster, p. 117 (quoting Devillers).

The scene early on 19 August in Hanoi as two platoons of Viet Minh troops strode through the populous quarters of Hanoi, marching to cries of *"mot, hai! mot, hai!"* (one, two! one, two!), is well described by Nguyen Duc Minh:

Though still poorly dressed and ill-equipped, these men were the first Vietnamese troops not commanded by foreign officers to march in Hanoi since the end of the nineteenth century! In a country which sets as much store by symbol and myth as Viet Nam does, the effect upon the masses was very great indeed . . .[35]

The shock waves burst upon the imperial court at Hue on 23 August. The Viet Minh sent an ultimatum to Emperor Bao Dai, with a deadline of 1330 hours. At that time a large Viet Minh crowd appeared, making a fearful noise outside the court. While the cabinet discussed the issue, news just happened to arrive which confirmed that two leading mandarins had been brutally murdered by the Communists — this was meant to assist the debaters to reach a speedy solution, and it succeeded in doing so. The shocked court disbanded and Bao Dai's abdication marked the end of the long and sometimes glorious Vietnamese monarchy. One of the murdered mandarins was Ngo Dinh Khoi, brother of the future South Vietnamese President Ngo Dinh Diem; he had served Bao Dai and was said to have been buried alive with his son, just one of the many victims of an unparalleled campaign of assassinations carried out at this time by the Party, led by what an OSS officer actually called a gentle "little old man sitting on his hill."[36]

Sacks described the abdication as an event of great significance, as the Vietnamese people, great traditionalists, saw in it the passing of the Mandate of Heaven from the Emperor to the Viet Minh and the Democratic Republic of Vietnam.[37] The French had earlier surrendered the Mandate when they were humiliated by the Japanese in March 1945,

---

35. Nguyen Duc Minh, p. 59.
36. Robert Shaplen, in his book *The Lost Revolution*, p. 29, tells how one OSS officer described Ho Ch Minh. Ho was flattering the OSS man, innocently asking about the US Declaration of Independence. The youthful OSS man reported that Ho was "an awfully sweet guy. If I had to pick out one quality about that little old man sitting on his hill in the jungle, it was his gentleness." Even today it is sometimes said that if Ho had been better handled earlier he would have turned out to be another Tito. This fantasy overlooks two things: he *was* well handled earlier, and when Tito broke away from Stalin the denunciations of him were led by Ho.
37. Sacks, p. 153.

although it took some time for them to understand that.

On 25 August the Viet Minh cavalcade reached Saigon. The situation was quite different in the south (Nam Bo), and the Viet Minh did not have everything their own way. Tran Van Giau, another alumnus from the Moscow school for revolutionaries, had been put out of action by the French after the abortive 1940 Communist uprising. The Japanese *coup* of 9 March had resulted in the release of many experienced cadres of all parties, and rival groups were rebuilt. On 14 August a wide spectrum of parties had formed the United National Front (UNF), in which the ICP was on paper a minority; but like the Viet Minh itself, the UNF was a vehicle for Communist ambition. Membership included the (Stalinist) Indochinese Communist Party of Ho Chi Minh and his southern lieutenant Tran Van Giau, the Cao Dai and Hoa Hao sects, the Advanced Guard Youth (later described by British Intelligence as militant and dangerous), the Trotskyists, and the Vietnam Independence Party. It turned out that the leader of the Advanced Guard Youth (or Vanguard Youth, as it is also called), Dr Pham Ngoc Thach, was really a member of the Indochinese Communist Party, and his organization supplied most of the early "muscle" for Viet Minh maneuvers.[38]

The attitude of the Japanese in the south was markedly different in technique, if not in substance, from that of their northern command; the high concentration of senior commanders and staff officers accounted for a somewhat less parochial outlook. While the Japanese were willing to turn the reins of government over to the Vietnamese, they preferred to exclude the Viet Minh, which was indistinguishable from its Communist brain and backbone. So the Japanese permitted the UNF to take over a number of public buildings and assume a posture of control.

Tran Van Giau immediately confronted the UNF, telling them that since they appeared to be a Japanese creation they would not be

38. An official SRVN source states: "At the outset, the 'Vanguard Youth' movement was one of Japanese inspiration, but unfortunately for the aggressors, they placed this organization in the hands of the Party sympathizers, intellectuals and students who, most of them, had entertained close relations with our Party." Led by Party cadres in key positions, "the Vanguard Youth movement developed at an unprecedented pace." These cadres met weekly, and were members of the Youth Organization for National Salvation. The Party went on to state that after meeting all evening, "the youth practised military drill overnight without feeling tired, and fearless of danger," which denotes an unusually high condition of fitness and stamina for the youthful cadres. The Vanguard Youth was the first group in Saigon to receive weapons from the Party. (From "Saigonese Youth in the 1945 Insurrection", *Vietnam Youth*, no. 122, March 1976, p. 20.)

recognized by the Allies. Only the Viet Minh, free from Japanese taint, would be acceptable. Lacking the broader historical perspectives of the Communists, the UNF collapsed in uncertainty, and by 25 August the Provisional Executive Committee for the south was formed, with Tran Van Giau in charge. As at Hue, huge demonstrations on 21 and 25 August helped the UNF members to make up their minds.[39] Of ten members of the Committee, four were listed as Communist and two as Viet Minh,[40] although at least one of the listed Viet Minh (Pham Ngoc Thach, of the Advanced Guard Youth) was a Communist. As Party histories say, the formation of the Provisional Executive Committee (PEC) completed the "August Revolution". In victory, the Party reiterated one of its most fundamental principles: "To make full use of the contradictions among the enemy ranks and take good aim at the main enemy", a principle which proved its value in the next thirty years. "The success of the Revolution does not come by itself, it must be prepared and won. The August Revolution took place within the span of only fifteen days but it had been prepared through fifteen years from the first days of our Party."[41]

The party was now in control in Hanoi, Hue and Saigon — the principal cities of Bac Bo (Tonkin), Trung Bo (Annam), and Nam Bo (Cochinchina) respectively — and the Japanese were helping the Viet Minh rather than the Nationalists.[42] In the last analysis the Japanese would have turned the government over to the devil rather than see the French return (provided the devil was Asian). The difference between the Japanese and the Chinese was that the Japanese would not be bribed.

The Party's critique of the August Revolution revealed that a major failure was their inability to seize the Banque de l'Indochine, which was the one institution the Japanese held back from the Viet Minh; another was the Party's failure to seize more arms from the Japanese, although Lieutenant-General Numata, Chief of Staff at Headquarters, Japanese Southern Army, later stated that the Japanese turned over quantities of arms to the Viet Minh. As the Party noted, Karl Marx had acknowledged that one cause of the failure of the Paris Commune in 1871 was its

39. On 20 August 1945 a car flying the Viet Minh flag toured the city, "rousing a bustling insurrectionist atmosphere among the population in preparation for the demonstrations of 21 and 24 August"(From "Saigonese Youth", March 1976, p. 21.)
40. Turner, p. 40.
41. *Thirty Years Struggle*, p. 97.
42. John T. McAlister, Jr., *Vietnam, The Origins of Revolution* (New York: Knopf, 1969), p. 253.

failure to capture the Banque de France, the "nerve center" of capitalist activity.

On 26 August Lieutenant-General Numata flew to Rangoon to negotiate the Japanese surrender to the British. The session was attended by Brigadier M.S.K. Maunsell, Chief of Staff to the newly-formed "Japanese Control Commission" (as it was then called) and former Chief of Staff to General Sir William Slim of the famed Fourteenth ("Forgotten") Army; Slim was now Commander-in-Chief, Allied Forces South East Asia. The Control Commission was placed under the command of Major-General Douglas D. Gracey, Commander of the 20th Indian Division. While the two Supreme Commanders, Admiral Lord Louis Mountbatten and Field-Marshal Count Terauchi, were working over their terms of reference, Ho Chi Minh was moving into Hanoi, now rapidly being cleared of opposition by Viet Minh "honor units" (assassination squads).[43] As the Party later noted, these liquidations were fundamental to the Viet Minh success.

It was vitally important for the Viet Minh that they should seize power before the Allies arrived, and thus appear as a *de facto* government to the occupying forces. They were under no illusions as to what would happen under any sort of Allied occupation (other than Russian). As early as December 1941, the Party had issued a communiqué which stated: "We must not nurture the illusion that the Chiang Kai-shek or British-American troops would bring us freedom." The Viet Minh would seek out allies everywhere, "even if they are only temporary, wavering or conditional ones." If the British-American forces helped the Viet Minh, "we could give them some economic advantages in Indochina."[44]

On 2 September 1945 (which happened to be the day of the formal Japanese surrender to the Allies in the person of General MacArthur), Ho Chi Minh proclaimed the founding of the Democratic Republic of Vietnam in Hanoi. Half a million people heard him make the announcement from the balcony of the opera house; the dramatic effect was heightened when a couple of American fighters flew low over the celebration,

43. Nguyen Duc Minh, pp. 56–7.
44. For comments on the allegations that senior OSS officers were privately negotiating business deals with the Party, see Devillers, *Histoire du Vietnam, 1940 à 1952* (Paris: Eds du Seuil, 1952), p. 202, or Lancaster, *The Emancipation of Indochina*, p. 143. For a different view see Buttinger's generally anti-French/British work, *Vietnam: a Dragon Embattled*, vol. 1 (New York: Praeger), pp. 343, 628–9. Devillers and Lancaster both had considerable first-hand experience in Indochina.

their white-starred insignia visible. The Viet Minh wasted no time in declaring that this was proof that the US Government supported the new DRV. Archimedes Patti, a virulently anti-Allied, pro-Viet Minh OSS officer, later stated that this exquisite timing was a coincidence brought on by pilot curiosity. It was only now that many Vietnamese people discovered that their new leader was the old Communist revolutionary, Nguyen Ai Quoc. A similar Viet Minh demonstration in the south ended in disaster. It was also called for 2 September to celebrate the Viet Minh's ascendancy, but in fact it proved the reverse, and the tragic results figured heavily in the actions of the future Allied commander in Saigon, General Gracey. Although the Viet Minh were nominally in control, several groups marched under their own banners. The Trotskyists especially were violently hostile to the ICP and Tran Van Giau, for they preached a more volatile line. The Cao Dai, Hoa Hao and Binh Xuyen bandits, among others, were their own masters. It was a huge rally, of perhaps a quarter of a million people. Given the loose overall control of a mob of this size, it was almost inevitable that violence would occur, and it did. It got out of control near the red-brick Catholic cathedral, when shots were fired from an unknown source. It has been suggested that French *agents provocateurs* were responsible, but this is questionable,[45] given the internment of most of the French security forces and the high state of fear of the French civil population. What seems more likely is that *provocateurs* of all hues were involved. A massive mob attack on a helpless French community, as in fact happened three weeks later, was not an unlikely event in this atmosphere.

A Catholic priest who was watching the demonstration, Father Tricoire, was dragged from the Cathedral after the first shots had been fired, stabbed repeatedly, and then finished off with a revolver.[46] The mob moved on, leaving a darkly dramatic scene behind. Father Tricoire's body, arms outstretched, lay on the steps of his Cathedral for over an hour. Five other French people were killed, and many were beaten and dragged off to prison. Much damage was caused, both political and physical.

45. Robert Shaplen, for example, leans to the view (*The Lost Revolution*, p. 5) that the Japanese were used as *agents provocateurs* by the French. Archival material and interviews with British and French officials who dealt with the Japanese at this time suggest that this would actually be the *least* likely explanation. The reason is that the Japanese so despised the French that they generally refused to work with them, let alone for them, and the Kempei Tei were the most virulently anti-French of them all.

46. Devillers, p. 154.

Tran Van Giau was embarrassed by the breakdown of march discipline and spent the next two days racing around Saigon to release as many imprisoned French people as he could find. But the harm was done, and the carefully cultivated myth of Viet Minh control was shattered, as it was to be again and again over the next few weeks. Just four days later the first Allied representatives arrived, in the form of a small British Repatriation of Allied Prisoners-of-War and Internees team, and they received first-hand reports of the riot from the now liberated Allied POWs, many of whom had formed units to protect the French civilians. These reports were sent back to Allied Headquarters and passed on to Rangoon to the senior officer most directly concerned, General Gracey, who, in his 4 September message to Field-Marshal Terauchi and from that moment on, reminded the Japanese of their obligation to maintain order under President Truman's General Order No. 1. As it turned out, he was not alone in insisting that the Japanese maintain order, for American and British local commanders from Korea and China to South East Asia relied on the Japanese security forces for some time to come.

On Ho Chi Minh's admission, there were only 5,000 Communists in Indochina at the time of the August Revolution. And there is little doubt that Communist ideology repelled the vast majority of Vietnamese people, hence the Party's constant use of cover organizations, fronts, alliances, and so on. How then did he do it? Irving, quoting Danielle Hunebelle in *Le Monde*, provides the following pithy comment:

When we say: "Ho Chi Minh is a Communist", the Vietnamese replies: "Ho Chi Minh is my father in the rice-paddy, my brother in the maquis. Do you wish me to take up arms against my father and my brother?" When we say: "But your father and your brother are fighting for Communism", the Vietnamese replies: "I am fighting for my independence. My father and my brother are fighting for their independence. As for your Communism, I have no idea what you are talking about."[47]

In the end, that may be as good an answer as any. Whatever the reason, it was especially during the August Revolution when Hồ Chi Minh, short on material and manpower but long on boldness and intuition, showed just what a magnificent political animal he was.

47. R. E. M. Irving, *The First Indochina War* (London: Croom-Helm, 1975), p. 136.

# 2

# THE FRENCH CONNECTION

In order to appreciate the emotional and unyielding post-war French attitude toward the future of Indochina, it is necessary to have some knowledge of the historic ties between those two countries. The following is a brief introduction.

In the seventeenth century French missionaries, mostly Jesuits, began to arrive in Vietnam, posing a challenge to the established religions and beliefs. Some of those French missionaries found their counsel sought by the imperial court. However, there were periodic purges when xenophobic Emperors forced the missionaries into hiding. In France, the influence of the Catholic Church (and especially the Paris Society of Foreign Missions, founded by the eighteenth-century Vicar Apostolic of Indochina, Pigneau de Béhaine) was so strong that the court was induced to send French warships repeatedly to bombard the Vietnamese. This was to secure the release of imprisoned missionaries (and to facilitate trade arrangements).

During the reign of Napoleon III, the French Government contemplated annexing Vietnam. The spreading of Catholicism remained a major factor, as did the need to compete with the British in Asia, and French control really began when Napoleon invaded (against the advice of many of his military and foreign affairs advisers). Napoleon was also encouraged to invade by his wife, who in turn was influenced by the Church. The French landed first (the Spanish were briefly involved as allies) at Tourane (later Danang), then turned south. By 1862 Cochinchina had become a colony, with Saigon as the major city. The rest of the French conquest, culminating in the final Franco-Chinese treaty in 1885, was a patchwork and haphazard affair, often resulting from the independent action of local commanders and swashbucklers. The experiences of Dupuis, Garnier, Rivière and the Black Flags (a group of Chinese brigands hired to fight the French), among others, are well recorded.

France took inordinate pride in Indochina; of all the colonies, it had pride of place. The military officers, engineers and administrators who closely followed the missionaries left their permanent memorials: the civil service, Vauban-type citadels, rail and road networks, education, industry, medicine, the immense feat of draining the Mekong marshes, the complex system of dykes in Tonkin, and more. All of this provided a livelihood for untold numbers of Vietnamese families. The Emperors were restored to their throne, albeit with limitations, and a Vietnamese militia was raised. Heroes were created during the course of the French conquest, and French schoolchildren eagerly read of them to this day. Indeed, so proud was France of her vaunted "civilizing mission" that she held regular and elaborate exhibitions to display to her metropolitan subjects the enormous benefits bestowed on the colonial peoples.

However, by contrast to the situation under other colonial administrations (the British, for example), the Vietnamese were confined to routine and generally menial jobs, for even lower-ranking civil service and police positions were filled by Frenchmen. This caused great local discontent; the unconquerable Vietnamese spirit produced recurring periods of unrest, and sometimes revolts, which were suppressed. Indochinese trade became tied to France.

The outbreak of the Second World War found the French armed forces in Indochina extremely weak and ill-equipped. In 1940 the Vichy Government appointed the controversial Admiral Decoux as Governor-General in place of General Catroux, who then joined de Gaulle. Cut off, the French had to bow to Japanese demands and opened up Indochina for transit; appeals to the United States and Britain for help had had no result. Although there was some French sympathy with the Allies, the *colons* remained generally Vichyite and cooperated with the Japanese, so that throughout the war Indochina remained the only colony in the Far East to keep the mother-country's flag flying. Viet Minh propaganda later played effectively on this Franco-Japanese collaboration. The French had other problems besides the Japanese. The Communists had received grievous wounds in the early 1930s, but they had not been quite finished off.

Concerning the mounting Japanese pressure, the French in Indochina felt obliged to follow the advice of their ambassador in Tokyo, and on 29 June 1940 Major-General Nishihara and thirty-five staff officers arrived in Hanoi to keep an eye on the borders and to collect intelligence. Four days earlier the Japanese had announced that part of their South China Seas Squadron would patrol the Gulf of Tonkin to monitor the embargo on goods to China. The collapse of France and the indecision of the new Governor-General, Decoux, contributed to the defeatist attitude of the French armed forces.[1]

---

1. The French Army now had one division in Tonkin, plus two "weak" divisions in Cochinchina and Cambodia. The Air Force could muster about twenty-five reason-

In early March the Japanese blockaded the border of Tonkin in an effort to choke off supplies to the Chinese. The flow of goods stopped on the two main routes to China (the Haiphong-Kunming railway and the Hanoi-Nanning road), and the third route via Kweiyang was being looked at. Rumors were also spreading that the Thais were considering granting bases in northern Siam to the Japanese to facilitate strikes against the Burma Road.

Early in August the French referred Japanese demands to the United States and Britain; these demands included the right of passage for Japanese troops and the use of naval and air bases in Indochina. The British Foreign Office attempted to enlist American support to put up a joint strong stand against the onrushing Japanese whirlwind, but the best they could get at this time was reflected in the bitter Foreign Office minutes: "The US refusal to do more than make a statement about the *status quo* seems categorical."[2] Added M. Esler Dening, Chief Political Adviser to the Supreme Allied Commander South East Asia and always the prophet in elaborating what was not yet called the Domino Theory (and who will figure prominently in this story): "I am afraid we must assume that US will do nothing, as usual . . . From Indochina it is but a step to Siam, and bases in Siam will at once put Malaya in grave danger. What we must do *urgently* is to stiffen up our defences as best we can in Malaya, and prepare for the worst. Because the worst is likely to happen." Before long the United States would join Britain in freezing Japanese assets, but as usual it was too little too late. For the present, business was business; Britain was about to become bankrupt through paying hard cash for American war supplies, and the Japanese onslaughts relied heavily on supplies of American petroleum and iron, also received on a cash and carry basis.[3]

On 4 August Lord Lothian, the British Ambassador in Washington, advised the Foreign Office of the Vichy Government's feeling that if Indochina were lost now it would be lost forever. On 5 August the Yugoslav Government passed on the Soviet information that the

---

ably effective planes; while the Navy had one old light cruiser plus a few smaller vessels. Against these the Japanese could immediately field eight, and possibly eleven, infantry divisions, eight battleships, twenty-four cruisers, five aircraft-carriers (each with 200 modern aircraft), sixty destroyers, and forty submarines.

2. GB, PRO, FO371/24719, Foreign Office minute by B. Gage, 6 Aug. 1940.

3. Thus vital oil, iron and other supplies continued to be sold to Japan until very late in the day, and it was likely that American metal sold to the Japanese was used in the carriers, aircraft and bombs which inflicted such damage on Pearl Harbor.

Japanese intended to seize Indochina and the Netherlands East Indies (now Indonesia). The Governor-General appealed directly to the United States for help, but the Japanese intercepted the message and confronted him with it. In the manner of Hitler and Vienna in 1938, they added that they would destroy Hanoi by bombing if their requests were not met.

The Japanese next demanded the right to use three airfields between Hanoi and China and to have 5,000 troops in Tonkin to defend the bases. They also wanted the use of all railways and set a deadline of 5 September for their ultimatum. The Foreign Office in London was following the drama, with difficulty, from long range. On 4 September, Dening noted: "The situation in Indo-China is at best obscure." It was not obscure to General Martin in Tonkin, who on that day agreed to the Japanese demands. To emphasize their seriousness, the Japanese sent their aircraft on "show-of-force" missions over Langson, and two companies of Japanese troops in battle formation crossed the frontier (but withdrew without making contact). The Chinese Ambassador in France, Dr Quo, thought that if the United States and Britain took a hard line over Japanese threats to Indochina, "they [the Japanese] would hesitate not once or twice, but thrice." In fact the French and Chinese did discuss joint defense plans, but nothing came of them.

The rest is well enough known. The Japanese pushed on, and when all hope of reasoning with them was lost, the United States suspended the trading of vital war materials to Japan, which unfortunately at this stage just about guaranteed the outbreak of war, for the occupation of Indochina was now essential for the Japanese. Japan's overriding concern at this time was to seize the Dutch oilfields in the East Indies, for the Allied embargo would immobilize the armed forces, and without the navy Japan's growth and even her existence were in jeopardy. The Japanese continued to bully the French, and by the summer of 1941 had garrisons in strategic bases throughout the whole of Indochina, including Cochinchina.

Their position in Indochina secured, the Japanese sprang south and west — to destroy white rule in Asia for ever. The British were driven back to India, the Dutch were locked up and the Americans were swept back to Hawaii. The French were later to prove that they could fight well in Indochina, but their collaboration with the Japanese brought them no honor at this stage.

The year 1942 saw the Japanese triumphant everywhere. The conquest of the American posts throughout the Pacific, the fall of Bataan and the fortress of Corregidor, the British surrender at Singapore, the rapid collapse of the Dutch and the subservience of the French — all heaped up the fires of Japanese chauvinism. In Europe a junior French general, Charles de Gaulle, whose war material consisted mainly of large charges of pride, was gathering together the scattered remnants of what had once been France. The French found refuge and strength in their African possessions, and it was from those bases that their long struggle to recovery was launched.

But although the French in Indochina were as tightly locked in as a ship in the pack ice, there were those Frenchmen who attempted to set up a resistance organization. This was extremely difficult given the long distances from Allied territory and the non-existent sources of supply. One remarkable Frenchman, involved in the resistance efforts from the start, provides an insight into the difficult beginnings of the movement. This was François de Langlade, who had been a rubber planter in British Malaya for nearly two decades. The smaller French staff left free in Asia were working closely with the British in Singapore. There was a feeling throughout the Malay archipelago during this period in 1941 that war was just around the corner. De Gaulle capitalized on de Langlade's administrative experience in the rubber industry by sending him to India, where he became the French Indochina (FIC) section of Force 136, working for Colin Mackenzie, its director, and collaborated closely in Force 136 plans for Indochina.[4]

With de Langlade in Delhi for the moment, a unique unit was being formed by the French in North Africa. This was the *Corps Léger d'Intervention* (CLI — Light Intervention Force), later renamed the 5th RIC, which missed its golden opportunity in Indochina, where it might have altered the course of history, because of the determination of the United States to eject France from there. The CLI was modeled loosely on the Chindits and was formed in Algeria during December 1943 by Lieutenant-Colonel Huard, who had seen long service in Asia. It was composed of 1,200 men who were specialists in various skills and Indochinese languages. The CLI would not be committed to combat as a unit, but would be dispersed throughout strategic areas of Indochina, its small parties forming cadres for an expanded resistance later.

At the end of January 1944 the men were divided into commandos dressed in the manner of British paratroopers but with Australian-style felt hats. The CLI's make-up and mission were similar to those of the US Special Forces in Vietnam a generation later. In a letter to Admiral

---

4. De Langlade brought out the news that the Japanese had very much exceeded their limit of about 32,000 troops, and now had close to 80,000 troops in Indochina; the British Ambassador in Bangkok refused to believe it.

Mountbatten, its prospective Theater Commander, Colin Mackenzie outlined the CLI's charter, which included political and military action. Its military tasks were

1. to form guerrilla zones in the hinterlands;
2. to sabotage strategic communications;
3. to work for the advantage of the principal Allies, primarily by assisting the initial cadres for units introduced by air; and
4. to make contacts with and restore the fighting morale of suitable elements of the old *Corps d'Occupation* and among the Police Force.

The CLI's political tasks were

1. to direct the operations of resistance groups which had already been organized in the country;
2. to report on the developing political situation in Indochina after the CLI had commenced operations; and
3. to take the preliminary essential measures in territory returned to Allied control which would restore French sovereignty, and to facilitate the eventual reestablishment of the regular civil authorities.

With the French thus laying the groundwork for re-entry to Indochina, de Gaulle ordered de Langlade to return to Indochina and go straight to Decoux. There was no definite course of action for Indochina at this time, but de Gaulle wanted information on the state of affairs there.

De Langlade's first try in 1944 was aborted when the United States authorities refused him permission to leave from Kunming, so he was forced to return all the way to India and use Force 136 facilities. The RAF flew him from the great Special Duty base at Jessore and dropped him into Indochina. It was, as de Langlade commented, "an eight hour flight to go over there, instead of half an hour". De Langlade's mission failed due to internecine disputes within senior French colonial ranks. General Aymé would have nothing to do with Free France and left it to Mordant to see de Langlade. De Langlade returned to de Gaulle and reported on the unsatisfactory results of his mission.[5] The meeting was brief. De Gaulle asked de Langlade, "Well, did you see Decoux?" De Langlade said no, at which point de Gaulle said, "Well, go back!", which he did.

This time de Langlade was allowed to stage from Kunming, because the OSS now needed information in Tonkin, and he arrived at Dien Bien Phu by aircraft, being spared the rigors of parachuting in again. He was

5. M. de Langlade stated that de Gaulle's memoirs give an accurate account of this episode.

now taken to Decoux in Hanoi by Colonel Robert (beheaded in the *coup* of 9 March 1945 by the Kempei Tei for his part in the resistance), and gave de Gaulle's message to the Governor-General. De Gaulle asked Decoux to keep completely apart from the resistance and refrain from interfering in any way. In return France was prepared to absolve him from post-war retribution. But Decoux was unable to resist the impulse to involve himself, and in de Langlade's words, "Instead he meddled — and went so far as to communicate with Vichy with a code we knew was bad. I had to stop the cables and go back and tell him." This summarized the greatest problem of the resistance throughout the war — the glaring security compromises. De Langlade was unhappy with the loose organization he found in Hanoi and, on the authority invested in him by de Gaulle, separated it from the fence-sitting senior officers and gave full control to the brave Robert; thereafter they preferred to work with younger men.

The resistance movement had two major purposes. The main reason for its existence was the hope of bringing out a large part of the French Army in Tonkin to China. These troops would later join the Allies in the war against the Japanese, as de Gaulle desperately wanted to get every man he could into the fight. There was no hope of getting the troops out from the south. The second purpose was the collection of information for Allied intelligence.[6]

The inter-Allied infighting over French involvement in the Far East is discussed later; suffice it to say that in January 1944 the French Committee of National Liberation took the first positive steps in that direction. General Blaizot was named Chief of the French Expeditionary Forces, Far East, and would head the French mission to Mountbatten's South East Asia Command headquarters in Ceylon. The French stressed that two conditions were necessary in order to put their military plans into effect: immediate contact between Blaizot and Mountbatten, and the introduction of French military representation in the Chiefs of Staff organization in Washington.

Chungking, Chiang Kai-shek's capital, at that time could easily have been a Hollywood creation. The British senior military representative

---

6. In this regard the resistance was extremely successful. Hundreds of thousands of tons of Japanese shipping were sent to the bottom by the China-based US 14th Air Force on information passed by the French. Other important targets were similarly struck. De Langlade reported a spectacular operation in 1944 when he asked for the bombing of a Japanese brigade assembled at the Hanoi railway station, and personally saw it carried out by the USAAF.

there was General Sir Adrian Carton de Wiart, a released POW, who had had an arm and an eye shot away and wore a black patch over the eye, and held Britain's highest award for valor, the Victoria Cross. He was now joined by the new Free French Ambassador, General Pechkoff, late of the French Foreign Legion, and also with one arm. General Pechkoff broke his journey in Kandy en route to Chungking. At SEAC headquarters, he said that while in the United States he had spoken to General Marshall and Mr McCloy, "both of whom had expressed sympathy for France and the restoration of the Empire." Asked about White House feelings, he stated that "a good friend" (reputedly General Donovan of the OSS) had recently seen President Roosevelt, and implied that "the wind in that quarter was not too unfavorable." If true, this had been a cynical playing on Pechkoff's fears, for the wind from the White House could not have been more unfavourable, and the French Mission at South East Asia Command, stalled in Europe, could only peer into Indochina from a distance and watch passing opportunities slip away.

Mountbatten continued to press for the installation at SEAC of the French Mission. His view was that the war would end in the foreseeable future, and, as reported by Dening, "these interminable delays will, if they result in General Stilwell obtaining strategic control of Indo-China, have a disastrous effect not only on the future operational prospects of his [Mountbatten's] Command, but on the whole British position in the Far East." In a memo to Dening, Mountbatten said that "poor General Blaizot, eventually driven nearly as mad as I have been by these delays, appears to have persuaded Mr Eden, through M. Massigli [Anthony Eden and René Massigli were respectively British Foreign Secretary and French Ambassador in London], to allow him at least to come out on a visit pending a final settlement between the President and the Prime Minister of the question of the Mission." As Mountbatten heard it, the British could not deal with Blaizot because he was de Gaulle's nominee, and de Gaulle was *persona non grata* with Roosevelt; this situation persisted even after Roosevelt accepted the facts of life and came to terms with de Gaulle. However, the time had come to act if future operations were not to be jeopardized.

On 1 September 1944, de Gaulle, enraged at the continued American refusal to sanction the movement of the *Corps Léger* to the Far East, and at the personal humiliations being heaped on him by US officials from the President down, ordered Frenchmen in Indochina to cease all cooperation with the Americans and to channel all intelligence information to the DGER[7] in Calcutta. This caused some problems, but the French resistance continued to supply the US 14th Air Force with vital target intelligence. The French in Indochina referred to the resistance efforts before 1 September 1944 as the "old" resistance and the organization after that date as the "new" resistance, reflecting the change of policy and direction from France. In the eyes of the old resistance in Indochina, conditions there and in France were similar, with Decoux a puppet of Japan much as Pétain was of Germany. After 1 September de Gaulle ordered Mordant, the Army Commander, to be his representative. When Decoux heard this, he retired Mordant from active service, saying he was too old to continue in his post, and replaced him with General Aymé, who wanted nothing to do with the Gaullists or the resistance. Aymé then told Mordant that since the Gaullist instructions stated that the Army Commander was to be in charge, then obviously it was Aymé, the General, and not Mordant (who was given the prefix "Monsieur"). Mordant then wired de Gaulle for clarification, asking who was to be in charge: himself or Aymé. De Gaulle replied that Mordant was in charge; Decoux remained at the top in name only. Therefore at that time the resistance ceased to be a "true" resistance, because the Government was no longer hostile and in fact received instructions from de Gaulle through the resistance.

As it happened, General Blaizot did go out to SEAC, arriving in Colombo on 26 October 1944 aboard the French warship *Dumont d'Urville*. Technically he was a visitor, but in fact he stayed. The high feelings at South East Asia Command over the Blaizot mission and the uneasiness regarding future developments were summarized by Dening: "I am sure the step is politically sound even though the Americans may shriek to high heaven at its impropriety." SEAC was envious of MacArthur's independence in the Pacific, for while Mountbatten adhered closely to guidance from the Chiefs, MacArthur was independent to a degree "not dreamt of in our philosophy, and I often think that we might on important occasions remind ourselves that we are not yet the 49th of the United States. I learned in strictest confidence that General Wedemeyer is destined to succeed Stilwell in China. He was with SAC in Cairo and knows of the decision. He is hardly likely to be on our side. So there may be trouble ahead."[8]

7. DGER (*Direction Général des Etudes et Recherches*) had replaced the old *Deuxième Bureau*. It consisted of the CE (*Contre-Espionnage*), SR (*Services des Renseignements*), and SA (*Service d'Action*).

8. GB, PRO, WO 203/5610, Dening to Sterndale-Bennett, Oct. 1944.

While Blaizot was on the high seas bound for Ceylon, General Juin, on behalf of the French Committee of National Liberation, outlined the role and composition of the French expeditionary forces for the Far East. French forces would be used mainly in actions leading to the liberation of Indochina. French ground and air units would initially be divided into two groups, one to operate in the Pacific (from New Caledonia) under US command, and one to stage from India under British command. But getting political approval to equip and move these forces to the Far East, in time for the Japanese surrender if not the March coup, would not be easy.

When Blaizot and his staff docked in Colombo, Dening and the SEAC headquarters Assistant Chief of Staff, Major-General Kimmins, went on board to welcome him. They all lunched in Colombo, then drove up to the pleasant town of Kandy, where Mountbatten's headquarters was located. Mountbatten received Blaizot, and the French were later entertained to dinner, when Mountbatten made a short welcoming speech. Blaizot sat next to Wedemeyer (who, reflecting Roosevelt's policy, had declined to accept the Blaizot mission in China Theater). What Blaizot had brought out with him was the nucleus of a force headquarters. Blaizot himself was described as "pleasant but colourless, a description which on first acquaintance would appear to apply as well to his staff". Wedemeyer left for Chungking a few days later. Again wistfully mentioning MacArthur's assumed independence, in which he informed his Chiefs of Staff, rather than consulted them, Dening wrote that "the extent to which [Wedemeyer] will cooperate is anybody's guess." As to Blaizot's mission, Dening and Mountbatten were of one mind and their views were reflected in a message from Colin Mackenzie, the Force 136 Commander, to SEAC: "Every step which registers a further *fait accompli* with regard to the basing of French activities in the Far East on SEAC as opposed to other Far Eastern theatres provides General Blaizot with an additional argument. SAC expressed his desire not long ago that we act in this sense, always provided that progress was made with the minimum of fuss."

In January 1945 the resistance in Indochina sent out word that the Japanese had moved 4,000 troops into Tonkin from Kwangsi, with possibly a division to follow. The Japanese were pressing for payments in the local piasters so exorbitant that the stability of that currency was threatened. The French authorities in Indochina saw these events as a hardening of Japanese attitudes and a warning signal of·an impending crisis, but Mountbatten said that it was not yet possible for SEAC to intervene directly in Tonkin. The French resistance had a difficult time in starting up and in carrying out concrete plans. Their source of support, Force 136 (SOE's special arm in South East Asia, immortalized in Pierre Boulle's *Bridge over the River Kwai*), had to fly tremendous distances to reach Indochina, and the OSS, just across the Tonkin frontier, could have made all the difference had they supported the French. But they officially refused to have anything to do with the French resistance movement.[9]

The Japanese *coup* of 9 March 1945 is examined in greater detail later, and it came as the French Provisional Government was beginning, slowly but firmly, to arrive at some practical measures for taking part in the war against Japan. Suffice it to say that the Japanese had an easier time of it due to what can only be described as the astoundingly lackadaisical attitude of senior French officers over security matters, and it took no geniuses in the Kempei Tei to piece the jigsaw together. So surprised were the French authorities that a delay of eight hours occurred before the Tonkin units were informed of the ultimatum handed to Decoux in Saigon.

The French, with great difficulty, succeeded in moving out about 5,000 troops into China, while scattered remnants found refuge in Laos. As expected, there was nowhere for the southern units to go. The Tonkin formations made the sort of fighting retreat which would have been immortalized elsewhere, but they were not later brought into the fight against the Japanese due to Chinese and American political objections. They remained in China, actually if not technically interned by the Chinese in less than pleasant circumstances.[10] The British Embassy in Chungking, sympathetic to the French, recorded the Franco-American friction over the exhausted French columns. When these troops first arrived across the frontier General Pechkoff, the French Ambassador, had a "stormy interview" with the American Ambassador, General Hurley, since the first American reaction to the arrival of the French had been "to get rid of them as speedily as possible".[11] The Americans,

9. One of the main arguments projected is that the OSS supported Ho Chi Minh because of the potential assistance his people could render in returning downed Allied aircrews. However, a vastly greater number of American fliers were cared for and returned at great risk by the French than by the Communists, who for thirty years have viewed American fliers as little more than bargaining chips.
10. See GB, PRO, FO371/46272 ("French Troops in China", July-August 1945), for the story of Mr Lionel Davis and how his small British "Ministry of War Production Unit" staff helped these French survivors.
11. GB, PRO, WO203/5561A, British Embassy, Chungking, to Foreign Office and M. E. Dening (SEAC), 18 May 1945.

reported the British Embassy, called the French "undisciplined, unequipped and destitute refugees and almost useless". The French hotly flung back that "despite all appeals for help they had had no assistance from the Americans in their own two-months fight with the Japanese," and what little help they did get from the British South East Asia Command had been subjected to American criticism. It was made clear to the US Ambassador and US Army headquarters that the French would strenuously resist evicting these troops from China. Pechkoff was further depressed on receiving a message from General Juin, who reported that the Combined Chiefs of Staff could foresee no immediate operations in Indochina and that the two French divisions could not be moved to Indochina in the immediate future. But, reported the British Ambassador, there had lately been a "sudden (and not explained) change of heart on the American side" to keep the French in China.

When it became evident that Allied help to the harassed French would be too little too late, the British and French began to concentrate on the problem of getting the *Corps Léger d'Intervention* to the East. Finally the US Chiefs agreed to the shift, provided that the British moved the CLI and took all responsibility for the operation — although by March 1945 the US Chiefs had still not formally replied to the request made in August 1944. Although the time had passed when the CLI could have done its best work, the British Chiefs thought that its cadres could still inject fresh blood and much-needed technical expertise into the French units slogging out of Tonkin. But even that moment passed as the CLI remained stuck in Algeria.

The British and Americans grew further apart over this issue, and the French Military Mission in Washington could as well have been in a revolving door, with their requests being tossed out as fast as they were submitted. Observing the situation, the Joint Staff Mission reported the position of the hapless French in trying to build up their armed forces, including the naval air arm:

In the replies they have been given from the Combined Chiefs of Staff they have received no encouragement whatsoever to think that their cooperation will be welcome, no promise that they will be given due warning when operations are being planned to liberate territories in which they are interested, and no indication that this situation is likely to improve in the future . . . We do feel that the attitude that has been adopted by the Combined Chiefs of Staff, largely of course on American insistence, is quite out of keeping with the current policy of our two governments to the French in Europe where they have been admitted to the EAC, the German Control Council and given a share in the occupation of

Germany. It seems only logical that this policy should be extended to the Far East. . . .[12]

In April the US Chiefs at last agreed to the CLI being moved but warned that due to a shortage of transport this was not a firm commitment as to time or the scope of their use in Indochina; they also assumed that their use would be coordinated with Wedemeyer. The CLI, now the 5th Colonial Infantry Regiment,[13] left their camp at Djidjelli for Algiers and embarked on 13 May for Ceylon, arriving on the 28th. Their new base was the "French camp" 20 kilometres from Trincomalee. Mountbatten asked for guidance from the War Office in London on the use of the French force, and back came the familiar reply: the War Office "can give no information" since the British were committed only to provide it with equipment, and the US Chiefs of Staff had expressed no view as to the use of the French in the war against the Japanese.

The French added to their own problems with the diversity of their chains of command, which their principal ally, the British, on occasion found confusing — as, no doubt, some Frenchmen did too. Mountbatten finally asked Blaizot for a diagram of the lines of command, the complexity of which did not appear on inspection to be justified by the numbers involved. Blaizot's paper to Mountbatten was based on a telegram from de Gaulle, which in British judgment resulted in no less than five equal French authorities. On 15 June de Gaulle approved the initial composition of the Expeditionary Corps for the Far East. He selected Philippe Leclerc, commander of the crack 2nd Armored Division, as its commander; Leclerc had wanted to go to Morocco, but de Gaulle told him: "You will go to Indo-China, because that is more difficult."[14] Leclerc's title was Commander of French Forces in the Far East, and he was eventually to replace Blaizot at Kandy, en route to Indochina.

---

12. GB, PRO, FO371/46321. Joint Staff Mission to London, 12 Apr. 1945.
13. The *Corps Léger d'Intervention* came into being on 4 Nov. 1943, and was renamed the 5th *Régiment d'Infanterie Coloniale* (RIC). The operational priorities of the 5th RIC were: (1) Moi country south of Pleiku, and north of the Great Lake, Cambodia — to enable landing operations in south Annam or the Cambodian coast and interrupt Japanese lines of communications areas and observe troop movements; (2) Annam Quadrilateral [Vinh-Thakhek-Savannaket-Quang Tri], plus the Tran Ninh Plain [Sam Neua-Paksane-Vientiane] — to enable Allied operations in Indochina to be insulated and to intercept Japanese movements between Siam, Annam and Tonkin.
14. Charles de Gaulle, *The Complete War Memoirs* (New York: Simon and Schuster, 1964), p. 926.

In July the Potsdam Conference ("Terminal") was held. Like Solomon in his wisdom, the politicians cut the Indochina baby in half, and as might have been expected it was not conducive to the baby's health. In August the two atomic strikes were made against Japan which ended the war. The US Chiefs hesitated to make their return journey to Washington via London because they might be accused by the Russians of "ganging up" against them. The British could not accept that argument, pointing out that the war with Germany was over and Russia was not at war with Japan. General Marshall had wondered if he should even attend the conference, because most of it was political.

In early August the Chief of the French Colonial Mission, Inspecteur des Colonies de Raymond, was in Calcutta. With him was Major Pierre Messmer, the High Commissioner-designate for Tonkin, while Captain (soon Colonel) Cédile, the acting High Commissioner for Cochinchina, was in Kandy. Cédile at the moment was in Burma observing the British Military Administration there. The British would (in addition to the eight Civil Administrators being trained in London) mobilize and train French administrators in Ceylon, but in deference to US attitudes, they gave no firm commitments regarding operations in Indochina, which forces might conduct such operations, or the eventual use of the Civil Affairs trainees (about 100).

With the end of hostilities with Japan, the French wanted to take immediate possession of Hanoi, Saigon, Hue, and Phnom Penh in order to establish French authority, ensure order, and release Allied prisoners-of-war and internees. Six DGER teams were standing by in Calcutta to parachute into these four cities, each team composed of four Frenchmen and two Vietnamese. These were reconnaissance teams, and when their reports were received, further civilian and military officials would follow.[15] Hanoi and Saigon were to receive two reconnaissance teams each, with single teams destined for Hue and Phnom Penh. If Wedemeyer were to decide to cooperate, General Alessandri would enter Hanoi from China.

By 15 August the awaited Japanese capitulation occurred, and Mountbatten's staff were frantically attempting to cope with their new and crushing responsibilities throughout South East Asia and the Netherlands East Indies. On 15 August Mountbatten asked London to send out

15. About 100 parachutists were introduced into Indochina by DGER in August and early September. Many were picked up by the Japanese, and General Gracey was asked on 6 September to obtain their release. Most of those in Viet Minh hands had been executed.

Civil Affairs officers with experience in France. "Regarding FIC, while planning here does not envisage occupation of any large areas, we are considering the composition of a projected SACSEA control commission to Japanese Southern Army headquarters at Saigon/Dalat which may have to control the area surrounding those headquarters." The words "control the area surrounding those headquarters" need emphasizing, for this is exactly what the Allied Commander (General Gracey) was directed to do.

On 18 August Mountbatten was told that Admiral Thierry d'Argenlieu would be nominated as High Commissioner and Governor-General.[16] In his capacity the Admiral would be senior to Leclerc, a turnabout from their respective positions in Africa. How he later personally wrecked the delicate negotiations being carried on between Ho Chi Minh and the French Government has been adequately described elsewhere. A terrible mistake was made in appointing him to that supreme post at such a crucial time.

We shall soon follow the course of events in Cochinchina, but it is necessary to follow, briefly at least, the initial French actions in Tonkin. The key man in the French operations was Pierre Messmer, who was designated High Commissioner for Tonkin, the dangerous and crucial protectorate which France needed to control as quickly as possible. Here the race with the Viet Minh was on. The appointment of administrators like Messmer and Cédile began a controversy which still continues today. These were the Gaullists, untainted by Vichy collaboration but new to Indochina. The question was whether to sweep the Vichy offi-

---

16. When Pierre Messmer, a man destined to become Army Minister, Defense Minister, and Prime Minister of France, was asked why d'Argenlieu had been appointed, he replied: "I never understood it . . . Anyway, I think it was a bad choice. He was an old man, and before the First World War he was a Navy officer. French Navy officers were very hard on colonial questions." After the First World War d'Argenlieu entered a monastic order, and remained there for some twenty years till he joined de Gaulle and received his Navy rank. Said Messmer, "He had been in a strict order, and he was strict when he came back into the service." (Personal interview, 1 September 1977.)

   François de Langlade provided an insight into the de Gaulle philosophy. He had met d'Argenlieu several times, and all correspondence between de Gaulle and d'Argenlieu passed through him. D'Argenlieu was "a bit of a disaster. But that was de Gaulle. The man didn't matter — what was important was the job, and any man should have been able to fill it." It was a view not shared by de Langlade who added, "We didn't have a very great choice, don't forget." De Gaulle was hesitant to give jobs to new people, and he "tried to help an old pal at the same time".

cials out completely and replace them with the new breed, or to keep them on and use their experience of the Far East.[17]

The original plan for reconnaissance teams was now modified in that the teams to be parachuted into Tonkin would restore French sovereignty to their areas. All teams passed through the SA (*Service d'Action*) section of DGER for final preparation before being sent in. Seven three-man teams were readied for Tonkin, and they were all dropped by RAF Special Duty B-24 Liberators from Jessore, near Calcutta. Their training had been given by Force 136. Messmer's civil mission wore uniforms for security reasons.[18]

Of the men sent in to Tonkin, few lived to tell of their experiences. All seven groups were captured by the Viet Minh, and only two survived and escaped out of Messmer's group. Two teams were returned by the Viet Minh after the Leclerc operations in Tonkin: the other four teams (twelve men) were executed, and one man in Messmer's group was poisoned. This was one of the many excruciating "might have beens" which characterize these few weeks bracketing the Japanese ceasefire.

17. Did the French replace too many of the old civil servants? Messmer answered:
    "A very good question. Many people think, even now, it was a mistake. It is not my opinion. The old civil service in Indochina, like the Indian Civil Service, had certain strong ideas about the policy to follow in Indochina, and were very strongly against people like Ho Chi Minh, Vo Nguyen Giap, and all the people who are dead now — Duong Bach Mai in Cochinchina. It was quite impossible to have through them any kind of cooperation with the Viet Minh. It was quite impossible.
    "De Gaulle's idea was, first, to replace French sovereignty in Indochina, and then to negotiate a new status with the government which had been in function then. It would have been more difficult to do this with the old civil servants from Indochina. To negotiate a new status would have been quite impossible."
18. Messmer recalled: "We were sent, seven small troops of three people, over North Vietnam (Tonkin and Annam) — two or three in the South. I was dropped at the foot of Tam Dao,[19] a large mountain not far from Vinh Yen. It was an awfully bad place to drop people because it was what was called the *Moyen Région*, Middle Region — that is to say not the mountains and not the plains, but a kind of country with small hills, terribly complicated, with numerous calcareous caves, and trees. An awfully bad place, and moreover a place where we always had a very bad political situation. The French were always in heavy difficulties in the Middle Region — it was simply a bad place to drop us." (Pierre Messmer, personal interview, 1 Sept. 1977.)
19. USAF officers in America's Vietnam war will never forget the gigantic Tam Dao massif. Always known to them as "Thud Ridge", it pointed straight to Hanoi, and at the base of it was located Phuc Yen airfield, the main North Vietnamese MiG fighter base.

Messmer himself is best qualified to pick up the story. "We left from near Calcutta — Jessore; RAF Liberator with Australian pilots."[20] A built-in "time cushion" brought his Liberator to its target area one hour ahead of schedule, so to kill time and make good his TOT (Time over Target) the pilot gave the team a look at the coast along the Gulf of Tonkin and lazily swept inland to view Hanoi. It was a daytime flight with the drop scheduled to be made at dusk. Said Messmer, "We saw Hanoi airport, with no flak at all — no Japanese planes, a very peaceful atmosphere. I told the pilot, 'Drop me here, this is a good place.' His response was, 'I am ordered to drop you over Tam Dao.' If we had decided to land [at Hanoi's Gia Lam airport] with the plane it would have been all right. But he had orders and he decided not to disobey orders — *but it was the day and the place to disobey orders!*"

Messmer added the following: "As a matter of fact, if our seven groups had dropped together, that is to say twenty-one people, we could have got through [the Viet Minh] because they were not well organized, and we should have succeeded in entering Hanoi. Without question. From a military point of view there is no doubt at all in my mind. They were not organized — they had small groups with old weapons, and no wireless, no telephone, no communications. With twenty people we should have passed through."

Had they dropped together and broken through to Hanoi, what might have happened? A strike at the Citadel would have released several thousand French soldiers incarcerated there in appalling conditions, the capable *Sûreté* would have re-established their networks, Ho Chi Minh would not have made his independence speech in Hanoi, and the French — back on the streets — could have dealt with the Chinese on more or less an equal basis. But for want of a nail the kingdom was lost. Who made the decision (against some questioning by the teams involved) to scatter and drop the groups separately? It was the old problem of officers in the field trying to present a realistic picture of conditions to the headquarters staff. Messmer was not impressed with the plan and was not sure who could have approved it. De Langlade, de Gaulle's right hand man as Secretary-General for Indochina, thought that the decision was probably taken collectively by two officers of the *Service d'Action* and

---

20. This is one of the inaccuracies in the portion of Ellen Hammer's *The Struggle for Indochina, 1940–1955* relating to this period in which she credits an American C-47 (implying the OSS) with dropping Messmer's team into Tonkin. Force 136 was compelled to make its attempts at checking the Viet Minh and supporting the French from long range.

*Services des Renseignments* sections, Crèvecoeur and Roos. Messmer was told by Roos to do it. Unfortunately, the plan was made before 9 March 1945 and was never changed, despite the fact that after the Japanese coup the French no longer controlled the country. When Messmer disappeared, Jean Sainteny was sent in to replace him as *Commissaire de la République*. Sainteny knew that Messmer had been captured by the Viet Minh and came down from Kunming as fast as possible, obstructed and humiliated at every step of the way by the OSS during those crucial days. His experiences are recorded in his book *Histoire d'une Paix Manquée* (Story of a Failed Peace).

The OSS men, including senior officers, were easily seduced by the Viet Minh who succeeded in maintaining the chasm between Americans and French. The usual "Friendship Association" was formed, this one "Vietnamese-American", promising to "send students to America". The American officers were so carried away with it all that at the Vietnamese-American Friendship Association's inaugural party, the audience was treated to the spectacle of the senior American officer and his aide going on stage to sing songs: "Lieutenant Unger, aide-de-camp to General Gallagher, sang a French Romance and was thunderously applauded. But the greatest success was General Gallagher's, who by order — once in a lifetime — of his aide-de-camp, went before the microphone for a lively performance."[21] This, for a senior Western military officer on a blatantly political occasion, was an astonishing action. In plain English, they were had.

On 30 September 1945, a US officer wrote an eight-page report on his experience in Tonkin. He had been sent to Ho's headquarters to establish an Air-Ground Aid Service (AGAS) communications net and to facilitate pilot rescue, and remained at Ho's camp from mid-June till the end of August. He came to know Ho fairly well while operating in the Tuyen Quang/Thai Nguyen/Bac Can triangle just north of Hanoi, and his report was a summary of the political situation from his vantage point near Ho, in the field. It was critical of the French record and of some of the OSS personnel, and said that the Viet Minh League had been backed by the Japanese, who "have given the Viet Minh a great deal of arms and

21. US Government Printing Office, *The United States and Vietnam: 1944-1947*, Staff Study no. 2 for the Senate Committee on Foreign Relations, 1972. Gallagher was later reprimanded for saying that there was "no question of restoration of the French protectorate in Indochina", and other remarks concerning French sovereignty. He later denied making these statements, but was told to stick to the narrow limits of his job as an advisor to Lu Han. (NA, RG165/336.2, Box 965.)

ammunition which they had taken from old French stocks." He stated that it appeared the Viet Minh enjoyed widespread support, and he criticized the continued lack of a firm US policy for Indochina. Further-more, "There is also the fact that several irresponsible American officers who arrived in Hanoi shortly after signing of the peace have made state-ments which should only have been given by the State Department. A Captain (now Major) Paddy [Patti] from OSS has gone on record with the statement that the US is wholeheartedly behind the VML [Viet Minh League] cause."[22] On 5 December 1945, Colonel Nordlinger, late of the American mission in Hanoi, reported personally to Abbot L. Moffat of the State Department. Moffat recorded that "Colonel Nordlinger commented that the younger American Army personnel and particularly the OSS group were extremely pro-Annamese and anti-French."

According to Sainteny, a man who personally held Ho Chi Minh in high esteem, the Americans in Hanoi, in playing the "anti-colonial" and "anti-white" game, helped to pave the way for Asiatic Communism. Sainteny asked himself why the OSS, "so rich in men of valor", sent such "short-sighted amateurs" to Tonkin during the critical August and September of 1945.[23] He prophesied that one day the United States would pay for its mistake, which was not confined to the local area.

And what was the Viet Minh reaction to the ease with which they were manipulating their American colleagues? Vo Nguyen Giap had no idea why the Americans had turned so venomously on their own French allies, but he was amused: "Soon after we returned . . . we also noticed that the Americans and the French in Hanoi seemed to dislike each other.

22.  NA, RG51, Box 6177, 30 Sept. 1945.
23.  Messmer summed up the effects of the OSS actions and the memorable feat of Ho playing off the various factions against each other in what some authorities regard as his finest hour:

> "We had heavy difficulties [with the OSS]. The problem was not easy. All our French problems in Indochina at that time, in '45–'46, are clear when you know that Roosevelt had decided to bar the French. I suppose he gave orders to the Officer Commanding in China — it was Wedemeyer — to manage the thing, so we had as many problems as possible. As a matter of fact we had awfully bad problems in north Indochina. At the same time we had no real problem at all in the south, where the British were in charge of the mission, especially in Cochin-china and Cambodia.
>
> "But in the north the OSS sent an officer to Hanoi, a Major Patti, who was sort of a counsellor to Ho Chi Minh. And Ho Chi Minh thought it was easy for him to play American off against French, and later to play French against Chinese when Leclerc was there." (Personal interview, 1 September 1977.)

[. . .] The American officer by the name of Patty [*sic*], for some reason we don't know, showed sympathy for the Viet Minh's anti-Japanese struggle.''[24] Of Potsdam even Giap wrote, ''Under American pressure, the French were left out of the operation'', but ''Gradually the Americans came to realize that we were not pro-Western 'nationalists' as they had expected.'' The rest is well recorded. The Chinese arrived in Hanoi and complicated the issue while the French were still off-balance.

In 1977, while much of the present work was being written, Michael Charlton presented a BBC radio series on Vietnam entitled ''Many Reasons Why''. It contained a concise history of events in Indochina in the 1940s while dealing with American's Vietnam war. In tracing the beginnings Charlton, who interviewed the main surviving participants, noted that when the Communists seized Hanoi and proclaimed the formation of the Democratic Republic of Vietnam in September 1945, American [OSS] officers, including Patti, stood beside the Communists and saluted the DRV flag. As Sainteny wrote, ''the infantile anti-colonialism of the Americans assisted to power a movement dominated by Communists with incalculable consequences.'' There is a photograph in *The Listener* magazine showing Patti and Giap saluting the Communist flag over the Hanoi citadel, in which the French were imprisoned. Charlton stated correctly that the British, in supporting France, ''engaged in what can only be called a running battle with the Americans over the post-war order in Asia'' when American officers in Kunming were blocking the return of the French to Hanoi, and allowing Ho Chi Minh to get there instead.

The selection of Patti to go to Indochina was odd, since the OSS had to bring him specially from Europe. He had to look at a map to discover the whereabouts of Indochina. He reported that General Donovan told him to avoid politics; if so, he carried out his orders in a strange way. Patti told Charlton that he knew of Ho's Communist background, and that Ho was using him; he did not mind because ''the use he made of us.was more one of image than substance.'' This revealed how lamentably little the Americans knew — and know — of Vietnamese culture in which symbolism is everything — image *is* substance. Charlton mentioned that it was clear in retrospect that the Viet Minh may have spent more time attacking and terrorizing their fellow-countrymen, and assassinating government officials, than the Japanese, and hinted that the OSS

24. Vo Nguyen Giap, *Unforgettable Days* (Hanoi: Foreign Languages Publishing House, 1975), pp. 18–19.

saw this; Patti replied that "there might have been some of that." Patti's version of the disbandment of the OSS offices in Hanoi made no mention of the fundamental reason for their departure: the new American consul in Hanoi packed them off as quickly as he could, before they could further damage long-range American interests. (The JCS history of the period, *The Indochina Incident, 1940–1954*, states that General Wedemeyer, Commanding China Theater, fired them.)

Charlton concluded that the show of American support for Ho Chi Minh (including an unfortunate fly-past of USAAF fighters at the independence ceremonies) left a deep impression on the Vietnamese people, one of whom became an important figure in the south. This was General Tran Van Don, who recalled that the "crucial fact" was that the Americans appeared to back Ho. In his view it was not popular sentiment but the visible support of the powerful Americans (in the form of some OSS officers) who put Ho over the top. Even Bao Dai, the Emperor, could not resist it. The French were treated as outright enemies by the Americans, who made sure that the unfortunate French prisoners remained locked up. Sainteny remembers that Patti used regularly to come by his place of confinement "to make sure we were really guarded by the Japanese — our common enemy", who had surrendered two weeks earlier but who still guarded them with fixed bayonets. The American officers inspected the Japanese guards on the French. According to Charlton, Ho was smart enough to know that the United States, not the Soviet Union, would determine events in Indochina, and it was "Americans who literally took revolution by the hand and accompanied it into Hanoi."[25]

25. Dennis Duncanson acknowledges Ho's gift for politics. Neither Ho nor the Communists won power by a simple "sentimental appeal to the mass of the people". Politics was not like that, and no Communist ever thought that it was — power grows from gun barrels. Duncanson rated Ho's performance higher than Lenin's. Lenin was a great writer, Ho was not. However, Ho "in his narrow field was . . . as a political manipulator, supreme." (*The Listener*, London, 22 Sept. 1977, pp. 357–60.)

Patti's book on his brief stay in Hanoi, *Why Viet Nam? Prelude to America's Albatross*, was reviewed for *The Times Higher Education Supplement* (London) by P. J. Honey, who summed up as follows: "Patti's account of the British in southern Vietnam, derived largely from communist propagandists, is inaccurate, misleading, and probably libellous. Lord Mountbatten believed that, had Britain disarmed the Japanese throughout the whole country instead of just the south, there would have been no Vietnam war and no communist regime. *Why Viet Nam?* would appear to prove him right. Instead of denigrating General Douglas Gracey, Patti would do well to ponder why China and North Vietnam, both in the American China

To return to our narrative, in the south it was a different story. The southern half of the two-pronged French re-entry into Indochina was led by Jean Cédile. As Pierre Messmer had responsibility for the north, Cédile was designated Commissioner for Cochinchina, or Southern Vietnam. He had been sent by the Gaullist Government to represent it at Mountbatten's headquarters and to study the British Army and British military administration. He was attached to the staff of the Director of Civil Affairs, Brigadier Gibbons, and travelled up and down Burma looking at Civil Affairs administration.

It was de Gaulle's wish that, since the Japanese had laid down their arms, a French presence must immediately be felt in Indochina. As Cédile stated: "General de Gaulle insisted that I be parachuted immediately so that there should be a Frenchman looking after French interests, and that the British would not be left solely in charge of the situation. This was not to imply a mistrust of the British, but obviously the situation required a French officer to be present."[26] Two days before he jumped, Cédile was taken to Jessore where the other small teams were being assembled. Then on 24 August, the RAF took several teams under his command, a total of about twenty-one men, in two or three aircraft and dropped them at their scattered drop zones all over Cochinchina and Annam. Said Cédile, "It was my first jump, and my only jump. I landed in a triangle between Soc Trang, Tay Ninh and the Cambodian frontier. We landed near some lakes, and it was the season of flooding. Our presence must have been revealed and in the middle of the night, at about eleven o'clock, we were attacked and captured by a Japanese company."

On landing, Cédile knew that he and his three subordinates could rely on little but their own wits. At that time there was no question of Franco-Japanese cooperation. Cédile's mission, according to his instructions, was to re-establish French authority as quickly as possible and to show the French in Indochina that France had not abandoned them and was coming back. Said Cédile, "We had virtually nobody, and the Frenchmen on whom we could count were the prisoners-of-war. The Allies too [POWs], such as the Dutch, the Australians and the British, were exceedingly cooperative. . . . The British sent units of

Theatre, fell to communism while Pakistan, India, Burma, Malaysia, Singapore, Thailand, and Indonesia are free independent states. South Vietnam resisted northern communism for thirty years, and its people still struggle even today. These developments did not come about by chance. *Why Viet Nam?* may well explain why Vietnam."

26. Jean Cédile, personal interview, 26 Oct. 1977.

the 20th Indian Division under General Gracey. There was never any doubt about cooperation with the British — there was 100 per cent cooperation.''

The Japanese interrogation of Cédile and his men was not a gentle one. The Japanese wanted to know if there were any more parachutists in the area, to which Cédile replied no, there were just the three of them plus the seven parachutes. (It must be kept in mind that the war was now over.) They were then marched to the local brigade headquarters, fording rivers en route, with hands bound behind their backs, and at times cruelly beaten. Cédile has never forgotten his treatment at the hands of the Japanese at the time of his capture by an ''élite Manchurian division''.

The higher-ranking Japanese officers ''understood that the game was up, but the troops — if we had stayed with them, things would have turned out very badly for us. They were not yet aware of the state of the war . . .'' When Cédile and his team arrived in Saigon they were kept in a school, along with some other parachutists who had been picked up by the Japanese. They stayed there for a few days, with little to eat or drink (the Japanese themselves were suffering shortages). Again, their stay at the school was not a pleasant one, and after a few days Cédile and two others managed to escape. He was precise in emphasizing that his break-out from the school was an escape, since the Japanese had them under what amounted to house arrest. Continued Cédile: ''We then went to the Governor-General's palace; it was on that day in fact that the Japanese guards were just leaving, to be replaced by the Vietnamese. My friends and I had taken a machine-gun from the Japanese. We went to the top of the palace stairs and opened fire from there, and somehow, luckily, the three Vietnamese guards just ran off. I then asked the Japanese to send us some guards to guard us and the palace, and they did so, and gradually the [Allied] troops began to arrive.'' It seems likely that Cédile and the French were now benefiting from the firm line being taken with the Japanese by Gracey in Rangoon.

The political situation in Saigon at this time (the beginning of September 1945) was extremely fluid and confusing. In Cédile's words, there were Japanese officers like one French-speaking colonel (referred to by Cédile phonetically as Imano) who knew that they had lost and had little to say. But there were others who were defying the official position of the government in Tokyo: ''One mustn't forget that these Japanese had in fact formed and armed some Vietnamese guerrillas. They armed and trained them against us. And that is why we very quickly found

Vietnamese guerrillas fighting against us, and in many places we even saw the Japanese commanding the Vietnamese commando troops. I'm not sure if the [Japanese] government knew anything about that; I am convinced that they must have had some inkling of it, but they always denied it when asked."

Cédile and his two companions broke out on the day before the massive demonstration of 2 September: "The Viet Minh believed that they would win and come to power and they were having demonstrations . . ." Of those disturbances Cédile said, "I'm convinced there were provocateurs among the French, but also especially on the part of the Vietnamese. It was the Vietnamese who were provoking the French, and the French reacted to these provocations instead of remaining quiet as we'd ordered them to do. Because, after all, we were not fools; we knew we were not the·strongest, but they didn't take heed of that and they retaliated by provoking the Vietnamese."

Cédile went up to Loc Ninh as soon as possible, to see the former Governor-General, Admiral Decoux. The Japanese were reticent about letting him go there, but he demanded to go, and by now Mountbatten had telegraphed the Japanese, saying that Cédile represented him and General de Gaulle, and that his safety was his (Mountbatten's) responsibility. Said Cédile, of Decoux, "I wanted to tell him that he had nothing further to do in Indochina and that he could go away. In fact, we sent him away in a very correct manner." Despite their reluctance to see Cédile go to Loc Ninh, the Japanese gave him an armed escort and, due to the worsening security situation, returned his revolver; but "they never talked much about politics, and if one asked them they never replied." Cédile had great trouble in simply communicating with the Japanese, and Imano appeared to be the only French-speaking Japanese officer available. Imano traced the course of events for Cédile, including the atomic explosions. He said that American troops were moving across the Pacific, Burma had already been liberated, and part of Siam was being attacked, so really there was no longer any hope for them.

In Saigon, said Cédile, "We immediately understood that things were going very badly." Although he had great difficulty in establishing contact with the Viet Minh authorities, there were problems from other quarters: "As for the French, they realized we were just a few officers with no arms, nothing. As soon as they saw a French uniform they thought that everything was fine and there would be no more problems now, no more occupation. There were provocations from both sides . . ." Cédile was explicit in recalling the fundamental problem, namely a lack of hard intelligence: "We had very little information about what was going on in Saigon, especially after the events of 9 March, when a lot of Frenchmen were eliminated; all our agents were either captured, imprisoned, killed, or went into hiding . . . In fact, some British officers in Lord Mountbatten's headquarters had asked us to send them what little information we could. But unfortunately I couldn't do very much about that, for when I was captured by the Japanese I managed to throw away all my coding instructions and cards and couldn't send them what little information I had."

Cédile reiterated his difficulty in getting the Viet Minh to a conference table, partly because of his own limited authority: "I found it very difficult to meet any of the authorities. The Committee for the South used to send me emissaries to tell me a few things and ask me what my government was going to do, but I really was not in any position to enter into negotiations because I myself didn't know what the situation was as I had left France some months before . . ." There were several critical lost opportunities in this history, and this is one of them. Although there now appears little doubt that de Gaulle fully intended eventually to grant independence to Indochina,[27] he can be faulted for not making his plans known to his emissaries, his Allies, and the Vietnamese. In any case, the Viet Minh initially avoided the French envoys. On the few occasions when Cédile did meet the Viet Minh representatives, his main efforts were directed to preserving the safety of the French civil population in Saigon. Meanwhile, he formed "a kind of embryo police force and intelligence force", preparing for the French arrival. Cédile provides a clue as to why the Viet Minh appeared reluctant to meet him: "They [the Viet Minh] were not very sure of themselves. They often gave out proclamations, many of them, and very often these contradicted each other." And referring to the period just before the arrival of the Allies, Cédile remarked to the author, "One of your compatriots was there, Peter Dewey." A good many people would soon have a lot to say about Dewey.

27. As he did with Algeria when he returned to power, de Gaulle intended to grant independence to Vietnam. But he was obliged to retire from politics in 1946, and the rise and fall of a succession of weak French governments made it impossible to prosecute the war effectively.

   Both Pierre Messmer and François de Langlade, who shared de Gaulle's innermost thoughts, are emphatic on this point. Both separately stated that de Gaulle had made up his mind to *grant* Vietnam and other colonies independence (as opposed to letting them *take* it), but it would first be necessary temporarily to re-establish French sovereignty exactly as it had been.

The first substantial French force to arrive in Indochina was commanded by Lieutenant-Colonel Jacques Massu, whose *Groupement Massu*, of the 2nd Armored Division, would soon be disembarking in Saigon. Massu, a soldier's soldier, had been hand-picked by Leclerc for the task.[28]

Leclerc went on to Tokyo to represent France at the Japanese surrender on the *Missouri*, after which MacArthur told him to rush as many French troops as possible to Indochina in order to re-establish French sovereignty. De Gaulle knew the difficulties facing the French in Indochina, and although he had resolved to grant autonomy to the Vietnamese within the French Union, it was unfortunate that his plans to grant them outright independence were not widely heralded. De Gaulle later wrote: "The Allies, applying their pre-established plan for the occupation of the country — Chinese north of the 16th parallel, British south, American missions everywhere — had fatally compromised the effect which the immediate arrival of French troops and officials and the disarmament of the Japanese by our force might have produced . . ."[29]

To summarize, history has now given its verdict on all the gross errors of judgment committed by some (but not all) of the American representatives in North Vietnam. Ho Chi Minh has emphasized the supreme importance of the American support he received at this time. By morally and materially supporting the Communists, and by fiercely opposing the return of the French, they ensured the survival of the Communists in Indochina. For this policy the United States would soon pay a heavy price — in prestige and in blood. Ho used the Americans during the last

28. Massu went on to become a four-star general in the French Army and a legend in his lifetime. He commanded the French paratroops during the Suez invasion of 1956 and used his power base in Algeria to topple the French Government and return de Gaulle to power. In a now classic operation (described by Jean Larteguy in *The Centurions*, from which the film *The Lost Command* was made), his airborne division, in a brutally efficient operation, cleared Algiers of the FLN and urban terrorists. During the leftist uprisings in 1968 Massu and the Army sustained de Gaulle in the Presidency. His iron-fisted methods of turning the tactics and techniques of urban terrorists against themselves have made him the bane of some writers, but his methods as a very tough and successful commander may well be studied in the Age of the Terrorist.

29. Charles de Gaulle, *War Memoirs: Salvation, 1944–1946* (London: Weidenfeld and Nicolson), p. 225.

year of the war and continued to use them during his seizure of power in Hanoi. It is no exaggeration to say that he made the American officers dance to his tune with embarrassing ease; he simply had to trot out the "anti-colonialist" tune. An iron curtain ultimately fell over North Vietnam, and 50,000 Americans were killed by Ho's men in the South a generation later. He used the Americans simply to legitimize his revolution, for the sight of American officers at his beck and call had a profound, if not decisive, influence on the Vietnamese masses. There are few Vietnamese today — whatever their politics — who would dispute this. Another short-sighted policy was the continued US veto over the transfer and employment of the *Corps Léger* in Indochina at a time when it could well have destroyed the Communists.

Was the effectiveness of the fight against the common enemy, Japan, reduced because of the American anti-French prejudice? The USAAF was more than willing to receive and react to target information from the French resistance in the field, as stated explicitly by François de Langlade and Marcel Mingant, but would not be seen having a Frenchman officially assigned to a US staff agency. For it was the French, and not the Viet Minh, who possessed the technical expertise, who knew intimately the factories, lines of communications and vital installations in Indochina, and how to inflict the maximum damage on the Japanese. And although the French *colons* collaborated to an unconscionable degree with the Japanese, there were enough Gaullists to form an effective resistance if they had been properly supported and exploited. Certainly the Viet Minh contribution to the anti-Japanese effort is now seen as, at best, minimal and ineffective. They, at least, were not naive; like their ideological uncles in China, they knew that the Japanese were done for, and for the Communists the real war was to begin when this one ended. They were delighted that the Americans were taking care of both the Japanese and the French for them.

Perhaps worst of all was the American policy of frequently humiliating the French at a personal level, starting with Roosevelt's treatment of de Gaulle and going down to open American contempt of the French in post-war Indochina. Some, certainly not all, of the OSS attitudes to the imprisoned French POW's bordered on the unbalanced — some showed not a spark of humanity, and no reasonable people would have permitted such suffering to continue, especially the suffering of Allies. France has never forgotten it. For both the Americans in that particular sphere and the Communists formed an unholy alliance of fanatics; the Communists classically illustrated their maxim that the end justifies the means, while the Americans exhibited their own brand of naivety and fanaticism in their rigid and nearsighted views of colonialism, reflecting a foreign policy based, as a Foreign Office official noted, on an event which had occurred two centuries earlier. And where fanaticism in any form enters the field, reason is often the first casualty.

One feature which stands out clearly in any discussion of this period is the apparent autonomy of the OSS, and the danger of permitting an agency of this sort to operate beyond the control of the theater commander. As will be seen, the OSS defied US Government policy under both the wartime Presidents. They covertly cooperated with the French resistance when ordered not to do so by Roosevelt, and refused to cooperate with the French after the war when policy changed under Truman. It appears that Wedemeyer did not have firm control over their activities in his theater; it is also likely that he was unaware of some of their operations. MacArthur was spared embarrassment and disaster because he refused to have the OSS in his theater. It is not generally known that the OSS did in fact supply the official French resistance movement with arms, although much less than the Viet Minh received later.

The British, especially, did their utmost to facilitate the return of the French, but de Gaulle was never reconciled to the fact that France did not reappear with "suitable dignity". But there was no question that de Gaulle knew that France could never again establish direct political control over Indochina, and he foresaw too that the French people themselves would ultimately provide the answer. On Indochina and related issues would they share his vision and see "the beams of a new dawn", or would they see "the last rays of the setting sun"?[30]

30. *Ibid.*, p. 931.

# 3

# THE JAPANESE IN VIETNAM

In all the discussions about Vietnam in recent years, the role of the Japanese seems to have been largely ignored or downplayed. Yet it was they who ultimately destroyed the position of the French in Indochina by occupying the country and successfully forcing their demands on them. When Japan collapsed, she did everything in her power to impede the claim of France to reoccupy her former possession. The Japanese turned over large stocks of arms, ammunition and money to the Vietnamese revolutionaries, and many Japanese deserters fought beside the Vietnamese rather than surrender to the Allies.

In March 1945, the Japanese dispensed with the trappings of French colonial rule and swept the French armed forces and civil administration into jail. In August, when Japan surrendered, the French were still locked up, and the Viet Minh were presented with the improbable spectacle of their former masters helpless, the Japanese silently cooperative, and the whole of Indochina ripe for the plucking as it had never been before — and never would be again. Not till later were the Japanese in the south ordered to retain their arms and go into action against the Viet Minh. The Japanese army thus continued fighting for several months after the end of the Second World War, but this time under the orders of the Allies — in rapid succession the Japanese had changed from former enemy to active ally. However, it was the initial Japanese occupation of Indochina which was eventually responsible for the post-war insistence by the British on Indochina being returned to France; the effective use that Japan had made of Indochina as a springboard to all of Southeast Asia had not been lost on them.

In discussing the role of the Japanese in post-war Saigon, it is necessary first to understand the reasons for their presence there. The political situation of Japan in the 1930s was marked by turbulence and uncertainty. In the middle of the decade the militarists obtained the upper hand and the idea of the Greater East Asia Co-Prosperity Sphere took shape. Japan invested Manchuria and created the vassal state of Manchukuo: if her grandiose ambitions for empire and influence were to be realized she would have to have access to a wider variety of raw materials than her own meager resources could provide.

In July 1937, with further Japanese encroachment into China, there occurred the famous "China incident" in which Japanese troops fired on the Chinese at the Marco Polo Bridge near Peking. Henceforth the Japanese referred to the larger Chinese war as the "China Incident". By 1940 they had pushed the surprisingly stubborn Chinese to the southern border, beyond which lay French Indochina. The French in the colony were naturally apprehensive of the bellicose Japanese behavior (especially when they became politically marooned following the defeat of their homeland by Germany). With the fall of Canton to the Japanese, the only reasonable supply routes to Chiang Kai-shek were via the Indo-chinese port of Haiphong, the Tonkin rail system, and the French-owned railway from Yunnan to Kunming. The Japanese exerted pressure on the French to close these routes, and finally took matters into their own hands by interdicting the Yunnan route by tactical air strikes.

The French government was not prepared to resist the Japanese with force unless the British and American governments promised support. The British replied that they would only go as far as the United States, and no farther. However, in response to this Cordell Hull, the US Secretary of State, felt that the British were shifting the burden of responsibility to him and he would have none of it. The result was that the French were forced to become more flexible in their dealings with the Japanese, who were fully aware of their tenuous position. On 19 June 1940, the Japanese bluntly demanded that the French seal off their border with China and permit Japanese inspectors to oversee the embargo on Chinese traffic. The French were prompt to respond to the Japanese demands, and on 20 June they replied that the border had in fact been closed two days earlier to gasoline supplies and trucks, and that they would expand the list of prohibited goods. They would, however, welcome the Japanese inspectors. The French offer was accepted and on 29 June a Japanese mission under General Nishihara landed at Hanoi. From there it fanned out, setting up a number of checkpoints at Haiphong, Hagiang, Laokay, Caobang, Langson and Fort Bayard. Most of these same places later became the scenes of bitter battles between the French and the Viet Minh.

The Chinese, of course, protested vigorously to the French and threatened to send their own armies into Tonkin. The French were now in the uncomfortable position of possibly being in the middle of the Sino-Japanese war. The Japanese were not at all satisfied with what they considered the lukewarm cooperation of the French, and their ambassador in Berlin was trying to persuade the Germans to put pressure on Vichy to cooperate more closely in Tonkin.

The Japanese made clear their need for new materials and rice, and the pro-Allied Governor-General, Catroux, asked the Allies for some tangible support. The British Far Eastern Naval Commander sailed up from Singapore and disappointed any hopes that Catroux might have cherished. The British simply had no power to spare.

The British ambassador in Tokyo, Sir Robert Craigie, was fully aware of the dangers inherent in the diplomatic maneuvering in South East Asia, and was himself subjected to considerable pressure from the Japanese. On 24 June 1940, the Vice Minister of Foreign Affairs told him that Japanese public opinion was solidly against Britain because of its support for the Chinese with war materials, and because British troops were still in Shanghai. Furthermore, the Japanese were in no mood to bargain over the Burma Road, over which supplies for China were being transported. The British Foreign Office were trying to determine whether (in the worst case of hostilities commencing) the war would be a local or a general conflict, for the Japanese were giving the British little room to maneuver. The Foreign Office was now satisfied that whatever happened Britain would be going it alone, for the United States was not prepared to take a firm stand against the Japanese. If the British were to give in to the Japanese demands over closing the Burma Road, further pressure could be expected. The British hoped to use the Burma Road as leverage in their efforts to extricate their Shanghai garrison, but they were under no illusions as to the difficulties involved, since the Japanese, in their clashes with the Russians, had demonstrated that they could wage violent local war without generalizing the conflict. To Craigie it was apparent that the younger group of Japanese officers were beyond reasonable control and might well murder the more cautious senior officers. The momentous issue of war or peace depended on the outcome of the struggle between the moderates and extremists in Japan.

The British, aware of their weakness in the Far East while they were concentrating on their fight for survival in Europe, fell back on their traditional diplomatic skills so as to buy time. Craigie told the Japanese that reports of arms shipments to China over the Burma Road were greatly exaggerated, and it was a fact that the amount was declining. Craigie asked the Vice Minister of Foreign Affairs if Japanese public opinion, under guidance from an interested party, was not making a mountain out of a molehill of this whole question.[1] The Vice Minister

---

1. Great Britain, Public Records Office, FO371/24666, Sir R. Craigie to Foreign Office, 25 June 1940.

was ready to agree with Craigie, but "it was obvious that Japanese public opinion, which had become greatly stirred," would not settle for less than a complete ban on the Burma Road traffic to China. The British were asked to put a halt to this flow of materials and to show "concrete evidence" that it had stopped; otherwise further, unspecified pressure would be applied. "Concrete evidence" would consist of permitting the Japanese Consul-General in Rangoon to go up and see for himself. The important point in this whole exercise was the American attitude. A firm American commitment to resist further Japanese aggression would largely decide the British reaction, but the Foreign Office predicted that it would get nothing but goodwill from the United States, and in this they were correct. The US continued to preach to the Allies but refused material support.

Craigie correctly advised the Foreign Office that this was not an opportune moment to take on the Japanese. The British had just extracted their Expeditionary Force from the beaches of Dunkirk while the Royal Air Force and the Luftwaffe were building up to the decisive air campaign of the war in the Battle of Britain. Craigie reluctantly recommended that the British accede to Japanese demands to close the Burma Road temporarily, but faced opposition from some of his colleagues. For example Sir Archibald Clark Kerr, ambassador in China, did not relish the idea, for while the Chinese might understand the French reaction to Japanese pressure, they might not forgive the British, who had not been beaten in war; he suggested archly that the orientals demanded a higher standard of morality from the British. His suggestion was to use the Shanghai garrison as a bargaining counter, and keep the Burma Road open. Craigie, nearer to the mood of the Japanese, disagreed, saying that the Japanese Army was determined to close the Road at all costs. The discussions on this subject were fascinating. Sir Frederick Leith Ross, of the Ministry of Economic Warfare, disagreed with Clark Kerr and favoured retaining the Shanghai garrison, while a majority in the Foreign Office agreed with Clark Kerr. L. S. Amery, Secretary of State for India, told the Foreign Secretary that Britain's position in the Far East was so weak that its only chance lay in a policy of boldness. If the Japanese started to fight now, Hong Kong must hold out as long as possible in the hope that the United States would come in before Singapore fell and the Navy was sunk. "To ask the United States for help beforehand is to my mind a waste of breath."[2] Lord Lothian, ambassador

2. *Ibid.*, Amery to Foreign Office, 28 June 1940.

in Washington, advised keeping the Road open. The War Cabinet reflected Amery's view that the United States was not prepared to increase pressure on the Japanese or take the initiative in a policy of conciliation. Craigie, knowing that the Japanese would plunge recklessly into a fight, continued to press for closing the Road. The idea was repugnant to him, but he thought that the Japanese could be taught a lesson when the Germans were defeated. The Burma Road was closed for three months as a compromise, but this was during the monsoon season when supplies to China would have been minimal.

In mid-July, General Nishihara raised the inevitable question of air bases in Tonkin. The Strike South faction in Tokyo was prevailing. The French, desperately stalling for time, replied that they would deny entry to Chinese troops, but the matter of air bases and transit rights for Japanese troops was a matter for negotiations between the French and Japanese governments. In August 1940, a French delegation travelled to Tokyo to engage in negotiations with the Japanese. Matsuoka, the new Japanese Foreign Minister, was not taken in by French stalling tactics and threatened force. The French finally gave in to these threats and recognized Japanese economic and political dominance in the East; they also granted the Japanese sweeping economic privileges while agreeing to permit the stationing of about 5,000 Japanese troops at three airfields in Tonkin and transit rights for the Japanese army along the Tonkin rail system. The Japanese claimed that these provisions were only to facilitate a favorable conclusion of the war with China, but it is doubtful if the French were satisfied with that explanation, even though the Japanese promised to recognize French sovereignty in Indochina. Despite these Japanese assurances, the French were still justifiably reluctant to allow the Japanese to get their foot in the door, and continued French delays in carrying out the accord were met with a threat by Nishihara to bring the Japanese Army into Indochina in early September. On 4 September, the day before the Japanese deadline, the French commander, Martin, signed an agreement which clarified the technicalities.

The new (Vichyite) Governor-General, Admiral Decoux, frustrated by the inexorable Japanese pressure, accused the British of subversion in Indochina by assisting Gaullists to leave Vichy territory. The Foreign Office, not wishing to give Decoux an excuse to act against British missions in Indochina, advised its consulates to suppress their natural inclinations to help the anti-Vichy French; however, Frenchmen who managed to reach British territory on their own would be given help in reaching Britain or Free French forces in Africa. This again reflected

Craigie's advice, which had been against making an issue out of the problem of Gaullists in Indochina, and the British were still contemplating "discreet" assistance to groups in Indochina. Decoux was also quite concerned over the possibility of a possible Gaullist coup by the army, fears which the army commander assured him were groundless. He was even worried about possible agitation from Singapore by his predecessor Catroux; also, the Chinese were threatening to blow up the railway at the Dedkay frontier station. After Catroux left Indochina he made the sort of assertions which became the common rationale for the French collapse: "It was not the French nation that was conquered, but its leaders. The crisis came too quickly for the people as a whole to assert itself. It was sold into bondage by men unworthy of a great and noble country."[3] In Indochina Catroux had himself been one of the leaders.

By January 1941, pro-Gaullist literature was passing from Shanghai through Singapore to Indochina. Although the British censors were withholding much of it, Decoux protested that the British Consul in Saigon was anti-French and supporting Thai claims to Indochinese territory. The British then entered into a "gentleman's agreement" with Decoux (the forerunner of a later and better-known gentleman's agreement over Indochina of which much will be said later), in which the British would fully ban all Free French propaganda to Indochina provided no Vichy propaganda was distributed in the Free French territories in the Pacific. From Tokyo Craigie reported that the French mission there was under strong pressure from the Japanese for allegedly being in accord with the British over Indochina. The Japanese declared that they were concerned that Anglo-French talks were going on in secret at the same time as the Japanese-French negotiations, and hinted broadly that Japanese Army commanders on the spot in Indochina might be hard to control.

In early 1941 Admiral Decoux, beginning his long and controversial double game, authorized the passing of military information to the British in Hanoi; there were now about 8,000 Japanese troops in Tonkin. Japan's increased unofficial activity in the area was reflected in its aircraft loss rate, when from 17 October to 1 December they lost thirty-six aircraft, seven through accidents while fourteen were lost over the Burma Road; this was a loss rate of nearly one aircraft a day.[4]

Significantly, evidence of Japanese interference in local politics was

3. GB, PRO, FO371/24342, Interview by G. Ward Price, *Daily Mail*, 26 Sept. 1940.
4. GB, PRO, FO371/27759.

uncovered even at this early stage. Pamphlets inciting the Tonkinese to rebellion were found in the baggage of Japanese officers, and there was "no doubt"[5] that the Japanese were giving arms, clothing and money to the Vietnamese resistance against the French. The French were considered especially vulnerable because of their long lines of communication and the increasing pressure being applied by the Thais; the British Foreign Office thought that the Japanese now regretted their promise to respect the integrity and sovereignty of French Indochina. The Foreign Office noted that the profile of the French administration in Indochina was not one to inspire confidence; in its view incompetence, corruption and defeatism were rife in high French circles, most officials seeming to be blind to wider issues and concerned mainly with their own salaries and pensions. Even Catroux was recommending a cautious policy in Indochina, for the Gaullists were in the minority. The "gentleman's agreement" also extended to the British and French naval commanders in the Far East, who refrained from firing on each other.

In Tokyo, Japanese policy was formulated by a series of Liaison Conferences between the Government and the service Chiefs of Staff.[6] Emperor Hirohito also had a large part in influencing policy.[7] These Liaison Conferences were started in late 1937, for by then the armed forces were so strong that the Government had to secure service approval for policy decisions; before long the conferences became paramount in the decision-making process, especially in foreign policy, Cabinet business being now largely confined to domestic affairs. The major decisions reached at the conferences were referred directly to the Emperor for ratification. At the 21st Liaison Conference on 3 May 1941, Foreign Minister Matsuoka discussed his trip to Germany.[8] The Germans had told him that in their view Japan should conquer Singapore at once, but the Japanese War Minister cautioned that Thailand and French Indochina would have to be occupied before operations could be undertaken in Malaya.

In April 1941 Winston Churchill, aware of the growing intransigence

5. *Ibid.*

6. *Japan's decision for War: Records of the 1941 Policy Conferences*, trans. ed. Nobutaka Ike (Stanford University Press, 1967). Ike and Bergamini are the chief sources of information for the discussions in this chapter on the making of Japanese policy and the decision to advance southwards.

7. See David Bergamini, *Japan's Imperial Conspiracy* (New York: Morrow, 1971), for an understanding of Hirohito's considerable influence on policy.

8. Ike, *Japan's Decision for War*, p. 26.

of the Japanese and the current crucial discussions on war policy, wrote a remarkable letter to Matsuoka, asking him to consider a number of questions.[9] Would Germany, without control of the air or sea, be able to invade and conquer Great Britain, and would it even try? It would be in Japan's interests to wait and see. Did Japan's joining the Triple Pact (the "Axis") make it more or less likely that the United States would enter the war, and if the former was the case, would not the "naval superiority of the two English-speaking nations enable them to deal with Japan while disposing of the Axis powers in Europe?" Was Italy a help or a hindrance to Germany, and was the Italian fleet as good at sea as on paper? Moreover, "Is it as good on paper as it used to be?" Would the British Royal Air Force be stronger or weaker in the coming year? Would the countries "being held down by the German Army and Gestapo learn to like the Germans more or will they like them less as the years pass by?" The United States and Great Britain had a combined steel production capacity of 90 million tons; if Germany was defeated again, would the 7 million tons of Japanese steel production be enough to sustain a "single-handed war"? Churchill concluded: "From the answers to these questions may spring the avoidance by Japan of a serious catastrophe. . . ."

At the 30th Liaison Conference of 12 June 1941, a policy document called "Acceleration of the Policy Concerning the South" was presented for discussion. The main points were the need for a military union with French Indochina in order to facilitate the movement of Japanese troops to Cochinchina, and for diplomatic preparation to be made in case force was used to achieve access to south Indochina. Furthermore, the Japanese must not shrink from war with the so-called ABD powers (Japan's major antagonists were referred to as the ABCD powers: the Americans, British, Chinese and Dutch) should they interfere with Japan's need for access to the south, including the coveted Dutch East Indies oil. In any event, an early decision was necessary, for the rainy season was approaching and much work was needed to bring existing Indochinese airfields up to heavy bomber standards.

Dutch East Indies oil was one of the main reasons for the relentless Japanese drive to secure bases in Indochina. In the face of a belated Allied embargo on oil shipments to Japan those oilfields took on an overriding importance. Without them the Japanese Navy would be immobilized, and without the Navy the growth of the Empire, or even its very existence, would be in peril.

9. GB, PRO, Premier 3/252–2, Churchill to Matsuoka, 1 Apr. 1941.

The only reason the Japanese did not move even more swiftly was the bitter infighting going on within the highest councils in Tokyo over whether to advance to the north or to the south. The "Strike South" faction won when Hirohito approved the General Staff paper on "Acceleration of the Policy concerning the South". The right-wing army faction, bolstered by important politicians such as Foreign Minister Matsuoka (who had spent some of his formative years in the United States) favored an attack on the Soviet Union rather than risk a war with the United States and Britain. This "Strike North" group lost influence when the Soviet Army inflicted a bad beating on the Japanese Kwantung Army in the Mongolian border area and official opinion held that the raw materials in the south were more important that allying with Germany against Russia. Moreover, 75 per cent of the Japanese Army were in China, and the Navy advised that they would need about fifty days in order to switch their preparations from south to north. The remarkable Soviet spy, Sorge, had also advised Russia that the "Strike South" faction was gaining influence, and the Soviets sealed the decision by promising to remain neutral in any future conflicts in the Pacific region.

The debate sharpened when Germany attacked Russia in June 1941, for Matsuoka estimated that the Germans would win, and if Japan attacked Russia from the East she would have a say in the post-war settlement. Tojo said that if Japan did not do something before the end of the year she might as well abandon the Greater East Asia Co-Prosperity Sphere. All the heady talk of going north or south received a slight dampening when Mr Kobayashi, Minister of Commerce and Industry, gave his opinion that if Japan's resources were used as a guide to strength, the country was not strong enough for war anywhere. The "Strike South" group finally won when at the Imperial Conference of 2 July 1941 the decision was made to go into Indochina, regardless of the risk of war with the United States and Britain.[10] Matsuoka himself was ousted when the Cabinet were asked to resign; he was replace as Foreign Minister by Admiral Toyada. The French were to be immediately told that Japanese forces would move south by 20 July; they had little option but to agree, and on 24 July the Japanese troops advanced to establish air and naval bases in southern Indochina, including Saigon.

As a result of this Japanese defiance of warnings by the Western powers, Japanese assets in the British Empire and the United States were frozen and sweeping economic sanctions were applied. The Dutch also

10. Ike, p. 77.

curtailed Japan's financial dealings in the East Indies, so that Japan was left with the basic choice of either stopping its advances or pushing on and probably going to war with the Western powers. The Navy Chief of Staff, Admiral Nagano, thought that if there had to be a war with America, victory would go to the Japanese now, but their chances would decrease with time. The Japanese were never fully confident of victory over the United States; they merely thought that if war were inevitable this was the best time to strike.

On 6 September 1941, twelve weeks before the attack on Pearl Harbor, a set of general principles was laid down at the Imperial Conference. On the question of the aims of a war against the United States, Britain and the Netherlands the conference stated:

The purposes of a war with the United States, Great Britain, and the Netherlands are to expel the influence of these countries from East Asia, to establish a sphere for the self-defence and the self-preservation of our Empire, and to build a New Order in Greater East Asia. In other words, we aim to establish a close and inseparable relationship in military, political, and economic affairs between our Empire and countries of the Southern Regions. . . .[11]

The Director of the Planning Board, Suzuki, spelled out Japan's situation in stark terms:

At this stage our national power with respect to physical resources has come to depend entirely on the productive capacity of the Empire itself, upon that of Manchuria, China, Indochina and Thailand. . . . Therefore, as a result of the present overall blockage imposed by Great Britain and the United States, our Empire's national power is declining day by day. Our liquid fuel stockpile, which is most important, will reach bottom by June or July of next year. . . . I believe that if important areas in the south were to fall into our hands without fail in a period of three to four months, we could obtain such items as oil, bauxite, nickel, crude rubber and tin. . . .[12]

The conference agreed that preparations for a war with Britain and the United States must be completed by the last ten days in October; at that time the weather in the north would be unsuitable for military operations. It was felt that to delay preparations past October would permit the United States to grow too strong. "A war with the United States and Great Britain will be long, and will become a war of endurance. . . . It would be well nigh impossible to expect the surrender of the United States." Then in a prescient statement which revealed a keen insight into

11. Ike, p. 152.
12. Ike, pp. 147-8.

the nature of American politics, the Japanese continued, "However, we cannot exclude the possibility that *the war may end because of a great change in American public opinion,* which may result from such factors as the remarkable success of our military operation. . . ."[13]

In mid-September 1941, French fears were realized as the Japanese demanded the right to garrison Indochina with a force of about 32,000 troops, and threatened to move in whether the French liked it or not. The hapless French, beaten at home and beset by scattered native unrest in Indochina, could only accept the Japanese demand. However, on 25 September a Japanese division attacked and annihilated the French garrison at Langson, on the Chinese border. The incident appeared to have been the result of independent action by the Japanese divisional commander, and peace was restored after a vigorous French protest. However, the lesson was well taken.

The new Japanese ambassador to Indochina, Kenkichi Yoshizawa (described by the press as an "able and patient negotiator", although he had had little success with the stubborn Dutch in the East Indies negotiations), left Kobe for Haiphong on 31 October 1941, arriving in Tonkin on 8 November. He was met by the Secretary-General in the absence of Admiral Decoux, and proceeded to Hanoi. There Yoshizawa announced that relations between the two countries had entered a new phase of cooperation and mutual prosperity.[14] With him were a strong staff.

On 4 November, 1941, at a meeting of the Supreme War Council, General Doihara asked: "What is the official excuse for this war against America, Britain and the Dutch?" In a remarkable statement the answer was given:

This is a clash between nations which have different world philosophies. The basic purpose of the war is to make the Americans do obeisance to us against their will — that and the Co-Prosperity Sphere to make us self-sufficient. Before we achieve these ends we must be prepared for a long war. Our immediate short-term ends are to break out of encirclement, undermine the morale of Chiang Kai-shek, seize the raw materials of the south, expel the Angol-Saxon race from Asia, make the Chinese and the peoples of the Southern Regions depend on us rather than the United States and England, open a southern route for closer ties between Asia and continental Europe, and get a monopolistic corner on the rubber, tin and other raw materials which the United States needs for military purposes.[15]

13. Ike, p. 153. Italics added. This was a remarkable prophecy in the light of the short-lived Communist military success during Tet in 1968, which was the beginning of the end for America in Vietnam.
14. GB, PRO, FO371/11278, Craigie to Foreign Office, Oct./Nov. 1941.
15. Bergamini, p. 812.

At the same meeting General Terauchi, Supreme Commander for the Southern Regions, betrayed a hint of anxiety in posing a written question to the Council in which he asked if there were not some way that a prolonged war could be avoided. He also sought guidance by asking what were the most important points to remember in Japanese administration of the occupied areas. The answer was:

First, secure raw materials; second, ensure freedom of transport for raw materials and personnel; third, in accomplishing these two objectives, we must not hesitate, as we did in China, to oppress the natives. On the other hand, we will not interfere in the details of government, as we did in China, but will make use of existing organizations and show respect for native customs.[16]

This explained why the Japanese allowed the Tricolor to fly in Indochina until 9 March 1945, when Allied pressure and an increasingly bold French resistance movement compelled the Japanese to round up and intern the French military and civil service units. The French had been doing an excellent job of running the country for the Japanese and effectively suppressing native unrest, while the Japanese were using Indochina and Thailand as firm bases for their attack on Malaya, Burma and the East Indies.

Admiral Decoux had reasonable relations (under the circumstances) with Yoshizawa, but in late 1944, when the Japanese were being pushed back everywhere, the latter was replaced by Matsumoto. The new man was not the gentleman that his predecessor was, and he immediately pressed the French to increase Japanese occupation expenses to 110,000,000 piasters a month,[17] a large increase and far in excess of what the Japanese really needed. What the Japanese did with this excess cash is a question that still remains unanswered, though some clues may be found in the post-war report by Lieutenant-Colonel T. H. Sweeny of the British Army's Pay Corps, after his detailed inspection of the records of the Bank of Indochina (discussed later).

In January 1945, Decoux had protested the new influx of Japanese troops in the north, saying that this was "an expression of mistrust" since the French already had troops in those particular areas. Furthermore, he asked the Japanese to reconsider in the light of the budding Franco-Soviet alliance. Matsumoto rejected Decoux' protests, and wired Tokyo, "So there is no turning back now." The French were also

16. *Ibid.*
17. Louis Allen, *The End of the War in Asia* (London: Hart-Davis, MacGibbon, 1976), pp. 98–9.

worried that the new demands for support of thousands of additional Japanese troops might bankrupt Indochina and bring on social upheaval. The French suspicions were well founded. In February 1945 there was discussion, in the greatly increased message traffic to Tokyo, of the need to invent a pretext for overthrowing the French regime. The Japanese began to talk of putting French forces under their control, for they thought that Indochina would be invaded and become a battleground — yet Japan's relations with France had to be considered.

The Japanese Supreme Council for the Direction of the War thought that the answer lay in the granting of independence to the peoples of Indochina. The Japanese Army in Indochina disagreed, saying that a balance of sorts actually existed, and that no new forces should be introduced into the equation. To sort out the differences between the civil and military officials in Indochina, Tokyo sent the Secretary of the Supreme Council, Mr Toko, to Indochina. (Because of Toko's visit, the cable traffic decreased and American cryptographers noted that these on-scene talks "spoiled a complete story in the available dispatches."[18]) As it was, in February 1945 Toko sided with the civil administrators in recommending independence for the states of Indochina, and the Supreme Council agreed. On 3 March the plan for the joint defense of Indochina was formulated.

Yoshizawa had earlier told Decoux that the Japanese would alter their policy in Indochina if Manila fell to American forces. In February 1945 Decoux, for a number of reasons, moved the seat of government from Hanoi to Saigon, and since the Japanese Supreme Headquarters was also in Saigon, it facilitated the Japanese *coup*. To ensure Decoux's presence in Saigon when they struck, the Japanese suggested that the Japanese-French Indochina rice agreement be renogotiated on 9 March 1945. On 4 March Decoux travelled to Dalat to visit his wife's grave, and (much to the relief of the Japanese) returned to Saigon on 7 March.

On 9 March General Tsuchihashi hosted a Japanese-French dinner, in return for a party at the Governor-General's residence a week earlier. At 1915 hours on the 19th, Tsuchihashi left the dinner and went to Army Headquarters. Only a few minutes earlier Matsumoto had met Decoux and said that a US landing was imminent and there was now an urgent need for closer cooperation between Japanese and French forces. What he meant was that French forces must be placed under Japanese control. Matsumoto presented the ultimatum to the stunned Decoux, demand-

18. NA, RG 457 MAGIC summaries, Jan. Feb. 1945.

ing an unequivocal answer by two hours later. At 2121 hours the orders went out to all Japanese units to execute their contingency plans.[19] At 2125 hours Navy Captain Robin delivered a reply to Matsumoto, who called it a rejection.

In the south the French were neutralized fairly easily, and the Japanese, during post-war interrogation, correctly blamed General Delsuc, commander of the Cochinchina division, for the French debacle during the early stages of the *coup*.[20] He had not only ridiculed Decoux's apprehensions, but had ignored a crucial piece of information unwittingly supplied by the Japanese: a Japanese airfield company commander had unthinkingly told his employees that he would be on duty during the night of the 9th,[21] and these, suspecting something was afoot, reported it to their superiors. Delsuc, however, failed to perceive the significance of the information, and when the Japanese ultimatum finally arrived, no one bothered to send immediate notification to the French Army in Tonkin. In Tonkin, thanks to the independent action taken by General Sabattier, the French reacted more intelligently. A double agent at Cao Bang had warned the French of the Japanese plan and, under the pretext of holding maneuvers, Sabattier had moved several battalions into the field when the blow fell. These troops made a fighting retreat to China.

On 9 March 1945, The Japanese Telegraph (News) Service *Domei* broadcast the following announcement from Imperial Japanese Headquarters in Tokyo:

Our forces stationed in French Indochina, owing to the utter lack of sincerity on the part of the French Indochina authorities, realized that the joint defense of French Indochina has finally been rendered impossible. Consequently, with a view to eliminating hostile influences, our forces decided to assume the duty of defending French Indochina on their own responsibility and commenced to take necessary measures on the night of 9 March.[22]

On 10 March the following momentous statement was released by Tokyo through a broadcast in German by the Japanese Overseas Service, which included the usual platitudes on the sincerity of the Japanese and the treachery of the French: "*We herewith also assure them* [the Indochinese] *that we shall unconditionally support what for many years had been their keenest desire for national independence — according to the main stipula-*

19. Allen, p. 105.
20. *Ibid.*, p. 109.
21. *Ibid.*
22. GB PRO, FO371/24719.

*tion of the Greater Asia declaration.''* Regardless of the stipulation, this was
it — a first concrete promise of independence[23] and it was something
from which the French never fully recovered, although it was later in
their power to turn the tide of independence in a more propitious direction. Consequently, on 11 March 1945 Emperor Bao Dai proclaimed the
independence of Vietnam.

In the British view there was more to the *coup* than the reasons
advanced by the Japanese. Having dispensed with the French, the
Japanese were now in full control of the Hanoi-Saigon railway; they had
previously been allotted only 2,000 tons a month whereas the total
monthly capacity was 5,000 tons. They also seized outright all coasters,
junks, buses, and so forth, for American air attacks had now severely dis-
located all Japanese shipping and movements. But more important was
the French refusal to make an open-ended commitment and pay out an
unlimited amount of piasters for the Japanese occupation expenses. In the
view of British intelligence, this was the actual occasion for the military
proposal to take over the country.[24] In January and February the French
paid out enough to cover actual Japanese expenditure, but it was only
one-third of the sum the Japanese demanded.

Following the *coup* the French were forbidden to leave town without authorization from the Japanese; all firearms, munitions, radios,
cameras, binoculars and typewriters were to be handed in, and no sale or
exchange of these items was to be allowed. The French were also forbidden to be out between sunset and sunrise, and meetings of more than
three people were banned. Outer doors of houses and apartments had to
be left open, and even an announcement was made ''to Frenchmen who
wish to become Quislings''. Although the Japanese were now admini-
stering the country directly, they could not manage entirely on their
own, and an appeal was made to the civil servants to keep them on the
job by promising to maintain their salaries. (This included 5,000 French
and 23,000 Vietnamese civil servants; also the important railway
workers, amounting to 300 Frenchmen and 16,000 Vietnamese.) Severe
punishment, including death, was promised for any actions deemed
detrimental to the Japanese Army, such as espionage, destruction of
communications and power plants, and a range of other offenses. On 11

23. This was the public version. The Japanese privately meant to keep an eye on the
    Vietnamese ''lest they should be off the rails, ridden by a mistaken idea of indepen-
    dence . . .'' (Gracey Papers, translation of Japanese version of the 9 March incident).
24. GB, PRO, FO371/46305, Enemy Branch, Foreign Office, and Ministry of
    Economic Warfare, 10 Mar. 1945.

March General Nagano and the 37th Division moved south from Kwangsi to Hanoi to reinforce General Mikuni and the 21st Division. By 13 March, the Japanese in Tonkin claimed to have captured 8,500 POWs (plus 1,000 killed), and a large booty of aircraft, land vehicles and weapons.[25] On 14 March the Japanese announced that the post of Governor-General was now held by the Japanese Commander. Matsumoto was Supreme Adviser in Indochina, Yokoyama was Adviser to the Annamite Government, Consul-General Kubo was Supreme Adviser to Cambodia, Consul-General Minota was Governor of Cochinchina, and Consuls-General Tatsuichi, Kawano and Kobase were Mayors of Saigon, Cholon and Hanoi. Spreading false rumors and removing Japanese posters were added to the list of punishable offences.

The Japanese listed ten "glaring incidents of treachery" which had led to the *coup*. These had occurred over a period of months, and included such things as French military preparations against the Japanese, the sheltering of Allied airmen, and the planning of a prayer meeting for the liberation of metropolitan France (they "went so far as to send an invitation" to Ambassador Yoshizawa, who banned it).[26] Despite the arrest and imprisonment of their compatriots, often in appalling conditions, many Frenchmen continued to work for the Japanese. In Saigon, the Opera House was turned into a centre for interrogation and torture by the Japanese, and some Frenchmen continued in their positions as prison warders.[27] But France's "Civilising Mission" in Asia was at an end. The *coup*, said Sainteny, had "wrecked a colonial enterprise that had been in existence for eighty years and that, despite its detractors, remains one of the glories of the French civilizing action in the world."[28] Worse, the blow fell just three days before the French were to execute an ambitious operation to destroy the Viet Minh. Thus, as Hồ Chí Minh is reputed to have said of the August Revolution, the Viet Minh did not really seize power, for there was no power left to seize. Continued Sainteny, "The Japanese . . . may not have disliked the idea of leaving behind them this time bomb represented by a Communist Vietnam. Besides, at this point the Japanese may have felt that political color was less significant than racial color. Then, as now, Asia must be left to the Asians: thus, the

25. *Ibid*. (New Delhi monitor of broadcast in French from Saigon).
26. *Ibid*.
27. Interviews with British officers in the Control Commission and Allied Land Forces French Indo-China.
28. Jean Sainteny, *Ho Chi Minh and his Vietnam*, trans. Herma Briffault (Chicago: Cowles, 1972), p. 38.

Japanese would not have lost the war completely, as Marshal Terauchi
was later to declare.''[29]

The defiant Count Terauchi,[30] promoted to Field-Marshal, was in
Saigon when the Japanese empire came to its cataclysmic end, and when
General Gracey arrived with the leading elements of his 20th Indian
Division to secure the Supreme Headquarters of the Japanese Army in
South East Asia.

---

29. *Ibid.*, p. 60. The United States through the OSS helped to plant this ''time bomb'',
    which was to explode in her own face just a few years later.

30. Terauchi was described by Laurens van der Post in *The Night of the New Moon*
    (Hogarth Press, London 1970) as ''a Japanese aristocrat of the oldest Japanese
    military school, a fanatical Imperialist of great independence of mind, imperious
    character, and with complete confidence in himself and in his own rightness of
    decision.'' He had independently ''made it quite clear to all his subordinate
    commanders . . . that they would be expected to resist the enemy in the classical
    samurai manner, if necessary committing harakiri in the event of defeat rather than
    falling alive into Allied hands'' (p. 57). Van der Post while a POW was told by a
    Korean camp guard that he had seen Terauchi's secret order to execute all POWs
    when the Allies closed in on the various camps through Southeast Asia. The
    Japanese were to kill first the prisoners, then themselves.

    Terauchi often acted independently of Tokyo, and it was rumored that he planned
    to ignore Hirohito's peace efforts and fight on; Hirohito's brother, Prince
    Chichibu, had to go to Saigon and talk to him. Maj.-Gen. Penney, SEAC Director
    of Intelligence, reported that the Control Commission in Saigon had seized plans for
    killing Allied prisoners-of-war and internees when the Allied invasions began
    (p. 145).

# 4

# BITTER HARVEST:
# ROOSEVELT AND INDOCHINA

President Roosevelt's peculiar hostility to the return of Indochina to France, and the reasons for it, will be discussed. This attitude was reflected in strained relations between the Allies on this matter, and caused severe problems between the two theater commanders (Mountbatten and Wedemeyer) and the operating forces down the line. Roosevelt's active opposition to the return of the French to Indochina ultimately assured the success of the heralded Communist "August Revolution".

When the United States became bogged down in Vietnam in the 1960s, there appeared to be little sympathy for her efforts from her major European allies. Some of the reasons for this go back to the early 1940s. Roosevelt could not conceal his dislike for de Gaulle, and was said to have made jokes about him at the Casablanca Conference in 1943.[1] In fact, the United States did not recognize de Gaulle until well after D-Day. Throughout most of the war, alone among the Allies, it recognized the puppet Vichy regime, and with the passing years Roosevelt's support for the re-establishment of the French empire waxed and waned in direct proportion to the US need for French assistance. In 1941 and 1942, the State Department informed the French that the United States wanted to see France restored to her pre-war grandeur, to include the repossession of her colonies.

On 7 December 1941, the day of the attack on Pearl Harbor, Roosevelt wrote to Marshal Pétain that it was essential to US vital interests that the French empire be preserved and that France continue to exercise jurisdiction and control over her colonies. Six weeks later Roosevelt sent a message to Pétain through Admiral Leahy, US Ambassador in Vichy, saying that it was important for the French to realize that he was "about the best friend they have; that one of his greatest wishes is to see France reconstituted in the post-war period in accordance with its splendid position in history. The word 'France' in

---

1.   Edward R. Drachman, *United States Policy Toward Vietnam, 1940–1945* (Cranbury, NJ: Associated University Presses, 1970), p. 15.

the mind of the President includes the French Colonial Empire."[2] But as
the war turned in his favor, Roosevelt became more confident in assert-
ing his ideas for post-war political settlements, many of them dis-
advantageous to his Western Allies.

Roosevelt's attitude to France disturbed British Cabinet officials.
Desmond Morton sent a note to Churchill saying that neither Roosevelt
nor the State Department understood that the Vichy Government did
not represent the French people. Morton wrote: "I feel that the linking-
together of the 'French' Government and the French people by the
President throughout his telegram is not accidental. The State Department have signally failed so far to comprehend what is going on in
France. . . . It looks as though the President has not the situation clear
either."[3] Roosevelt had mapped out a sort of grand scenario of world
events, which included the elimination of the British and French
empires.[4] As La Feber and others have pointed out, Britain became
financially strapped in the war. A belligerent for longer than any other
nation except the Germans, she was forced to pay in hard cash, securities,
and trade arrangements for American war supplies until she could pay no
more, and Lend-Lease came into being in 1941.

A week after Roosevelt's election to a third term, Churchill sent him
an urgent message. In it he described the desperate situation in Europe
and told Roosevelt the stark fact that Britain was going bankrupt by
having to pay so heavily for American supplies, and would soon run out
of money. Wrote Churchill, "The moment approaches when we shall
no longer be able to pay cash for shipping and other supplies."[5] To quote
La Feber, "The United States had tried to weaken British rule and gain
post-war American access to the colonial and Dominion areas at the
Atlantic Conference of August 1941, but a compromise had to be
devised when Churchill refused to be cornered."[6]

In July 1943 Anthony Eden, the Foreign Secretary, prepared a note for
Cabinet discussion on his views on "the French position and the
American attitude thereto".[7] Earlier that year, on 2 January 1943, Eden

2.  Great Britain, Public Record Office (hereafter PRO) Premier 3/187, Roosevelt to
    Churchill, 29 Jan. 1942.
3.  *Ibid.*, D. Morton to Churchill, 2 Feb. 1942.
4.  Walter La Feber, "Roosevelt, Churchill, and Indochina: 1942–1945", *American
    Historical Review*, vol. 80 (1975), p. 1279.
5.  Churchill as quoted by Robert A. Divine, *Roosevelt and World War II* (Baltimore:
    Johns Hopkins University Press, 1969), p. 38.
6.  La Feber, "Roosevelt, Churchill and Indochina", p. 1279.
7.  PRO, Premier 3/181–8, Eden to Churchill, 13 July 1943.

had informed the United States of the British view that the central
French administration of the French empire should be formed in Algiers,
a move privately supported by General Dwight D. Eisenhower, who
knew that Roosevelt opposed it. The United States never replied to
Eden's message, and Eden wrote that the Americans did not want to see
a strong Free French administration and "the growth of an independent
spirit" in Free France, and thought that "any French authority with
whom they deal should comply without question to their demands."
The merger of the two French anti-Nazi factions (those respectively of
Generals de Gaulle and Giraud) was "unwelcome" to the Americans,
who "would have wished, if this had been possible, to disrupt the
Committee of Liberation, to eject de Gaullist members from it, to set up
in its place a puppet committee . . ."

Eden went on to recall the strong US pledges to the French on the restoration of their empire, and the fact that Roosevelt was now going back
on his promises. What was worse, it was said that Roosevelt wanted to
remove part of metropolitan France itself, including the provinces of
Alsace and Lorraine, and incorporate it into a new buffer-state, to be
called "Wallonia". It appeared that the United States had "little belief
in France's future" and, continued Eden, "Dr Benes has told me, since
his return from Washington, that the Americans are not so much anti-
Gaullist as anti-French . . ." Eden then outlined the main reason why
Britain supported the restoration of France, a position from which it did
not waver in the coming crucial three years. Since containing Germany
would be Britain's "main problem" after the war, a powerful France
was needed to balance the Anglo-Soviet treaty securing "Germany's
eastern flank". This was vital whether or not the United States joined
NATO. The entire British policy towards France was to be governed by
this consideration, for twice in this century the French had "stood
between us and the assault of the German aggressor". Everything must
be done to restore French self-confidence. Furthermore, feeling against
the Americans was rising in France and in North Africa due to the
Americans' attitude towards France and "their open hostility to the
Gaullists". Finally, "Europe expects us to have a European policy of our
own and to state it." Eden had tried his "best to bring the United States
Government to a more sympathetic outlook towards Gaullists and 'the
more active of the resistance movements', but without success."

At that time, in presenting his own views on the situation to the War
Cabinet, Churchill took exception to a remark made by Roosevelt
during a press conference, namely that there was "no France at the

present time".[8] As Churchill mentioned, recalling his earlier visit to Washington, "the President almost every day gave me some paper or other showing his annoyance with de Gaulle." Roosevelt's response to de Gaulle's growing strength was an imperious order to Eisenhower in North Africa to forbid the Committee of National Liberation (Free France) to meet, but Churchill persuaded Roosevelt not to send it. As Churchill put it, "I have repeatedly stated that it is in the major interests of Great Britain to have a strong France after the War and I should not hesitate to sustain this view. I am afraid lest the anti-de Gaullism of the Washington Government may harden into a definite anti-France feeling." At Tehran Stalin said that he had no time for the French generally, adding that they had collaborated with the Germans. Roosevelt agreed (despite being the only Ally to support the collaborationists), and went on to say that "no Frenchman over 40, and particularly no Frenchman who had ever taken part in the present French Government, should be allowed to return to position in the future . . . The first necessity for the French, not only for the Government but the people as well, was to become honest citizens."[9]

In keeping with his own peculiar concept of the post-war world, Roosevelt engaged in a bizarre performance. On 16 December 1943, he received the Chinese and Turkish Ambassadors, the British Minister Sir Ronald Campbell (Halifax, the Ambassador, was sick), the Egyptian Minister, and the Soviet and Iranian First Secretaries. During this meeting Roosevelt made the following statements, telling his audience that they "must not repeat to anyone what he said".[10] He had, he said, "been working very hard to prevent Indo-China being restored to France," who during the last hundred years had done nothing for the Indo-Chinese people under their care. They were still as poor and as uneducated as ever and this state of affairs could not be allowed to continue. Roosevelt thought that the Indo-Chinese were not yet ready for elective institutions of their own, and should be put under some sort of UN trusteeship, under which they would begin to govern themselves, something in the Philippine manner. Roosevelt acknowledged the probability of future trouble with the French, but said it had to be done. Peace must be kept by force, and world policemen (the US, Great

---

8. PRO, Premier 3/181–8, Churchill to War Cabinet, 13 July 1943.
9. United States, *Foreign Relations of the United States* (hereafter FRUS), *Diplomatic Papers, The Conferences at Cairo and Tehran, 1943* (Washington, 1961), p. 485.
10. PRO, Foreign Office 371/41723, and Cabinet 122/812, Halifax to Eden, 16 Dec. 1943.

Britain, the USSR, and China) were necessary who would need certain strategic bases from which to operate without bringing up questions of sovereignty. As La Feber has pointed out, "FDR's anti-colonial idealism was firmly rooted in the determination to protect American spheres of interest with military force." Roosevelt went on to mention Dakar, which could be a threat to the whole Western Hemisphere if in weak hands.

Eden immediately flashed the message to Churchill, who replied from the Mediterranean: "I have frequently heard the President express these views about Indo-China and Dakar and have never given any assent to them . . . One can hardly suppose any intention on the part of the United States to take territory from France forcibly without agreement with France after a French Government has been formed on the basis of the will of the French people." Churchill then intimated that Roosevelt did not know what he was talking about in regard to Dakar, "as it was only made available to the Allies by the voluntary action of Admiral Darlan and had hitherto resisted all other shocks." Furthermore, said Churchill, "For the above reasons I am of the opinion that if we are officially apprised of these declarations we should give immediately a perfectly clear indication that we have no part in them. . . . You should also recur to the various declarations on behalf of the integrity of the French Empire which have been given by the President from time to time."[11] Eden then instructed Halifax to speak to Secretary of State Cordell Hull about it, and to ascertain whether it was a concerted White House/State Department policy, and whether the President remembered the many American promises to France and had considered all of this "in light of a possible post-war security system in that region". On 4 January Halifax saw Hull, who said he knew no more than Halifax did. The latter, thus assuming that this was not a concerted American diplomatic effort, pointedly reminded Hull "of the fact that the United States Government had given various undertakings concerning the French Empire in terms more explicit than any which he had employed". Hull acknowledged this "and said that he did his best from time to time to remind the President" of the matter. Halifax concluded with his own opinion, "This is all a bit woolly."

In Southeast Asia, as elsewhere, Roosevelt's words were noted. Lord Louis Mountbatten, Supreme Allied Commander South East Asia, and his Chief Political Adviser, Esler Dening of the Foreign Office, both

11.  PRO, Premier (Prem) 3/178–2, Churchill to Eden, 21 Dec. 1943.

viewed Roosevelt's remarks with alarm. A hostile France would not
only make the future Allied invasion of Indochina a more difficult
operation, but it would rule out the possibility of establishing resistance
nets in the country (an operation which Mountbatten was now secretly
conducting). Mountbatten immediately sent word of Roosevelt's comments to his SEAC Chief of Staff, General Browning: "I attach an
astonishing telegram. I am afraid that, by speaking to the Chinese,
Turks, Egyptians and Persians, the President is scarcely likely to achieve
that degree of secrecy which he enjoined upon his hearers." If the French
were now to be excluded from Indochina, "then I think the French
should be told now, since not to tell them would be an act of treachery.
To tell them now would be to prejudice forthcoming operations in
Europe, as also in due course in Indo-China." Hostility could be
expected in Indochina, and the French, "far from collaborating half-
heartedly with the Japanese as they are now, will do all they can to
obstruct our entry." This new policy would hamper Allied intelligence
and subversive activities there. "We are already faced with the arrival of
the Corps Léger d'Intervention, and if we are not going to give Indo-
China back to France we had better be chary about using Frenchmen."
As well as SEAC, Special Operations Executive (SOE) in Europe were
upset by Roosevelt's remarks, since they now feared a hostile population
both in metropolitan France and in the colonies. From Asia Dening
wrote of his concern over the American Asian policy, for he saw Indochina becoming the key area in South East Asia in the future. "In view
[of] the hopelessly unsatisfactory position of Americans' activities in and
from China . . . consider vital that we should do everything in our
power [to] prevent destruction of our cooperation with French."[12] The
Indochina trusteeship plan being advanced by Roosevelt was to involve
around half a dozen members of various nationalities, including a
Russian, an American, and perhaps a Chinese, "to educate them for self-
government".[13] Presumably it would be a democracy based on the
Philippine model; but it was not clear what the Chinese and Russians
would contribute to the idea of representative government.

Halifax next went straight to Roosevelt, and on 18 January 1944 the
two met over lunch. Roosevelt had meanwhile received a note from Hull
describing his talk with Halifax, and mentioning Halifax's question as to
whether the President's comments "represented his considered view".

12. PRO, FO 371/41723, Dening to Foreign Office, 3 Jan. 1944.
13. Drachman, *United States Policy Toward Vietnam*, quoting Samuel I. Rosenman
    (ed.), *The Papers of FDR*, XIII (New York. Harper and Row, 1950), p. 562.

The President, reported Halifax, "gaily interjected" that they did. And on Halifax's comment that, in view of the company in which Roosevelt's remarks had been made, they no doubt would get back to the French, Roosevelt again cut in with "I hope they will."[14] Roosevelt then went on to expound "the usual case" for depriving the French of Indochina, and said that Stalin thought it a good idea (as well he might, since his agent Ho Chi Minh was working very hard to do just that). Churchill, continued Roosevelt, had refused to discuss it, as Roosevelt said that he had discussed it twenty-five times with the Prime Minister, "or perhaps discussed is the wrong word. I have spoken about it 25 times but the Prime Minister has never said anything." Halifax pointedly reminded Roosevelt of the President's promises to restore the French, but "The President did not think that his pledges about the French Empire were of importance." Halifax told Roosevelt that "quite apart from his pledges which were primarily his own affair", he did not like the trusteeship plan. To the Foreign Office he wired, "He might one of these days have the bright idea that the Netherlands East Indies or Malaya would go better under international trusteeship."

When pressed on British and Dutch possessions, Roosevelt said that the cases were different. Halifax said, "I then asked him whether he did not think that however long it might take, it was in all our interests to get France on to her legs again as a great power and that if she started off with a good slap in the face like this she would be permanently resentful which would not at all be helpful." Halifax persisted, but Roosevelt "was not taking it all too seriously", and kept on about the hopelessness of the French. Roosevelt concluded by remarking, "Well, tell Winston I gained or got three votes to his one as we stand today." Halifax, worried, wrote, "I am left feeling that he has got this idea in his mind a bit more than is likely to be wholesome."

In London, a memo by Mr Foulds, a Foreign Office official, on Halifax's paper noted that "President Roosevelt continues to push his idea that France should not be allowed to recover Indo-China and evidently pledges are not to be allowed to stand in the way . . ." Mr Butler (also of the Foreign Office), referring to FDR's remarks on three votes to one, commented, "I don't understand the President's remarks about gaining votes," to which someone pencilled in "US, USSR, China = 3; UK = 1".[15] Churchill was not impressed with this sort of alignment, or voting. He and Stalin represented irreconcilable ways of

14. PRO, FO 371/41723, Halifax to Foreign Office, 18 Jan. 1944.
15. PRO, FO 371/41723, Foreign Office Minute by Mr Foulds, 22 Jan. 1944.

life, and as for Chiang Kai-shek, "I cannot regard the Chungking Government as representing a great world-power. Certainly there would be a faggot-vote on the side of the United States in any attempt to liquidate the British Overseas Empire."[16]

Despite the strong British opposition to Roosevelt's trusteeship scheme, the Foreign Office was trying to avoid being forced into a needless confrontation with the United States over France, and as a sop to Roosevelt tentatively agreed to the idea of "police station" bases in Indochina: "Our policy for Indo-China . . . might best be achieved by the establishment of some system of United Nations bases in Indo-China, rather than by depriving France of her possessions."[17] When Churchill was asked by the Foreign Office to go straight to Roosevelt over this impasse about France and her possessions, he declined to do so at that time. He wrote to Eden and Lord Cranborne, the Dominions Secretary: "I think it a great mistake to raise this matter before the Presidential election . . . On this point the President's views are particular to himself. The war in the Far East may go on for a long time. I do not consider that chance remarks which the President makes in conversation should be made the basis for setting all this ponderous machinery in motion. Nothing is going to happen about this for a long time." Churchill advised Eden to "develop a very strong movement on this issue from the Foreign Office through the State Department and leave till a later stage any direct communication between me and the President." As Churchill told the Cabinet at the same time, "It would be better to delay. One can always concede."

Many people in the State Department shared the Foreign Office's alarm over Roosevelt's hostility to France. Foreign Office frustration was reflected by Sir Alexander Cadogan, its Permanent Under Secretary: "I cannot follow the purpose of a policy of estranging progressively, and often to our own disadvantage, the only French authority that at present exists. I don't understand it — I don't know what is at the back of it . . . I can only infer that the Prime Minister, knowing as we all do President Roosevelt's — or Admiral Leahy's — sinister intentions regarding Indo-China, is careful not to do anything that might imply recognition of French rights there." Eden wrote that he agreed with Cadogan and shared "his concern at consequences of treating [the]

16. La Feber, "Roosevelt, Churchill, and Indochina", quoting Churchill, p. 1280.
17. At the Cairo conference Roosevelt casually offered Indochina to Chiang. Chiang, far more knowledgeable about the long history of Sino-Vietnamese relations, firmly declined the offer.

French Committee in this way in every sphere''. Eden wrote to Churchill and mentioned, among other things, that Lord Selborne (of SOE), the Chiefs of Staff, and Mountbatten were all in favor of the French taking part in political warfare in the Far East. To this end they wanted the *Corps Léger d'Intervention* moved to the Far East for operations against the Japanese. The French were also pressing the British to move the CLI east, and to permit the establishment of a French Military Mission at SEAC Headquarters. Churchill demurred, noting American opposition to these moves. It was pointed out that the Dutch mission was established at SEAC without referring to Washington, but Churchill was unmoved as the President had peculiar feelings about Indochina. The time was not yet ripe.

In the Pacific, US Government pledges to René Pleven and General Giraud were repeated "word for word" to the French leader, Admiral d'Argenlieu. These were relayed by the US Consul at Noumea, and "The fact that this statement was issued in New Caledonia is perhaps of interest since the ports of the French Empire, the future of which is debatable, are, in addition to Indo-China, the French islands in the Pacific.''[18] These French islands figured prominently in the US Pacific invasion strategy.

Once again Roosevelt needed French cooperation, and so temporarily ceased his vendetta against France. The British Ambassador to Free France, Duff Cooper, wrote to Churchill that de Gaulle had been surprised by a visit from Admiral Fenard of the French Military Mission in Washington. Fenard said that he carried a personal message from Roosevelt to de Gaulle, saying that the President knew of the latter's belief that Roosevelt did not like him, but that the opposite was really the case and he would be pleased to receive him in Washington. De Gaulle told Duff Cooper that he was "completely mystified" by it. This was a few weeks before the vital D-Day invasion of Normandy. Yet four weeks earlier Roosevelt had told Churchill, when Churchill had pressed the President to receive de Gaulle, "I will not ever have it said by the French or by American or British commentators that I invited him to visit me in Washington. If he asks whether I will receive him if he comes I will incline my head with complete suavity and with all that is required by the etiquette of the eighteenth century.''[19] A few days later Roosevelt wrote to Churchill, commenting on the latter's forthcoming talks with

18. PRO, FO 371/41723, Barclay (Washington) to Mack (Foreign Office), 6 Jan. 1944.
19. PRO, Premier 3/121–2, Roosevelt to Churchill, 12 Apr. 1944.

de Gaulle: "All good luck in your talk with Prima Donna . . . please for the love of Heaven do not tell de Gaulle that I am sending him a 'friendly message to come over to see me' . . . I decline absolutely as Head of the State to invite him to come over here." Churchill in reply referred to American press attacks on his references to Spain, and said that Britain was closer to these problems than America and had no wish for a hostile Spain, either, after the war. Churchill told Roosevelt: "We should not be able to agree here in attacking countries which have not molested us because we dislike their totalitarian form of government. I do not know whether there is more freedom in Stalin's Russia than in Franco's Spain. I have no intention to seek a quarrel with either."

Roosevelt's crude personal attacks were not confined to de Gaulle. In 1942 Vice President Wallace had passed a message from Roosevelt to Chiang Kai-shek in which the President had said that Britain did not think that China was a world power, adding that "Churchill is old," and a new British Government without him would be more sympathetic to China, and perhaps even give Hong Kong to China. When Roosevelt suggested to the British that they should think about giving up Hong Kong as a gesture of goodwill, Eden swallowed and noted caustically that he had not heard of the Americans making any similar offers of self-sacrifice.[20] Roosevelt also said, "We shall have more trouble with Great Britain after the war than we are having with Germany now."[21]

On 22 June 1944, when the Normandy operations appeared to have some chance of success, Halifax wrote a note to Churchill and Eden stating that the French delegation in Washington, long on the receiving end of American scorn, now had copies of correspondence between the US Government and Vichy in the 1940–2 period concerning Indochina. These were said to show that Sumner Welles "consistently urged Vichy to make every concession to Japan and to acquiesce in all Japanese demands. After Pearl Harbor, fearing that Vichy might publish the correspondence, the United States Government gave an unqualified undertaking that they would support the return of Indo-China to France in all circumstances."[22]

This brief political overview may facilitate understanding of the military problems in Southeast Asia, of which Indochina was the stick-

---

20.  La Feber, "Roosevelt, Churchill, and Indochina", p. 1280, quoting the Hopkins Papers, box 138, Bk. 7, "Memorandum — Hopkins-Eden Visit", 29 Mar. 1943.
21.  *Ibid.*, p. 1279, quoting Charles Taussig Papers, FDR Library, box 52, "Resumé of a Number of Conversations with Sumner Welles", 30 Nov. 1942.
22.  PRO, Prem 3/178–2, Halifax to Churchill and Eden, 22 June 1944.

ing point. In 1943, spurred in part by Roosevelt's apparent desire for post-war supremacy in South East Asia, the British created a new major command in the area, South East Asia Command (SEAC), with Lord Louis Mountbatten as Supreme Allied Commander, South East Asia (SACSEA). SEAC was an Allied Command, although primarily British. As directed by the Chiefs of Staff, SACSEA's prime duties were twofold: to wear down the Japanese forces, especially the air forces (and compel the Japanese to divert resources from the Pacific Theater), and to maintain and broaden contacts with China in the joint effort. By now all American hopes that China would be the place to defeat Japan had long since vanished and the Pacific strategy was proving tremendously successful.

When the Japanese thrust to India was stopped during the desperate battles at Imphal and Kohima, and General Slim's 14th Army began to grind the Japanese Army down, Mountbatten thought about the future assault that would be necessary to eject the Japanese from the South East Asian mainland. But before any Allied landings could take place in Indochina it was necessary that a great deal of "pre-occupational" work be done, resistance nets organized, native levies raised, intelligence data gathered, and so on. One problem was that Chiang Kai-shek, supported by the United States, regarded Thailand and Indochina as lying within the Chinese area of operations, and Chiang was reluctant to omit these areas from his theater because of the resulting adverse effect on Chinese morale. It was a matter of "face". Since the US Chiefs of Staff in 1942 had complicated matters by unilaterally declaring that Siam and Indochina lay in the US (and thus Chinese) sphere of operations, Mountbatten had to see Chiang Kai-shek about working out an arrangement whereby Indochina could be considered open territory for military operations. Since it took years to develop resistance nets, Mountbatten could not afford to wait any longer before doing something in Indochina. He proposed to Chiang that the Chinese and British be free to attack Indochina from the north and south respectively, the political boundaries to be decided later according to how quickly the forces advanced.[23] Mountbatten then asked Chiang if he objected to the British sending agents into Indochina and Siam; Chiang had no objections provided he was kept informed. This was the "Gentleman's Agreement", worked out through the good offices of Lieutenant-General

---

23. PRO, WO 203/5608, Gen. Somervell's Notes on the Mountbatten-Chiang Kai-shek Conference, 8 Nov. 1943.

Brehon Somervell, Chief of the US Army Services Forces, who was on a
visit to Chungking from Washington at the time. The US Chiefs of
Staff had no objection to this arrangement, for they thought that the
Chinese would get there first anyway, and were in general agreement
with the views expressed by the Generalissimo at Sextant (the Cairo
Conference): that if the troops were landed in those countries (Thailand
and Indochina), the boundaries between the two theaters were to be
decided at the time in accordance with the speed with which the respective forces advanced.

SEAC, as could be expected, had some teething troubles at first, not
the least of its problems being the Deputy Commander, the US General
Stilwell. With the senior Allied political leaders openly at odds over
South East Asia, the antagonisms were often reflected in the field.
Among the troops, some Americans sneered at SEAC, saying it had been
formed to "save England's Asian colonies". The British in turn
wondered where the Americans had been in the two World Wars until
1917 and nearly into 1942. These feelings were not universal in South
East Asia, but were prevalent enough to be of real concern. By early 1944
SEAC was aware that Stilwell had been conducting a press campaign in
the United States to undermine Mountbatten's strategy, while advancing his own plans to defeat the Japanese with Chinese troops under his
command. Dening expressed his deep concern, saying:

. . . the latest animosity of General Stilwell, which has made the existence of
SEA Command so uneasy ever since it was established, is now manifesting itself
in a more virulent form. I have discussed the telegrams with General
Wedemeyer who said that, whatever else his faults, he had always been given to
understand that General Stilwell was at least honest. It now appeared that he
was not even that, and General Wedemeyer found that very hard to forgive. I
have in my own mind no doubt that, in spite of Admiral Mountbatten's defence·
of him in Chungking last October, General Stilwell has been disloyal to him
throughout . . . and there have been strong suspicions that General Stilwell has
been active in trying to undermine our position with Chiang Kai-shek.[24]

Dening concluded: "Such activities on the part of an American officer
holding the position of Deputy Supreme Commander are difficult to
excuse . . . There is little doubt that the general attitude of US troops in
this theatre is influenced by the Commanding General. It is doubtful
whether this very unsatisfactory state of affairs can continue indefinitely
without doing active harm to the cause for which British and American

24.  PRO, FO 371/27861, Dening to Foreign Office, 23 Feb. 1944.

troops are fighting together.'' Eden sent Dening's message to Churchill.

Mountbatten had earlier intervened with Chiang Kai-shek on Stilwell's behalf. When Mountbatten went to Chungking in October 1943, Dr T. V. Soong told him that the Generalissimo was finding Stilwell intolerable and wanted to be rid of him. Mountbatten supported his deputy and refused to be associated with a campaign to remove him, and indeed insisted that Stilwell be informed of all this. When told, Stilwell was crestfallen, but cheered up when Mountbatten assured him of his support. Things improved in China after that, and Stilwell expressed his ''gratitude and devotion'' to the Supreme Allied Commander — but this was not to last long. He soon continued to undermine Mountbatten, submitting papers on SEAC to the US Chiefs without Mountbatten's knowledge. In Delhi, at a meeting of senior officers to discuss strategy, Stilwell publicly humiliated Wedemeyer, who had discussed a paper, and went on ''in a very ill-tempered manner'' to describe his own strategy — a drive on Canton. He refused an invitation to meet the Viceroy and left. As Dening noted, the great danger lay in the growing inter-Allied friction which was being openly inflamed in Stilwell's headquarters, and which was embarrassing to the US officers at SEAC.[25] Wedemeyer said that Stilwell was now an American hero, and the British must not agitate against him in an election year, even though he agreed that it was outrageous for Stilwell to send his representative to the United States to begin a press campaign without informing Mountbatten, the theater commander, and called Stilwell ''mean''.[26] Stilwell was warned by General Marshall to stop it or be fired, and the SEAC representative in Washington met divergence on South East Asia policy ''round every corner''. It was not clear to the British exactly what the US South East Asia policy was.

The French, rebuffed and humiliated by the United States, were in the unenviable position of having to go for help, begging bowl in hand, asking for some ships here, a few planes there, perhaps some equipment for a couple of divisions or transportation to move troops to a crucial area. In

25. Mountbatten had earlier said that no matter what their nationality, all agencies in SEAC would operate under his orders or go out (a reference to a ''quasi-military organization'', which meant the OSS). It was for this reason that Gen. MacArthur refused to have the OSS in his Pacific Theater; their loyalties were too frequently divided, they inclined on occasion to make their own policy, some of their major conclusions were projected on inadequate field intelligence (e.g. on the Chinese Communists), and a good many of their appointments seemed to have been based on personal or political connections.

26. PRO, Cab. 122/1162, SACSEA to Eden, 3 May 1944.

late 1944 the French offered a marine division of colonial troops to be used in warm climates, but the US Chiefs declined the offer. In January 1945 the French requested six "Liberty ships" and two tankers to move their own people, and were turned down. The British, in the war for a very long time, could now only refer them to the Americans for major supplies. But de Gaulle never accepted a reduced role for France. Force 136 had proposed three possible courses of action in Indochina, and in view of the political realities the course of action involving a lower level of risk and investment (pure sabotage) was adopted. French support in Indochina was to go a long way to ensure Allied success when the time came to invade. It was thus becoming more difficult to exclude the French from "reasonable military participation", for they would not be willing to keep SOE (Force 136) fully informed of events in Indochina pending acceptance of the Blaizot mission. Dening noted: "The situation in Indo-China has grown very delicate with the disappearance of the Vichy regime, and I feel that the FCNL will wish to take early steps to influence it to the advantage of France . . . The Americans seem to have no constructive ideas on the subject except that they want to exclude us." According to Dening, it really made no difference who attacked Indochina, but French help would certainly be needed in any case; the main point was to strike a blow against Japan. "If we are prevented from doing this by American obstruction, then I think the outlook is gloomy both militarily and politically."

Mountbatten had been urging Eden to push for the establishment of the French mission at SEAC, and Eden in turn had been pressing the Combined Chiefs for a decision. Since SEAC was an Allied command it was necessary to consult the Combined Chiefs. Eden's prompting took on more urgency as he foresaw the Japanese *coup* of 9 March 1945: "With the progress of the operations in France the days of the Vichy regime are numbered and, when it disappears, it is possible . . . that the Japanese will eject Admiral Decoux's government in Indo-China and take over the administration themselves. Should that happen there would be added scope for subversive operations by the special corps [the CLI]." However, the problem was complicated because "The United States Government have given more specific guarantees than we have ourselves about the restoration of the territorial integrity of the French Empire." Roosevelt's problems in this area were increasing. The French were growing stronger, and Averell Harriman, the US ambassador in Moscow, had his eyes opened to the true nature of the victorious Soviet government: "There is every indication the Soviet Union will become a

'World Bully' wherever their interests are involved unless we take issue with their present policy. When they turn their attitude in that direction this policy will reach into the Pacific and China as well . . .'[27]

At SEAC Mountbatten was trying to prod the politicians into a decision on Indochina; the day was not far off when his planners would be concentrating on that area. Both Siam and Indochina were vital to him because Japanese reinforcements and supplies had to transit those countries to reach Burma and Malaya. Although he had been supporting covert operations there, it was now urgent for full-scale pre-occupational activities to begin. It was important that resistance forces be in position to interfere with Japanese lines of communication as required by British offensive operations in Burma, and be ready to promote large-scale resistance and revolt in conjunction with future operations following the reconquest of Burma. He requested an early decision on the boundary question, especially since the Allied leaders were meeting in Quebec. As it was, Churchill did not raise the Indochina issue with Roosevelt; he had given up on the President in this matter and had decided to do what he thought best. He had had a great deal of trouble in just getting the United States to accept British support in the Pacific fighting. Churchill eventually cabled the President asking him to support the verbal agreement reached between Mountbatten and Chiang Kai-shek in November 1943. When queried by Eden about pursuing it further, Churchill decided that there was no need to do so and instructed Eden to proceed with proposals by the Chiefs of Staff and to inform Mountbatten accordingly so that he could get on with his work.

At noon on 28 October 1944, Roosevelt announced the recall of General Stilwell and the splitting of the China–Burma–India (CBI) Theatre into two new theaters, China Theater and India-Burma Theater. Major-General A. C. Wedemeyer was to head the former, and Lieutenant-General D. I. Sultan the latter. For SEAC, the end of CBI meant the start of new problems. When China Theater was formed, the US Chiefs had unilaterally decided to place French Indochina in the new command, in contradiction, thought Dening, of the Mountbatten/Chiang Kai-shek agreement. Mountbatten wanted the British Chiefs to contest the point about French Indochina, since the announcement coincided with the arrival of the French Military Mission to his SEAC headquarters. French and British officials at SEAC were dismayed, for the

27.  PRO, Prem. 3/396–4, Harriman to Hopkins and Roosevelt, 12 Sept. 1944; repeated by Churchill to Eden.

US-Chinese partnership would now have veto power over SEAC plans in Indochina, plans which had taken months and years to formulate and which were now being put into operation. The French forces which had planned to drop in and set up resistance groups in the North, and who could possibly have stamped out the still small Communist groups in the hills, were now stalled by active US opposition to their plans.

In SEAC's view, Wedemeyer had been relatively reasonable while in his former position as Deputy Supreme Allied Commander at SEAC. But as soon as he assumed command of China Theater and became deputy to Chiang Kai-shek, he began actively to oppose SEAC in Indochina, with far-reaching consequences. Mountbatten reported that Wedemeyer now not only opposed the ''Gentleman's Agreement'' but ''went so far as to declare that General Somervell had no authority to negotiate (which is interesting when one recalls that in the early days of this Command, General Wedemeyer was in complete support of the Supreme Commander's attitude). He seemed to have forgotten that the President and the US Chiefs of Staff favoured this agreement (see COSSEA 6 of 1943).''[28]

On 27 October 1944 Mountbatten announced the arrival of General Blaizot and the French mission. By November 1944 Blaizot, anticipating a Japanese move against the French, wanted to send small parties to Indochina to organize resistance and sabotage. But Wedemeyer, following his instructions from Roosevelt, was adamant, and his attitude placed an increasing strain on inter-Allied relations. In this atmosphere Dening met Wedemeyer for a discussion of the problem and was taken aback by the intensity of Wedemeyer's feelings:

Until General Wedemeyer told me with conviction that there would not be a British Empire after the war I had hoped that the tension would be eased out here with the removal of General Stilwell and the conclusion of the Presidential election. Now however I fear that the situation may well deteriorate further. At present the question of whether to prop up a tottering China with props which may not hold, or to hit the Japanese hard where we have the forces to do it, seems already resolved in favour of the former. If props hold, America will get the credit and if they do not, we shall get the blame . . .[29]

So the Allies went their separate ways in South East Asia.

28. PRO, WO 203/5561A, Dening to Foreign Office.
29. PRO, FO 371/41746, Dening to Foreign Office, 9 Dec. 1944. When interviewed by the author on 29 Nov. 1980, Gen. Wedemeyer did not recall making the remarks on the future of the British Empire attributed to him here.

At a meeting held on 7 December 1944, chaired by Mountbatten's Chief of Special Duty (i.e. clandestine) Operations, Air Vice-Marshal Whitworth-Jones, it was decided to ask Force 136 to update their proposals for pre-occupational activity in French Indochina. However, they were to confine themselves within certain ground rules. Due to the delicate situation in Indochina between the French and Japanese forces, all operations which might provoke the Japanese into action against the French were prohibited. Furthermore, no act of resistance was to be intitiated without orders from General Blaizot, acting with the authority of SACSEA.

A review of past and present operations was conducted. During three series of operations, codenamed "Belief", "Polka" and "Radical", eighteen sorties with RAF B-24 Special Duty Liberator bombers had been flown into French Indochina up to 1 December 1944, out of forty-six which had been planned and approved.[30] The "Belief" sorties dropped transmitters and receivers to form a communications net, while the "Polka" operations were designed to introduce demolition stores into the country. These operations had succeeded in establishing a radio network within French Indochina, with twelve stations now in communication with the Force 136 War Station in Calcutta; introducing a very limited amount of stores for training purposes; and carrying out three pickup operations (using smaller aircraft) by which leaders of the resistance movement inside French Indochina had come out for discussions, and one of General Blaizot's staff officers had been sent in to hold discussions within Indochina.[31] These modest operations were conducted at the maximum possible range of the aircraft, and in addition to the support given to the extensive Force 136 operations in Burma, Thailand and Malaya. Much more could have been accomplished with a coordinated Allied policy on the resistance.[32]

30. These were professionally tremendously demanding missions, involving 18–20 hours of predominantly evening and night flying to reach pinpoint targets in the most appalling weather and terrain to be found in Indochina. They were scheduled around the monthly full moon periods.
31. Major (later Colonel and Gouverneur, France Outre-Mer) François de Langlade, the personal representative of Gen. de Gaulle at this time. (Personal interview, 3 Sept. 1977.)
32. The French have often been criticized, especially by American writers, for the modest nature of their resistance efforts. In fairness it must be realized that the British, adopting Force 136's Course A, contributed to keeping the resistance at a low level, while the United States officially refused to have anything to do with the French in Indochina.

In late 1944 a new "Indo-China Council" was imposed on Admiral Decoux by the resistance movement to make sure that he did not act in a manner contrary to the interests of the French Provisional Government of de Gaulle.[33] As yet, there had been no Japanese reaction to the Council, the formation of which was announced by a broadcast in Vietnamese on 3 December 1944. At that time the Supreme Federal Council of Indo-china was dismissed and the new Indochina Council was formed, to "be responsible for all interests of Indochinese countries and advise the Governor-General on efficient methods for ruling the country. All decrees and laws issued by the Governor-General will be discussed and assented to by this council before execution." The Japanese very likely knew what was happening, but were not yet ready for a showdown with the French.

The British were given responsibility for South East Asia at the Quebec Conference in September 1944, in which the United States decided to concentrate on the Pacific strategy. With the US abdication of interest in South East Asia, Force 136 now came to life in Indochina. In January 1945 the plans were put into effect to try to build up the French in the interior by dropping in arms and supplies to resistance groups.

The RAF had ten squadrons available for Special Duty. Seven of these were equipped with B-24 Liberators, modified with dropping slides, long-range fuel tanks, and navigation homing equipment. One squadron had B-24 and Halifax bombers, one was a Catalina flying-boat squadron, and one had B-24s, C-47s and Lysanders for short field take-offs and landings. There were eight other squadrons which could make special supply drops when called upon: seven of C-47s and one of Halifax bombers. The special dropping slides on the Liberators made it possible for a stick of up to four men to be dropped on the same run. The C-47s were used for the narrow valleys of Burma, which were hazardous for B-24s. These missions took their toll of men and machines. The 358 Squadron alone lost fourteen Liberators, which were listed as crashed or missing on Special Duty operations. Some aborted missions were due to "Lack of confidence of the Captain", while others pressed too hard in dangerous conditions and crashed. For these crews there were no targets destroyed, no rolling stock shot up, no enemy killed — no glamor, in fact. Their missions were secret, involving long and lonely night flights of great technical difficulty, but were often the sole reason that many resistance groups stayed alive, judging from their field reports sent back

---

33.  Interview with Col. de Langlade, 3 Sept. 1977.

to the aircrews. Given this start and the limited resources at hand, Force 136's expanded plans were now put into operation. On the night of 22/23 January 1945, eleven Liberators of 358 Squadron took off from Digri, headed for target areas at Lang Son, in northern Tonkin, and Hanoi under Operation "Bazaar". Only two missions were successful, and several which were begun could not be completed because of the appalling winter weather. All target areas reported 10/10 low cloud cover, and some aircraft dropped their stores where they estimated the drop zones to be. Three of 358 Squadron's B-24's failed to return.

In February, Headquarters SACSEA sent to Headquarters ACSEA (Air Command South East Asia) a study called "Incidents Involving SD Aircraft".[34] In it was quoted a message from General Carton de Wiart, the British military representative in Chungking. De Wiart's first paragraph had been originally delivered for circulation the usual way, but the second had been transmitted in a private sealed letter from Air Vice-Marshal Whitworth-Jones to Admiral Mountbatten. The first paragraph said, "It is reported that a few days ago [date not given] three Liberators operated into French Indo-China without warning the 14th USAAF in the normal manner. General Chennault has told General Carton de Wiart that had the Americans been carrying out an operation, the British aircraft might well have been destroyed." The sealed message reported that "General Carton de Wiart was informed by General Chennault that 'sometime ago' two British Liberators had entered Chennault's area without giving previous warning. As a result the Liberators had unfortunately been destroyed."[35] Whitworth-Jones ended by saying "I am to request that these two assertions be examined and a report rendered. It is possible that the Liberators referred to by General Chennault as having been inadvertently destroyed by the Americans are two of the Liberators lost on a recent SD operation. The other incident is not understood." This was a grave situation indeed.

Because of the secret nature of the operations the results of the subsequent investigation were not released. The investigation revealed that the loss of the two, and perhaps three, bombers had been a logical outcome of the Mountbatten-Wedemeyer dispute over activity in Indochina. Earlier, when General Donovan, head of OSS, came through Ceylon he had been disturbed at the atmosphere created by the dispute,

---

34. PRO, Air 23/3595, "Incidents Involving SD Aircraft", 19 Feb. 1945.
35. When American aircrews began flying missions over Laos and North Vietnam in the mid-1960s, much of the area was still uncharted, with huge blank squares on the charts reading "Relief Data Incomplete".

and the resulting adverse effect upon clandestine operations, and he strongly urged Mountbatten to take up the question of French Indochina with Wedemeyer personally. While Mountbatten and Wedemeyer were talking, SEAC's Special Duty Branch chief issued orders to ensure that Mountbatten would not be compromised: no operations to French Indochina were to be staged through China, routine exchanges of information with 14th USAAF were suspended "in the interests of safety", and cover bombing and leaflet drops were stopped, although SD operations without cover bombing or leaflet drops could continue. When the talks between the two senior Commanders were over, Mountbatten, having made his point about security, authorized a return to the routine exchanges of information with the 14th Air Force warning system. However, the B-24s were launched just before the resumption of this exchange. It was recommended by the Special Duty branch, and accepted by SACSEA, that all concerned adopt a "sealed lips" policy over this tragic occurrence, and that if a detailed investigation were carried out the results should remain a secret. (Night intercepts were carried out by 14th Air Force P-61 Black Widow fighters equipped with radar. A cursory check of their operation logs showed that during this period, at least, they destroyed more Allied than Japanese planes; they had also recently mistakenly destroyed an American B-24.)

These difficulties in the field still mirrored the higher-level differences in Washington, London and Paris. In January 1945, Halifax was still fighting the Indochina battle with little success. On 3 January he had seen the US Secretary of State, Mr Stettinius, who said that the President still thought that any military or political action on Indochina was premature, and preferred to discuss the situation with Churchill. Halifax persisted, telling Stettinius that the President was not considering Mountbatten's urgent military arguments for operations in Indochina. Stettinius said that he could do no more, so Halifax decided to go again directly to Roosevelt. When he saw Roosevelt a few days later, he told the President of his disappointment with Stettinius's reply on the Indochina question, a reply based on instructions from Roosevelt. Wrote Halifax, "The President launched off into his general ideas about the future of Indo-China with which we are generally familiar. I said that I was not concerned to argue those at the moment, and the point of our suggestion, to which we attach great importance, was that Mountbatten should be free without delay to get some parties of Frenchmen into Indochina to do sabotage work which might hamper Japanese communications into Burma." The President replied that if the British thought it important they should tell Mountbatten to go ahead and do it and ask no questions. The Foreign Office were unsure about the meaning of this "off the record" remark by Roosevelt, but thought that it should be sent to all commanders in the field; however, it was not to be quoted officially, as it did not represent a formal endorsement or commitment by the United States. If Mountbatten was getting by in his challenge to the Americans, then "Let sleeping dogs lie", in Halifax's words, and press on. If Mountbatten intended to expand his operations, then Halifax would confidentially tell General Marshall of Roosevelt's comments and Marshall could pass it on to the appropriate American commanders.

From SEAC Dening advised Eden that in view of the President's attitude it would be wiser now to stop pressing him. Dening thought that if Mountbatten pressed on in Indochina, acting on the assumption that the "Gentleman's Agreement" was still valid and there were no grounds for disagreement, Roosevelt might have to accept "an already firm situation". Roosevelt was being reinforced in his Indochina ideas by Admiral Leahy, former Ambassador in Vichy. As J. C. Sterndale-Bennett of the Foreign Office Far Eastern Department noted, "The obstruction seems to be partly the President's political ideas about Indo-China and partly the alleged desire of Admiral Leahy to get Indo-China out of SEAC." Within twelve months the United States would have done a complete about-face and was strongly urging the British to keep Indochina in SEAC, but by then continued American obstruction and subversion of the Allies in Indochina had made this impossible. During the same week, on 9 January 1945, Sterndale-Bennett minuted that the Foreign Office had proposed to the State Department, as far back as August 1944, that the French Military Mission be established at SEAC, the *Corps Léger d'Intervention* be moved to the Far East, and the French be allowed to participate in political warfare in SEAC. Up till then, because of Roosevelt's attitude, the United States had not even replied to the proposals. The British in fact went ahead with the Mission. As Sterndale-Bennett wrote, "After all the war cannot stand still and we have been waiting 5 or 6 months for the President's reply." So Blaizot's move, originally a temporary measure pending US approval, was now regarded as permanent. The French were under suspicion of having a foot in each camp, desperately trying to make sure that they would return to Indochina. Continued Sterndale-Bennett, "It is highly unsatisfactory that we and the Americans should be fencing with each other in this way . . . it is also high time we knew where we stood with the US Government as regards the broad general principle of whether Indochina is to remain

French.'' A Foreign Office memorandum of 18 January 1945 reflected this maddening stalemate, noting that theater commanders could not agree on courses of action in Indochina because of the risk of upsetting Roosevelt, and the British were precluded from taking official action because the President's remarks to Halifax were made off the record.

At the same time, while the Foreign Office and Roosevelt were sticking to their positions, the acrimonious and unproductive sparring continued between SEAC and China Theater. As reported by Dening, SEAC received a message from Wedemeyer ''who, this time, seems to be determined to challenge our whole position''. Wedemeyer said that his directive included French Indochina, and this was recognized by the British Chiefs of Staff (this was news to Dening). Furthermore, if SEAC had bomber sorties available for use to China Theater he would pick the targets at his own headquarters. Said Dening, ''So that is that,'' and went on, ''If there were any prospect at all that his Command could, in the foreseeable future, attack Indo-China, one could see some point in his claim from the military point of view. But this is impossible.'' Wedemeyer was claiming that he should have full control of all forces and activities in French Indochina. Dening (and the Japanese) thought that MacArthur, using Luzon as a springboard, stood a far better chance of invading Indochina. Dening, alarmed at the long-term implications of the US Indochina policy, was determined that SEAC should hold fast. ''I think, therefore, that we should stoutly resist General Wedemeyer's attempt to usurp the sole authority for this job.'' Although Force 136 was not heavily involved in China, ''Indo-China, on the other hand, is another matter. As you know, Force 136 have been the guiding light there, and but for them the French, who I believe are now contributing very valuable intelligence, apart from any other activities, would have been unable to get going. The Supreme Commander has just urged that we should let sleeping dogs lie. Unfortunately the dogs have failed to remain asleep.'' Dening persisted in trying to find some way out of the impasse but Wedemeyer remained unmoved. Dening noted, ''I am afraid it is only too clear that the Americans are, for what are purely political reasons, trying to block something which is militarily sound.'' Even if MacArthur was able to mount the initial assault from the Philippines, any pre-occupational activities in Indochina would be invaluable to him.

At the Tet festivities in Paris, de Gaulle flatly rejected Roosevelt's ideas of trusteeship for Indochina. France, said de Gaulle, would be her own trustee. A Foreign Office planning paper had anticipated his remarks by recalling, a week earlier, that former Governor-General Albert Sarraut had described Indochina as "the most important, the most developed and the most prosperous of our colonies". Any attempts arbitrarily to confiscate it "would be passionately resented" by France and have incalculable results not only in the Far East but in Europe. It would also "put in question the future of all other Far Eastern colonial possessions (including our own) which have been overrun by Japan." French Indochina was of considerable importance to Great Britain. It had been used as a stepping-stone for attacking Malaya, and British interest, "by means of special strategic agreements within an international security scheme", lay in making sure it did not happen again.

The planning paper mentioned an ominous possibility: namely, that if Russia entered the war against Japan she might show an interest in French Indochina. The position of Indochina was peculiar to begin with. De Gaulle was saying that France was at war with Japan, but the Japanese did not recognize his Provisional Government and therefore did not regard themselves as being at war with France. Japan regarded Indochina as linked to Vichy, with which she had certain agreements and rights, but the Vichy Government no longer existed. Roosevelt was guaranteeing trouble in Europe and Asia by persisting in trying to take Indochina away from France, and the Allies were not able to prosecute the war fully in Indochina because of these fundamental differences between the US and British/French senior commanders in Asia. The only people gaining anything from this unfortunate deadlock were the Japanese and the Communist-led Viet Minh.

The problem of the post-war status of Indochina now loomed over everything. With de Gaulle's Provisional Government rapidly gaining strength, it was difficult to see how Roosevelt could persist in his present attitude. But he now postponed discussions on Indochina. On 6 February 1945 the US Ambassador to China told the British Ambassador in confidence that the absence of any declared American policy on Indochina was embarrassing for him. He had asked Roosevelt to make a move, perhaps at a three-power meeting, but had had no luck so far. In a memorandum of 1 January 1945 to the Secretary of State, Roosevelt had written, "I still do not want to get mixed up in any Indochina decision. It is a matter for post-war. By the same token, I do not want to get mixed up in any military effort toward the liberation of Indochina from the Japanese." Dening's frustration showed in his correspondence with the Foreign Office. He was by now despairing of convincing Hurley and Wedemeyer of the long-term dangers of their obstructionist policy in

Indochina. When Dening saw them on 20 February, Wedemeyer told him that he was "180 degrees at variance" with Mountbatten over Indochina.[36] Wedemeyer again openly aired his own suspicions of British intentions everywhere, telling Dening that Britain did not want a unified China. Dening said that he simply had no time to prove him wrong. Wedemeyer then went on to express contempt for the French in Indochina, and doubted that they would be of any use in ejecting the Japanese. Dening sighed, "Someday some better man that I may find time to convince General Wedemeyer that we are not as sinister as he thinks we are. It will be a difficult but worthwhile task."

While these talks were taking place General Carton de Wiart sent Churchill a report of his own conversation with General Pechkoff, the French envoy to Chungking. Pechkoff went to see de Wiart "not as a French Ambassador but as a soldier"; reflecting French fears of a Chinese move, he said he had information that two Chinese divisions and some Americans were on the Indochina border, and the Americans were known to be helping the Vietnamese revolutionaries. He said the French would fight if the Chinese entered Indochina. De Wiart also sent General Ismay further information on the seemingly irreconcilable problem in South East Asia. "Wedemeyer was quite frank to me about his plans, and I think he, for military reasons, would like to see the Indo-China question solved. It would simplify military operations and give him an opportunity of doing something big; scattering his army, just to occupy the Japanese, is a poor role for a Commander, and would leave everything for MacArthur."[37]

Mountbatten now met Wedemeyer in Calcutta and took up the issue of his "gentleman's agreement" with Chiang Kai-shek. Mountbatten recorded, "I warned him that it was my intention to confirm personally from the Generalissimo in Chungking that he regarded his gentleman's agreement with me as still binding, and I particularly invited General Wedemeyer to have one or two representatives present when I made this statement. After demurring, he finally agreed that he would arrange for General Gross (his Chief of Staff) and an American interpreter to be present." Wedemeyer reiterated his opposition to the agreement, and Somervell's lack of authority to negotiate, and now said that he was going to tell his superiors in Washington about it. Mountbatten thought he knew one of the reasons for Wedemeyer's suspicions. It went back to the previous year when the "seed of distrust was firmly

36.  PRO, FO 371/46304, Dening to Foreign Office, 21 Feb. 1945.
37.  PRO, Prem 3/185–3, de Wiart to Ismay, 23 Feb. 1945.

implanted in Wedemeyer's mind in July 1944." At that time Force 136 made an "unfortunate mistake" in infiltrating a French officer to Indo-china bearing a letter of introduction from General de Gaulle.[38] Wedemeyer had some justification for his suspicions, but the quarrel between the two theater commanders hindered operations in that vitally important area. When Kunming airfield was closed to Force 136 operations on 24 January 1945, the Saigon area and Cambodia had to be omitted from Special Duty plans due to extreme flying ranges from Jessore.

The British War Cabinet took note of the slowdown of operations in French Indochina, and of Wedemeyer's idea that his new position over-rode the Chiang-Mountbatten agreement, which at the moment was Mountbatten's bridge to Indochina. "Early in January he told Admiral Mountbatten 'that he would have to inform the US Joint Chiefs of Staff that the Supreme Allied Commander was still acting on his agreement with the Generalissimo' and he expressed great astonishment on being told by Admiral Mountbatten in reply that instructions to United States Commanding Generals were of no special concern to the British Chiefs of Staff and certainly did not give General Wedemeyer any Allied rights over Indo-China."

On 13 January SEAC wanted to call forward the *Corps Léger d'Intervention*, then in Algiers, to engage in guerrilla operations in Indo-china. Wedemeyer was opposed to this, but there were sound political and military reasons for turning them loose now. When the SEAC staff had reached agreement, General Wheeler, the American deputy, threw a bombshell into the plan; he produced a telegram from the US Chiefs which he had previously hidden, forbidding the movement of French forces to the Far East, and said that "Admiral Mountbatten as an Englishman could do what he liked but as the Supreme Commander of an Allied Command he was not entitled to take such action without the authority of the Combined Chiefs of Staff."[39] On 4 March 1945 Eden asked Churchill to try to stop "the present sparring" between Mount-batten and Wedemeyer, which would lead to trouble. Eden asked if the Prime Minister would "consider an approach to the President", for "no other course is likely to produce a decision." As the problem was explained to Churchill, the British Chiefs of Staff had asked the Com-bined Chiefs to approve increased French participation in the Far East. The US Chiefs, reflecting Roosevelt's views, had for several months

38.   The officer was Col. de Langlade. (Personal interview, 3 Sept. 1977.)
39.   PRO, FO 371/46304, Dening to Sterndale-Bennett, 2 Feb. 1945.

now refused to reply. But the President had meanwhile told Halifax that he was prepared to turn a blind eye to Mountbatten's pre-occupational activities in Indochina, but now Wedemeyer was the problem. Since Wedemeyer was in Washington at this time it would be a good idea to send a message to Roosevelt.

Unfortunately, in the midst of all this, the long-dreaded event occurred when the Japanese on 9 March finally struck down the French, an event of calamitous consequences. The Communist-dominated Viet-Minh, with American help, now had a free hand to accelerate the build-up of their own movement. On 12 March General St-Didier, of the French Mission in Washington, asked the Combined Chiefs to send help to the beleaguered French columns in Indochina. The reply was not helpful, and no increase in the French staff at Chungking was to be permitted. Wedemeyer would meet Blaizot if necessary, and look into the situation. At this time Wedemeyer was returning from Washington to Chungking, and the British Chiefs and the Foreign Office were hoping to persuade him to return via London. He begged off this, and on 12 March Ismay told Churchill that the US Chiefs had probably dissuaded Wedemeyer from stopping off in London lest those crafty British sway him from his plans for a great offensive by the Chinese armies, which would settle the Indochinese question once and for all. Churchill was in fact preoccupied with bigger things, and this flaring Indochina problem was something of a nuisance. Before writing to Roosevelt he asked General Ismay, "Let me have a short note, not more than one page, on what has happened in Indo-China since the beginning of the war. How is it there are French troops and a Governor-General there now? Are they survivors of the Vichy period? Have they not yet joined up with de Gaulle? I have not followed the affairs in this country for some time."

In Paris on 13 March, on hearing of the inactivity of the USAAF concerning help for the retreating French forces in Indochina, de Gaulle summoned US Ambassador Caffery and said that he had received word that US forces had refused to assist the French, and the expeditionary forces for Indochina were stalled because the Americans had prohibited their movement to the Far East. He said he failed to understand American policy. In a cold fury he turned on Caffery: "What are you driving at? Do you want us to become, for example, one of the federated states under the Russian aegis? The Russians are advancing apace as you well know. When Germany falls they will be upon us. If the public here comes to realize that you are against us in Indochina, there will be a terrific disappointment and nobody knows to what this will lead. We do not want to become Communist; we do not want to fall into the Russian orbit, but I hope that you do not push us into it.''[40] While the French survivors were trudging into China, pursued by the Japanese, memos were circulating in the State Department that the French were using their reverses for publicity. James C. Dunn, for example, reflected the views of many at State in commenting on the frantic French appeals for help as the Japanese struck: ''I personally think that the French are making a great fuss over the Indo-China resistance for political reasons only and in an effort to smoke out our policy.'' They were not alone; many Americans were also trying to ''smoke out'' a policy on Indochina, and it was acknowledged that US commanders in the field were embarrassed over the lack of a policy.[41]

The War Cabinet's initial assessment of the *coup* revealed that for the moment the Japanese action appeared to be limited to major centers. Eight of the radio stations, built up originally during the ''Belief'' sorties, went down, although fifteen were still up. There was an urgent requirement for drops of food and arms to the retreating French columns. On 11 March, four RAF B-24 aircraft loaded with arms had flown to the French in the vicinity of Thai Nguyen, in Tonkin; two sorties were successful. One of the few places where the Japanese surprise had not swept the French away was at Moncay, in far northern Tonkin, where the French reported that their troops had surrounded the Japanese and no Japanese reinforcements had yet arrived; but they badly needed supplies to sustain their fight. On 16 March the War Office informed the Foreign Office that RAF Liberators were being diverted to drop supplies to the French, but the USAAF just across the border had announced that they would drop nothing to the French unless authorized by Washington. On 17 March, with the RAF straining to sustain the French in this fighting retreat, Churchill finally wrote to Roosevelt that he had heard that there were ''certain difficulties'' between Mountbatten and Wedemeyer about operations in Indochina. He went on to bring Roosevelt up to date on those operations:

---

40. US, FRUS, *The British Commonwealth, The Far East*, p. 300.

41. On 5 Feb. 1945 Maj.-Gen. Craig wrote in a memo on Indochina to General Handy of the Army Staff that the ''French and British representatives have repeatedly of late attempted to ascertain the US policy regarding French Indo China. Our policy is a direct quotation of the President . . . strictly a 'do nothing' policy. . . . The execution of such a policy has caused repeated difficulty for our field commanders.'' (United States, National Archives [NA], RG165 [OPD], 336TS, 28 September 1945, FW1.)

Under existing decisions of the Combined Chiefs of Staff Indo-China is still within the China Theater. But Mountbatten has a vital interest in Indo-China as well as in Siam since it is through them that runs the Japanese land and air reinforcement route to Burma and Malaya; and as you know he has an oral understanding with Chiang Kai-shek that both he and the Generalissimo shall be free to attack Siam and Indo-China and that the boundaries between the two Theatres shall be decided when the time comes in accordance with the progress made by their respective forces. The Generalissimo agreed after Sextant that this understanding extended to pre-occupational activities.[42]

Churchill concluded by saying that General Wedemeyer "feels difficulty in recognizing this oral understanding," and "harmful friction" could come about. He suggested that they clear it up by addressing the oral agreement, "which seems a sensible and workable agreement." Roosevelt replied five days later, but much had happened in the interval.

On 18 March the news from Indochina was worse. On behalf of the French Government, the Head of the French Naval Mission in Washington begged the Combined Chiefs of Staff for help, particularly for the 1,000 French troops at Moncay who were resisting the Japanese and crying out for arms and ammunition; the latter was of particular urgency since Japanese policy had been to keep the French Army short of ammunition. In Chungking General Gross was asked to parachute Bren guns and sixty cases of ammunition stored there. He refused to do so, citing (it might be thought somewhat cattily) previous French requests that the US stop sending arms to Indochina. These earlier requests had, of course, referred to American support of Communist revolutionaries who were the Viet Minh's backbone. The French Government stated that if help were not forthcoming immediately the battle at Moncay would be over. The French, over "such a misunderstanding . . . would deeply resent not to see our Allies bring them immediately all possible help in their traditional brotherhood;" they urgently requested help from the US 14th Air Force sitting across the border in China. From Washington, in his memo to the Cabinet, Field-Marshal Wilson, Head of the British Joint Staff Mission (to the Combined Chiefs of Staff Committee), said that if anything was to be done for the French it must be done quickly. In his view the US Chiefs of Staff would support General Gross and refuse to permit the 14th Air Force to aid the French.

On 18 March, the same day as Churchill's message was en route to Roosevelt, General Marshall received a message from General Gross, which Marshall passed to Field-Marshal Wilson without comment. At

42.  PRO, Prem 3/178–3, Churchill to Roosevelt, 17 March 1945.

this critical juncture while the French were being cut to pieces across the border by the common enemy, the best Gross could do was to complain again of SEAC's philosophy that so long as they did not stage out of China they could operate in Indochina without receiving permission from Wedemeyer. Wilson cabled the British Chiefs: ". . . If military considerations were the only factors that had to be taken into account . . . a solution could be found which would be acceptable to both Wedemeyer and Mountbatten. But the difficulty in the background all the time is political . . . HMG [His Majesty's Government] on the one hand wish to foster the French resistance movement and the USG [US Government] on the other take an entirely contrary view. We want to work with the French and make increasing use of French manpower to increase clandestine resistance to the Japanese but feel that the American inclination is to exclude the French altogether."

Churchill had by now had enough. On 19 March he wrote to Wilson asking him to tell Roosevelt and Marshall that "it will look very bad in history if we were to let the French force in Indo-China be cut to pieces by the Japanese through shortage of ammunition, if there is anything we can do to save them." He went on to hope "that we shall be agreed not to stand on punctilio in this emergency."[43] Wilson immediately saw Marshall and asked him to tell Wedemeyer to help the desperate Frenchmen at Moncay. Should Marshall be reluctant to do so, or Wedemeyer refuse, then the British would tell the US that Mountbatten would do it for them anyway, while keeping Wedemeyer informed. Actually, Mountbatten was already helping the French as best he could, and the British Chiefs had asked Mountbatten if he could increase the present scale of air support for the French groups operating in Indochina. On 20 March, clearly despairing of an American change of heart and prompted by the terrible condition of the French in Indochina, Churchill decided to go all out. He brushed aside Wilson's caution that Indochina was in the US sphere and ordered Mountbatten to do everything he could to assist the surviving Frenchmen. When Marshall heard of this he immediately ordered Chennault to start helping the French, but China Theater did not respond.[44] On 21 March Mountbatten replied to London. With an eye on the political implications he wrote that it was never his intention

---

43. PRO, Prem 3/178-3, Churchill to Wilson, 19 March 1945.
44. In later years Gen. Wedemeyer refused to discuss the broad aspect of his operations in Indochina when approached by the historian Bernard Fall, saying that his instructions were still classified. He did, however, discuss them with the author in 1980 (see Appendix to this Chapter).

to supply French regular forces, but the Japanese coup had now mixed the French regular forces and underground together. His previous policy had been to establish a radio net with the underground and supply selected centers with limited quantities of arms and supplies for training and future use by guerrillas. The supply problem had been of the utmost difficulty due to the extreme distances and bad weather. In one month (from 6 February to 6 March 1945) only twenty-eight of seventy-seven Liberator sorties had been successful. He could possibly have done more, but political considerations (American objections) had stopped him from accepting a French offer to operate two squadrons.

In the United States, the French could not even get credit for their belated struggle. On 21 March Edward W. Barrett, of the Office of War Information, asked the State Department if his office could now publicize the story of French resistance to the Japanese. The answer was that since French resistance had now collapsed he should adhere to previous guidance, which policy was "quite rigid, emanating, as you know, from the most authoritative sources". At about this time a note from State's European Affairs ("EHD") to "Jamie" (presumably James C. Dunn) called the latter's attention to the fact that the US Military Chiefs were "strongly" against sending Ambassador Caffery a copy of a cable which stated that Chennault's help to the French "does not (repeat not) represent a commitment for military aid. No such commitments can be given." As it was, the cable was never sent, as "EHD" wrote: "The substance has been incorporated in the draft note to be handed the frogs [French] here."

On 22 March Roosevelt, having delayed, replied to Churchill's request that Wedemeyer honor the Mountbatten-Chiang agreement. He said he knew about the agreement, and "This appears perfectly sound to me." However, he noted the obscurity in the agreement in dealing with pre-occupational activities, and thought that Chiang (through Wedemeyer) had insisted on controlling all non-Chinese clandestine activity in Indochina. So Roosevelt essentially did not accede to Churchill's request, and went on to say that Wedemeyer should have the final say. Since the two theater commanders were independently running their own air operations and intelligence, there was a possibility of confusion which "might result in placing the two theaters unintentionally in conflict" (Roosevelt may have had in mind the destruction of the RAF "Liberators").

On 24 March 1945, Ambassador Caffery and Samuel Rosenman, Roosevelt's Special Counsel, called on de Gaulle in Paris. As they were leaving, de Gaulle said to Caffery, "It seems clear now that your Government does not want to help our troops in Indo-China. Nothing has yet been dropped to them by parachute." Caffery muttered some excuse about the distances involved, but de Gaulle snapped, "No, that is not the question; the question is one of policy, I assume."[45] De Gaulle was correct; official American policy was to deny aid to the French. Marshall had no objections to helping them, but left the final decision to Wedemeyer, who later stated that he had little to spare from his own stocks.[46] On 1 April 1945 John J. McCloy, Assistant Secretary of War, wrote from Europe that trouble was brewing in France over the lack of American help for the French survivors in Tonkin. And on 7 April Mr Matthews of the State Department reported that Ambassador Caffery was being embarrassed by de Gaulle's charges and asked for information on US assistance to the French in order to counter this criticism. But as of 9 April, nearly three weeks after Marshall's authorization, nothing had been dropped, and at this time Marshall himself told his senior commanders in China that the State Department's requirement for only "token assistance was appropriate."[47]

45. US, FRUS, *The British Commonwealth, The Far East*, p. 302.
46. Personal interview, 1980.
47. This token assistance was authorized at Ambassador Caffery's request, to deflect de Gaulle's bitter criticisms. (NA, RG 165/336.2 France, Box 972.) As of 2 April no supplies had been dropped to the French. By 9 April, a month after the Japanese attack on the French and after the fight was essentially over, an American Memo for Record stated, "Aid given to French Indo-China to date consisted of a few aerial supply drops, actually resulting in inconsequential assistance. It is contemplated that the same system will apply in the future." However, on 14 April China Theater was reporting that no supplies had yet been dropped, and Marshall had to ask why so many reservations were being placed on aid to the French. (NA, RG 165/336.2[OPD]; RG 165/336.2 [France], Box 972.)
    A major problem seemed to be Leahy, the political Admiral. More than once Leahy is seen stepping in to gut any moves which might have helped Free France. For example, during discussions over the proposed move of the *Corps Léger* to Indochina, the Joint Chiefs of Staff (in para. 2 of a proposed memo to the Secretary of State) wrote that from a "military point of view it would appear advantageous to permit operations of the proposed Corps Léger d'Intervention in that area as proposed in the aide memoire of the British Embassy." Leahy deleted this paragraph over the questioning of John J. McCloy, who thought that if this was the military advice of the JCS, they should say so; McCloy wrote that "the second [paragraph] should not be deleted if it in fact represents the considered judgment of the military people . . ." Even some sections of the State Department were not pleased with the memo, but Leahy brought them into line. (NA, RG 165/336B, 15 Apr. 1945.)

Unfortunately for the poor French, not only was the United States not helping them, but it seems that US aircraft also bombed the little French firepower that existed. On 13 March William R. Langdon, American Consul General at Kunming, wrote to Washington to say that the "main body of white French troops in Indo-China", about 12,000 in number, were "surrounded by superior Japanese forces and threatened with annihilation or capture, its artillery ammunition having been destroyed, probably by accident, a short while ago by the 14th USAAF"[48] (which appeared to be inflicting damage on the British, French, Japanese, and other Americans alike). Perhaps if 14th Air Force had accepted a French liaison officer at their headquarters, incidents like this could have been avoided. Continued Langdon, "[The French] have asked for weapons, but our weapons are reserved for our own specific purposes. They have asked for air support, but that is not on our program. They have asked for transportation to Chungking on Army planes for members of their Military Mission, but it has not been granted." Little by little the British were turning away from the Combined Chiefs on Indochina, beginning with their giving Mountbatten the green light to go all out to supply the retreating French columns. The United States was advised that the British would inform the French why the CLI could not be moved; the British were "reluctant that the odium of this refusal should fall on us."

On 30 March the British Chiefs of Staff examined Roosevelt's reply to Churchill, and, on their strong recommendation, Churchill replied to the President, reiterating Mountbatten's vital interest in Indochina and saying that it made more sense to fly supplies direct to South East Asia from India or SEAC rather than via the long and indirect route over the Himalayas, and India was the great base supplying both China and South East Asia. But he now finished with trying to evoke a sense of urgency in Roosevelt and stated that he was empowering Mountbatten "to conduct pre-occupational activities in Indo-China from whatever base appears to be most suitable", keeping Wedemeyer informed. He did not even say *south* Indochina. Of Mountbatten's directive, Churchill amended this sentence by hand to read, "You may conduct from whatever base appears most suitable the minimum pre-occupational activities in Indo-China which local emergency and the advance of your forces require." Churchill's note to Roosevelt continued, "Now that the Japanese have taken over Indo-China and that substantial resistance is

48. NA, RG 226/125233S/13 March 1945 (OSS Report).

being offered by French patriots, it is essential not only that we should support the French by all means in our power, but also that we should associate them with our operations into their country. It would look very bad in history if we failed to support isolated French Forces in their resistance to the Japanese to the best of our ability, or if we excluded the French from participation in our councils as regards Indo-China.''

By 30 March, when Churchill's directive was en route to Mountbatten, General Chennault, the US 14th Air Force Commander, still had not done much to help the French. This is a puzzling part of the story, for he wrote in his autobiography (published just four years after these events) that he strongly opposed the policy of refusing aid to the French columns falling back in the hills, and wanted very much to help them.[49] However, the recently opened archives tell a different story. In a telegram to his superiors, when he was acting Theater Commander in Wedemeyer's absence, he complained that the British were helping the French at Son La and Moncay, and said that the ''French continued representations for assistance to their resistance groups in Indo-China.'' As an excuse he reported: ''Fluidity of situation, bad weather conditions, and non-availability of surplus equipment have materially limited action.'' He then stated that this sort of thing (the RAF B-24s assisting the French) would give a bad impression, as people might think that the Americans were now helping the retreating French columns.[50] He went on to say that any assistance to the French must be weighed against a return value for effort expended.

In this complaint to Marshall, Chennault said that on 14/15 March a shot-down 14th Air Force pilot reported seeing British B-24s dropping

49. Bernard B. Fall, in *The Two Vietnams*, quotes a couple of paragraphs of Chennault's autobiography *Way of a Fighter* (New York: G. P. Putnam's Sons, 1949), p. 342: ''. . . Orders arrived from theater headquarters stating that no arms and ammunition would be provided to French troops under any circumstances. . . . The American government was interested in seeing the French forcibly ejected from Indochina so the problem of postwar separation from their colony would be easier . . . I carried out my orders to the letter but I did not relish the idea of leaving Frenchmen to be slaughtered in the jungle while I was forced officially to ignore their plight.'' Fall goes on to comment that ''Wedemeyer actually complained to the British SEAC commander that the latter's transport planes were overstepping operational boundaries by parachuting equipment to the dying French'' (*The Two Vietnams*, p. 57). At this time the archives were still closed and Fall was unaware of Chennault's similar complaints, which call into question the alleged soul-searching in Chennault's autobiography.

50. PRO, Prem 3/178–3, Chennault to Marshall, 30 Mar. 1945 (repeated Joint Staff Mission to British Chiefs).

food and supplies to French forces at Son La, among which were cases of American K-rations! Also, on 20 March two Allied (RAF) Liberators had dropped supplies and arms to French forces at Moncay. Some of the supplies had fallen beyond French reach, and luckily, exclaimed Chennault, friendly Chinese had picked up these few crates. While protesting that Mountbatten should coordinate operations in Indochina with Chungking, his main problem seemed to be that these actions "may lead to erroneous reports of China Theater operations in French Indo-China." The supplies he mentioned, which but for the Chinese might have fallen into Japanese hands, consisted of a few machine-guns and twenty tommy-guns, plus of course those K-rations — not likely to make much of an impact on the Japanese war effort one way or the other. But these complaints reflected a corporate state of mind.

On 31 March the British Chiefs pressed Churchill for action on moving the *Corps Léger* out to the Far East. Churchill replied that he was reluctant to over-burden the President, who was already hard-pressed and "I like to keep him as much as possible for the biggest things," noting also that "the telegram he sent me [on pre-occupational activities] was obviously not his own." On 3 April he told General Hollis of the War Office that he was prepared to bring it up to Roosevelt "in a day or two". What he really meant was that he had decided to act and would simply inform the President. Churchill's attitude reflected the mood of the Foreign Office. On the question of command boundaries and the despatch of the *Corps Léger* to the Far East, the Foreign Office noted that it had been more than three weeks since the French Ambassador had appealed to the British for help. Wrote Sterndale-Bennett: "The time has come to grasp this Indo-China nettle and to tackle the Americans on the whole issue;" the British had no wish to "lose respect by our subservience in this issue." The next day they acted.

On 5 April Admiral Fenard again wrote to the Combined Chiefs about the CLI. The French resistance in Indochina needed reinforcement cadres. Since the French troops were obliging the Japanese troops to fight them (Japanese who could be used elsewhere), it was desirable to keep those Frenchmen in good fighting condition. He had thus been instructed by the French General Staff to ask for permission to transport 100 officers and men of the CLI to the Far East; these men were familiar with Indochina and the resistance in that area. The remaining CLI men could go aboard one of two French cruisers, the *Suffren* or the *Georges Leygues*. The British Chiefs supported this approach, and now the Combined Chiefs had no objections, for this was also the day when the

British instructed the Joint Staff Mission to inform the US Chiefs that they would be sending the CLI to the Far East.

As the Combined Chiefs were studying Fenard's message, in South East Asia Mountbatten was preparing for a visit by Wedemeyer. Both their plans were now overtaken by events and a face-to-face meeting was overdue. When Wedemeyer arrived at SEAC, Mountbatten went over the whole history of the negotiations, and took his visitor into the top-secret Clandestine War Room to show him also the extent of SEAC clandestine activity in South East Asia. The meeting was reported to the Foreign Office by H. N. Brain, of Dening's Foreign Office staff at SEAC. Brain said that the two commanders had had a long talk on French Indochina, during which Wedemeyer was under the impression that the "gentleman's agreement" had never been approved by higher authority in Washington and was "astounded" when shown evidence of its approval by both the President and the US Chiefs. Wedemeyer admitted that he must have seen these papers while on Mountbatten's staff, but said that the British had accepted the inclusion of French Indochina in his sphere of operations. Mountbatten retorted that the British had never been consulted about it and had thus considered it "purely a question of control of American forces and as such no concern of ours". The talks did much to clear the air for the moment, even if they did not ultimately settle the issue; however, Wedemeyer was reaffirmed in his power to veto operations which conflicted with his own. As they talked, Mountbatten asked Wedemeyer if he could now tell the Chiefs of Staff that they had "buttoned up" these problems, to which Wedemeyer replied "Certainly." Mountbatten reported that Wedemeyer "once more assured me that nothing was further from his mind than to exclude British activities as long as they contributed to the overall effort against Japan."

As Wedemeyer returned to Chungking the Foreign Office received a folder from Colonel Taylor of SOE, containing a message from Colin Mackenzie (Commander of Force 136) in Delhi. Mackenzie's message was an update of the French-Japanese fighting in Indochina, and contained the following main points. The French were continuing to cause the Japanese trouble, and some of the initial sabotage plans were carried out. Three special groups introduced had successfully recruited about 100 guerrillas. "If we had [the] 5th Regiment [CLI] thus ensuring further special groups [the] position would have been most promising." The French troops were getting tired and their morale was declining. The main deficiencies in Indochina now were of transport (to carry

essential supplies), a fresh supply of young officers (the absence of whom
was preventing columns from being split into smaller guerrilla parties),
and the continued holding back of the CLI (which constituted a breach
of faith). As things stood, Mackenzie continued, all the sacrifices and
effort would be in vain as the group faced extermination, with the exception of those columns falling back to China. Force 136 had requested
SACSEA to send in jeeps and trailers, and were wanting to drop in a
couple of liaison officers as a gesture, but the real answer lay with the
Combined Chiefs of Staff. Mackenzie described a particularly depressing
incident which had occurred on 29 March, when the Americans flew in
two sorties (possibly 10th Air Force C-47s), one for their own needs
(presumably OSS exfiltration), and one to evacuate six US airmen (who
had been brought out by the French). For the ragged and desperate
Frenchmen around, this studied callousness had its effect: ''In neither
plane were there any stores, not even medical stores or cigarettes.
American name is mud repeat mud with French and British alike in this
whole episode.'' Mackenzie pulled no punches: if the British did not go
all-out to help, ''our position will be little better than that of the
Americans.''

On 12 April Franklin D. Roosevelt died, worn out by his heroic
efforts to carry the burdens of the wartime presidency. Churchill and he
had enjoyed a warm personal relationship; their disagreements had been
political. When FDR had earlier sent a birthday message to Churchill,
the Prime Minister responded: ''I cannot tell you how much I value your
friendship or how much I hope upon it for the future of the world,
should we both be spared.'' And after the 1944 Presidential election
Churchill told Roosevelt (8 November 1944):

I always said that a great people could be trusted to stand by the pilot who
weathered the storm. It is an indescribable relief to me that our comradeship will
continue and will help to bring the world out of misery . . . things are afoot
which will be remembered as long as the English language is spoken in any
quarter of the globe, and in expressing the comfort I feel that the people of the
United States have once again cast these great burdens upon you. I must avow
my sure faith that the lights by which we steer will bring us all safely to anchor.

Now the pilot was dead.

On the narrow issue of his Indochina policy, La Feber may be as close
as any with his comment that ''The President's Indochina policy in
1943–4 is a case study of how supposed idealism, in this instance anti-

colonialism, can blend perfectly with American self-interest,''[51] — a drive for post-war access to new markets and new materials, and influence in the new countries of the future. But in the end, like many other policies of limited vision, it did not work out that way.

The accession of Harry S. Truman sparked a debate which still continues as to whether he carried on or departed from Roosevelt's policies. Although it may be argued either way, what followed appeared to favor the ''break'' theory. Still, some of the old prejudices lingered on. Just before de Gaulle visited Washington in 1945 for an initial meeting with Truman, the President asked an experienced newsman to sum up de Gaulle. When told that the French leader could hold his own against anybody, Truman banged the desk saying, ''Dammit, why doesn't anybody ever tell me the truth! The State Department's always been telling me de Gaulle is stupid.''[52] Within a few days of his assuming office, Truman wrote to Churchill noting that Mountbatten and Wedemeyer appeared to have patched up their quarrel, and that Wedemeyer had been instructed to do what he could for the French resistance groups. The British Chiefs considered that the directive, ''although not altogether satisfactory, . . . is a great advance on anything that the American Chiefs of Staff have hitherto been prepared to do in this matter, in that it implicitly recognizes that Admiral Mountbatten is entitled to have plans, intuitions and intelligence as regards Indo-China.''[53] With Roosevelt's death francophobia in Washington diminished, even if it did not vanish, and Wedemeyer was told not automatically to oppose Mountbatten.

If Truman assumed that the Wedemeyer-Mountbatten dispute was at an end, he was wrong. A couple of days after he had written to Churchill, Wedemeyer wrote a ''Personal'' letter to Mountbatten and Wheeler (with copies to General Marshall and Cordell Hull in Washington).[54] It opened all the old wounds. He professed ignorance of the Mountbatten-Chiang arrangement. Also Hurley, US Ambassador in Chungking, had had several conferences with Chiang about theater boundaries and areas of operational responsibility, during which Chiang had made available his copy of the formal minutes of the meetings in October 1943. Wedemeyer ''carefully reviewed'' those minutes and reported that he could find ''no reference concisely to

51.  La Feber, ''Roosevelt, Churchill, and Indochina'', p. 1294.
52.  Pierre Galante, *The General* (London: Leslie Frewen, 1969), p. 124.
53.  PRO, Prem. 3/178–3, General Ismay to Churchill, 20 Apr. 1945.
54.  PRO, Prem. 3/178–3, Wedemeyer to Mountbatten *et al.*, 16 Apr. 1945.

French Indo-China and Siam''. He stated that the basis for his discussions with Mountbatten and Washington was "the so-called gentleman's agreement based on information furnished by Mountbatten.''

Chiang Kai-shek reaffirmed the two stipulations in what Wedemeyer repeatedly called "the so-called gentleman's agreement'', namely that both theaters might launch attacks on Siam and French Indochina, with the political questions to be discussed at Chungking. But Wedemeyer insisted that Chiang had stipulated that these arrangements must be made in advance, agreeing only to that proviso, and had not agreed to operations being conducted by Mountbatten or anyone else from outside China Theater into China Theater's area (French Indochina and Siam) without his prior clearance; and Somervell's notes were said to confirm Wedemeyer's claim. Wired Wedemeyer, "I am now placed in a position of revealing the fact that Mountbatten has either unwittingly misinterpreted the Generalissimo's intention and desire as expressed in 1943 or that the Chinese are attempting to abrogate commitment made in so-called gentleman's agreement.'' He said that he was thus in a "delicate position" as he did not want to stir things up between Allies. This was strong stuff. Mountbatten, whom Wedemeyer had all but called a liar, was stung by this and hit back immediately. He wrote to London, saying that since Wedemeyer had sent this message to Marshall and Hull, implying that he (Mountbatten) had deliberately distorted the Generalissimo's wishes and that the question of clandestine activities in French Indochina and Siam were never the subject of a gentleman's agreement between the two, perhaps the Joint Staff mission in Washington would now place the true version before Marshall and Hull by forwarding a copy of his reply to Wedemeyer.[55]

But while the Chiefs fiddled, the French resistance flickered and then

55. PRO, Prem. 3/178–3, Mountbatten to Wedemeyer (repeated to London from Washington), 20 Apr. 1945. Mountbatten stated that he understood that the problem of clandestine activity in Indochina had now been settled at the highest level, but "As a matter of record, however, I should like to point out that I am not surprised that the formal minutes of the meetings held in October 1943 contain no references to French Indo-China or Thailand. It has never to my knowledge been suggested that they did; and this in fact is why the subsequent gentleman's agreement was ever necessary.''

   He then went over the history of his talk with Chiang, and Chiang's request that he be kept informed of SEAC's clandestine activities in his areas. Mountbatten replied that "I will of course do the same as you do!" But since he had "from that day to this received no information whatever" from anyone in China "concerning activities in FIC or Siam'', he had, "in view of the known lack of security in China'', refrained from telling Chiang about SEAC's activities.

died. The US Chiefs, in now agreeing to the move of the CLI, still found it necessary to add the stipulation that, although authorizing the move, they could not offer "any assurance as to the timing or scope of employment of the *Corps Léger d'Intervention* in Indochina". The fundamental reason for the quarrel between Wedemeyer and Mountbatten over Indochina had largely disappeared. In Mountbatten's case, there were not many Frenchmen left to organize, and their ragged and starving remnants had either escaped across "friendly" borders or been killed. The OSS in the north now had a pretty free hand with Ho Chi Minh and the Viet Minh. Mountbatten's sharp reply to Wedemeyer had its effect. After having shown the message to Marshall, Wilson wired the War Cabinet and Mountbatten: "I think you may dismiss from your mind any anxiety you may have had about this verbal agreement."

Even as Marshall was telling Wilson that the Indochina question was settled, Wedemeyer continued to press his objections, and an apologetic Foreign Office told Mountbatten that "this tiresome question seems to elude all our efforts to reach a satisfactory settlement." And on 6 May 1945 Mountbatten was forced to write to Wedemeyer and remind him that French Indochina had originally been in South East Asia Command, but that the United States, without asking anyone, had decided to give it to Chiang Kai-shek for face-saving reasons. But in his dealings with Mountbatten, Wedemeyer continued to miss the point that the whole purpose of the gentleman's agreement lay in keeping it unofficial so that the Generalissimo would not lose face with the Chinese people while letting Mountbatten operate. At the same time Mountbatten sent his deputy, General Wheeler, to see Wedemeyer, after which he wrote to Anthony Eden:

. . . I don't think you will be left in any doubt as to the true position, namely that while Wedemeyer was on my staff, he was supporting me enthusiastically over the question of our operating in French Indo-China. Now that he has gone as US Commanding General in the China Theatre, and Chief of Staff to the Generalissimo, he seems to think it is his duty to try and upset all the agreements which he has subscribed to before, in the mistaken notion that he is looking after American interests, in preventing the British or French from getting a foot into French Indo-China.

Mountbatten then addressed the emotive issue: "Fortunately for British interests, he has behaved in such an unfriendly manner to the poor French in Chungking, and been so unhelpful about their wretched troops who have been driven across the Chinese border," that the French would be even more well-disposed to the British. Now that

Burma was liberated there was a better chance of driving to French Indochina.

The acrimonious exchanges between the two senior commanders gradually took on a more personal note. As the debate continued into May, Mountbatten informed Wedemeyer of his intention to fly particular clandestine sorties into Indochina, giving details, target areas, and so on, while noting that he had so far failed to receive any reciprocal information from China Theater. Wedemeyer replied on 25 May, with a copy to the US Chiefs: "Your message 106 was referred to me and I regret and express surprise that you have adopted course of action revealed in your message. It has never occurred to me that you would presume that you had authority to operate in an area contiguous to your own without cognizance and full authority of the commander of that area." While complaining that Mountbatten was not giving him suf-ficently detailed information on clandestine sorties, Wedemeyer con-tinued, "You did show me diagrammatically your plans for Indochina but time was so limited when I was in Kandy, it was impossible to exa-mine or evaluate them in detail." Wedemeyer, who failed to see the need for reasonable air support for clandestine activities (as stated in a previous message to Mountbatten), said he found it "difficult to comprehend the urgent operational necessity of your operations in this theater." By this Wedemeyer was referring to a message from Mountbatten stating that he had given Wedemeyer the necessary information and could wait no longer for a reply as several parties in Indochina depended on the supplies, and the sorties were already being carried out.

After pointing out that Mountbatten was contradicting the General-issimo's wishes, Wedemeyer concluded: "Your action clearly indicates that we have been unable to agree in what I consider an important matter and therefore I have no alternative but to refer the entire matter to the US Chiefs of Staff." Mountbatten's attitude, backed by the British Chiefs, was now one of inviting Wedemeyer to refer his complaints to whomever he wished. Indochina was too important to permit pro-Western elements to be overwhelmed through American obstruction. On 30 May 1945 Wedemeyer asked the War Department to suspend lend-lease aid to British clandestine organizations in South East Asia Command pending resolution of his disagreement with Mountbatten. However, this was not deemed practicable since in the China and India/Burma Theaters (as noted in an ABC memo) the United States was in fact getting "considerable assistance from [the] British through reverse lend-lease." But Mountbatten did win a few. By COSSEA, 16

May 1945, he was informed that the US Chiefs had told General Sultan, Commander in India–Burma Theatre, to place all OSS activities in Thailand under the more experienced Force 136 group; thus in Thailand at least the mistakes of Indochina were averted.

As Allied operations in South East Asia were increasingly successful and the focus on Indochina sharpened, the dispute between the two theater commanders worsened. Marshall deplored the bickering, and added that Ambassador Hurley (in Chungking) was not helping by sending out "strongly worded telegrams on the subject with a strong anti-British bias". He also thought that it would be a pity if "good relations should be jeopardized over a dispute arising over matters of such low importance as clandestine operations in Indo-China, when placed in relation to the overall primary task of the attack on Japan." A few weeks later, in early June, Marshall (whose attention was not riveted on Indochina) was to write an exasperated note to Wilson: ". . . There must be an extraordinary importance to the clandestine operations being carried out by Mountbatten in Indo-China to justify the possible creation not only of ill will but of a feeling that there is a lack of good faith." Marshall — like Lieutenant-General Browning, Mountbatten's Chief of Staff — thought that if the press exploited this it would be to "our serious disadvantage all over the world".

Marshall's comments gave cause for hope, but a week later it was back to square one. Wilson now reported that Marshall had, for some unknown reason, reversed himself on Indochina and had surprised him by writing that the Combined Chiefs of Staff could not do much from this distance. Wrote Wilson, "I have a feeling that there is more in it than meets the eye and he probably does not wish to commit himself to writing." Another week later, on 16 June, Wilson had another talk with Marshall, during which Marshall said that he had heard no more about Wedemeyer, but was now worried about what had grown into an open feud between the two top American officials in China Theater: Hurley (who was backing Chiang Kai-shek "at all costs") and Wedemeyer (who felt that the Communists had some military value against Japan). Wilson also reported that Drew Pearson, an American newspaper columnist who seemed to have access to anything he wanted, had printed the texts of several secret messages between Hurley and Wedemeyer on that subject, plus a "graphic description of a 'near fist fight' at a Chinese cocktail party between Hurley and Wedemeyer's Chief of Staff".

The British were now approached by the French for facilities to train about a hundred French administrators. As the Foreign Office noted, "The idea is that these men when trained would be available for cooperation with whatever Allied force may eventually go into French Indo-China." It is likely that the French had a pretty good idea which Allied force would go into at least part of Indochina. The British, who had historically been less specific than the Americans in absolute guarantees to the French, agreed to the request, with the proviso that their use or commitment in Allied operations in French Indochina could not be promised. And in keeping with the increasing divergence of views the Foreign Office continued, "We see no reason to consult the US Government" but would keep them informed "without repeat without asking for observations". As Sterndale-Bennett told Dening, this was done so that the British could not be accused of working behind the Americans' backs. The French must also have been betting on British forces initially entering Indochina, for back in March 1945 Massigli, the Free French ambassador in London, had proposed to Sir Alexander Cadogan that a Civil Affairs agreement be worked out for French Indochina, similar to that agreed for metropolitan France. (The French had approached the United States but had been rebuffed.)

Things were now slowly coming to the boil. A decision on more than just clandestine activities in Indochina would soon have to be made. The US Chiefs of Staff, having bypassed the Japanese army, scented victory in the Pacific and were rapidly losing interest in South East Asia. Mountbatten could go ahead and mop up the Japanese there, while they concentrated all their considerable energies on the thrust to the heart of Japan. So the US Chiefs agreed to an earlier British suggestion that from the military viewpoint French Indochina should be divided at 15° N. latitude; however, Chiang should be consulted. The United States also proposed that she should turn over all her responsibilities in the South West Pacific Area to SEAC, to concentrate on the drive to Tokyo and free herself from the anticipated post-war turmoil in those areas; the turnover date was to be 15 August. Unfortunately this was done at the last moment, and the increased responsibilities put a terrific strain on SEAC. The US Chiefs were now interested in South East Asia only in so far as it affected overall Allied operations and Lend-Lease requirements.

On 18 July the British Chiefs responded and concurred, but called on the US Chiefs to support a move to transfer South Indochina to SEAC. On 22 July the British Chiefs, after examining the lines of communication in Indochina, altered their proposals slightly to make the 16th Parallel the line of demarcation between commands. As to the politics of it, the French were getting stronger and US policy now reflected an abrupt change of direction, as noted in this Foreign Office memo:

. . . I confirm that nothing was said by the American delegation during the trusteeship discussion to imply that French authority in Indochina was not acknowledged by the United States Government. . . . In particular at one stage the Australian delegation put forward a proposal the broad effect of which would have been that the General Assembly could in certain circumstances decide to put people's colonies under trusteeship whether the colonial power concerned liked it or not. The United States was as firm in its opposition to this as anybody.[56]

At the Potsdam Conference the Combined Chiefs of Staff highlighted the shifting emphasis from Europe to the Pacific. "The invasion of Japan and operations directly connected therewith are the supreme operations in the war against Japan . . . No other operations will be undertaken which hazard the success of, or delay, these main operations." This confirmed SEAC in its secondary role.

Mountbatten's primary task was to open the Straits of Malacca. He was also to complete the liberation of Malaya, keep the pressure on the Japanese on the Burma-Siam frontier, capture key areas of Siam, and establish bridgeheads in Java and/or Sumatra for subsequent clearance of those islands. But the task of the Commonwealth Force in the main invasion against Japan took priority in SEAC resources and staff effort. A key decision taken here by the Chiefs was to assign operations in southern Indochina to SEAC, "since these are more closely related to those of South East Asia Command than to those of China." The Chiefs recommended an approach to Chiang by the President and the Prime Minister, with a view to perhaps later adding all of Indochina to SEAC. Had that happened, the subsequent history of Indochina might have been different.

The Potsdam Conference covered a lot of ground: war reparations, Polish frontiers, administration of the·Ruhr, Yugoslavia, war crimes, the break-up of the great German industrial cartels. It also brushed Indochina. Acting on the advice of the Combined Chiefs, Truman and Churchill agreed to send a message to Chiang. The Foreign Office had long recommended the direct personal approach, and that it should be emphasized that the division of Indochina was for operational purposes, to secure China's flank. The US Chiefs preferred a governmental

56.   PRO, FO 371/46323, A, Poynton (Colonial Office) to Sterndale-Bennett, 23 July 1945.

approach, which the Foreign Office thought would lead to interminable delay — perhaps that was the reason. In fact the British Chiefs, in concurring with the FO, felt that "further reference to the US Chiefs of Staff, who have now returned to America, on method of approaching [the] Generalissimo would lead to undesirable delay." At any rate, on 1 August a message went to Chungking saying that the President and Prime Minister would send personal notes to Chiang, suggesting that southern French Indochina be assigned to SEAC. Midway through the conference the British electorate threw the Conservative Churchill out of office and ushered in more than six years of government by the Labour Party with Clement Attlee as Prime Minister. The personal messages to Chiang were similar. Prime Minister Attlee wrote and informed Chiang that on the advice of the Combined Chiefs of Staff he and the President thought that for operational purposes part of Indochina south of 16° N. latitude should come under SEAC.

At Kandy, SEAC officials were relieved at winning a battle (if not the war) over Indochina.[57] Yet Dening, whose brilliant political prophecies were nearly always fulfilled, was worried as he noted: "The division of French Indo-China by the parallel of 16 degrees north, if persisted in, is going to cause a lot of trouble. . . . The division is purely arbitrary and divides people of the same race, while raising new and unnecessary problems to divide French civil administration between here and Chungking."

The war had been over for three days and Dening's forebodings were well-founded. As we shall see, Mountbatten's urgent preparations to speed a force to Indochina received a setback when General MacArthur, in his capacity as Supreme Commander of the Allied Powers, directed subordinate theater commanders to delay landings in Japanese-held territories until his surrender ceremonies in Tokyo were completed. This directive had enormous consequences in Indochina, for a political vacuum was created which was happily filled by Communist leadership. That leadership is still there.

57. See Appendix to this Chapter, p. 117.

Ho Chi Minh, 1945.

*Above*: Group at Tan Son Nhut airfield, Saigon, with (centre) Vice-Admiral Lord Louis Mountbatten, (back to camera) Major-General Douglas Gracey, (centre right) General Sir Miles Dempsey, and (far right) Major-General Brian Kimmins.

*Left*: Esler Dening with a Thai envoy.

The arrival of General Leclerc at Tan Son Nhut airfield, 5 October 1945, with (centre left) Brigadier D.E. Taunton and (centre right) Major-General Gracey.

*Above*: Admiral d'Argenlieu (left) receiving a Japanese sword from Major-General Gracey, who had just received a scroll of honour as a *Citoyen d'Honneur* of Saigon.

*Below*: The 2/8 Punjab Regiment marching past the Cathedral in Saigon on their way to embark.

## APPENDIX

I interviewed General Wedemeyer after this book had been completed. Previously, in correspondence, I mentioned the serious results (from the Anglo-French view) of his running dispute with Mountbatten, and the General wrote back to say that the dispute was neither as serious nor as personal as I had described it. I then sent him excerpts from this chapter, adding a list of issues I thought important to discuss. The General appeared surprised by this material and he and his biographer had spent a week reviewing all papers connected with what I have called the ''Mountbatten-Wedemeyer dispute''. As our meeting began, he asked if I intended to change this chapter. I said I could not, since I was unable to alter archival material; much of it was from British sources, and it could be understood that it might not be entirely complimentary.

The General stated that he had been interviewed by about twenty historians in the last ten years, but none had brought this sort of material to his attention. He then gave me a copy of a moving letter he had written to the British Ministry of Defence on the death in 1979 of Mountbatten, at whose state funeral he represented the United States (reportedly at Mountbatten's request).

General Wedemeyer repeatedly returned to the archival material in which the dispute between him and Mountbatten appears to put him in a bad light. He considered the messages derogatory and humilitating. While he had an excellent memory, he appeared to be unaware of the existence of the problem and correspondence.

In Mountbatten's defense I pointed out that, regardless of the chaotic situation in Washington, most governments rightfully expect to keep their private affairs private, and when Mountbatten wrote his reports the fifty-year rule was in effect in the United Kingdom. This was not reduced to thirty years until the 1970s. Thus he fully and reasonably thought that none of the principals would be alive when the archives were opened — in this case it would have been 1995.

Wedemeyer later declined to permit publication of portions of the interview. He took exception to the archival material presented here, and intends to address these issues at some future date.

There are two conclusions I drew from my talks with General Wedemeyer. The first is that it seems clear that Chiang Kai-shek told Mountbatten one thing and Wedemeyer the opposite — telling each what he wanted to hear. There also seems no doubt that he did indeed agree privately to Mountbatten's operations in his area, then adamantly opposed them to Washington. So both men were under the impression that they were right and the other was obstructionist (Wedemeyer) or opportunistic (Mountbatten). It was further complicated by the fact that Wedemeyer thought that the decision to divide Indochina was taken by the Combined Chiefs of Staff (and thus with British concurrence) — whereas Mountbatten declared that as it was a unilateral decision by the Americans it was no concern of his.

The second concerns Wedemeyer's surprise at the depth of unhappiness in

SEAC at his actions while in China. This suggests one of two things: a notably inefficient communications system (including message distribution), or the interception and withholding of key message traffic somewhere in his headquarters. At this date the appropriate communications logs (of messages received and sent) would probably not be in existence.

I have already touched on the activities of the OSS, and the long-term results of their actions. If the French were to be opposed, why did not the OSS, with their considerable resources, build up the nationalist, as opposed to Communist, groups? It is not enough to say that the Communists were well organized; so is the Mafia. The OSS was playing at policy-making. Much of their conduct, such as the murder of Klotz, came as a shock to Wedemeyer (yet Mountbatten had written to him about this particular incident). More seriously, Wedemeyer's initial anger at Mountbatten's reports to London was restrained when it appeared that he never saw many of the reports which Mountbatten had sent to him pointing these things out. It does appear that there were also messages going from SEAC to London, concerning Wedemeyer, that Wedemeyer did not see.

Wedemeyer appears to have been a man who rigidly adhered to his instructions, and when he moved to China he looked out for Chiang's interests as strongly as he had earlier supported Mountbatten. The problem appears to have been Chiang Kai-shek. Why did Chiang do it? Was it to divide and conquer, from his relatively weak military position? Was he playing the Americans against the British and French — to get rid of the latter, knowing that the former would also leave after the war? There are still many questions to be answered. After all, the Chinese are noted for historically playing one set of barbarians off against another.

# 5

## FIRST ENCOUNTERS

By early August the staff at Headquarters South East Asia Command were anticipating the end of hostilities. Although the war was still going on, and operations planning continued, senior staff officers were beginning to be aware of the immense problems associated with post-war re-occupation duties. Final planning for "Zipper" (the assault on Malaya) was in progress, and the 20th Indian Division, an experienced fighting formation under a singular commander, was marked as one of the spearhead units in the invasion force. According to guidance given by SEAC to the Civil Affairs staff in planning their re-occupation tasks, the two essentials were that the Japanese should comply fully with British instructions, and secondly that law and order should be maintained "in regard to populations of occupied countries".[1] This was the bedrock which underlay all re-occupation policies.

The sudden cessation of hostilities caught the British unprepared to assume peacetime occupation duties. The situation was best described by General Slim, Commander of Allied Land Forces South East Asia (ALFSEA): "The area of South-East Asia Land Forces had suddenly expanded to include Malaya, Singapore, Siam, Indo-China, the Dutch East Indies, Hong Kong, Borneo, and the Andaman Islands . . . In two of them, Indo-China and the Dutch East Indies, nationalist movements armed from Japanese sources had already seized power in the vacuum left by the sudden surrender. . . ."[2] Heavy burdens were placed on his forces, commitments which were expanding almost beyond capability while his troops were being released and demobilized by the new Labour Government in response to political pressures at home.

On 13 August the British Chiefs of Staff laid down the priorities for re-occupation after Singapore: Indochina, Siam, Java and Sumatra. Indochina was placed first on the list because Saigon contained the headquarters of the Japanese Army in that part of the world.

Earlier, while these discussions were taking place, the Duke of

---

1. Great Britain, Public Record Office, WO 203/4422, SACSEA to Political Intelligence Department and Far Eastern Bureau, Foreign Office, 15 Aug. 1945.
2. Field-Marshal Sir William Slim, *Defeat into Victory* (London: Cassell, 1956), pp. 529, 530.

Windsor and a British diplomat called on President Truman, who told them that he had just received a report from the Swiss Chargé d'Affaires in Washington; a telegram just received by the Japanese Legation in Berne from Tokyo "did not contain the message awaited by the whole world." Truman remarked sadly to his visitors that he now had no choice but to order the dropping of an atomic bomb on Tokyo. As it turned out, Nagasaki and not Tokyo was bombed, and the Japanese capitulated. But when they agreed to lay down their arms on 15 August, the position was one of an armistice or ceasefire, not a formal surrender.

In mid-August the British and French Governments agreed by memorandum on the broad objectives of Allied forces in Indochina. These were the disarming of Japanese forces, the liberation of French authorities, and the maintenance of public order. They further agreed that the French would be responsible for the administration of Indochina, and that this French administration would possess the powers of a state of siege.[3] The agreements signed later (in September and October) were in the form of five memoranda, and covered such areas as administrative control and currency. The big question was whether speed of occupation or a show of force was more important in the establishment of an Allied presence in Japanese-held territory. And what were to be the priorities of occupation? More specifically, the SEAC Headquarters Joint Planning Staff stated that any occupying force would have a number of tasks besides accepting a Japanese surrender. British forces would be faced with the immediate re-occupation of as many key points as possible, and then would have to dispose of Japanese forces, speedily evacuate Allied prisoners-of-war and internees, preserve law and order, protect vital installations (and food and arms supplies), prevent sabotage and looting, provide for the relief of the civil populations, and take emergency steps to rehabilitate key facilities until these responsibilities could be taken over by civil authorities. But before all this could be done it would be necessary to hold a number of meetings with Japanese envoys to agree on principles and clear up various key matters. There would be no negotiations regarding terms, as the Japanese surrender was unconditional.

The SACSEA team nominated by Mountbatten to meet the Japanese at Rangoon was headed by his Chief of Staff, Lieutenant-General Browning, who was to meet his counterpart, Lieutenant-General Tatazo Numata,[4] of Field Marshal Count Terauchi's staff. But before the

---

3.  PRO, FO 371/46307, 16 Aug. 1945.
4.  Personal interview with Brigadier M. S. K. Maunsell, Chief of Staff, Headquarters

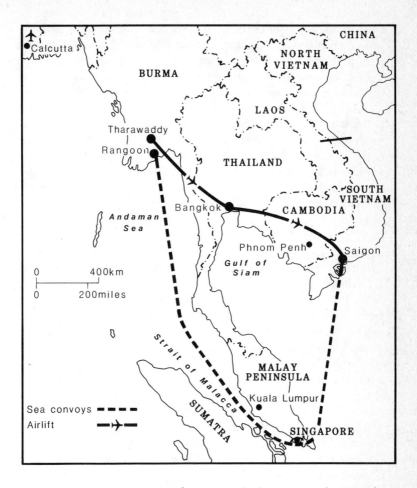

Movement of British/Indian forces to Indochina, September–October 1945.

two sides met a number of things happened, one of which may have had profound effects on the course of events to come. This was MacArthur's general order to his subordinate commanders to hold all re-occupation plans in abeyance until after the Japanese surrender (see below).

Talks on the functions of the nascent Saigon Control Commission centered on controlling the headquarters of the Japanese Expeditionary Forces in the Southern Region (also known as Japanese Southern Army) as a first priority. It was hoped that the Control Commission would accompany General Numata back to Saigon in late August, and the Commission was placed on twenty-four hours' notice to move from 0900 hours on 18 August. Mountbatten had earlier been confidentially told by the Prime Minister at Potsdam about the atomic bomb, and was thus anticipating an early Japanese capitulation. His staff were trying desperately to anticipate future movements, but hastily drawn contingency plans were being changed almost as fast as they were conceived. Underlying the changes of plan was the question of Japanese intentions, which could not be assessed until the Browning-Numata talks had taken place. But planning could not wait until the last moment.

The Joint Planning Staff (JPS) and Dening were agreed that a strong escort was required for the Control Commission, but French Indochina was at that time "low on the order of priority", and in view of the strength of Japanese forces there a fairly large initial occupying force would be needed to ensure the Commission's safety. Therefore, "We must either considerably delay the mission so that it has some force to protect it or we must accept that the Commission is sent in earlier with about two companies as escort and that the Japanese can be trusted."[5] The latter was done, although the initial force was incapable of doing more than protect the mission. It certainly could not control the Japanese headquarters or enforce correct behavior by the Japanese. In fact the Japanese were not really brought under control for several weeks, until General Gracey finally had his whole division in Saigon.

While all this was going on, and occupation forces were being assembled and in the process of being dispatched to a number of widely dispersed areas, a message was received from General MacArthur which caused an uproar at Kandy. On 19 August Major-General Penney

---

SACSEA Control Commission No. 1 (Saigon Control Commission), 20 Apr. 1977.

5. Papers of General Sir Douglas D. Gracey; also PRO, WO 172/1778, JPS Paper 185, 22 Aug. 1945; WO 203/4566.

(Director of Intelligence, Headquarters SEAC), visiting MacArthur's headquarters in Manila, cabled Browning that MacArthur had strongly requested that all subordinate commanders (including Mountbatten) delay any operations to or landings on Japanese territory until he had accepted the formal Japanese surrender in Tokyo on 28 August.[6] MacArthur's reasons were, first, that the Japanese had so far only declared a willingness to accept the Potsdam terms, and had actually signed nothing — they appeared to be stalling and the only orders to date from Tokyo to the field concerned a cessation of hostilities — and secondly, any unilateral action by theater commanders would "prejudice the whole peace settlement". Thirdly, Field-Marshal Terauchi might not obey any orders from Mountbatten, and the developing situation could have incalculable consequences. MacArthur's blunt final words to Penney were "Tell Lord Louis to keep his pants on or he will get us all into trouble." Mountbatten told his representative in Manila, Lieutenant-General Gairdner, and Penney to tell MacArthur that Wedemeyer and the Soviet Marshal Malinovsky were contravening his orders, and added, "Tell him that I will keep my pants on if he will take Hirohito's off." Gairdner informed Mountbatten that MacArthur was adamant, and that precipitate action would jeopardize good relations between the Commonwealth and the United States. In a reply which he kept from MacArthur's view, Gairdner telegraphed, "As a personal view I would urge utmost caution as air is electric."[7]

At his 17th (Miscellaneous) Staff Meeting on 20 August 1945, Mountbatten read out the telegram from MacArthur: all re-occupation plans were suspended until 28 August or until the surrender in Tokyo. As it turned out, a typhoon delayed the actual signing in Tokyo Bay, and the formal surrender was not effected until 2 September. Mountbatten told his staff that "he was at a loss to understand why General MacArthur should wish to impose such a dangerous delay." He personally preferred to see the Japanese experience defeat in the "unmistakable form of successful invasion of their homeland". The Russians, he noted, had ignored all this formality and had kept on fighting to achieve their goals. He shared MacArthur's distrust of the Japanese, but did not support his reasons. For Mountbatten, the longer the Japanese were given to

---

6. PRO, Cab 88/39, Mountbatten to British Chiefs of Staff, 21 Aug. 1945. However, an OSS plane landed in Hanoi on 22 Aug. carrying 16 Americans and 5 Frenchmen, including Sainteny.
7. PRO, WO 172/1778, Gairdner to Mountbatten, 21 Aug. 1945.

recover, the harder they would be to control and the more evasive they would become. He particularly drew attention to the fact that only he seemed to be obeying MacArthur, as Wedemeyer and Marshal Malinovski were not acting in accordance with his request. As some of Mountbatten's re-occupation forces had put to sea six days before the receipt of MacArthur's telegram, Admiral Power expected a 30–40 percent casualty rate in small ships due to mechanical breakdown and the adverse winds brought by the monsoons. The forces in the small ships would also run out of food and water, and even the larger ships could not hold at sea for long.

The Control Commission thus got off to a late start. The original plan called for transporting the Commission and one infantry battalion to Indochina by sea on 27 August, to arrive in Saigon on 2 September. As it happened, 2 September was the date of massive rioting inspired by the Viet Minh, but the British, delayed by MacArthur's ruling, were not in Saigon to prevent or control it. Thus, had it not been for MacArthur, British/Indian troops would have been in Saigon earlier, before the Viet Minh could have consolidated what power it had. And had not the Americans been fiercely opposing the French in their struggle to return to Indochina, the same could be said for the occupation of Hanoi.

A parallel concern was the fatal effect of the delay for the Allied prisoners-of-war. Many of the dying POWs were being moved by the Japanese at that very moment. Terauchi had not responded to broadcasts from SEAC, and MacArthur declined to assist in contacting Terauchi through facilities in Tokyo. Mountbatten felt that he could delay his operations no later than 28 August, or his dispersed re-occupation forces would have to return to their bases. He requested support for his plans from the British Chiefs of Staff, who initially agreed but were overruled by their political masters and on 22 August were obliged to direct Mountbatten to conform completely to MacArthur's wishes.

The effect of MacArthur's edict was outlined by the Commander of Allied Land Forces South East Asia. Describing the operations being readied, or already being executed — namely to move the 7th Indian Division to Siam, 20 Division to Indochina, 5 Division to Singapore, 3 Commando Brigade to Hong Kong, and 26 Division to Sumatra and Java — General Slim wrote:

All these operations were about to begin, indeed the first ships of the Malayan force were already at sea and all headquarters buzzing with activity, when, on 19th August, a very considerable spanner was thrown into their busy works . . . He [General MacArthur] decreed that the formal surrender in South-East Asia could take place only after it had been ceremonially completed in his own theatre. This, though inconvenient, might not have mattered so much had he not ordered, also, that no landings in or re-entry to Japanese-held territory would be made until he had personally received the formal surrender. . . .[8]

Dismayed senior commanders in SEAC, many of whom saw something more personal in MacArthur's edict than the officially listed reasons, had weighed the consequences of his orders to remain in place. After satisfying themselves that the Japanese would obey the Imperial order to cease hostilities, which was confirmed at these Rangoon negotiations, they decided, on humanitarian grounds, not to be confined to obeying the letter of MacArthur's edict. Slim led the resistance:

But the delay could have had most serious consequences for our prisoners in Japanese hands. Admiral Mountbatten . . . decided, in spite of the ban on landing, to fly in help to the prisoners. Our men and those of our Allies were daily dying in their foul camps; thousands were at the limit of weakness and exhaustion. Had he delayed for even a few days in sending supplies and relief personnel, many more would have died pathetically at the moment of rescue.[9]

And finally, in a statement which remained the touchstone of his policy towards the Japanese: "There can be no excuse for a nation which as a matter of policy treats its prisoners of war in this way, and no honour for any army, however brave, which willingly makes itself the instrument of such inhumanity to the helpless." The records of 232 Group (RAF) state that as a result of the sudden delay in operations to occupied territory, POWs were left waiting on the airfield for up to thirty-six hours with only a cup of tea to sustain them.[10]

As soon as the Japanese delegates returned to Saigon, Operations "Birdcage" (leaflet dropping) and "Mastiff" (supplies and medical personnel) were put into effect. By MacArthur's estimate there were still up to 7,000,000 Japanese under arms. The Japanese armies in the field were still generally undefeated and they were very conscious of that fact. It was emphasized at SEAC that Japan's position was the reverse of Germany's. For Japan, capitulation was at the center first; for Germany, it had been in the field first, when her forces were defeated, and surrender at the center came later. The Japanese were still capable of stiff fighting, and surrendered only when ordered to do so by the Emperor. In the Southern Regions, Luzon fell completely only after receipt of the

8.  Slim, *Defeat Into Victory.* pp. 530–1.
9.  *Ibid.*, pp. 531–2.
10.  PRO, Air 25/1022, Operational Record of 232 Group (Transport).

Imperial order to cease hostilities, and Terauchi would not begin negotiations until the arrival (on 19 August) of Prince Kanin, a member of the
Imperial family, bearing the Emperor's decree.

In a reply to Browning, Mountbatten stated that although ALFSEA
would provide most of the personnel for Saigon, the Control Commission "would be a HQ SACSEA responsibility". The initial SEAC post-
war garrison commitments were formidable, and it was under these pressures that Mountbatten resisted Leclerc's pleas to include the whole of
French Indochina within SEAC's responsibilities. As Mountbatten
reported, he was not keen on military grounds to take responsibility for
all of Indochina; this was due to his shortage of resources.[11] Leclerc
pursued this point, and Esler Dening, at Mountbatten's request, called
on Leclerc on 22 August to state the Foreign Office and Allied position.
The General, reported Dening, "spoke with considerable vigour" on
the question of boundaries in Indochina, and preferred that the Japanese
should stay on until Mountbatten (with French forces) could take over,
rather than let the Chinese in. Even if the boundary question remained
unsettled, there would be no problems if the Chinese stayed out of Indochina. Dening replied that the problems were with Chiang and
Wedemeyer. But both were in agreement about the overall importance
of Indochina which, in the view of the British Chiefs of Staff, was the
"key to the defense of South-East Asia".[12]

As always, the big question which pervaded all planning discussions
was the attitude of the Japanese. Field-Marshal Terauchi, having now
received a royal decree, was able to negotiate, but there remained the attitudes of fanatical subordinates.

At last the day arrived for the long-awaited meeting with the Japanese.[13] The British sent a twenty-man delegation to Rangoon. The main
party left Kandy on 25 August in two C-47s. The second aircraft con-

11.  PRO, WO 230/5608, draft SEACOS, 30 Aug. 1945.
12.  PRO, Cab 96/9, Far Eastern Committee, "Policy Towards Siam (Annex II)", 14
     July 1945.
13.  As Brigadier Maunsell, who participated in the negotiations as General Slim's
     representative, said: "British Intelligence had an idea that Japanese headquarters
     didn't really know where its units were . . . . Japanese Intelligence and Kempei Tei
     divulged nothing. The Rangoon meeting was held to learn if it was possible to call
     a ceasefire which would be effective, and would [Japanese] units respond to it. The
     first meeting between the Japanese and Allies in SEAC was to discuss the ceasefire
     and to tell the Japanese what information the Allies must have *now* — where forces
     were, etc., and where the POW camps were." (Personal interview, 20 Apr. 1977.)

tained Esler Dening, Maunsell and Brigadier Gibbons of the Civil Affairs branch. The Japanese delegation consisted of three officers and two interpreters. Their most junior officer, Lieutenant-Colonel Tomura, was later described by Maunsell as a capable and intelligent man "around whom everything seemed to revolve." The other two were Numata and the Assistant Chief of Staff, Rear-Admiral Chudo. At the start of the meeting, a "letter of attorney" was handed to Browning by Numata, who identified himself as Chief of Staff of the Japanese Army in the Southern Regions, appointed by Field-Marshal Terauchi to represent him at the preliminary negotiations. He said that he wished to make his salutations to the representative of the Supreme Allied Commander South East Asia on the occasion of the winning of the war by the Allied forces, and to express his admiration of the manner in which they had conducted it. He also expressed regret that the arrival of the Japanese delegation had been delayed by late receipt of orders from General Headquarters in Tokyo. He had brought with him the data required by the Allies. He felt honored to be able to attend the meeting with Lieutenant-General Browning and the other gentlemen, and expressed gratitude on behalf of the Japanese for the privilege and honor of being permitted to wear swords.

Browning wanted assurance that the Japanese surrender would be smooth and quick, as between two Imperial forces, and in accordance with the traditions and usages of war. Numata responded that Terauchi was confident the surrender would be accomplished in accordance with the august command of His Majesty the Emperor. He added that the "suspension of arms" was a complete surprise to most units of the Japanese forces, especially at the far posts, and the order to lay down their arms was received with a disappointment and chagrin which could readily be imagined. It was not so much winning or losing as going against the ancient traditions of *Bushido*. Terauchi had had a difficult time getting his subordinate commanders to agree to the ceasefire, but he was sure that it would be done.

Browning asked if Numata knew of the surrender being scheduled for signing in Tokyo on 2 September; he understood that an Imperial envoy had brought some information to Field-Marshal Terauchi. Numata replied that when Prince Kanin arrived in Saigon on 19 August, nothing definite had been decided, and he still had no official confirmation of the exact date. Browning asked Numata when the agreement signed at Rangoon would become effective, and Numata replied that these agreements were separate from the general armistice to be signed in Tokyo and would become effective from the date of signature. Numata's brief concerned only matters pertaining to Terauchi's area of command.

Browning then listed four Allied requirements which had to be met immediately. These were for day and night Allied reconnaissance flights over Japanese territory, the sending of supplies and medical staff to POW camps, free movement of Allied ships in Japanese waters, and mine-sweeping in Japanese-controlled waters — all these conditions to be effective from 28 August. Numata agreed to these requests. Browning asked how many days it would take for news of the surrender at Rangoon to reach all Japanese forces. Numata replied that most of the command could be reached in less than a week, emphasizing that Terauchi's area contained widely scattered forces. The longest delays would be in reaching forces in New Guinea, parts of Borneo, the mountain districts in the Philippines and parts of Burma west of the Sittang River — places with very limited communications. "We want your sympathy," said Numata, since Terauchi wanted to carry out these orders as soon as possible. Browning then said that there were certain other points to be raised, in addition to the four requirements already stated. These concerned the Control Commission's move to Saigon and the moving out of certain areas by the Japanese, and he ended the first day's negotiations by saying that the two staffs would meet later and work out the details. The Japanese were then handed a number of documents and a list of further information required.

The next day, 27 August, the two sides met again. The Japanese had closely studied the demands presented the day before, and Browning opened the session by asking Numata if he had understood them. Numata replied that Terauchi had given him a note for Mountbatten and asked permission to read it aloud, as it had a bearing on the present talks. In it Terauchi reiterated his intention to cooperate, but expressed concern at the present declining state of law and order in parts of his command. He also wanted advance notice of the arrival of occupation forces. Numata explained that this was necessary because the Japanese had to move out of their present lodgings and build tents and bamboo and leaf huts in the countryside in order to make room for Allied forces. Terauchi then made a strong appeal to be able to disarm the Japanese forces himself through the existing Japanese command chain, otherwise problems might arise. He also suggested that certain units of the Japanese forces should retain their arms, "not exceeding machine-guns", in order to maintain discipline among themselves and law and order among the civil population. Terauchi went on to request that officers, warrant officers and NCOs be permitted to wear swords or bayonets. Other questions touched on places of assembly and quartering of troops, communications equipment, transport, clothing and medical supplies for outlying areas, and leaving the currency systems unchanged for the sake of stability. The British received the impression from this that Terauchi's basic idea was that the Japanese should not be treated as prisoners-of-war. Numata again mentioned the importance of deferring to the special spirit and traditions of the Japanese forces so as to ensure a successful conclusion to the negotiations. He said that he had in fact just left a sick bed, bringing a doctor with him, in order to attend the meetings. If these requests were not granted, his role would be reduced to one of a messenger and he would be ashamed to return to Saigon.

Browning did not respond directly, but asked if the Japanese had further questions. Rear-Admiral Chudo then pointed out that things were not so simple. Field-Marshal Terauchi had been given control of all Nippon forces in February 1945, but since naval operations had ceased, responsibility for the Navy now rested upon the Commander of Naval Forces in Southern Waters. Numata added that as there were no important questions, he would like to add some views of his own. He suggested that some of the discussions could conform to Terauchi's note, and a few other points could be amended. He also proposed to express his views on each article of the final document. In the first part of the main body, perhaps the words "in accordance with the direction of General Headquarters, Tokyo" could be inserted at an appropriate place. Browning interrupted to say that Numata did not seem to understand that he had been asked if he wished to raise questions for clarification, not to criticize the orders. Numata then said that he had no questions and perfectly understood the orders. The agreement was signed on 28 August 1945.

Dening's report on the Rangoon conference reflected his continuing suspicions of the Japanese. The terms of the formal surrender ceremony at Singapore had been worked out, but he was convinced that the general Japanese attitude remained unchanged. Except in Burma, their armies had not been defeated and their outlook was thus not that of a defeated nation. There was, he said, a lot of talk about *Bushido*, and regardless of the surrender terms they would try to preserve its "spurious legend" The high command would obey the Emperor, but he was apprehensive of the lower echelons. The Japanese envoys had at first tried to avoid putting their official seals to the documents, "but this had been speedily rectified." To Dening it was of overriding importance that Field-Marshal Terauchi's authority be supported, and that he be held "personally

responsible'' in the area of his command. It was in the light of this political guidance that General Gracey pinned responsibility for the disturbances in Saigon a few weeks later on Terauchi. Mountbatten's assessment of the negotiations corresponded with Dening's; the SAC wired
London that the Japanese attitude in this theater was that the game had
been drawn, since they had not been defeated militarily or as a nation.
Numata said that ''it did not matter so much to the Japanese whether
they lost or won a war; far more important to them was the preservation
of the spirit of *Bushido*, or in other words the spirit of militarism.'' Actually Mountbatten was soon to have cause to appreciate the lingering
Japanese spirit of *Bushido*, for without active Japanese assistance in Indochina and Indonesia the British casualty rates would have been such as to
cause a political uproar.

   One unpleasant surprise lay in store: the last-minute US withdrawal
from the Control Commission. A crucial part of the Commission was its
signals unit, which would handle all message traffic, ciphers, and so on.
Since South East Asia Command was an Allied command, Mountbatten
had designated nine members of a US Signals Company, which was part
of the SEAC staff, to accompany the Control Commission to Saigon.
Although it would be two weeks before the Mission actually arrived
there, the American withdrawal came when it was on daily alert to fly
out at a moment's notice. At SAC's staff meeting on 28 August 1945,
Brigadier-General Timberman, commanding US forces in South East
Asia, abruptly announced that owing to the rapid demobilization program and ''certain administrative difficulties'' it was preferable that US
signals personnel should not accompany the British to Saigon. Mountbatten, knowing his politics, agreed, although it had earlier been made
clear to Timberman that there was a desperate shortage of signals units,
and the tiny American unit was scheduled to be in Saigon for only six
weeks before being replaced by ALFSEA resources. As it was, there were
absolutely no replacements for these nine Americans and their equipment, and no fully-staffed signals office was available to General Gracey
for several weeks.

   That this episode left a bad taste all around was evident in Mountbatten's sharp reply during a staff meeting on 8 September to another ill-
considered objection by Timberman, this time to French involvement in
the occupation of Saigon. Timberman thought that the reoccupation of
Indochina had ''nothing to do with the French''. Mountbatten retorted
that when he had been in Berlin a few weeks before, General Marshall
had asked him how soon he could receive French forces for employment

in Indochina, and how he proposed to employ them. Therefore "it was not a question of the French being nothing to do with Indochina." It was apparent at SEAC that the United States was avoiding the difficult problems and leaving the hard-pressed British to cope with the violent political explosions in Indochina, Java, Sumatra, Burma and Malaya. With far greater resources, the United States restricted her responsibilities to garrison duties in Japan, Okinawa and the Philippines, none of them European colonial territories.

The Control Commission had by now to share equal billing with Headquarters Allied Land Forces French Indo-China (to be referred to as ALFFIC). The same senior officer headed both organizations. Both commands were sailing into uncharted waters. The Civil Affairs branch at SEAC headquarters was barely big enough to guide British military administrations in the reconquered British possessions, but was completely overstretched when the South West Pacific Area (SWPA), including Indochina and Indonesia (the worst problems), was added to SEAC's area of responsibility. The same applied to the Foreign Office representation on the Political Affairs Staff. As late as 17 August Dening reiterated his unease over the arbitrary division of Indochina: "The division of French Indo-China by the parallel of 16 degrees north, if persisted in, is going to cause a lot of trouble." It was Dening's urgent prompting of the Foreign Office, in early August, which speeded the general agreement on Civil Affairs between Paris and London. The United States had refused to talk to the French about Civil Affairs agreements in any part of Indochina.

As early as 2 August the senior SEAC Civil Affairs officer, Brigadier Gibbons, had written that his Civil Affairs Division was "now becoming inadequate for the efficient processing of the Civil Affairs policy matters which have to be submitted to the Supreme Allied Commander". Worse, there was no Civil Affairs Division at ALFSEA headquarters, from which the occupational ground forces were going to be drawn, forces which would need up-to-the-minute guidance in their duties from Civil Affairs experts. For it would not be the Control Commission personnel who would have to take to the streets to meet the rioters, snipers and guerrillas, or protect local populations, or escort food convoys, rescue hostages and mount sweeps and patrols and come into direct contact with the civil populations — it would be the land forces, which had no Civil Affairs personnel whatsoever. The Civil Affairs branches in Europe (Italy, Germany etc.) were fully staffed, but in South East Asia, where the problems were truly dangerous and civil war was imminent, the Civil Affairs branch was understrength.

One fundamental problem which affected all of SEAC's plans was the acute shortage of transport. As Slim later noted, his air transport capability was halved as soon as the ceasefire was announced, when the United States immediately prohibited further use of all Lend-Lease equipment (unless bought for cash, which was unavailable to SEAC). US policy continued to the very end to cause annoyance — as when, on the Japanese laying down their arms, the USAAF immediately cancelled spare parts for eight types of aircraft including 200 C-47s of the types used by ACSEA; altogether 1,600 American aircraft and gliders would soon be unserviceable. Under the new rules an aircraft had to be grounded before a spare part could be requested, even on a cash and carry basis.

The Japanese were to remain an enigma until Allied forces actually met them face to face. Some of the Japanese forces were in a truly ghastly state. The Burma Area Army had received no reinforcements whatsoever since December 1944, and units simply disappeared from the rolls as they were destroyed. The Japanese 18th Army in New Guinea had had no supplies since April 1944. Some units were reduced to cannibalism, and records indicate that US airmen were killed and eaten in New Guinea by starving Japanese soldiers. At the ceasefire the Japanese commander appealed for food to enable his troops, riddled with starvation, beri-beri and malaria, to march to the concentration areas. Indochina was in better condition, at least in the south. The north suffered from famine because the transportation system, devastated by Allied bombings, was unable to move surplus rice from south to north. However, the condition of prisoners-of-war in Indochina was far better than in other areas, like Malaya and Siam, largely due to French people smuggling medicines, food and other supplies into the camps.

The Japanese High Command was hampered by an extremely crude and ineffective communications system, and it seems clear that Japanese actions regarding nationalist movements in different countries were frequently the result of independent decisions by individual commanders. At this time, Mountbatten cabled Terauchi, "I would remind you that the preservation of property intact and the maintenance of law and order are responsibilities agreed to by your plenipotentiary at Rangoon." The Field-Marshal was ordered to take disciplinary action against Japanese commanders who violated these strictures. The first warnings to him on the maintenance of public order thus came from the Supreme Allied Commander, and not from the head of the Control Commission.

Mountbatten ordered Terauchi to return Numata to Saigon, this time with powers to give orders to Japanese forces throughout South East Asia. On 31 August Gracey told Mountbatten that Terauchi had cabled a suggestion that the Control Commission remain in Rangoon for the time being and maintain contact with Saigon through Numata in Rangoon. Gracey agreed with this suggestion. Numata was to return to Rangoon on 4 September to stay there and return to Saigon with the Control Commission. SACSEA advised ALFSEA and 12th Army that "The Control Commission will thus begin to fulfil its functions, as enumerated in the Directive issued to General Gracey from this Headquarters on 29th August, at Rangoon instead of Saigon and will act at Rangoon as the intermediary for the passing of SEAC's orders direct to such Japanese commanders as he may wish to instruct."

Mountbatten was worried about reports that General Itagaki in Singapore had vowed to fight on rather than surrender, but on 1 September Terauchi denied this, saying that this sort of disobedience to the Supreme Commander could never happen in the Japanese Army. Terauchi also told Mountbatten that he had difficulty in walking and standing and would not be able to attend the grand surrender ceremony in Singapore. He also delayed sending Numata back to Rangoon because he would not authorize him to issue orders in the name of the Supreme Commander.

The old British-American dispute over Indochina persisted to the end. On 31 August Mountbatten, who had kept his small clandestine parties intact in the north, received a message from Headquarters BRITCHIN (British Forces China), stating that there was no relaxation of the anti-British/French attitude by US China Theater headquarters. BRITCHIN reported that the US attitude was that, since the war was over, there was no longer any need for SACSEA to support the French resistance movement, and if the French were in need they should contact the Chinese.

On 31 August Dening reported on the Rangoon conference to Sterndale-Bennett at the Foreign Office. The Japanese had been dignified, but obviously under strong emotional stress. Dening reiterated his fears: "They do not consider that they have been defeated and say so quite openly" — namely that they had laid down their arms on the Emperor's orders. Wrote Dening, "We are thus in a position that, in a few days time, we shall be setting out to disarm an undefeated army . . . There was every evidence at Rangoon that they have not changed in one respect, namely, their capacity for evasion." With Gracey's mission in mind, Dening continued, "As we are everywhere going in inferior strength in the first place, the situation is still fraught with danger, . . . If, therefore, [Terauchi's] authority is undermined too early, there is no knowing what will happen."

On 2 September MacArthur completed the long-awaited ceremony in Tokyo Bay, and SEAC intercepted a radio report from an eye-witness describing conditions in Hanoi, where 5,000 French officers and civilians were imprisoned in the citadel, and there had been scattered attacks on the defenseless French population. There was a paradox in Hanoi in that the bodies of people who had died of starvation were piled on the Doumer Bridge while the fine shops were stocked with silks and fine clothes and the Hotel Metropole was serving six-course meals. The Japanese were not suffering.

On 4 September a paper titled "Situation in Indo-China, as on 1st September 1945" was published. It was pertinent to SEAC Headquarters since General Gracey and the Control Commission were only nine days away from Saigon. The general summary took note of Japanese intrigue with the revolutionary groups, and stated:

The Southern Regions, which are of the most immediate interest to SEAC, are unfortunately those on which we possess the least information . . . On the 27th August a revolutionary government (Communists and Viet Minh, jointly) proclaimed the Republic of Southern Viet Nam. Since then, events have taken a grave turn and the revolutionaries have proclaimed a state of siege. Great confusion reigns at Saigon. The Communists have seized crossroads and strategic points and have cut off electricity. Newspapers have been suspended . . .

The report went on to say that the Viet Minh had killed a member of an SA team dropped in on 31 August, and concluded: "Only an armed force can restore order . . . The Japanese game in French Indochina leaps to the eyes."

Gracey did have some knowledge of conditions in Saigon. A US Dakota doing OSS work had landed at Tan Son Nhut to extricate a few American prisoners-of-war in Saigon; it departed on 3 September. An OSS sergeant engaged on RAPWI (Repatriation of Allied Prisoners-of-War and Internees) passed on the information that the airfield was in good condition, the Japanese "nauseatingly helpful", and there were about fifty Japanese aircraft on the field (transports, fighters and fighter-bombers). The Continental Palace Hotel was intact and in good condition but crowded with French refugees. Public services appeared to be in order, and the "City [was] beflagged and bill-posted by Annamese welcoming the Mission". The Japanese appeared to be in control, although there were about 1,000 "badly armed" Annamese in the streets (contrary to British orders to the Japanese to disarm the revolutionaries). The POWs were well organized and in good condition. The report continued, "PW of all nationalities cannot speak too highly of French assistance often at great risk. Sympathies are entirely with [the] French and many [POWs] stated they wished to remain to help them."

It has been mentioned earlier that by now the Control Commission was officially established and working in Rangoon, and General Gracey was already acting as the Supreme Allied Commander's agent in communicating with Japanese supreme headquarters in Saigon. President Truman had also earlier told Prime Minister Attlee that the Japanese were being held responsible for the maintenance of public order in territories occupied by their forces. It was in this context that Gracey sent a sharply worded telegram to Terauchi when news of French deaths in Saigon reached Rangoon. Gracey said he had heard that a French officer had been killed in Saigon and another severely wounded by the Annamites, who were also molesting other Europeans. He reminded Terauchi that under the local Rangoon agreements and in accordance with the Supreme Allied Commander's orders he was personally responsible for the maintenance of law and order in French Indochina and the protection of Allied nationals. Terauchi was then told to tighten discipline in his forces.[14] Thus, while still in Rangoon, Gracey began to stamp his authority on the Japanese headquarters. Terauchi was also ordered to release Cédile and other Free French officials and to arrest the Japanese officers involved in what were regarded as hostile acts against Allied representatives. The Japanese did not heed Gracey's strictures to the letter, and in Cédile's case merely removed their guards to make way for ones provided by the Viet Minh.[15]

On 5 September, Mountbatten addressed Terauchi on the worsening situation in Indonesia. On 19 August, four days after Japan's announced surrender, the Field-Marshal had (apparently unilaterally) declared the populous island of Java to be independent, with Sukarno as President. Mountbatten now ordered him to retract his declaration, but it was too late. Terauchi at first denied responsibility, but on 7 September he admitted his part in this matter, but said it was done "according to the orders I have received from the Imperial Headquarters", and he had discontinued further efforts after the Japanese peace overtures.

At the SAC's 279th Staff Meeting on 5 September, Gracey's message

14. PRO, WO 203/5608/5644, Gracey to Terauchi, 4 Sept. 1945.
15. Jean Cédile, former Commissioner and Governor of Cochinchina; personal interview, 26 Oct. 1977.

to Terauchi was discussed. General Slim backed Gracey's firm line by reporting that "Field-Marshal Terauchi had been given clear instructions that he was to maintain law and order." On 5 September, also, the first medical team was parachuted into Saigon under Operation "Mastiff", to work through senior camp officers. Supplies had been dropped into the camps since the Japanese had agreed to it on 26 August, the date of Numata's arrival in Hong Kong. On 6 September the first uniformed British troops arrived at Tan Son Nhut airfield, a small detachment (less than a platoon) of the 1st Battalion, 19th Hyderabad Regiment of India (1/19 Hybad). They were a token escort for the 20th Indian Division advance party, which consisted of an Intelligence team, Engineers, an RAF detachment and medical officers. This advance echelon brought radio sets with which to send back first-hand reports of local conditions to General Gracey in Rangoon. Accompanying them were the RAPWI staff — and Royal Navy Surgeon-Captain Birt, specifically sent by Mountbatten to authenticate Terauchi's claimed infirmities.

As the first heavily-laden Dakotas climbed slowly out of Bangkok for Saigon on 6 September, worsening weather severely restricted the operations of the RAF transport squadrons mounting the fly-in. The ferocious monsoon thunderstorms had already literally torn aircraft to pieces in mid-air, and 345 Wing alone had just lost, due to bad weather, nine aircraft within a few weeks, two having broken up in violent air and seven having crash-landed in paddy-fields throughout Burma. En route to Saigon the cloud base was about 9,000 feet, with the weather gradually getting worse as the aircraft neared Tan Son Nhut. However, after just crossing the Grand Lake in Cambodia the Dakotas were able to descend and follow the roads leading to Saigon. Before they landed, the two leading ones overflew the city center, with pilots and passengers taking a good look as they circled over Saigon.

As could be expected, there was much uncertainty as to how the Japanese would react to these visitors. A Royal Air Force Squadron-Leader who was in the second plane described his emotions: "We went in without any real knowledge of whether the Japanese Command would imprison us, or impound our aircraft or cut us up into small pieces. . . . Lord Burleigh (I believe that was his name) was on the other plane . . ."[16] "Lord Burleigh" went with the Japanese to the Continental Hotel "to discuss with the Japanese authorities the question of our

16.  Personal interview, 17 Aug. 1977.

taking over all the POWs, to take them back to hospitals in Rangoon. This was our first concern, to get our prisoners out . . ." With these last-minute details arranged, the first aircraft departed; returning to freedom in it were the first twenty-five British prisoners from Indochina. The aircraft, its crew and passengers were never seen again after departing the Bangkok refueling stop; piloted by the squadron commander, it was caught in a thunderstorm over the Gulf of Martaban and broke up less than forty minutes out from Mingaladon. The second aircraft was immobilized at Tan Son Nhut, having burst a tire on landing.

Continued the officer, "I remember being met on the runway by all the Japanese generals lined up in their uniforms — they were all looking very smart with their Japanese swords." The Canadian pilot got out and, "the Canadian being a very extrovert and happy-go-lucky people," saluted the ranking General (probably Numata) and shook his hand. "I came after the plane crew . . . I had only a week before seen the emaciated Prisoners of War, lying in the hangars of Don Muang airport and they were in such a shocking condition, with bones sticking out of their bodies, that this was etched into my mind, and the idea of shaking hands with a man who was responsible for this to happen was just beyond my capability. . . . He offered his hand and I just walked past him." He saluted the other generals and entered a waiting car, chauffeured by a Japanese soldier. This first party was then driven to the Continental Palace Hotel, where a large crowd of French and Vietnamese had gathered, drawn by the circling Dakotas.

While the 20th Division's advance party was becoming acquainted with local conditions and radioing back reports to General Gracey in Rangoon, the Squadron-Leader decided to visit the POW camps. Because of the Dakota's burst tire he was now stuck in Saigon, and he thought he should tell the prisoners that the war was over and they would soon be back in safe hands and in hospitals for treatment. He also wanted to tell them of the latter stages of the war. So he left the hotel and walked up Rue Catinat (later renamed Tu-Do), a main street which led from the Cathedral to the river. He asked directions to the POW camp from the first person he met; it was a fortuitous meeting, and the stranger, who happened to be a Laotian prince who later married the American heiress Barbara Hutton, personally took him to the camp. The officer, to his surprise, was allowed into the camp by the Japanese. The prisoners turned out to be fairly well informed and knew about the atomic bomb. In at least one of the French camps the prisoners, after hearing of the war's end on their hidden radio, had negotiated with the

Japanese colonel in command, with the result that inside the camp they were left in complete control while the Japanese continued to maintain a guard on the outside, a matter of "face". [17]

Since there appeared to be no problems on the Japanese side regarding the repatriation of Allied POWs, the big remaining question concerned the state of public order, the political situation and the disturbing number of armed revolutionaries at large, especially since more detailed reports of the recent riots were now being made available to the Control Commission and to Allied Land Forces French Indochina. On 6 September, as the RAPWI team and the detachment of 1/19 Hybad troops were arriving, General Manaki sent a message to General Gracey in Rangoon expressing, in his capacity as commander of Japanese forces in South Indochina, his regrets at the rioting and the killing of Frenchmen, but assuring Gracey that the situation was well in hand; calm prevailed and things were not as bad as they might seem.

Terauchi had stubbornly defied Mountbatten in one matter. He was ordered to send Numata back to Rangoon on 4 September, and to empower Numata to issue orders in his (Terauchi's) name. This Terauchi absolutely refused to do, and the British had no option but to accept it. Wrote Terauchi, "My right of command over all the forces in the Southern Region is endowed directly from the prerogative of the Supreme Command of our Emperor and I am in no position to hand it down to any junior officer."

Surgeon-Captain Birt examined the Field-Marshal, and diagnosed that he had suffered a slight stroke resulting in mild residual paralysis in the left leg. Birt reported that Terauchi would be capable of going to Singapore for the surrender ceremony. On 8 September Terauchi cabled his thanks to Mountbatten for sending Surgeon-Captain Birt to examine him; he indicated that he did *not* intend to go to Singapore for the surrender, intimating that Birt had concurred in this. Mountbatten decided that Terauchi might be considered a martyr if he were forced to attend, and excused him; General Itagaki, Seventh Area Army commander, signed on his behalf. Before long Terauchi was examined again, by a board of doctors from the 20th Indian Division medical staff. Their findings showed him to be regressing rapidly.

On 8 September Gracey sent Numata back to Saigon with the second advance group, and two days later he accused Terauchi of violating the terms of the Rangoon agreement by permitting movements of Japanese

---

17. Letter from M. Vallat, Secretary General of the Federation of the Indochina Resistance [Federation des Reseaux de la Résistance en Indochine], 31 Oct. 1977.

forces, reports having been received in Rangoon that Terauchi was paying off and disbanding bodies of Korean and Formosan troops, including POW guards who would probably be wanted for trial as war criminals. The sole task of the first arrivals (6 September) had been the care and repatriation of the POWs and internees. The second group was responsible not only for RAPWI problems, but also for procuring information on war criminals, protecting American property such as it was, and surveying the political climate and vital points (including the airport, power station and docks); early reports were radioed back to Gracey in Rangoon. Numata arrived with orders from Gracey to release all French parachutists still in prison, disarm the Viet Minh police, establish law and order with Japanese forces, and establish a curfew in Saigon and Cholon; the riot of 2 September had prompted these orders.

A day earlier, on 8 September, Mountbatten had passed on to the Chiefs of Staff Leclerc's request to fly 500 troops of the 5th RIC to Tonkin to support the French resistance "who are in a very serious situation". Leclerc returned from Tokyo during this period and, to expedite matters, reduced his request: he called for sixty paratroopers to be flown in aboard three Dakotas to Vientiane or Luang Prabang. While in Tokyo MacArthur had told Leclerc that he should get as many French troops to Indochina as possible, and tell Mountbatten that the two of them were in agreement. The Chiefs replied that Leclerc should be told to ask Wedemeyer in China, which Leclerc knew would be a fruitless exercise; he did, however, strenuously object to the presence of Chinese troops in Laos, for there were no Japanese troops there. At it happened, the Chinese were not interested in the Japanese in Laos; they were more interested in profiteering, and stayed in Laos long enough to harvest two opium crops.

During the next forty-eight hours, hundreds of men and several different battalions prepared to begin a journey to what almost all of them thought would be a welcome change from Burma to a "land flowing with milk and honey".[18] As the first major fly-in started on 11 September, the troops' expectations were at first fulfilled, but the euphoria was brief.

---

18. *Frontier Force Regimental Magazine*, Feb. 1946, vol. III, no. 1, p. 38.

# 6

# GRACEY ARRIVES IN SAIGON

Because General Gracey's role in post-war Saigon has generated much heat, if little light, it is necessary to examine his terms of reference as a preliminary to any intelligent assessment of his actions. A proper definition of his directive is precisely what has been missing or misrepresented in most accounts published to date of the Allied involvement in French Indochina.

The Potsdam decisions, reached at the highest policy-making level, have already been discussed in their relation to Indochina. Since the Chinese were militarily and politically incapable of action in Indochina, the decision to assign the northern half of the country to China was taken at American insistence for the purpose of saving Chiang Kai-shek's "face". This arrangement also permitted the United States to enter behind the Chinese and work for the exclusion of France from Indochina. After the political decisions had been made, the British Chiefs of Staff in turn delegated the responsibility for occupying the south to the theater commander, Lord Louis Mountbatten. They sent him a broad overview of British tasks following the surrender of Japan. In reference to the first task ("Reoccupation of key areas of occupied territories, in order to secure effective control and to enforce surrender and disarmament of Japanese Armed Forces"), Mountbatten "should not occupy more of French Indo-China than is necessary to ensure the control of the headquarters of the Japanese southern armies."[1]

Mountbatten created two distinct organizations to deal with the problems of French Indochina, both commanded by the same officer, Major-General Douglas Gracey.[2] The first of these was made up from South East Asia Command resources and was responsible directly to Headquarters SEAC; this was the numerically smaller Headquarters SACSEA Commission No. 1 (the Control Commission). The second organization was Headquarters Allied Land Forces French Indo-China (ALFFIC), a far larger organization containing British and French military forces, including the 20th Indian Division and supporting units. To

1. PRO, Cab. 105/165, COSSEA 314, British Chiefs of Staff to Supreme Allied Commander South East Asia, 13 Aug. 1945.
2. See Appendix A following this Chapter, pp. 161–4.

appreciate the role of the Allies in Vietnam more clearly, it is necessary to understand from the beginning that these two organizations had only one thing in common: their commander (and even that was nominal, for Brigadier Hirst actually ran the 20th Division in Gracey's name, Gracey being preoccupied primarily with Control Commission affairs).

The two organizations were tasked by two separate headquarters and reported to separate headquarters. The Control Commission was tasked by and reported directly to Headquarters South East Asia Command (Mountbatten). Allied Land Forces French Indo-China was tasked by and reported directly to Headquarters Allied Land Forces South East Asia (Slim), going through 12th Army for routine matters. As Head of the Commission, Gracey was given nine tasks, which revolved around controlling the Japanese theater headquarters.[3] The lineage of Gracey's directive as Commander of Allied Land Forces French Indo-China will be discussed in descending order.

President Truman's General Order no. 1 directed the Japanese to maintain law and order in their occupied areas until Allied forces could take over. Force Plan 1, "The Occupation of French Indo-China", drawn up by the Headquarters South East Asia Command Joint Planning Staff (JPS), reflected the agreed Allied policy by stating that "the eventual reoccupation of FIC is a matter for the French,"[4] and this statement dictated the conduct of the whole operation. The objective was to introduce a force into Southern French Indochina "in order to control Japanese Southern Army Hq, to concentrate and evacuate Allied prisoners of war and internees and to disarm Japanese forces," and to maintain public order while these primary tasks were being accomplished. There would be two phases to the occupation, Phase I coinciding with the British occupation and Phase II with the takeover by French

3. As Chief of the Control Commission, Gracey had the following tasks: to assume control of Headquarters Japanese Southern Army and supervise the surrender; transmit Mountbatten's orders to Japanese headquarters; obtain information regarding Japanese dispositions and supplies; control Japanese communications; study the RAPWI problem and render all possible aid; report on Indochina's lines of communication, airfields and the port of Saigon; open river and sea approaches to Saigon, using Japanese resources; reduce the size of Japanese headquarters as soon as possible; and maintain liaison with the local French Government, keeping Mountbatten informed. (Gracey Papers, Control Commission tasking, 30 Aug. 1945; also in GB, PRO, Air 23/2375 and WO 203/4566.)

4. Gracey has been widely quoted as having made this statement before departing from Rangoon (Ellen Hammer has him in India) for Saigon. In fact, in dealing with news reporters he carefully confined himself to repeating verbatim this statement from his supreme headquarters.

military forces and civil affairs personnel. Under "Army Consideration" the following was directed:

The primary task of army forces will be to secure the Saigon area, including control of Japanese Southern Army Headquarters. Other tasks which should be undertaken as soon as sufficient forces are available include:

(*a*) disarming and concentration of all Japanese surrendered personnel.
(*b*) collection and evacuation of Allied Prisoners of War and Internees.
(*c*) maintenance of law and order and protection of vital installations.
(*d*) apprehension of war criminals.[5]

On 23 August the Commander-in-Chief, Allied Land Forces South East Asia, General Slim, issued ALFSEA Operational Directive no. 8 to his four senior subordinate commanders — Lt.-Gen. Stopford (12th Army); Lt.-Gen. Dempsey (14th Army); Lt.-Gen. Christison (15 Indian Corps); and Lt.-Gen. Roberts (34 Indian Corps). This directive discussed the broad outlines of reoccupation tasks and priorities, and followed the guidance laid down by the Joint Planning Staff. In carrying out the plans "to effect the military occupation of Burma, Malaya, FIC [French Indo-China] and NEI [Netherlands East Indies]", the general policy for all area commanders would be: (*a*) disarm and concentrate all Japanese forces, (*b*) protect, succour and subsequently evacuate Allied prisoners-of-war and civilian internees, (*c*) establish and maintain law and order, (*d*) introduce food and other civil affairs supplies, and (*e*) set up the appropriate civil administration.[6] The general priorities for reoccupation were now — in order — Malaya, Saigon (FIC) and Burma; Siam; the Netherlands East Indies. In keeping with Mountbatten's directive, Allied commanders were ordered to control the Japanese through their existing chain of command.

The ALFSEA directive (Operational Directive no. 12, 28 August 1945) to Gracey was prefaced with the clarifying statement that these tasks were separate from those of the Control Commission; in that capacity he would be directly responsible to SACSEA. As Commander of Allied Land Forces French Indo-China, Gracey "will come directly under command Commander-in-Chief, Allied Land Forces, South East Asia." He would remain under 12th Army until his arrival in Saigon, at which time he would report directly to General Slim at ALFSEA. The following tasks were given to General Gracey as Allied Land Force Commander:

5. PRO, WO 203/5444, SEAC JPS Force Plan 1, "Occupation of French Indo-China", 31 Aug. 1945.
6. Gracey Papers, ALFSEA Operational Directive no. 8, 23 Aug. 1945.

(*a*) secure the Saigon area, including Headquarters, Japanese Southern Army.

(*b*) disarm and concentrate all Japanese forces in accordance with the policy laid down in this headquarters' letters 10028/G(0)1 dated 19 and 28 Aug. 45.

(*c*) maintain law and order and ensure internal security.

(*d*) protect, succour and subsequently evacuate Allied prisoners-of-war and internees.

(*e*) liberate Allied territory in so far as your resources permit.

You will give such directions to the French Indo China Government as are required to effect these tasks [these directions are pertinent to the *coup* of 23 September 1945]. In these matters you will consult the senior French Land Forces Commander.[7]

This ALFSEA directive, the basic document relating to "Masterdom" (code name for occupation of French Indochina), was retransmitted to the 20th Indian Division. These directions for the Land Force Commander have been presented in some detail to show that the one common thread through all command levels was the maintenance of public order; this thread, it will be seen, extended to the Foreign Office as well.[8] Thus by the end of August Gracey, who was supervising the Control Commission from Rangoon, had his directives in hand.

The Foreign Office minutes reflect the concern felt in London over the delicacy of the problem of keeping public order. It was suggested that General Gracey himself was asking that the impending civil affairs agreement with France should not commit him to maintaining law and order, since he wished to concentrate on the Japanese. Dening echoed the general unease over this potentially dangerous issue by telling the Foreign Office that he was worried about the attitude of the French civil affairs officer at SEAC headquarters. He warned that the British should be wary of committing themselves to becoming involved in law and order, and recalled that there was a history of resistance in Indochina, long before the Japanese arrived in South East Asia. The French would claim that the resistance movements were Japanese-inspired and would call on British troops to quell Annamite[9] uprisings. Having said that,

7. Gracey Papers, ALFSEA Operational Directive no. 12, "Masterdom", 28 Aug. 1945; also in Great Britain, Public Record Office, WO 203/2066.

8. Writers critical of Gracey appear to be unaware of these orders. For example, Ellen Hammer, quoting Devillers, said that Gracey was under "strict" instructions only to disarm the Japanese and not to get involved with keeping order; she states that he disregarded his instructions (*The Struggle for Indochina 1940–1955*, p. 115).

9. The contemporary word "Annamite" (referring generally also to South Vietnamese) and "Vietnamese" will be used interchangeably throughout, depending on the context.

Dening recognized that French civilians were in real danger from internal disorders. He wrote prophetically: "I think we should avoid at all costs laying ourselves open to the accusation that we are assisting the West to suppress the East. Such an accusation will rise very readily to the lips of the Americans and Chinese and would be likely to create an unfavourable impression throughout Asia."[10] Dening concluded by acknowledging the difficult task which lay ahead of Gracey: "I do not know the answer but I feel I should warn you of the situation which is likely to arise and the difficulty with which the Force Commander will be faced in Indo-China."

Dening's message reflected the worry felt throughout South East Asia Command at the prospect of becoming involved in what the British (with their long experience in it) called Internal Security duties. For the Army it was one of their most difficult and least rewarding tasks, which they would avoid if at all possible. This question was raised when the draft Anglo-French civil affairs agreement was sent by the Foreign Office in London to South East Asia Command for comment. It was specifically met head-on by Brigadier E. Gibbons, who had wide pre-war experience as a civil administrator in Africa and was now Chief Civil Affairs Staff Officer at SEAC headquarters. In his reply Gibbons noted that the message [COSSEA 314] had defined a limited British role in Indochina, and he objected to paragraph 5(c) of ALFSEA Operational Directive no. 12 to General Gracey; this, "which charges him with the task of maintaining law and order and of ensuring internal security, apparently without limitation of area, looks overwide."[11] For the same reason he objected to the London text of the Anglo-French civil affairs agreement (Memorandum no. 1), which "could well lead to serious commitments, political as well as military, and it is recommended that a less definite undertaking, which should be subject to the Allied Commander-in-Chief's primary task not being compromised, should be substituted for it."

The Foreign Office minutes, in commenting on Dening's note of caution on how far to commit British forces to law and order, noted that the War Office had echoed Dening's question, especially in regard to Cambodia. The fact was that not enough troops were immediately available for the job: "From the military point of view the main difficulty is

10. PRO, FO 371/46308, Dening to Foreign Office, 9 Sept. 1945.
11. PRO, WO 172/1782, Headquarters SEAC War Diary, Memo by Brig. Gibbons to Conference Secretariat minutes, 5/266; 7 Sept. 1945; also in WO 203/5562 and WO 203/4452.

that owing to the very small number of British forces involved it will be quite impossible for the Allied Commander-in-Chief to ensure the maintenance of public order if so requested by the French authorities.''[12] In fact the draft memorandum was reworded to reflect these fears, and now stated that the French would ask the Commander, ALFIC (Gracey) to maintain law and order in particular areas where necessary. The final draft stated that involvement in the maintenance of law and order anywhere but in the British key areas was to be referred to Mountbatten for decision. It can thus be seen that the British responsibility in this area was never an issue; the only question was the physical extent of involvement, and the highest political and military officials were agreed that the Commander of Allied Land Forces was charged with the keeping of public order in his key areas, which included Saigon.

In his examination of the London text of Memorandum no. 1, Gibbons made the following remarks. The principal effect of the memorandum was to "place squarely upon French shoulders responsibility for conducting the administration of the country''.[13] A second result was to lay General Gracey open to demands from the French to maintain public order "in such areas as the French authorities might invite him to take over". In view of this, the areas to be occupied must be more clearly defined and qualified. Gibbons went on to warn Mountbatten of the "considerable" consequences, political and military, of taking on the maintenance of law and order in other than the "occupied areas", and reiterated that Gracey's directive seemed to him dangerously wide. Finally, Gibbons recommended deleting the appropriate paragraph (5c) in the ALFSEA directive and replacing it with "a less definite undertaking of assistance in maintaining order, subject to this not involving interference with the proper discharge of the primary tasks". Furthermore, French forces should come under Gracey, but if the French were to be responsible for the rest of the country, an independent French Command in Indochina was "immediately necessary".

As it turned out, the force of Gibbons' argument persuaded Mountbatten to give further definition to Gracey's responsibility for law

---

12. PRO, FO 371/46308, 10 Sept. 1945 [F6636].
13. PRO, WO 172/1782, Gibbons Memo, 7 Sept. 1945. A compelling reason for limiting the British role in Saigon as much as possible was the extreme sensitivity of the French over any apparent encroachment on their rights there. In 1945 the French and the British were diametrically opposed in their basic philosophical approaches to colonial affairs, and Gibbons and others thought that the best thing to do was to limit as severely as possible any British role in French Indochina. (Brig. Gibbons, telephone interview, 20 Jan. 1977.)

and order, but the establishment of an independent French Command was simply not feasible at that time. Also, the War Office had told Mountbatten that it was under "considerable pressure" from the Foreign Office and French authorities to complete the draft civil affairs agreement. (Thus Gracey should have received an amendment to paragraph 5*c* of ALFSEA Operational Directive no. 12, literally as he was leaving Rangoon for Saigon.[14] As he later wrote, he in fact appears not to have been notified of this crucial change until after the French *coup*. At Mountbatten's direction, Slim provided Gracey with the final — and only — amendment to his directives, reemphasizing that the French were to be responsible for civil administration. In these designated key areas, Gracey was directed to "exercise full authority over both military and civilian but working through French Civil Adm[inistration]. Outside such areas Adm will rest solely with French authorities exercising powers of state of seige." Gracey was told that he would not have responsibility for law and order outside the key areas unless called on by the French and approved by Mountbatten.[15]

Foreign Office minutes of that time noted that British troops were "not to subdue unruly elements in the country apart from the Saigon

14. Gracey Papers; PRO WO 203/5644, ALFSEA to Saigon Control Commission, 12 Sept. 1945. This was the amendment whose text is as follows:

    Para Five C ALFSEA OP Directive Number Twelve dated 28 Aug is being amended in view of a memorandum defining adm[inistrative] and jurisdictional questions connected with the presence of Allied Forces in FIC. Memorandum still in draft stage pending approval by War Office [,] SACSEA and French Authorities. Amendment will not be issued until paper finally approved . . .

    Your primary task as defined by SEAC Directive to you dated 30 Aug is by controlling HQ Japanese Southern Army to enforce the surrender and disarmament of all Japanese Forces. You will report earliest possible the areas you require to occupy to ensure this control and any other area necessary to ensure release of RAPWI. This need not necessarily include all of Saigon as indicated in para Five A of ALFSEA Directive Number Twelve. Such areas defined as key areas.

15. It was this part of the directive which Gracey, according to Mountbatten, purportedly disregarded in "exceeding his instructions" by his proclamation of 19/21 September. Gracey in fact never left his key areas, never had any intention of doing so, and wrote that anyway he did not receive this amendment until later. The proclamation (discussed later) was a warning to groups rampaging throughout the country that the Japanese were charged with maintaining law and order. In any case, Gracey had no means by which he could personally enforce it had he wanted to, and these proclamations were the normal occurrence throughout the areas of British responsibility in South East Asia.

area, as that will be left to the French. It was noted that under the surrender terms the Japanese were also responsible for maintaining law and order, and that reports were being received of small parties of Japanese joining Viet Minh attacks on the French. There was complete anarchy in areas controlled by the Viet Minh (which was recognized as a largely Communist organization); these areas were experiencing a rapid economic deterioration, and (anticipating Gracey's proclamation) would have to be administered under martial law.[16] The Foreign Office was also aware that the advance party in Saigon had reported great unrest and agitation and had urgently requested the dispatch of British troops.

In the various writings about the Saigon occupation it is surprising to find no mention of the most important consideration of all, namely what may be called the ''Athens connection''. Experience of events in Athens, shared by many of the staff officers in the headquarters of South East Asia Command, engendered extreme reluctance to become involved in Saigon and was ultimately responsible for the dispatch to Gracey of the amendment to ALFSEA Directive no. 12, restricting his role as far as possible without making his trip to Saigon completely useless. It was also the reason why at first Mountbatten seriously considered withholding the rest of Gracey's division from him, in the mistaken belief that if Gracey were so weakened he could never become involved. As has been mentioned, the palpable Allied weakness in the early stages produced, as usual, only the reverse result by encouraging the Viet Minh to aim higher and become more intractable. It was a lesson which Western leaders had to learn and relearn. The influence of the Athens operation was so important to the planning of the occupation of Saigon that we should discuss it briefly before moving with Gracey to Saigon.

In 1944, with the Germans no longer a factor in Greece, Britain sent General Scobie to provide general humanitarian relief for Athens, which was invested by the EAM (National Liberation Front), a large Communist guerrilla group. Although the need for guerrillas was by then at an end, the EAM and ELAS (National Popular Liberation Army) refused to disband. Not long after Scobie arrived (with the Greek Government) the Communists, surprised by the weakness of the British occupying force, made a violent bid to overthrow the Government and seize power. By this time they had (as in Vietnam) set up a provisional government and eliminated most of their rivals, and were in control of the whole of Greece except for Athens and Salonika. The British, forced in bitter

16. PRO, FO 371/46308, Foreign Office Minutes, 8 Sept. 1945.

street fighting to abandon the RAF headquarters, barely sustained themselves until reinforcements arrived; then, using tanks in the streets, they
pushed the Communists out of Athens.

   Churchill appears to have been genuinely hurt by Roosevelt's lack of
support or sympathy. In a message to Roosevelt he wrote:

You will realize how very serious it would be if we withdrew, as we easily
could, and the result was a frightful massacre, and an extreme left-wing regime
under Communist inspiration installed itself, as it would, in Athens. My
Cabinet colleagues here of all parties are not prepared to act in a manner so dis-
honourable to our record and name . . . Stern fighting lies ahead, and even
danger to our troops in the centre of Athens. The fact that you are supposed to
be against us, in accordance with the last sentence of Stettinius' press release, as I
feared has added to our difficulties and burdens.

   Roosevelt had gone so far as to suggest disbanding the famous (and
anti-Communist) Greek Mountain Brigade and the Sacred Squadron.
With Roosevelt more and more influenced by Stalin, Churchill again
dug in by himself:

The disarmament of the Greek Mountain Brigade, who took Rimini, and the
Sacred Squadron who have fought so well at the side of British and American
troops, would seriously weaken our forces, and in any case we could not
abandon them to massacre. . . . In the midst of our bringing food and relief for a
Government which has no armed forces, we have become involved in a furious
struggle. I have felt it much that you were unable to give a word of explanation
for our action . . .[17]

   Roosevelt made a lame reply about American public opinion and the
local political situation. In the words of Brigadier E. C. J. Myers,[18] the
senior British officer intimately involved in Greek guerrilla operations
(one of many officers who went from the Mediterranean to South East
Asia Command), the British "got their fingers severely burned" in the
Athens insurrection. To them Gracey's occupation of Saigon appeared
analogous to Scobie's operation, and they feared the possibility of his
being dragged into a civil war, with the events of Athens repeating
themselves exactly in Saigon. Hence it was that successive restrictions
were placed on Gracey's freedom of action until the very safety of his
initial force was in jeopardy. This too was the reason why Dening, a

17. PRO, Prem 3/472, Churchill to Roosevelt, 14 Dec. 1944.
18. Brig. E. C. J. Myers, personal interview. Brig. Myers was later sent to Saigon to
    investigate the political situation. He wrote a book (*Greek Entanglement*) on the
    Greek resistance.

most talented political officer, made his comment that should the British be involved in a fight against the native revolutionary government, accusations would "rise very readily to the lips of the Americans."

Gracey's original plan called for him to occupy the following areas: Saigon/Cholon/Thu Dau Mot; Mytho; Nha Trang/Ba Ngo; Phnom Penh; Dalat. In view of the amendment of 12 September, he was directed at the last moment to confine his key areas still further. He was thus limited to the Saigon area until in October the Chiefs of Staff authorized him to expand his control to include Thu Dau Mot and Bien Hoa.

The mechanics of the move of the Commission and the 20th Indian Division[19] to Saigon were contained in a document entitled "Force Plan 1", published by the Headquarters SEAC Joint Planning Staff. Both "Army Considerations" and "Political Considerations" ("a matter for the French") had already been discussed, as had Phases I and II (the occupation of key areas and follow-up by French forces). The document stated that political advice would be available from the Foreign Office representative to the Commission (it did not, however, become available till late September). Headquarters SEAC recognized a series of VPs (vital points) which were considered to be targets for immediate seizure by Allied forces: the power plants, wharf area, foundry, ship repair and barge building works, navy yard and arsenal, and machine shops in Saigon and Phnom Penh, Cam Ranh Bay base, Nha Be oil storage depot, Tan Son Nhut airfield, and Saigon Radio. These were modified later in view of the restrictions added to the Allied Land Force Commander's tasking. It was reemphasized that the Japanese were responsible for the maintenance of law and order in conformity with President Truman's General Order no. 1.

Japanese troop strength in French Indochina was listed as 71,000. Of these, 40,000 were in the south, primarily in three divisions (2nd, 22nd and 55th), one Independent Mixed Brigade, and headquarters and non-divisional troops in the Saigon area. In Saigon were located the headquarters of Southern Army (with a detachment in Dalat), part of 38 Army, and the 2nd Division, which had recently been withdrawn from Burma for reforming (8,000 men). The remaining 9,000 included Navy and Air Force strength.

A source of trouble later was the policy of using the Japanese to guard their surrendered weapons until relieved by the Allies, but with the

---

19. For the history of the 20th Indian Division, make-up and movement of forces to Indochina, taskings of the land, sea and air forces etc., the author's Ph. D. dissertation (School of Oriental and African Studies, London University) can be consulted.

British area of control now practically reduced to Saigon city, not much else could be done in the first few weeks. At the senior Allied commander's discretion, a small number of rifles only could be issued to Japanese forces for self-protection. Exceptions were made to the general policy of treating the Japanese as Surrendered Personnel — which left them under their own officers, responsible for their own maintenance — in the case of members of the following groups, all of whom were subject to immediate arrest: the Kempei Tei (the "Japanese Gestapo"); the Tokumu Kikan (intelligence organization); the Hikari Kikan (Japanese/Indian organization); General Staff intelligence and associated personnel; war criminals, and guards of POW and internee camps. Gracey also carried with him a booklet containing "black" and "grey" lists, recording the names of sixty-four prominent known or suspected French and Vietnamese collaborators.

At last the time came to fly the main party of the Control Commission and escort into Saigon. The troops that flew in (excluding the small detachment of 1/19 Hybad which had flown in a week earlier) were two companies of 1/1 Gurkha Rifles (GR), and two companies of 1/19 Hybad, plus 80 Brigade headquarters and a tactical headquarters. Gracey might have been expected to take one of the other Gurkha battalions first, such as the 3/1 Gurkha Rifles, which had been in the division from the beginning, fought at Imphal and marched down through Burma. The 1st Gurkhas were relative newcomers to the 20th Division, but they were Gracey's old regiment, so he picked them to be his own escort. The fly-in began on 11 September and most of the troops arrived the next day so as to be in place when the senior officers (such as Gracey and Maunsell) arrived on the 13th.

The Gurkha advance party was led by Lieutenant-Colonel Cyril E. Jarvis, the battalion commander. On 10 September, 151 Gurkhas, including the battalion headquarters, motored down to Hmawbi. The airfield was in a chaotic state, reflecting the fact that major decisions were still being made at the very last moment. It was not till this date, for example, that the decision was made to substitute the 114th Field Regiment, Royal Artillery, for the 2nd Indian Field Regiment (making the 114th the only British troops in French Indochina, apart from the smaller RN and RAF units — the rest were Indian, Gurkha and French). The decision to limit Gracey's area further was still two days away. Wrote the 1/1 GR recorders: "The complete absence of any administrative arrangements for reception, which was to be so typical of the next few days, was here first apparent.''[20] At 0900 on 11 September the Gurkhas left for Mingaladon, where at 1245 they began the journey to Saigon in seven sorties, arriving in Bangkok at 1600 hours for an overnight stop. Here too the Gurkhas were not greatly impressed: ''At Bangkok, reception arrangements were less than inadequate; no one had heard of the hot meals so facilely promised in Rangoon.''

On 12 September the group began the final leg at 0530, arriving at Tan Son Nhut airfield at 0900, where they waited for an hour before being driven into Saigon by the Japanese. The barracks was an Annamite girls' school. By evening, guards were posted on Gracey's residence, the mission compound, and the signal exchange. Arriving with the Gurkhas were two companies of the Hybads, who immediately took over guard duties at Tan Son Nhut airfield, one of the prime VPs. The headquarters of 80 Brigade were located in the Japanese staff quarters, across the street from the headquarters Southern Area Army (in the south-west of Saigon). At 1200 hours on 12 September, the Control Commission closed down in Rangoon and simultaneously opened in Saigon.

The RAF, having noted that morale flights over POW camps had finally met with intense anti-aircraft fire, described their arrival in Saigon on 12 September: ''The outward welcome accorded to the Allied Forces from both the French and Annamese alike on our entry into French Indochina was decidedly embarrassing. Our Forces obviously found themselves in a divided house.'' A large crowd of French civilians had gathered at Tan Son Nhut to cheer each aircraft of 62 Squadron as it taxied to its parking spot. The RAF reconnaissance parties immediately inspected Japanese Air Force installations at Tan Son Nhut. The arms

20. PRO, WO 177/7769, War Diary 1/1 Gurkha Rifles, 10 Sept. 1945. There was a reason for this not atypical state of affairs, and it is provided by Maj.-Gen. Pyman, Slim's Chief of Staff, who as far back as 15 August had foreseen the confusion: ''This theatre quite unready for surrender. There was no plan at all . . . to meet such a situation. [. . .] Neither Supremo nor Cs-in-C had given consideration to any plan to meet the new surrender conditions . . . *five days after first warning of surrender and no approved plan*.'' And that was not all: ''We could not even speak to 12 Army at Rangoon and could just to 14 Army at Secunderabad.'' Furthermore, the entire planning concept left much to be desired, for the Joint Planning Staff drew up plans on the Supreme Allied Commander's orders. But ''SAC emphasized that these planners formed a part of the staff of their respective Cs-in-C. Cs-in-C did not appear to be aware of it . . . The main danger was an old and obvious one, namely that the planners produced papers for SAC which the Cs-in-C were not prepared to accept.'' (Pyman Papers, Diary of Maj.-Gen. H. Pyman, Liddell Hart Centre for Military Archives, King's College London.)

discovered tallied with the Japanese lists, but it was emphasized that there was no way of proving that the lists were accurate: "Judging by the aggressive attitude of the Annamese towards the French at this period, it may well have been that considerable stocks of Japanese arms had not been declared."[21]

Gracey then received a message from these first arrivals to say that all was prepared for his reception, and he and the senior staff landed on 13 September, touching down at Tan Son Nhut at 1400 hours. As his Dakota came to a halt in the reception area, the door was opened and his personal bodyguard of seven Gurkha soldiers scrambled down the steps and fanned out around the aircraft. Gracey stepped out, followed by his Control Commission Chief of Staff, Brigadier Maunsell. The entire field was strongly surrounded by Japanese troops. Across the tarmac were about eight senior Japanese officers, including Lieutenant-General Numata and the senior officers of the Army, Navy and Air Force; Terauchi was not well enough to be on hand. Off to one side was a small group of Vietnamese, whose presence neither Gracey nor Maunsell had anticipated. Said Maunsell of them: "We didn't know who they were — they were just a little group which turned out to be the Viet Minh." They started forward, talking, to intercept Gracey, but at that moment the Japanese stepped up, saluted and bowed to Gracey, who walked past the Viet Minh to the waiting Japanese generals.[22] The preliminaries over, Gracey asked to be taken to his headquarters. The Viet Minh came forward again to speak but Gracey waved them aside and entered Terauchi's "wonderful" old Chrysler convertible for the drive into Saigon. The road to Saigon was lined with Union Jacks and a cheering throng; most of the French population were in the streets to greet the senior Allied officers.

So ended the beginning of the occupation of Saigon, with the troops expecting a pleasant sojourn in the Paris of the East and soon to be disappointed. The following are two typical recollections. Colonel Jarvis mentally noted that most of the cheering crowds were Vietnamese, who outnumbered the French. All the troops expected a largely ceremonial role, so when Jarvis was asked what he wanted from the regimental

21. PRO, Cab 106/113, Air Chief Marshal Park's report (ACSEA), Aug. 1945, p. 2159, para. 399.

22. Brig. M. S. K. Maunsell, personal interview, 20 April 1977. Gracey, described by all his colleagues as very quick-witted, made an instant decision to walk straight to the Japanese, as the Allies had not recognized the Viet Minh revolutionary government.

center in India, he asked for the bagpipes to be sent out to add a little class to the guard mounting. The pipes were also said to be good for the morale of the *colons*. But what really excited spectators was the order "For inspection — draw *kukris*!" — the *kukri* being the distinctive Gurkha weapon, with a large curved blade. However, he soon wished that he had brought the battalion mortars instead.

Major Peter Prentice, a twenty-year-old captain and company commander, noticed how poorly armed were the first British/Indian troops to arrive in Saigon. The infantry companies brought only small arms — rifles and one or two light machine-guns, having left the medium machine-guns and mortars behind. The word had not yet filtered down to the soldiers that troubles might await them, the ceremonial role being prominent in their planning: the Gurkhas made sure that they arrived with white belts and gaiters to add smartness to their honor guard. The first few days did indeed correspond with their expectations, although the Gurkhas, accustomed to sleeping out in the open during the Burma campaigns, could not adjust to the soft beds provided for them, and slept on the floor beside the beds.

On 12 September a total of 1,091 men and 26 tons of stores were flown in, and on 13 September 211 men and 11 tons. On the return legs 9,271 POWs were evacuated to Bangkok. Most of the personnel flown in were Control Commission, RAF, RAPWI, hospital, Pay Corps, and engineer staff. No more than a third were infantry, and taking into account rest periods, sick calls and so on, there were probably no more than a light company of soldiers — perhaps a hundred men — on duty throughout Saigon at any period. So predominant was the idea of a peaceful role that perhaps as many as a third were immediately appropriated by senior officers as batmen (valets), drivers, and so forth.

On the morning of 14 September, his second day in Saigon, Brigadier Maunsell decided personally to reconnoiter Saigon and Cholon — in Terauchi's car — to try and get the feel of the city, checking "for normal traffic control, the state of the shops, the markets, whether Cholon was active, and so on". A Union Jack flew on the car's bonnet in accordance with a decision that only officers of flag rank might have this privilege.[23] Maunsell found Saigon fairly quiet, and half under the

---

23. Gracey, in keeping with standard international practice, directed that only officers of one-star rank or above ("flag rank") would be permitted to fly a flag on their cars. This was to denote rank, so no national flags were generally allowed. The local OSS senior officer, Lt.-Col. Peter Dewey, complained about it to Maunsell, who would not back down, so he went to Gracey. Said Dewey, "It is necessary for me to

control of the Japanese "who only acted when they felt like it". The Viet Minh claim to control the city was "a laugh" — they had no control, and the one or two traffic policemen on duty were French. The shops were open, and Maunsell particularly recalled the "absolutely marvellous" flower market, something he had not seen for five years. In short, Saigon seemed to illustrate that daily life goes on regardless of what is happening at the top. At that moment there was no sign that Saigon was anything but a "completely and utterly quiescent city"; Maunsell reported to Gracey that if there was underlying dissent it was extremely difficult to recognize.

That afternoon Cédile arrived at Mission headquarters for a long talk with Gracey and Maunsell. He was described as "awfully nice, charming, liberal-minded — a scholastic man rather than military". He was doing an extremely difficult job waiting for Leclerc, who was "an explosion" in himself. Cédile knew Leclerc, and did not wish to aggravate the situation by committing him to policies which might later have to be disavowed; he was in a position familiar to officers in every generation, of having responsibility but not authority. Occasionally he "let his hair down" with the British, expressing supreme contempt for most of the French in Indochina; they were considered the collaborators with the Japanese, disloyal and active resisters to Free France. It now struck Gracey and Maunsell that they might well have serious difficulties with the French as well. But during these early days French information was valuable.

On 15 September the Commission distributed leaflets throughout Saigon and Cholon, telling the population that the British/Indian troops had certain tasks to perform and that the populace must maintain "the strictest order and discipline" throughout. Another leaflet stated that "in certain areas Europeans have been attacked, killed, and wounded, by extremist elements of the population," and that the peace and prosperity

fly the Stars and Stripes because of my work." Gracey reminded Dewey that his work should not take him to places where he found it necessary to seek protection under the American flag. Furthermore, Dewey was told that, in keeping with standard practice, he might paint the Stars and Stripes on his vehicles; he was also told to lash a large American flag over the radiator grill of his vehicle. After Dewey was killed some members of the staff thought that the ban on flying a relatively tiny national flag was a contributory factor. This is, at the least, questionable. As Maunsell later recalled, Dewey was unquestionably up to shady things, for his presence was reported "in a number of places with a number of people which called for an explanation the Control Commission never got." (Personal interview, 20 April 1977.)

desired by all "can only be prejudiced by these outrages committed by irresponsibles". The message concluded: "Be warned that such criminals will be tracked down and punished. All persons found guilty of promoting civil disorder will be severely dealt with."

Even at this early date the activities of the OSS detachment were so blatantly subversive to the Allied command that within forty-eight hours of his arrival Gracey felt compelled to summon its chief, Lieutenant-Colonel Peter Dewey, to appear before him. The small OSS team was in Saigon only because the occupation was an Allied effort, and it had only two relatively straightforward tasks: "One, to watch over American interests, including POW property. Two, to assist British Counter-Intelligence Staff."[24] The latter directive was concerned largely with the compilation of information on war criminals. Dewey, however, did not confine himself to his directives, but spent much of his time in and out of obscure alleyways and cafés in his dealings with the Communists and the Viet Minh. But it is very difficult for a Caucasian to escape notice anywhere in the Far East, and Dewey's activities were recorded, step by step, by everyone — the Japanese, the Vietnamese, the French and the British intelligence personnel. In the event, his machinations were more of a nuisance than of any great harm to the Allies; however, he was a danger to himself and his group, and despite repeated warnings from the British he consistently refused either to cooperate with the Allies or indeed to associate with them in any way. He deliberately maintained his villa and office outside the British area, and rejected all suggestions that he was at risk out there. The whole episode would have been of no importance had he not been needlessly assassinated at the hands of the Viet Minh. More will be said of this later.

Warned by Gracey on 15 September to confine himself to his assigned tasks and stop subverting his Allies, Dewey complained to his headquarters in Ceylon: "At General Gracey's request I must discontinue assistance to managers [of] American interests, collection of documents, and war crimes investigation [these were in fact the tasks to which Gracey asked him to confine himself], until directive for this work and presence Embankment [the code word for the OSS mission in Saigon] is clarified. There is no other US authority in Saigon."[25]

In his report to the Foreign Office in London, Dening commented on the displeasure caused at all levels by the OSS activities, and reported that

24. PRO, WO 203/4932, Browning to Gracey, 14 Sept. 1945.
25. *Ibid.*

Gracey was dissatisfied with OSS actions in his area.[26] Dewey had appeared and informed Gracey that he was charged with consular duties, but Gracey had been informed by the Chiefs of Staff that the only tasks permitted OSS by SACSEA were the repatriation of POWs and internees of special interest to them, the procurement of information on war criminals, and the protection of American property. If the US Government had wanted a uniformed officer to discharge consular duties, wrote Dening, then it should first have approached the Supreme Allied Commander.

I am afraid that what lies at the root of the matter is that OSS applies to go to places to fulfill one or more stated purposes only to engage in other activities which they do not disclose, which makes a very bad impression. There is nothing very sinister in undertaking Consular functions but there is no reason why Supreme Commander should not be consulted in the first instance.

As his first meeting with Dewey, Gracey had caught him in a clumsy lie.

Jean Cédile shared the attitude towards the two OSS heads of mission, Patti in the north and Dewey in the south, of all who had any dealings with them, namely strong personal dislike. The British senior officer in Hanoi described Patti as "an awful man", while Dewey in Saigon was remembered variously by British and French alike as "not at all a nice man", "a very unattractive man — not a man many people liked", "an unpleasant man", and several opined that they were scarcely better liked by their own colleagues. It was said that such interest as was aroused by Dewey derived from his being the nephew of New York Governor Thomas E. Dewey, a former Democratic Party presidential candidate. The Americans in Saigon deliberately shunned the society of both French and British, and even boycotted the *Cercle Sportif*, neither of which can have helped them in their task of information-gathering.

On learning one day that an American plane was about to deposit a passenger in Saigon, Cédile ordered the new arrival to be detained. It was Colonel Dewey, who freely admitted his OSS mission, saying "of course he knew we were on the same side."[27] Cédile later recalled: "I reproached him for not informing us of his coming and told him 'We could easily have shot you.' I told him, after all, at that time we were all a little bit trigger-happy." Dewey replied that he had come by himself, "without any troops, without anybody else", just to look around, and he did not intend to see anyone in particular (which, in Mingant's case at

26. PRO, FO 371/46308, Dening to Foreign Office, 20 Sept. 1945.
27. Governor Jean Cédile, personal interview, 25 Oct. 1977.

least, was not entirely true). Cédile released him.

Captain Marcel Mingant of the French colonial forces had been a captive of the Japanese since March, and was in the hospital in Saigon when Dewey arrived there. Dewey had apparently been given his name by OSS headquarters in Ceylon or China, and so sought him out. Mingant left the hospital temporarily to meet Dewey at the Continental Palace Hotel, where they talked for a while about the general situation, after which Dewey asked if they might meet again in eight days, as he had business in the countryside at that time. Mingant warned him against travelling in certain areas, but Dewey said, as he did repeatedly in Saigon, that his American nationality would protect him. When Mingant returned to keep the rendezvous he learned that Dewey had been murdered.[28] Saigon was the scene of continuing isolated murders, usually in areas far from the scattered presence of Gracey's small force.

On 16 September General Slim, Commander-in-Chief, ALFSEA, arrived in Saigon to make a personal assessment of the situation. He immediately recognized the virtual impossibility of Gracey's task, and took back with him the strongest recommendation to Mountbatten that the rest of Gracey's division should be sent to him as quickly as possible. Gracey was not only short of troops; on this date he sent an urgent plea to SEAC for additional typists and clerical staff, for his officers were becoming bogged down by administrative duties.

On 17 September Gracey held his first plenary meeting with Field-Marshal Terauchi, the Japanese Commander-in-Chief. However, Maunsell had earlier been sent by Gracey to visit him at his residence in the south-west of Saigon, and had then instructed Terauchi to order the Japanese to acknowledge British orders immediately — for which he would be held personally responsible. It was a "fairly typical set of instructions from victor to vanquished". This had been Terauchi's first meeting with the British. In the hall of the house, Maunsell had been surprised to see on a table six glasses and a bottle of "Dimple" Haig Scotch whisky, a brand he had not seen since 1940. He discovered that Terauchi had several cases of it downstairs. Maunsell sat down as he had been briefed to do, and told Terauchi that because of his age and infirmity he could be seated. Terauchi replied, "I will never be seated in the face of a representative of my conqueror." Maunsell responded, "As you wish." The interpreter then read out each paragraph of the instructions while the old man stood there, his head bowed, and said that he would

28. Col. Marcel Mingant, personal interview, Oct. 1977.

ensure that these were carried out as the Supreme Allied Commander wished. He then asked, "May I say something?" To Maunsell's affirmative reply Terauchi said, "Tomorrow is the anniversary of the death of the Emperor Meiji." Maunsell only later learned that this was the Emperor who had decided that Japan should be westernized. Terauchi continued, "I was brought up the son of the Japanese ambassador to the Court of Saint James." He then burst into tears, and struggled to finish: "I fought for an understanding between my country and yours until the outbreak of hostilities, and no shame can be greater than mine that I am the leader of a vanquished army in the face of my conqueror." This scene was repeated later in the presence of Mountbatten. It was Maunsell's opinion that Terauchi was fast approaching senility, and although he did his best to carry out the British instructions, he was continually undermined by his intelligence staff and the Kempei Tei, who created great problems with their anti-British and anti-French activities. Maunsell had believed that the Japanese could be controlled by very stringent orders, but later found that the British had underestimated the large number of them who were collaborating with the Viet Minh. It was not forgotten too that Terauchi had been accused of encouraging the harsh treatment of captives. When Terauchi came face to face with Gracey, it was again emphasized to him that he was personally held responsible for Japanese activities. Terauchi finished by asking about the ceremony in which he was to hand over his sword. He asked Gracey to tell Mountbatten that he wanted to hand over his special sword, which was in Tokyo, and not his "comparatively rough everyday sword", and expressed regret at being unable to go to Singapore to sign the instrument of surrender himself.

At this time Gracey told Mountbatten that it was essential to occupy the Thu Dau Mot/Bien Hoa/Lai Thieu area north of Saigon, in which the main body of Japanese forces would initially be concentrated. Gracey said he fully understood the "position vis-à-vis the French Administration". Slim approved this proposal but Gracey was not permitted to carry it out at that time.

On 17 September the 1st Gurkhas took over a second arms storage area from the Japanese, to be relieved in turn by the French — a pattern which was followed until the British left Indochina, for the Japanese would not cooperate directly with the French. Now with sole responsibility for guarding two substantial arms storage areas, the French began the process of rearming the ex-POWs of the colonial forces.[29] Also on

29. Gracey Papers, rebuttal to Headquarters SEAC report of the British occupation of Saigon, 3 Oct. 1946; also, Brigadier Taunton's report on operations of 80 Brigade.

that date there occurred the incident which probably did as much as any-thing to persuade Gracey to act against the Communist-led Committee for the South. Until then he had been fully occupied with his efforts to control the tens of thousands of heavily-armed Japanese with his few hundred soldiers; he remained powerless to stop the growing anarchy in a city for which, by Allied direction, he was personally responsible. Japanese intelligence staff were actively opposing him and abetting the Viet Minh, the French appeared to be about to confront him with a further problem, and to add to his existing worries, the Viet Minh now decided to call a general strike. Their decision proved to be a miscalculation of some magnitude, for hitherto Gracey had simply not had time to notice the Viet Minh, let alone take any steps against them. By putting the city at peril they forced him to drop everything and con-centrate on them. It was the first of many serious miscalculations for which the Viet Minh leader, Tran Van Giau, was eventually removed from office by the Central Committee in Hanoi.

The ensuing situation was described in part by F. S. V. Donnison, who wrote that on 17 September the Viet Minh proclaimed the establish-ment of the "Independent Government of Viet Nam" while claiming the right to govern all of Tonkin, Annam, and Cochinchina. As Donnison correctly noted, "In fact, however, the republic had at this time little or no authority and there was no effective civil administration, and no maintenance of order whatsoever." The French population was being attacked, and inflammatory broadcasts and press articles flowed from Hanoi and Saigon. Most important, "the Republic, whose govern-ment was Communist in character, [could not] count upon the mass of the Annamite people for these, nationalists though they may be, were by no means all supporters of Communism."[30] Commenting on Gracey's problems, Donnison pointed out that it was some time before Civil Affairs Staff officers arrived, that no financial adviser was attached to the Commission or the Allied Land Forces Commander's headquarters, and that "no political adviser became available until some ten days after the arrival of General Gracey." Mountbatten was later to criticize Gracey, but the Commission was the SACSEA Control Commission, and thus ultimately the responsibility of Mountbatten himself, including these serious staff omissions.

On the day of the general strike, the Viet Minh directed all Vietnamese to leave French employ and ordered markets to be closed to

30. F. S. V. Donnison, *British Military Administration in the Far East, 1943-1946* (London: HMSO, 1956).

the French from the next day. SEAC radio monitoring services had intercepted an English-language broadcast from Saigon Radio which
described three ways in which the Viet Minh could oppose the French
reoccupation. They could engage in ''(*a*) active resistance, (*b*) boycotting
the French population, (*c*) a general strike''. The second and third measures were now in effect. The Viet Minh attitude at this early stage was
already inflexible: ''They feel that any compromise now would be a
defeat. . . .'' At 2230 hours on 17 September, fifteen armed Viet Minh
police tried to enter the power house, but were turned away without
incident by the 1/19 Hybad platoon leader, Havildar Kan Singh. The
next day, the workers in the power house stopped work for two hours,
saying that they were afraid of being beaten by the Viet Minh for possessing French passes. They were then offered British passes, but still feared
retribution. The matter was resolved and protection was guaranteed
after a meeting between the manager and the workers' leader.

With the Viet Minh attempting to strangle the city, the airport and
the port of Saigon now took on an even greater importance. The
Brigadier in charge of movements and transportation wrote: ''The local
political situation is of interest as it may become a factor affecting work
in the port. At the present, public services appear to be in the hands of the
Viet Nam party, a puppet government established by the Japanese.'' The
party demanded independence and was ''violently anti-French''. With
Cédile's approval, a meeting was held between the Brigadier, the Royal
Navy Commander and Viet Minh party officials. The Viet Minh leader
said that he was willing to restore all port facilities and operate under
British direction alone. A Port Sub-Committee was formed, which
included two Viet Minh officials, and the plan worked. The British
senior officer reported: ''If promises are kept, the civil [Vietnamese]
authorities will be responsible for such matters as labour, lighting,
cranes, machinery and pilots. Detailed planning has started and at the
present time there seems a reasonable hope of success but the situation
may well become complicated when French civilian authorities become
available to take over. . . .''[31]

The British were perfectly content to collaborate in the docks with the
Viet Minh provided that common goals were met, and entertained no
particular preference for the French, whose arrival, everyone knew,
would signal the start of trouble. But although these local accommoda-

---

31. PRO, WO 203/4020, Saigon Control Commission, Progress Report no. 1 to
    Headquarters SACSEA, 18 Sept. 1945.

tions with the Viet Minh were made, they contravened the Allied charter which forbade official contacts with such groups — it was expressly laid down that all civil administration was to be French only. Yet many years later, when the British officers concerned had retired from active service, not one of them, from Chief of Staff to company commander, expressed any anti-Viet Minh or pro-French sentiments. In fact most had favored Vietnamese independence. Even when the British/Indian troops were fighting the Viet Minh, the feeling was more of professionals having to do a job than anything else. Major C. U. Blascheck, commanding D company, 3/1 GR, said later: "We had no antagonism towards the Viet Minh on our arrival. We knew that independence was coming for India, and thought that the Vietnamese should also have their independence — and we were all largely sympathetic to them." (In the early days, Blascheck had come across a Viet Minh military recruiter and, as requested, joined him in a spot assessment of potential recruits lined up in the street.) Anger occurred in isolated cases of torture and mutilation of Indian soldiers or where cases of mutilation of French women and children were found.

Meanwhile, the fly-in continued — intermittently because of atrocious weather. On 18 September, in view of the worsening local situation, 1/1 GR relieved the Japanese guarding the Majestic and Continental Hotels (where most of the Mission staff lived). By that afternoon, General Gracey and the Control Commission had spent five full days in Saigon (see Appendix B, pages 164-6).

## APPENDIX A

Douglas D. Gracey was born in Gorakhpur, India, in 1894, the son of an Indian Civil Service officer. He attended Sandhurst and in 1914 was commissioned in the Indian Army. In 1915 he saw action with the Royal Munster Fusiliers, and in 1916 joined the 1st Battalion, the 1st King George's Own Gurkha Rifles, beginning a lifelong association with the Gurkha regiments. (Three decades later this battalion, 1/1 GR, accompanied him to Saigon.) Gracey was wounded during World War I, received the Military Cross and bar, and was mentioned in despatches. Over the years he held a series of appointments in the Middle East (including Palestine and Persia) and India, and in 1942 was given the task of raising the 20th Indian Division. It turned out to be one of the premier units of 14th Army, being instilled with Gracey's own spirit and reflecting the special personal interest he took in the welfare of his troops.

Gracey spoke fluent Gorkhali and could converse in the various tongues of his Division. On one memorable occasion he turned a tongue-lashing into a cheer when at the front he came across some soldiers who had not made an effort to dig in against Japanese artillery. After forcefully pointing out the effects of artillery on exposed infantry, he immediately asked them if they knew how much he cared for the safety of his soldiers and their families at home. He never had to do this again. During the course of the war Gracey developed a hatred for the Japanese primarily because of their inhumane treatment of captives and civilians. He had said on more than one occasion that it was not hard to be a great commander if the acceptance of unlimited casualties was of little importance. He told his company and platoon commanders to be intimately familiar with the problems and situations of their men: their villages; their wives, parents, uncles and aunts; who had just died, and so on. In this way the Division would be more than just an efficient fighting formation; it would be a happy family. Slim, another Gurkha officer, rated the 20th Division as one of the best (if not the best) divisions in the 14th Army.

Brigadier Woodford, former Commander of 32 Brigade, wrote a typical description of the man:

> What sort of man was Douglas Gracey? My answer is inevitably coloured by my personal regard and affection for him. Before I took command of 32 Brigade, I was his G. 1 [Chief of Staff] on HQ 20 Indian Division from the beginning of our offensive in the fall of 1944 up to the crossing of the Irrawaddy. Consequently I was in daily contact with him and got to know him very well indeed.
>
> I have never served a better commander. He was clear-thinking and decisive and, in my opinion, had an exceptional understanding of the workings of the minds of the Japanese Divisional Commanders against whom he was fighting.
>
> He had raised, trained and led 20 Div. himself and made it into the fine fighting formation it was. . . . He was personally known to every officer and man in the Division and I believe that his personality, his constant concern for his men and their trust in him were responsible for the exceptional standard of discipline and efficiency it always maintained. He was not a publicity seeker and I think he may have hampered his chances of more rapid promotion by his plain speaking to some of the higher-ups if the interests of his troops were likely to be overlooked [this view was shared by Brigadier Taunton of 80 Brigade]. For this we were truly thankful because no other Commander could have taken his place in our hearts. (Letter to the author, 9 August 1973.)

Major P. G. Malins, late Royal Indian Army Service Corps, wrote the following in 1981:

Although Douglas Gracey and 20 Indian Division which he commanded were in French Indo China for less than five months, because of all that happened afterwards culminating in the complete takeover by the Viet Minh 30 years later, a vast literature has since appeared, seeking to trace events back to those days. Few of those who have written about that period . . . ever knew Douglas Gracey.

He has been portrayed by many left-wing writers as an imperialist putting down an independence struggle. Nothing could be further from the truth. . . .

My first sight of Gracey was standing on a little hill at Palel outside Imphal, as I arrived to join the Division. I saluted him, and although he did not know me he saluted with a warmth and a smile that made me feel instantly wonderfully welcome. He was like that to everyone in the Division right up until he died in 1964. . . .

In Burma Gracey acted as though he was personally responsible for the lives of every single man under his command, and never forgot the slaughter he had seen on the Somme. He constantly emphasized to everyone as we led the advance to Rangoon on the right flank that while casualties were inevitable, "men are the most precious thing we've got — use them with the greatest care. . . ."

He had a very clear mind, an ability to grasp detail rapidly, to get to the essential factors and to make decisions quickly without equivocation, and to provide clear-cut orders for their implementation. He was a splendid communicator verbally and on paper, quick in speech, thought and discussion. While not suffering fools gladly he was equally a good listener who did not suborn his subordinates and allowed us full scope to put over our views. His decisions were invariably the right ones . . .

The result was that we all had total confidence in Gracey and morale could not have been higher . . . We called the brief divisional history 'A Happy Family' and it truly was, with Gracey a much loved and revered father figure to us all. . . .

In my opinion he was an ideal man for the very difficult situation which faced us in French Indochina. He was totally competent professionally, he had a great concern for human life and was the antithesis of the pugnacious, blockhead type of commander. He had a very great regard for Eastern peoples through his long service with the Indian Army, and had direct experience with the Indiansation of the Army and of Indian aspirations for independence. . . . He did not believe he had special political sagacity and recognised that while he had to make decisions these must be based on good advice from political specialists. He was a Conservative of the old school, and while he was slower to share the views of us younger men who were impatient to see independence for India and other colonial territories, he recognized this as inevitable. . . .

Gracey was not in a position to make a personal judgment on whether or not to recognize any government but the French in accordance with the directives he had been given. Had he allowed the Annamites to continue to occupy public buildings in Saigon and to put themselves forward as a provisional government he would have acted in direct contravention of the instructions he had received from Mountbatten based on the decisions agreed by the Allied powers.

Gracey was awarded the CBE for his part in the Imphal battle and the CB for the taking of Mandalay, Rangoon and the Irrawaddy crossing. At the particular request of Pakistan, he became the first Commander-in-Chief of that country's Army at independence, and on his retirement in 1951 was showered with letters from his former soldiers, one of whom wrote: "You are going much against the wishes of thousands of soldiers whom you so dearly loved and patronized like your own kith and kin. From the hearts of my heart I reveal this once again that I shall miss you most." Thereafter he did exemplary work as Chairman of the Royal Hospital and Home for Incurables in Putney, West London, where after his death from a sudden heart attack in 1964 a grateful Pakistan built a Gracey Memorial Pavilion in his honor. The first military hospital built in independent Pakistan was also named after him.


# APPENDIX B

In October 1946, by then a Lieutenant-General and engaged in building the Pakistan Army prior to Partition, Gracey responded to the official South East Asia Command (i.e. Mountbatten's) version of the occupation of Saigon, which appeared to hold him responsible for every difficult situation and to praise Mountbatten for every success. This official report possibly formed the basis for Mountbatten's Section "E" report to the Combined Chiefs, which has been used by historians ever since in writing of these events.

Gracey was not a man to go quietly to the block. In his rebuttal he pointed out obvious errors (e.g. the confusing of Saigon with Surabaya) and attacked what he considered gross distortions, innocent or fabricated. Because what he wrote is little known, despite its importance, and because of the personal criticism leveled at Gracey by some well-known historians, much of it is included here. This complements the "Report of the Saigon Control Commission", the "History of 20th Indian Division," and "Build-Up of 80 Indian Infantry Brigade" (written by Brigadier Taunton and his staff).

Gracey's rebuttal to the proposed SEAC history ran as follows:

1. The chapter on FIC gives a false impression of the situation and of events. There are many inaccuracies and chronology is incorrect . . .

2. *The Story*

Shortly after VJ day General Gracey was summoned to Kandy, where the situation was discussed in conference with SAC and General Slim and their

Staffs. Two directives were issued, one by SEAC dealing with the evacuation of prisoners of war, the control of the Japanese Southern Army HQ located at Saigon, and the disarmament and concentration of Japanese forces in Southern FIC, and the other by ALFSEA dealing with the action of the troops to carry out the above. This latter specifically stated that General Gracey was to keep law and order in FIC south of the 16 degrees parallel. He was to command all the Allied troops in FIC and he was given to understand that he would have the whole of his 20th Division to carry out his tasks . . .

Commenting on his pre-departure knowledge of the Saigon situation, Gracey stated:

3. It was known at the time that an Annamite government was in power, put there by the Japanese [Gracey also knew that it was Communist-led] . . . 4. . . . the Japanese commander was ordered to maintain law and order, to ensure the safety of all French and other nationals, to stop handing over arms to the Annamite forces, and not to recognize the Annamite government, which, in accordance with general Allied policy, being a Japanese-sponsored government, was not recognized by the Allies.

Gracey then traced the evidence of anarchy in Saigon:

5. It was evident at the time that the situation was very tense in FIC, particularly in Saigon, and that the Annamite and Communist Chinese press was inciting the Annamite troops, police and government supporters to acts of violence against all other nationalities who did not support the puppet government, particularly against the many French people and loyal Annamites.
6. A serious riot, in which several French civilians were killed by Annamite police and armed forces, took place on September 2nd, and was only stopped from assuming very serious proportions by the very courageous action of various released British and Australian prisoners of war who were unarmed, and the few RAPWI officers who had already been flown in. [This was apparently surreptitious, for we have found no documentation for this. Terauchi, on 5 September, did report negotiating with a Major Pias about the condition of the POWs.] In the outlying districts, similar demonstrations, accompanied by unpleasant incidents, took place.
It was clear that the Annamite puppet government, vociferous on paper as regards democratic and even communistic plans for the future, was quite incapable of keeping law and order. It was also clear that there was a very large hooligan element out to make mischief, many of whom were criminals of the worst type, who had been let out of jail in March 1945, and many of whom were in possession of arms. It later became clear that this criminal element largely composed the Annamite government army. (Gracey Papers, rebuttal to Headquarters SEAC report of the British occupation of Saigon, 3 October 1946.)

Gracey's pre-departure information was further described by a former member of Force 136 who accompanied the Commission to Saigon. This was, roughly, as follows: "Saigon was in a state of anarchy, with no group solidly in control. . . . After Gracey's arrival it was by no means certain that the Viet Minh had the support of the population, and intelligence reconnaissance sorties through Saigon confirmed this. People in outlying villages were angered by Viet Minh terror tactics which included impaling nonconformists on stakes, and so on." (Lt.-Col. the Hon. Hugh Astor, personal interview, 26 June 1977.)

# 7

# CRACKDOWN

On 19 September, 4/17 Dogra began the move to Saigon, and echoing a theme common throughout the 20th Division and RAF personnel, the Dogra chronicler wrote: "It seemed strange at first to have to depend on Jap drivers and Jap MT until our own arrived, but we got used to it, and the Japs' discipline was excellent."

The first of Gracey's airborne punch arrived on 19 September, the Spitfires of 273 Squadron. The squadron had been looking forward to the move to Saigon: "Morale is boosted once more owing to the squadron moving . . ., this time into liberated territory. . . ." On 11 September, ten Spitfires left their home base at Mingaladon for Bangkok, where they had a delightful stay. On 19 September, the 273 Squadron log continued: "The planes left Bangkok today with the pilots in high spirits, hoping Saigon lived up to its name, 'Paris of the East'." Then, echoing the familiar shock, "Everyone a little dazed with having Japanese chauffeurs and guards, the Japanese being fully armed."

At the Supreme Allied Commander's 80th staff meeting of 19 September, it was stated that Headquarters SACSEA had received copies of monitored broadcasts from Saigon and Hanoi. These repeated the text of Gracey's proclamation. The "so-called Viet Nam Government" had made the broadcasts, and Mountbatten ordered Gracey to seize Saigon Radio from the Viet Minh immediately and to begin censoring all broadcasts, this despite his strictures to Gracey to avoid interfering in local affairs. Dening addressed the assembled officers and spoke, for the record, of the wider political implications of the problems in French Indochina:

"The Supreme Allied Commander said that he wished to reiterate, for the sake of Press guidance, the intention of British policy in FIC. The object of HM Government, in sending British troops into FIC, was fourfold — to control Field-Marshal Terauchi's headquarters, which commanded the Japanese Armies in the Southern Regions; to disarm the Japanese; to release and repatriate Allied prisoners-of-war and internees; and to maintain law and order until the arrival of French forces. He stressed that HM Government had no intention of using British forces in FIC to crush resistance movements."

Hugh Astor had earlier spoken to Tran Van Giau about curbing the inflammatory rhetoric being broadcast over Saigon Radio, to no avail. When he accompanied the troops who finally dislodged the Viet Minh from the radio station, it suddenly occurred to the British that it was no good without the transmitter, which was some distance away, so they made a hectic dash and seized it before it could be sabotaged.[1]

Gracey now had temporarily to suspend his other activities to deal as a matter of urgency with the Viet Minh, who had interposed themselves between him and his task of disarming and concentrating the Japanese. It is not difficult to understand why the Viet Minh decided to force the issue within a week of the British arrival. Seventy thousand Japanese constituted an excellent diversion from their activities; of course their presence also added confusion to the local scene, especially since many Japanese were aiding, training, and even leading Viet Minh forces. Once the Japanese had been concentrated and repatriated, the Viet Minh would become more exposed, and would lose a source of arms. With the passage of time the French would return in greater strength, lessening the chances of a successful Viet Minh seizure of power. The optimum time for the Viet Minh challenge was obviously while both British and French forces were far weaker than they were themselves, and while the Japanese were still present in strength. But Gracey adopted a course of action which the Viet Minh had probably discounted: he applied pressure on the Japanese to control the situation until the Anglo-French forces became strong enough to take over.

The Viet Minh did not confine themselves to inciting the general population; they now attempted to subvert Gracey's own soldiers. Their propaganda leaflets were left in British/Indian troop areas and quarters, and Vietnamese made propaganda through personal contacts. One leaflet, an "Appeal to the Indian Officers and Soldiers among the British troops", said in part that both Indians and Vietnamese were fighting for freedom, and another called the Indians "heroic sons of Gandhi".[2] This attempt to turn the Indians against the British proved ineffective for one obvious reason: there was hardly a single Indian soldier who did not know that negotiations were well under way to grant Indian independence. And the fact that the Indian Army was an all-volunteer, professional army made them less susceptible to subversion anyway.

Gracey reported the events in a telegram to Mountbatten, the subject of which was the "Internal Political Situation in FIC with special refer-

1. Hon. Hugh Astor, personal interview, 26 June 1976.
2. Gracey Papers.

ence to Annam''. He said that on his arrival on the 13th he had interviewed Colonel Cédile, General Leclerc's representative, who had traced
the recent history of the area, including the abdication of Bao Dai and the
Saigon riot of 2 September. The Annamite Government's control was in
name only, no legal writ was in evidence, and pillaging and looting were
increasing. Gracey wrote that after having personally examined the
situation for six days he decided that ''although the situation was not
serious, the Annamite Government constituted a direct threat to law and
order through its Armed Police Gendarmerie and Armed Garde Civile.''
Furthermore, the Vietnamese press were daily becoming more violently
anti-French, and Vietnamese propaganda was ''aimed at subverting
British troops against the French.''[3]

Gracey now moved to exert his influence by announcing to all factions
that he was freezing the situation. He would clamp down on the press, as
the newspapers were inciting disorder, and order the Viet Minh leader
Tran Van Giau to stop requisitioning buildings, return appropriated property, hold his forces in place, and furnish a list of Viet Minh armed
police and militia. He was also to be given a copy of the proclamation
Gracey intended to issue two days later, on the 21st. The three figures
responsible for the proclamation were Gracey, Brigadier Hirst (the division's Artillery commander who ran the 20th Division for Gracey) and
Maunsell.[4] It was, according to Maunsell, formulated in a period of

---

3. Maj.-Gen. S. Woodburn Kirby *et al.*, *The War Against Japan*, vol. V: *The Surrender
of Japan* (London: HMSO, 1969), p. 229.
4. The proclamation itself was as follows:
   1. With the unconditional surrender to the Allied Nations by all Japanese Forces
   signed in the name of the Emperor of Japan at Tokyo on 2nd September, 1945, the
   Supreme Allied Commander of all Allied Forces in South-East Asia Command,
   Admiral Lord Louis Mountbatten, GCVO, KCB, DSO has delegated to me,
   General D. D. Gracey, CB, CBE, MC the command of all British, French and
   Japanese forces and all police forces and armed bodies in French Indo-China south of
   16 latitude with orders to ensure law and order in this area.
   2. Let it be known to all that it is my firm intention to ensure with strict impartiality that this period of transition from war to peace conditions is carried out peace-
   ably with the minimum dislocation to all public and utility services, legitimate
   businesses and trade and with the least interference with the normal peaceful activities and vocations of the people.
   3. I call on all citizens in the name of the Supreme Allied Commander to cooperate
   to the fullest extent to achieve the above object and hereby warn all wrongdoers,
   especially looters and saboteurs of public and private property and those also carrying out similar criminal activities, that they will be summarily shot.
   4. The following orders will come into immediate effect.

increasing disorder and tension; part of it was actually written by him, and part by the intelligence officer on the Commission. It was evident to them that the Viet Minh were set to challenge the Allies for control of Saigon. These three officers discussed the situation well into the night, and decided that time was running out for them and that they must act immediately. Ironically, Gracey acted for precisely the same reason that the Viet Minh did, for he thought that if he delayed, the Allies would be outdistanced by both factions, the Viet Minh and the Japanese. The latter were by then already wondering whether the British really did exercise control, and indeed a major concern of the three was the question of what the Japanese were thinking.[5]

> (A) No demonstrations or processions will be permitted.
> (B) No public meetings will take place.
> (C) No arms of any description, including sticks, staves, bamboo spears, etc., will be carried except by British and Allied troops and such other forces and police which have been specially authorized by me.
> (D) The curfew already imposed on my orders by the Japanese authorities between 2130 and 0530 repetition 0530 hours in Saigon and Cholon will be continued and strictly enforced.

"The Proclamation given above is being thoroughly bill-posted in all languages on 21 September throughout Saigon and Cholon under Japanese arrangements," wrote Gracey to Mountbatten. Great Britain, Public Record Office, WO 172/1784, Gracey to Mountbatten, 20 Sept. 1945.

5. In a personal interview on 20 April 1977, Brigadier Maunsell said: "We were terribly thin on the ground. They [the Japanese] still had their arms — we still hadn't disarmed them. They still had their ammunition — they still had access to it. We still distrusted every action the Japanese took. We talked at times as to whether there was any likelihood of a sort of kamikaze aspect. There we were — we'd been there for days, we appeared to be losing control, nobody appeared to be very excited by our arrival — mostly because they realized we had no teeth, no real teeth, and if one's going to be really honest, I believe that it was for two reasons: one was that we felt we had got to act, and number two, we felt (which is understandable if you've just finished a war) that it was well within our terms of reference to act on that basis, because we felt it was ninety-nine and nine-tenths to do with law and order."

Maunsell remembered the occasion well: "Douglas Gracey felt very strongly about this aspect of his responsibilities, for he felt that unless the country was pacified, and quickly, none of his other tasks could be successfully accomplished. But most of all, he felt that under the terms of his original directives he'd been given tasks to do, which must be done, and this was an essential preliminary to doing any of them and within his terms of reference." At 3 a.m. Gracey padded into Maunsell's room and awakened him. Gracey said, "I've been thinking, we haven't time." They discussed it again, and decided to act. Maunsell stated one more reason why Gracey acted: "Throughout all this Gracey was thinking that he must make certain that whatever action he took would support, would buttress, would under-

Brigadier Maunsell was delegated by Gracey to give Tran Van Giau a copy of the proclamation which would be published on the 21st. So on 19 September he ordered Terauchi's car and drove up to the front of the *Hôtel de Ville*, which was still occupied and guarded by the Viet Minh and the Committee for the South. It was a short drive, since Gracey's residence was next door and he had only to drive around the block. A rumor had spread that something important was afoot, perhaps initiated by senior French officials, for as Maunsell drove around the *Hôtel de Ville* he was cheered by crowds of Frenchmen. Proclamation in hand, Maunsell ascended the steps and entered the building for the first time, and then paused in complete astonishment at the scene which confronted him. As far as the eye could see, there were scattered groups of totally unconcerned Vietnamese around their cooking pots, which were bubbling over open flames and exuding thick smoke and pungent aromas. Half-naked urchins tumbled about the floor. The City Hall was little more than a squatter's haven. As Maunsell said later, it was not quite what he had expected from the Provisional Government of South Vietnam. He asked at random where the Government was located, or where its head could be found. No one spoke English, so he picked his way around and asked in French. Finally, someone nonchalantly pointed upwards; Maunsell walked upstairs, followed by another officer, wondering whether he was wise to do so. A number of rooms led from the landing, some with doors closed. The absence of any signs of authority or organization was complete. .

One door was, somewhat conspicuously, shut tight, and Maunsell thought that if anything was going on, this was where it would be. So he advanced, opened it, and discovered a meeting in progress. One man lay on a sofa, some were sitting at a table, another man stood looking out of the window. Half of them did not appear to be taking any interest in what was going on in the room. But one man got up immediately — Tran Van Giau. He blinked furiously in his agitation at being confronted by a British officer in uniform, having been given no official warning of the visit. Maunsell announced, ''I come in the name of General Douglas Gracey,'' and asked Tran Van Giau in French if he understood. He then handed Tran Van Giau the proclamation, bowed to him and the assembled company, ''who had so far evinced not the slightest interest in the entire proceedings,'' and departed.

pin, would excite the body of support for the French that we were told on hand was there.''

Maunsell could not believe that the group he had seen were in real control. He was "ready to believe that they possibly had pockets of control, or that they were in touch with various elements or groups." But atrocities were being all too frequently committed, and the photographs seen by the Commission staff were chilling. In retrospect Maunsell was not prepared to say whether or not the Committee for the South were responsible for these acts, or agreed or disagreed with them, but he was certain they had little knowledge or control of what was really going on. This was his feeling in all subsequent dealings with the Viet Minh, and his lasting impression of them: "Good talkers, quite attractive men from an intellectual point of view; but of those that I met, I would not have thought that executive control was ever going to be their strong suit."

Gracey's proclamation was made public on 21 September. The curfew announced in it was meant to go into effect immediately, but the problem arose as to how it should be enforced and policed. The British had only two battalions, the French were of little real use, and at this moment there were no plans to use the Japanese in a fighting role; Gracey was "trying desperately not to fall into the trap of using them, for severe criticism would follow."[6] On the night of the 21st, Maunsell sent two intelligence officers, including the head of the Control Commission's intelligence staff, with a small bodyguard, to go twice around Saigon and Cholon during the curfew and report on its observance. The reconnaissance party reported back that the curfew was not being observed, especially by the Japanese. The Cholon dance halls and night "establishments" were operating at full blast, and numbers of Japanese soldiers were frequenting these places. That same night a drunken Japanese soldier hit a French officer, which added to the problems. Furthermore, neither the Viet Minh police nor the French population were paying any attention to the curfew. The next day Gracey and Maunsell talked about it. If there was a curfew and the British were unable to enforce it, they would look very silly.

Several members of his staff were pressing Gracey to use the Japanese troops, but he resisted it "step by step, hour by hour". Maunsell clearly remembered Gracey's hatred of the Japanese, and his feeling that if he rearmed them this would be seen as weakness on his part. There was one way by which the need for large-scale Japanese rearmament might be avoided, and that was to speed up the establishment of effective French control over the city. But eventually the use of the Japanese became unavoidable, and Maunsell remembered some nights when he and

6. *Ibid.*

Gracey wondered if they would live to see the morning. Although both had seen a lot of war, street fighting was new to them, and the nightly sounds of mortars and small arms were magnified in the city.

Gracey had no illusions as to what Mountbatten's reaction would be. In telegraphing the Supreme Allied Commander he said that despite appearances he had acted "only in the interest of the maintenance of law and order" after consulting the senior French representatives. To have employed the Japanese or French would have exacerbated the situation. He wrote that the Japanese would have allowed "a considerable number of wanted Annamites" to disappear, while using the French "would have precipitated bloodshed; further, there were not enough French troops available.[7] Mountbatten, in his reply to this telegram, told Gracey that his proclamation was contrary to ALFSEA'S directive, but since the 20 Division Commander was "the man on the spot", the SAC would support him. But he made it clear that only Japanese and French and not British/Indian troops were to be used to enforce his orders outside the key areas. Any French request for British help outside key areas was to be referred to HMG through Mountbatten. Mountbatten later wrote that while he appreciated the gravity of the military situation in Saigon, he felt that Gracey had exceeded his authority in addressing his proclamation to all of Southern Indochina and not just the key points. Since such a proclamation might have been taken as government policy, "I warned Major-General Gracey that he should take care to confine operations of British/Indian troops to those limited tasks which he had been set."[8]

However, Gracey could not wash his hands of the kidnappings and murders of civilians outside his key areas — and, as we have seen,

---

7. PRO, WO 203/4273, Gracey to Mountbatten, 23 Sept. 1945.
8. Vice-Adm. the Earl Mountbatten of Burma, *Post Surrender Tasks*, Section E of the Report to the Combined Chiefs of Staff (London: HMSO, 1969), p. 287. It is said that the Supreme Allied Commander had reacted angrily to this action by Gracey, although Mountbatten's response is presented far more smoothly in his report to the Combined Chiefs. There was nothing essentially wrong with this sort of proclamation, and it was the accepted thing to do in areas of Allied occupation. Evans in Bangkok and Hawthorn in the NEI had done exactly the same thing. The controversy arose over the wording of the first paragraph, which implied that Gracey was empowered to keep law and order in all of French Indochina south of 16° north latitude. That would have been true but for the amendment of 12 September, which limited his responsibility for law and order to key areas only. But as will be seen, there is doubt as to whether Gracey had actually received this amendment before 25 September, at which time Evans in Bangkok and Gracey in Saigon were both restricted to key areas and told to refer questions of extra-perimeter public order to SACSEA.

Mountbatten's instructions to Gracey were not crystal-clear. Having registered his displeasure, the SAC then said that he approved of Gracey's proposed military measures: making Terauchi personally accountable for Japanese behavior, clearing the approaches to Saigon, and extending and consolidating his perimeter. Mountbatten reported that after consulting Generals Slim and Leclerc, and in view of the situation in Saigon, "I telegraphed to the Chiefs of Staff on the 24th September that I considered that Major-General Gracey, in issuing his proclamation, had acted with courage and determination in an extremely difficult situation." If "the riots he feared had developed," his small force and the French population might well have been in grave danger. Gracey was in a dangerous situation, and there is no doubt that, had he waited for the trouble to erupt before acting, he would have been more severely criticized and there would have been casualties on both sides. At that moment it was only a battle of words and wills. But Mountbatten touched on the fundamental problem: "I was told that French forces, with Civil officials, would be responsible for the administration of the country, Civil administration being carried out by the French even in the key areas in which my forces would be operating."

The Viet Minh chose to meet Gracey's attempt to assert his authority by challenging him head-on; they immediately called for a complete strike. Gracey reported this to Mountbatten and said that he did not expect armed resistance, that there were alternative sources of labor (notably the Japanese), and that many workers would resume work when the threat of victimization by the Viet Minh was removed. The Viet Minh, although calling for an intensified strike, sent a letter to Gracey. The "Executive Committee of Southern Viet-Nam Republic" stated that it was doing "its best to make the population accept your decisions" in order to give the country "an example of calmness and dignity" while cooperating with the British forces. However, they wanted to draw Gracey's attention to some of the more unpopular measures, notably the crackdown on newspapers, which they declared "will be a serious handicap for the Government regarding the control of public opinion." (The "control of public opinion" by the Viet Minh press was precisely why, among other reasons, Gracey had acted against them.) They declined responsibility for future incidents, and again asked Gracey to lift the newspaper suspension so that "we shall be in a measure to control all rumours which are being spread in Saigon." Gracey considered this a "definite climb-down from previous utterances", and commended the Viet Minh for their "prompt obedience" to his orders, "which has shown me that wise counsels have prevailed." Acknowledging the effect of his newspaper suspension on the public, he said he was "now willing to receive application for the renewal of publication of all papers that are owned by men of integrity and high repute." He had already directed that a close look be taken at how Radio Saigon could serve the "best interests of the country".

Earlier as Maunsell was delivering the proclamation to Tran Van Giau, the Control Commission's senior intelligence officer wrote to Major-General Penney, Director of Intelligence at SEAC, calling his attention to the Commission's lack of expert guidance on political, financial and Civil Affairs matters. On 19 September Gracey had telegraphed directly to Mountbatten: "The deficiency from my staff of 2 CAS [Civil Affairs Staff] officers and one Foreign Office representative is becoming increasingly serious. Advice on political problems is essential and I would therefore be most grateful for arrival these officers urgently."[9] The complaint of the Commission's intelligence officer was discussed in Kandy, and Mountbatten responded by hastening the departure to Saigon of Harry Brain (later Sir Norman Brain) of his Political Affairs Staff; he also asked the War Office in London to speed up the assignment of two Civil Affairs officers to SEAC. Dening sent his own assessment to the Foreign Office: "A situation is arising which is even more serious than I had contemplated since objection is being taken at the very outset to the presence of British troops as supporting French Imperialism." He thought it likely that both the Japanese and Chinese were behind the various revolutionary movements in Indochina, and felt that the British could not escape their duty of liquidating the Japanese headquarters and evacuating the Allied POWs and internees.

Dening then, apparently independently, arrived at the same conclusion as Gracey and his senior officers in Saigon when he wrote: "That objective can only be attained if law and order are maintained in areas occupied by British forces." Furthermore, "unless the population of the areas concerned are willing to maintain law and order themselves, steps may have to be taken to enforce it, but in that case the populations concerned will themselves be responsible for such action as may be necessary." Dening concluded: "I fear, however, our forces are going to have a difficult time and will require all the support HMG can give them . . ."[10] This message, sent on 20 September, was probably written on the 19th as Gracey was preparing to do just what Dening thought must

9. PRO, WO 203/4932, Gracey to Mountbatten, 19 Sept. 1945.
10. PRO, WO 203/5644, Dening to Foreign Office, Tel. No. 506, 20 Sept. 1945.

happen if they were to get anything done. It is interesting to note that the senior Foreign Office representatives appear to have been consistently closer to Gracey's thinking in these problems than Mountbatten. The most senior military officers,· Mountbatten excepted, also consistently backed Gracey, as will be seen.

Mountbatten told the Chiefs that Gracey's proclamation left him with two possible courses of action: to give Gracey his full support and assume responsibility for administration throughout the whole of southern French Indochina, or to restrict the area of his responsibility to the control of the Japanese Supreme Headquarters only. The latter option represented the narrowest possible interpretation of the Chiefs of Staff direction. Mountbatten emphasized that the first option, which he called Course A, would require a full division to implement until the French were ready to take over. He also thought that it exceeded his instructions. Course B required Leclerc to reaffirm the proclamation, which in Mountbatten's opinion would be dangerous to revoke. Leclerc was willing to do this, but only after the arrival of the 9th DIC. Mountbatten recommended the adoption of Course B, which meant that the senior French officer would have to be instructed by the French Government to exercise civil and military control outside the key areas. Course A would also entail SACSEA controlling all French forces and Civil Affairs until Leclerc should assume that responsibility. Mountbatten told the Chiefs that Leclerc had "expressed his warm appreciation of what Gracey had done." Leclerc thought that French forces under SEAC control could operate outside the key areas. Mountbatten anticipated general unrest in Indochina, but did not see how he could divest himself of the "responsibility for the maintenance of law and order which is a normal military responsibility of a Commander".[11]

While Mountbatten admonished Gracey over the proclamation, he himself posed the same questions to the Chiefs of Staff, saying "In fact we cannot have it both ways." Either South Indochina was within SEAC's area, or it was not. And if not, Mountbatten's boundary "must be redrawn to exclude it," placing on France the full responsibility for law and order, the wellbeing of the ex-POWs, disarming of the Japanese, and apprehension of war criminals. That was precisely what Leclerc was pondering aloud. In a telegram to the French Government he asked how, if Gracey were to be restricted to Saigon only, the British could control, disarm and concentrate the Japanese, most of whom were

---

11. PRO, WO 172/1784, SACSEA to Cabinet, 24 Sept. 1945.

scattered throughout South Indochina. Again under Course B, Mount-batten seemed to think that the Chiefs were hinting that he should stop the build-up in Indochina, but Leclerc protested vigorously that the plan called for a division (the 20th Indian) and it would be dangerous now to renege on this. Leclerc discussed the situation in a telegram to the French Minister of War. He reported that Gracey's proclamation was "very important in Mountbatten's eyes in light of restricted instructions received from London. These new instructions were badly defined . . ." Said Leclerc: "I declared that General Gracey had in my opinion taken the best possible measures in the circumstances because if he had shown any weakness the situation might have become critical."[12]

Mountbatten, speaking officially, had requested that Leclerc suggest to the French Government that a "precise and detailed declaration" be made promising independence and dominion status to Indochina. Leclerc wrote that in the SAC's view this declaration ("taking into account the important differences between British Imperial aims and local conditions in Indo-China") would have two positive effects: it would stop the fighting, since independence would have been promised; and it would have a "beneficial effect on English opinion especially and on the American attitude". The last phrase was significant. Gracey's strong stand had set off vociferous left-wing complaints in the press.

The proclamation thus generated a great deal of controversy, and much was said and written about it, for and against. Everyone but Gracey, it seemed, had something to say about it. But Gracey *did* express himself on the subject in his long-buried, little-known rebuttal to Mountbatten's scribes at SEAC headquarters which provides insight into his predicament and, more important, challenges the published allegations that he was an unfeeling blimp who disobeyed orders and did all he could to resurrect the colonial system. It now appears that Gracey had never received the ALFSEA amendment which limited his responsibility for law and order to the key areas of Saigon, despite Slim's visit to the city, and there are indications that some of the SEAC staff deliberately sought to make a scapegoat of him, influenced perhaps by loyalty to Mountbatten and Mountbatten's concept of his place in history.

Gracey objected strongly to the SEAC staff's version of events covering the period of the proclamation. In October 1946 he wrote to the SEAC Recorder that the SEAC version "is *not* in chronological order,

---

12. PRO, FO 371/46308, Leclerc to Minister of War, repeated SACSEA to Cabinet, 24 Sept. 1945.

and gives the impression that the Allied commander was insubordinate and irresponsible.'' He added: ''It is absolutely untrue to say that 'the proclamation covered the whole of FIC' [It referred, of course, only to *southern* FIC, Gracey's area of responsibility]. It is not correct to talk about key areas at this stage. This is most misleading. The question arose later.''[13] The SEAC report apparently went further, for Gracey correctly denied threatening to use '' 'all the weapons at my disposal.' This I did much later in a pamphlet dropped over certain Annamite rebel forces, when it was absolutely necessary to do so, to prevent unnecessary bloodshed.'' Gracey tore into the SEAC report: ''Surely, the Recorder is confusing the operations in FIC with those in Sourabaya! [scene of some of the worst street fighting in the Netherlands East Indies] The proclamation could under no circumstances have been interpreted as coming from 'the sovereign government of a state' as the Allied commander clearly stated what his forces were in the country to do.'' It is not mentioned in any of the SAC's reports that Sir Alan Brooke, Chief of the Imperial General Staff and thus Mountbatten's superior, fully backed Gracey in this affair. In the same document Gracey wrote: ''It was obvious to all in Saigon at the time — and the later acceptance by the COS [Chiefs of Staff] in their COSSEA 366 of the measures taken confirm this view, coupled with what Lord Alanbrooke himself said to me personally — that the proclamation was essential in the form and at the time of its publication.'' (Lord Alanbrooke met Gracey during his visit to the Far East in December 1945.) Brigadier Maunsell later confirmed that all three senior officers in the Allied Command agreed that issuing the proclamation was well within their terms of reference.[14]

13. Gracey Papers, Correspondence with SEAC Recorder, 3 Oct. 1946. Gracey appears to refer to Telegram NGS, 106 (WO 172/1784, Mountbatten to Gracey, 24 Sept. 1945).
14. Brig. M. S. K. Maunsell, in a personal interview on 20 April 1977, said: ''Gracey would never knowingly embarrass Mountbatten or His Majesty's Government. We didn't think at that moment that we were wrong. If I had thought that Gracey was doing anything wrong I would have stopped him. It was an absolute, plain, . straightforward misunderstanding.'' Maunsell also questioned the timing of the limitation of Gracey's area of responsibility. In backing Gracey after thirty-two years of silence, his deputy concluded: ''Well, I can't prove it, and furthermore it's no good me saying it because Dickie Mountbatten will say I'm wrong . . . it's a long time ago.''

I was never able to see Lord Mountbatten. During the writing of this study (1977) his private secretary replied to my note, saying that Lord Mountbatten was particularly interested in Indochina, and at his request I sent some mainly archival

Finally, by Mountbatten's account, one of Slim's reasons for visiting Saigon was to assess the strength of forces required by Gracey to fulfill his tasks. But Gracey was never told that Headquarters SEAC was even remotely considering withholding his division. The consequence might well have been catastrophic, for Gracey predicated all his actions on having the entire division to back up his decisions. Gracey wrote later in retrospect: "It was during this time [from 25 September onwards] that the Allied commander was warned that the whole of 20th Division might not be made available for FIC, *and was also ordered to restrict the activities of British forces to a perimeter*, which was large enough to ensure the safe working of the port of Saigon, the safety of the airfield, and the speedy concentration and disarmament of the Japanese forces in Southern FIC."[15]

But while Gracey was struggling to control events in Saigon, another small crisis erupted within SEAC headquarters itself, over a letter written by Leclerc to Mountbatten; it generated anger in some quarters and evoked a spirited response from the SEAC staff. Although an archival copy was undated, the letter was probably written on 17 or 18 September, for the furious responses from various SEAC staff agencies are dated 19 September. Leclerc, of course, received information regularly from his officers in Saigon, and helplessly he watched from afar the growing anarchy and intimidation of the French population. Having seen France humiliated there, he, like de Gaulle, desperately wanted to make sure that French troops restored French sovereignty in Indochina. And, like de Gaulle too, he wanted to make sure that French troops should arrive before Gracey had solved the problem for him and for France. Leclerc's letter to Mountbatten had the effect of a bomb going off at SEAC headquarters.

Leclerc began by saying that he and his officers appreciated the friendship shown to France by Mountbatten, his officers and the British government, but that despite all public declarations and diplomatic

material which the former SACSEA was to read on his impending vacation in the Bahamas. After that, repeated requests for the return of my material went unanswered. Mountbatten was aware of my research, for he later asked Hugh Astor if he had talked to me. When I later interviewed Lt.-Gen. Sir Brian Kimmins, Mountbatten's Assistant Chief of Staff in SEAC and a man who owed his high rank to his former superior, I felt that we never really came to grips with the hard questions.

15. Gracey Papers, Correspondence with SEAC Recorder, 3 Oct. 1946. Author's italics.

negotiations, there existed "beyond all doubt . . . certain people who desire to kick us out of North Indo-China." There was "only one method of contesting such a manoeuvre: that is the rapid arrival of French troops in sufficient numbers." Leclerc stated that this was "why several weeks ago I bid high for the move of the 9th Division," which was armed and ready to go from France. However, Paris had just informed him that the War Office in London had stated that SEAC had not yet asked for the transport to move the 9th Division. Leclerc was now asking Mountbatten to try and overcome the damaging delay by making this a top priority request. He knew that the SAC would object and cite other urgent commitments, but Mountbatten "must recognize that the situation is not at all the same as far as France is concerned." Britain had met great difficulties in the theater, but because of her power the "final outcome has never been in doubt." Leclerc explained by contrasting Burma and Indochina: if a month should be lost in restoring order to Burma, it would be serious but would not in any way undermine Britain's position there. However, if the 9th DIC arrived a month too late, "the problem of the final issue of Indo-China rears its head." Leclerc pointed out another way of buying time for France, namely "by parachuting a few men into regions where guerrilla forces are still resisting against the revolutionaries. I refer to Laos." The SAC had promised help, "yet one month after my arrival it has not been possible to do anything along these lines, whilst our adversaries do not bother to respect all the mutual agreements." It was obvious that in both cases pretexts could be found "against such a weak operation". But the fact that would stand out to the French and to world opinion was that "sixty Frenchmen could not descend in time to succour their friends, although all the material means for so doing existed." Leclerc ended by saying that he did not know if this double protest on his part would "be of any use whatsoever, but what I can definitely assert is that if I fail in the task which has been entrusted to me, to return Indo-China to France, all Frenchmen will know the reasons for it."[16] The French staff at first tried to soften the impact by translating the last phrase as "All Frenchmen will want to know the reasons for it."

There were serious charges in this letter, and the result was a spirited defense by the SEAC staff agencies involved with the French. Every SEAC division associated with the French rose to rebut Leclerc's charge that Mountbatten, for whatever reason, had delayed — perhaps

16. PRO, WO 203/5611, Leclerc to Mountbatten, n.d.

fatally — the transfer to Indochina of the 9th DIC. Everyone from Kimmins to the Special Duty people pointed out the inconsistencies in the French effort, and their own great efforts to support it. Browning's staff added that "Gen Le Clerc's veiled allusions to 'certain men' who 'wish to see us thrown out of Northern FIC' (para 3) can only produce ill feeling and lack of enthusiasm by the British for a task which already entails for us endless diplomatic complications, considerable expenditure of British resources and no small danger of British forces having to fight." The staff officer had missed the point here, for Leclerc had clearly been referring to the pro-Viet Minh American OSS officers in Hanoi. It was repeated that it would have been useless to ask Wedemeyer for permission to drop French parachutists into Laos. According to SEAC, the sixty French parachutists were to protect about 120 French internees, including women and children, since there were no Japanese troops in the Vientiane area. On 17 September Mountbatten had decided to try again to secure approval from Wedemeyer, who was rigidly opposed to the French, but on the 18th the French let it be known that the internees had been evacuated to Thailand some days earlier. Thus "it can only be assumed that the French thought that SAC would look upon this operation with less favour were he to realise that its object had altered." Finally, Leclerc was ignoring the fact that the 5th RIC had "been equipped up to the maximum number of men available to be ready to go in with 20 Div", the equipment coming by air and "white-hot" priority rail movement. "In addition we have undertaken to accept the Combat Comd of 2 Armd Div without any French maintenance backing. We cannot accept more without inviting a breakdown. A base organisation designed for one div. cannot possibly maintain $2\frac{1}{3}$ divs."

Having amassed these examples of British endeavour and French fickleness and ingratitude, Kimmins suggested that "Gen Le Clerc be made to appreciate the need for diplomatic finesse in this theatre," and that his staff "be enlightened as to the world shipping situation and receive an explanation of all the factors involved in its detailed allocation within the India/SEAC Commands." If the French "fully understood the tasks to which SAC and C-in-C India are irrevocably committed, whether it be politically, economically or merely in connection with the movement of occupation forces, they would be less distrustful of our motives and more appreciative of our assistance."

The Foreign Office was following the unfolding drama in Saigon with interest, and it is evident that the professionals in the Foreign Office were closer to Gracey's thinking than were the newly-elected Labour government and Mountbatten at SEAC. For it was Gracey who was resisting, with all the limited means at his disposal, the "revolutionary outbreaks" feared by the Foreign Office. A lengthy memo by Mr Wilson-Young noted that Britain would have to proceed very carefully in Indochina; as a colonial power, she wanted to see a "smooth and gradual" evolution towards progressive self-government; "revolutionary outbreaks" would "have an unsettling effect on the native populations of our own territories in South East Asia and in the meanwhile might also affect the quantity of rice available for export to famine areas."[17] Again, clearly in line with Gracey's understanding, the minute continued, "The responsibility of SACSEA extends under General Order No. 1 up to 16° N . . ."

The British recognized that there was not a single advantage to be gained by having their forces in Indochina; the Americans, Chinese, and French would all object for their own reasons. If their troops suppressed the revolutionary outbreaks, the Americans and Chinese would complain; if they failed to do so, the French would complain. Wilson-Young noted that the delay in calling forward French forces (the 9th DIC) was caused by SEAC's "concern about the provision of their supplies". The Foreign Office view, as stated below, echoed Leclerc's later question to Mountbatten: "In view of the delicate political situation would it not be advisable to give a higher priority to the provision and transport of supplies for the French troops, even at the cost of operations elsewhere, so that French troops can be allowed to proceed to Saigon without delay?" The French wanted the first troops to Indochina to be white, which is why the 9th Division was now being preferred to the Madagascar Brigade. But the transportation for 9 DIC could not be allocated until Mountbatten called for the troops. He had not yet done this, but the Foreign Office "might suggest to the Chiefs of Staff that this be done without any further delay."

Wilson-Young was not to know that Leclerc at that time was suggesting the very same thing to Mountbatten at SEAC headquarters. He presented an official view from London, which rejected Dening's suggestion that "our position should be made clear to the world in an official pronouncement stating that our sole object is the liquidation of Japanese headquarters at Saigon and of the Japanese forces in Indo-China south of 16° N and to evacuate Allied prisoners of war and internees and that

17. PRO, WO 371/46308, Foreign Office Minutes by Wilson-Young and others, 20 Sept. 1945.

when it is accomplished our forces will be withdrawn.'' Declared Wilson-Young, ''The trouble with this suggestion is that it might well be interpreted as an indication of our intention to wash our hands of all internal developments in Indo-China and as indicating that we do not even accept responsibility for the maintenance of law and order.'' The result would be that ''The revolutionaries would regard this as an invitation to proceed with their activities and the French, who have been pressing us in vain for months for transport to carry their troops to Indo-China, would feel that their worst suspicions of our motives were confirmed.''

Again in line with Gracey, Wilson-Young thought that the Supreme Commander could not ''allow the position to drift,'' and it would be advisable to say that while the Force Commander (Gracey) had no instructions to become involved in the country's internal affairs, he could not carry out his main tasks of ''liquidating the Japanese situation'' and working the problem of prisoners-of-war and internees if he tolerated ''activities on the part of any political groups which did not serve to contribute to the orderly administration of the country pending the resumption of control by the French. If approved, this suggestion might be put urgently to the Chiefs of Staff.'' The suggestion was approved by the Eastern Department and the Chiefs soon released Gracey from the restrictions imposed on him by Mountbatten. So the Foreign Office and the Chiefs of Staff overruled Mountbatten, and it seemed that practically everyone except the SAC supported Gracey.

It is sometimes said that troubles come in threes, and it happened to be true of SEAC headquarters. Even before the reverberations from Leclerc's letter and Gracey's proclamation had died down in Kandy, the staff were confronted by a third crisis — the *coup* of 23 September. ''*Coup*'' is perhaps an exaggerated term to apply to the event in question, for if Gracey had had sufficient British/Indian units at his disposal, perhaps little more would have been heard about it and 23 September would have passed by unremembered.

# 8

## COUP D'ÉTAT

Although political problems were rapidly coming to a head in Saigon, the build-up of the 20th Division and ancillary units remained slow and ponderous. This was due largely to Mountbatten's reluctance to "get involved" in Saigon. While Gracey anxiously awaited the arrival of the rest of his division, these sorely-needed battalions were languishing in temporary transit camps in Burma, their commanders doing their best to keep the men occupied.

Although the build-up of his force was proceeding at what seemed to him a painfully slow pace, Gracey carried on with his methodical plan for disarming the Viet Minh police — a job the Japanese should have done. These operations, carried out over a period of several days, led up to the "*coup*" of 23 September; the combined Franco-British action on the morning of that day was only the culmination of these events. The seizure of the central jail on 20 September was part of the process. Another key move was the takeover of two main banks in Saigon, the Yokohama Specie Bank and the nearby Bank of Indochina. The Yokohama Bank was to be closed permanently, and its seizure was planned as a surprise move to preclude the Japanese from destroying any remaining documents and securities. The Bank of Indochina was to be closed temporarily "in order to evict Jap controllers and secure their books and documents which will then be handed over to the French authorities."[1]

Leclerc had made the French position quite clear. He professed himself unable to accept Mountbatten's restricting Gracey so severely, for the Supreme Allied Commander's commitment, "which is under the terms of Potsdam and Tokyo", was "to disarm all Japanese forces South of 16° North". He stated that "disarming Japanese troops brings trouble if they are not replaced by other troops for the purpose of maintaining order. Therefore, the maintenance of order is a SACSEA responsibility until such time as sufficient French forces are available to relieve British troops." Leclerc, like Gracey in Saigon, had little doubt that much of the troubles in Cochinchina and Annam were the work of "bandits and

---

1. PRO, War Diary 1/19 Hyderabads, O.O. no. 4, 20 Sept. 1945.

assassins taking advantage of the gap which must occur between the Japanese and Allied occupations. I have showed that the political unrest was backed unofficially by the Japanese who have never renounced their aspirations for their future programme for a Greater Asia.'' Leclerc had no doubt that ''Any sign of weakness or lack of agreement would play the game of the Japanese and might lead to grave consequences for the future of the white races in Asia. It is essential that Great Britain continues their previous action until the arrival of the 9th Division.''

On the 21st, Lady Louis Mountbatten came to visit the POW camps in Saigon, and this was one of the few occasions when female members of the Viet Minh were in evidence. As soon as Lady Louis' presence in Saigon became known, Viet Minh women made their public appearance. Maunsell at first had no idea who they were. ''They were attractive and intellectual, aged between 30 and 45, and like the men were great idealists and talkers. But, like the rest of the Viet Minh, they made claims to control which were seldom supported by facts or personal observations.''

During the night of 21/22 September, 1/19 Hybad took over two more police stations and the civil jail immediately to the west of the Colonial Artillery barracks, relieving armed Viet Minh police as part of the continuing process of methodically replacing the Viet Minh officials by the French. Following these actions, 212 armed Viet Minh were escorted away for questioning. The Hybads also took control of the Treasury, and at the same time 1/1 GR surrounded the Saigon Post and Telegraph Office and took it over from the Viet Minh. As Brigadier Taunton wrote a few weeks later, ''The stage was now set for the *coup d' état* by the French to take over the civil administration in Saigon from Annamites.''[2] This remark by Taunton confirms Gracey's own suggestion that he planned to remove the Viet Minh as soon as possible from the few official buildings they were guarding. Gracey would have preferred to wait for the arrival of greater Allied forces, preferably French, which would have resulted in the easing of the Viet Minh to one side. But the fact that by 20 September Mountbatten had still not called forward the 9th DIC — Leclerc alleged this and was supported in his allegation by the Foreign Office — left Gracey to grapple with the problem alone. It therefore became very much a question of who would strike first — Gracey or the Viet Minh. Gracey himself wrote:

---

2. Gracey Papers, ''Report on Operations — 80 Indian Infantry Brigade, 22 Oct. 1945.

On the arrival of the Allied Control Commission on September 13th, the situation was appreciated afresh and it was quite evident that unless the puppet government was evicted and the French government reinstated almost immediately, in fact strong measures taken, not only would the puppet government's hold on the country be consolidated and their plans for subversive action and hooliganism be made firm, but also landing by air and sea of troops and supplies would become daily more hazardous. All this would be playing into the hands of the Japanese, and would seriously delay their disarmament and concentration.[3]

This is significant because it suggests that Gracey may have decided at an early stage slowly but firmly to prise loose whatever grip the Viet Minh claimed to have on Saigon. Slim visited Gracey in Saigon on 16 September, and undoubtedly discussed with him in full, and approved, the operations for the transfer of power which were planned for the coming week and which were already occurring at that moment.

On 20 September the radio link between Terauchi and SEAC headquarters was broken; all traffic now passed through the Control Commission. By the following day Gracey's force numbered about 1,500; atrocious flying weather had prevented more of his soldiers from reaching Saigon. Despite his advance warning to the Committee for the South, the proclamation did not deter attempts by the Viet Minh to subvert his troops. One of the more bizarre attempts to split the Indians away from the British was revealed by a leaflet addressed directly to "Indian Soldiers", which tried to spread confusion by stating that Gracey had been killed; it may indeed have been meant for release to coincide with Gracey's assassination.

Gracey's hand-written comments on his personal copy of the Control Commission's official report of the period 13 to 23 September provide perhaps a greater insight into the situation than does the official report itself. This document traced the situation in Saigon, describing the growing anarchy and lack of public order, and how the illegally constituted revolutionary government was terrorizing the general population through murder and brutality. The report stated that, to carry out Gracey's tasks,

. . . it was clear that the situation of inactive mob rule then existing could not be allowed to continue; it was of the greatest importance, not only to Saigon and Cholon but also to the remainder of French Indo China, that administrative services should be made to function properly as soon as possible and that,

---

3. Gracey Papers, Correspondence with South East Asia Command Recorder, 3 Oct. 1946.

therefore, law and order and proper security must first be reestablished in the Saigon-Cholon area. It was therefore inevitable that the French should re-establish control with, as a first step, the assumption of police responsibilities and the necessary disarmament of Annamite armed elements.[4]

Under the last paragraph is the pencilled question, "Can they [the French] control any better than the Annamites?" It was a moot point, as Gracey's government was committed to recognizing France's sovereignty over her territories in Indochina. On the first page of the report (which dealt with the recent history of events), the pencilled comments express satisfaction with the summary, saying "Good". At the bottom of the page the following was written by hand: "A good exposition of the case, which is an almost exact parallel with Burma. If only the French would promise progressive sovereignty to be complete at a very early date (say two or three years) *and* the Annamites would be equally ready to meet them, the situation might clear up." But since neither condition was likely to be fulfilled due to the extreme intransigence of both sides, and Gracey knew it, all parties concerned proceeded with their own plans for future action.

To make the operation as bloodless and as easy as possible, Gracey's own troops had unobtrusively disarmed the greater part of the Viet Minh police during the previous few days. It was left to the French, perhaps for reasons of *amour-propre* as much as politics, to legitimize the operation by completing the final and largely ceremonial steps in the plan. Most of the installations in Viet Minh hands had already been taken, one by one, without resistance, by the British troops, after which many of them had been handed over to French forces. It was a brilliant operation and marked a departure from the traditional concept of the violent *coup d'état*, for it avoided confrontation between French and Viet Minh. It was left to the French to add the finishing touches, and that is when the problems began — but even then it remained a relatively bloodless operation, for only two participants were killed, both of them French.

A considerable body of literature has been published about the *coup*. Different versions vary in their closeness to the facts, but no single account is wholly correct. Cédile did indeed see Gracey about the French

4. Gracey Papers, "Saigon Control Commission, Political Report, 13th September, 1945, to 9th October 1945," n.d. The preceding paragraphs described Gracey's main tasks in his capacity as Commander of Allied Land Forces as securing the Saigon area, disarming the Japanese, maintaining law and order and ensuring internal security.

role in the *coup*, but as we have seen the French did not have the domi-
nant role in the eviction of the Communist-controlled Viet Minh
"government". As the French were rearmed, they began to reconstitute
their units; it was necessarily a rushed process involving much impro-
visation. As Cédile said, "We had a body of officers, and by force of circumstances we began to form little commando groups, putting them in
charge of a captain or a commandant, but they were not real units."[5]
(Before Gracey's arrival, British, Australian and Dutch ex-POWs armed
with bamboo staves did invaluable service in maintaining public order in
Saigon.)

On 21 September SACSEA queried Gracey on assurances from the
French Mission at Kandy that trained, hand-picked French troops were
on hand; a "large number of French and loyal Annamite troops" were
now said to be available in French Indochina for internal security duties.
At the same time Gracey wired Mountbatten that no official civil
government existed, and order was being kept by the Japanese with
Allied troops at selected vantage points; the Viet Minh were on guard
over many public buildings. But "Viet Minh claims to be de facto
government and to have resisted Japs throughout. Both claims childish.
No legal processes exist and ample evidence in fact [that they were]
puppets of Japs and actively cooperated." The Viet Minh police were
carrying out arbitrary political arrests and were suspected of murdering
some of the first French parachutists to arrive. The spot-check of a Viet
Minh jail (referred to by Brigadier Maunsell) on 19 September

revealed numerous political prisoners [including] two French officers who parachuted FIC and two French sailors. These [were] released. Only one European
French national voluntarily released by alarmed Annamite governor . . . .
French population has been very nervous with many wild rumours current.
Confidence now returning. Viet Minh violently anti-French . . . . Woefully
short security personnel who have many heavy increasing tasks unusually
complex situation.[6]

On 21 September, also, a cryptic intelligence summary had been
cabled from the Control Commission in Saigon to SACSEA, which said
in part:

Political situation and low strength own troops hitherto precluded much intelligence action. Interim period used collect info through staff meetings [with the]

5. Jean Cédile, personal interview, 26 Oct. 1977.
6. PRO, WO 172/1784, War Diary, Headquarters South East Asia Command,
   Gracey to Mountbatten, 21 Sept. 1945.

Japanese [and through] activities other agencies. Progress satisfactory and plans in hand action when circumstances permit . . . No effective civil government exists.[7]

In other words Gracey was gradually removing the Viet Minh and restoring French control, and would take decisive action at the propitious moment. His proclamation was discussed at the SAC's 27th Miscellaneous Meeting on 22 September. Mountbatten told those present that Gracey had acted outside the scope of his "more recent instructions" (which he had apparently never received) in that his proclamation was addressed to all of FIC south of 16° N., but went on to say that "the root of the difficulty lay in the contrary instructions given in different paragraphs of the original telegram" [from the Chiefs of Staff].[8] The first paragraph directed Mountbatten to reoccupy key areas of Japanese-held territories, to enforce the surrender and disarmament of "Japanese allied forces", and to effect the earliest possible release of Allied prisoners-of-war and internees. The third paragraph gave as a particular task control of the headquarters of the Japanese Southern Armies. Because of this apparent diversion Mountbatten was going to ask the Chiefs for definite guidance.

Evidently some blunt and spirited discussion took place at this meeting. Dening said to Leclerc that it was his opinion that "serious trouble in FIC would cause world-wide political repercussions, and that it was therein that the true danger lay." These were indeed prophetic words. The SEAC Director of Plans wanted to halt the build-up of Gracey's forces and limit the use of troops to Terauchi's headquarters. He made another poorly thought-out suggestion that the Spitfires and Mosquitos should take care of quelling any disturbances. General Slim interjected at this point, that he could not accept that the British forces were in Saigon only to control Terauchi's headquarters. He said that the British had three additional objectives: to disarm the Japanese, bring back the Allied prisoners-of-war and internees, and maintain law and order, at least in the Saigon area. He also did not think they could do it cheaply, for the Air Force would not be of much help in putting down "riotous outbreaks". At this point Mountbatten said that he was going to repeat Gracey's telegram to the Chiefs, with two alternative courses of action to reflect the two contradictory instructions he had received, pointing out the advantages and disadvantages of each. The Chiefs

7. PRO, WO 203/3861, INTSUM (Intelligence Summary) No. 1, 21 Sept. 1945.
8. COSSEA 314.

should then give a definite ruling. A telegram from the War Office, dated 18 September, also appeared to limit British responsibility to Japanese headquarters. Mountbatten's Planning Staff, on a majority vote, recommended that the British build-up should cease and that British/Indian forces should withdraw from French Indochina as soon as possible.

Captain Goodenough, RN, and Group-Captain Spotswood, RAF, were in favor of stopping the build-up of Gracey's forces. The third member of the Planning Staff, the Army's Brigadier Blacker, strongly disagreed, on the grounds that the Supreme Allied Commander could not avoid responsibility in French Indochina until the Combined Chiefs of Staff agreed to the formation of a separate French command there. All problems connected with the disarming, guarding, and evacuation of the Japanese were definitely the SAC's responsibility, besides providing limited administrative support for the French. Should the British build-up cease and the French be pushed into assuming full control before they had sufficient strength, it was highly probable that they would get into trouble and demand assistance from the British. Under the SAC's control the French forces could be confined to tasks commensurate with their strength. The establishment of a separate French command must coincide with the withdrawal of British forces.

Mountbatten appeared to be playing down the seriousness of the situation in Saigon. He thought he could control Saigon with a single brigade, and said that he hoped it would not be necessary to send all of 20 Division there. Major-General Pyman, ALFSEA Chief of Staff, pointed out to Mountbatten that 80 Brigade's vehicles were still in Burma and were due to arrive with the remainder of the division. Mountbatten thought that a possible solution would be for British forces to control Saigon and the airfield while "incidentally offering sanctuary to women and children in the event of rioting". The telegram he proposed to send to the Chiefs would suggest "two definite alternative courses of action, founded on the two contrary instructions he had received and the different factors of the situation". If the Supreme Allied Commander was confused, it is hardly surprising that some of his subordinates were not clear as to what British forces should do in Saigon. It was surprising that it took so long to direct the Chief's attention to what appeared to some officers to be contradictory directives.

The SAC's 28th Miscellaneous Meeting was attended by Mountbatten, Slim, Leclerc, Dening and other senior officers. Mountbatten drew Leclerc's attention to Gracey's telegram, which contained the text of the proclamation, and summarized the political situation in Saigon. Mountbatten concluded his discussion by saying that "it was not quite clear, from instructions which had been received from London, what were his precise responsibilities in French Indo-China, and it might be that the action which had been taken by General Gracey was too wide." Mountbatten repeated his intention to seek clarification from the Chiefs of Staff. Leclerc asked how Gracey was supposed to disarm the Japanese in southern Indochina if he was to be restricted to Saigon only. Mountbatten replied that this was the point he would make with the Chiefs, and Leclerc suggested that Mountbatten could "add in his telegram that the measures taken by General Gracey had in fact ensured the maintenance of law and order with small forces under extremely difficult conditions." Mountbatten agreed to do this.

Dening next expressed the Foreign Office view of the political question, pointing out that it was not strictly accurate to say that French Indochina south of 16 degrees North was a purely British responsibility. It was the SAC's responsibility "under the Combined Chiefs of Staff", to which Mountbatten commented that this was why US Brigadier General Timberman was at the meeting. Dening went on to say that political movements were a French responsibility, although admittedly it was "very difficult to divorce the military and political responsibilities"; but he advised that the British should not become involved in "political manoeuvring on French sovereign territory". This was sound advice, if difficult to implement, but it appeared to run directly counter to the recent directive from Mountbatten to Gracey to suppress Saigon Radio. Leclerc responded by saying that he wanted the British to keep law and order only until he was in a position to assume command and responsibility himself. Mountbatten asked him to urge the French government to proclaim publicly the autonomy of Indochina, and he replied that he had already urged de Gaulle and d'Argenlieu to do so; he then turned to Dening and asserted that it was "fallacious to argue too closely any superficial comparisons between the political situation [in Indochina] and the political difficulties in different countries; similarly, there was no common solution." Leclerc believed that "looting and brigandage" were the main problems in French Indochina and that the people were not overmuch concerned with politics. Dening diplomatically replied that he would pass on Leclerc's remarks "on the true nature of the present unrest" to the Foreign Office. Earlier during the meeting Mountbatten had pressed Leclerc to assume responsibility for south French Indochina on 5 October (the proposed date of his arrival in

Saigon); by that time 3,250 French troops should be ashore. Leclerc had pointed out that between 1,000 and 1,200 of these troops would be ex-POWs from the 11th RIC and of only "mediocre value". He was no less anxious than Mountbatten for an early takeover, and pointed out that French Indochina was "three quarters the size of France, and he could not reasonably be expected to assume such enormous responsibilities with a force of only 3,250 men." He agreed with Slim that he would assume responsibility when 9 DIC arrived in Saigon, and suggested that "General Gracey would likewise be in a position to exercise full control only when a full British division had arrived in Indo-China."

Mountbatten thought that the British and French commands should be separated, with the British being confined to Saigon and the French assuming responsibility for the rest of the country. This was contrary to what Dening had just said, and Leclerc could not accept it. He thought the suggestion unworkable and wanted the French to remain under British command for the time being, although he would agree that the British should restrict their activities to the Saigon area. Leclerc said he understood that the British government had accepted full responsibility for French Indochina south of the 16th parallel, and thought it "inequitable" that they should abandon this responsibility when France was not yet able to take it on. He would be quite willing to take over as soon as he had sufficient strength (the 9th DIC) "even if the situation was still difficult." Meanwhile, he would go to Saigon immediately after the rest of 5 RIC had arrived, and give Gracey all the assistance he could. Mountbatten said he would convey the thrust of Leclerc's argument to the Chiefs of Staff. At the end, Brigadier-General Timberman interjected the thought that "any improvement in the lot of Asiatic peoples would be well received by the American public."

On 22 September SEAC informed Gracey that two Civil Affairs officers were on their way to him from Britain, and Brain, a member of Dening's Political Affairs staff, should be arriving in Saigon at any time. At the same time the SEAC Joint Planning Staff issued the second draft of Paper Number 201, "Handover of FIC to the French", which, by citing the telegram COSSEA 350, suggested a reduced commitment for British forces. This telegram from the Chiefs said: "In view of French willingness and ability to provide forces you should do your utmost to reduce the British forces sent there as soon as possible." French willingness was fine, but the forces were not yet in Saigon and the War Office seemed to be suggesting that it would not be necessary to wait for the

French build-up before beginning the British withdrawal. A halt in the British reinforcement program was recommended, although Dening held that the British departure should coincide with French agreement to assume sole responsibility in Indochina. SEAC was considering sending the third brigade of 20 Division (100 Brigade, scheduled to arrive in Saigon around 14 October) directly to Borneo from Rangoon, withdrawing it from the scheduled Masterdom convoy. All of this was being discussed as the final touches were being applied to the approaching *coup* in Saigon.

Back in Saigon, Cédile met Gracey for a last-minute discussion of the impending removal of the Viet Minh from the few buildings they still held. As Brigadier Maunsell recalled, the *coup* was the idea of Cédile and another Frenchman. The latter, reputed to be a Gaullist and the possessor of many medals won in the First World War, had been vouched for by Cédile. It was the "profound belief of Cédile and others (who continually advanced it) that the coup would be a simple affair, as indeed it turned out to be." About three days earlier, "in tremendous secrecy", Cédile and his associate had said, "we'll go up to the Viet Minh outside one of the police stations [the headquarters], and we'll do *that* to them," making a sweeping gesture with his arm, "and it will be over. And all our friends, now silent, will throng to the French."[9] Years later, when asked of Gracey's worry that the *coup* might misfire, Cédile replied: "Yes, there was the risk of an accident, of course, and he had the responsibility. But he accepted it and he agreed with me. He understood me and . . . I managed to convince him. And he said, 'Well, you're a brave young man and we're going to help you, my dear boy.' He was very kind."[10] This statement verifies Maunsell's argument that Cédile had convinced Gracey that the quickest way to resolve the "sticky" situation was with a lightning takeover by French forces (although it is not impossible that Gracey, having already made up his own mind, may simply have gone through the motions of becoming convinced by the two Frenchmen).[11]

9. Brig. M. S. K. Maunsell, personal interview, 20 Apr. 1977.
10. Jean Cédile, personal interview, 26 Oct. 1977.
11. In an interview on 20 Apr. 1977, Maunsell said: "Douglas Gracey was an emotional man, but he always required facts and information, proof — but he couldn't get proof. But he became enthusiastic about it [the *coup*], and enthusiasm was a great part of Gracey's make-up. . . .

"The two Frenchmen converted Gracey and got him enthusiastic for this cause. After all, if the French could consolidate power quickly, the British could wind up

The *coup* was a combined Anglo-French operation, with the preliminary steps being taken almost exclusively by the British. Queried
about joint planning, Cédile agreed that there was liaison: "For
example, two nights before 23 September, the Gurkhas occupied the
Police Commissariat. The Viet Minh were in blockhouses and bunkers
and it was this pressure point which we took which helped the British
troops when they became involved in the clashes. They helped very
much on 23 September and then they left it to us. Obviously the plan had
been made because the attack was made on all sides to free Saigon . . ."[12]
    Brigadier Taunton reported to Gracey the gradual takeover of vital
points during the previous few days, culminating in the Hybads taking
the two police commissariats, the Treasury and the *Maison Centrale* from
armed Annamite police, and the Gurkhas taking over the Post and Telegraph Office on 21/22 September: "The stage was now set for the coup
d'état by the French to take over the civil administration in Saigon from
Annamites." During the night of 22/23 September the French had
taken over Viet Minh police posts, the town hall and so on, and established guards on the five bridges over the Arroyo de l'Avalanche. On the
23rd the 1st Hybads had surrounded and taken over the Yokohama and
Indochina Banks. Taunton also mentioned that "When taking over vital
points from the Japs, the policy was British take over and hand to French
later." Further, "when taking over from Annamites, in the main, Japs
took over first and handed over to British;" but "it was very apparent
that the Japs had not adequately disarmed the Annamite police."[13] On 22
September the final outline of the *coup* was contained in 80 Indian
Infantry Brigade Operational Order no. 13.[14]
    The French force actually used was a mixture of 5 RIC, 11 RIC (ex-
POW) and armed civilians; 11 RIC had been reconstituted only a few
days earlier. As Cédile said, the French POWs were not released on his
arrival in Saigon because the Viet Minh had threatened to shoot them:
"So I had to negotiate very carefully with them and eventually we let the

---

and go home quicker. This would be the way to unite the French in a Verdun-like
spirit and they would be able to properly prepare for Leclerc's arrival. And, above
all, their friends among *les Annamites* would all come out and rally around the Tricolor. It was repeated so many times that the British came to believe it in the total
absence of any other information."
12. Cédile interview, 26 Oct. 1977.
13. Gracey Papers; "Report on Ops — 80 Ind Inf Bde," by Brigadier Taunton, 22
    Oct. 1945.
14. See Appendix following this Chapter, pp. 206–7.

prisoners out almost individually and we put them into houses where there were women and children, but it was just a few days before 23 September that we rebuilt and rearmed these units.'' This explained why the French death toll was kept relatively low during the days between the 2 September riots and 23 September. Around the earlier date, Cédile described the ex-POWs as weak, some with no shirts, and armed only with bamboo staves. Fighting had been hand-to-hand, and when grateful civilians gave them ''bottles of spirits'' the effect on weakened bodies was immediate.

One reporter described the *coup* as follows:

As clocks chimed 0300, a ragtime, grim silent army of 300 men, armed to the teeth, padded silently along the deserted streets. The Coup d'Etat was beginning and Saigon was about to become French again. This was the culmination of an incredible week of turbulent rumour and imminent uprisings. Who would strike first? Would it be the Annamese, angry, confident, truculent? Or the French? ''Three o'clock Sunday morning'', the word went round: and 300 tough men went out to take a city.[15]

Each Frenchman involved wore the Cross of Lorraine on his shoulder. Christopher Buckley of the London *Daily Telegraph* quoted a British officer as saying (of the French), ''They have the opportunity of a lifetime for starting with a clean sheet a liberal policy for the joint running of the country.''[16] Writing of the action, Buckley gave perhaps the most balanced report of the day's events:

The total number of casualties in the course of the night's and morning's shootings are trifling — two French killed and four wounded, one Annamese killed [not a single Vietnamese was killed in the whole operation], and an unspecified number, perhaps some dozens, more or less roughly handled.

It has been established that no casualties occurred in the taking over of the town hall . . . The Annamese were taken by surprise and the French troops, in accordance with orders, fired at the walls and roof.

Buckley then described the unnecessarily brutal conduct of the French, citing the breakdown in French discipline:

It hardly seemed necessary that women and striplings should be kept seated on the ground with their hands above their heads several hours after the shooting had stopped in the center of Saigon. This I saw. Such treatment was entirely contrary to the orders issued by Col. Cédile and Col. Rivier.

15. PRO, WO 203/5023, Emory Pierce's Story, 23 Sept. 1945.
16. PRO FO 371/46308, *Daily Telegraph* (London), 24 Sept. 1945.

Buckley warned that the Vietnamese might well react violently to such wanton provocation by the French. He had introduced his story by saying, "The solution of the problem of rule in Indo-China will depend primarily upon French ability to exercise tact and conciliation." In the afternoon the city was quiet except for some sniping in the northern suburbs.

On the morning of the 23rd the Post, Telephone and Telegraph Office was handed to the French at 0600 by 1/1 GR; the jail was handed over at 1130. However, a mass escape was attempted when the prisoners saw the French resuming control, and a number of prisoners and Vietnamese warders ran away. The mutiny was contained when the Gurkhas took back control of the jail at 1400 hours.

What should have been a simple and painless operation got out of hand for one reason: the state of mind of the French ex-POWs and civilians. After their harsh experience of imprisonment and humiliation at the hands of the Asians, the French population went wild on seeing the Tricolor flying once more over the city hall. Had the French troops maintained their discipline, the French civilian population would in all probability have been held in check, but mob hysteria, like fear, is contagious. One of the British officers who arrived in Saigon within hours of the *coup* stated quite simply that fear underlay the French reaction in the wake of the *coup*.[17] The Japanese had permitted the Viet Minh to take over guarding the 11th RIC, and on the 23rd the sight of the fleeing Viet Minh proved too much and the French, back on top, lost control of themselves.

Gracey's only serious worry about the *coup* was the behavior of the French, and he had repeatedly stressed the need for discipline above all to Cédile and Rivier, who assured him that the French troops were well-officered and tightly controlled. Maunsell said later:

There is no doubt that Gracey thought that it would be a pushover — he believed Cédile and had been told it innumerable times. The information the British had about the Viet Minh was that they would not resist. The information about the French was that Cédile had tight control over them, that this was not at all a difficult task, and would be simply done — and that once done, it would provide a substantial, useful step forward for the furtherance of the gradual takeover from the British by the French.

Most of us had been fighting the Japanese since '42 and had not seen our families in three or three and a half years. Newsmen and latter-day academics did not understand the British frame of mind in this regard . . . We were not inter-

17. Lt.-Col. E. Gopsill, personal interview, 12 Dec. 1977.

ested in anything past defeating the Japs. . . .

Suddenly, the war was over, and I went to Rangoon to meet Numata — this was the first inkling of an unwelcome postscript to the war. All talk was about the Japanese — no one had ever heard of the Viet Minh.

Mansergh [NEI], Evans [Siam], Gracey [FIC] — all talk was once they got the Japs under control in those various places, there wouldn't be any other trouble . . . It never entered our heads that there would be a problem caused from any other source than the Japanese . . .

Until the draft "Masterdom" plan was produced, neither Gracey nor Maunsell had given the matter much thought —

Then it started to dawn on us that this was going to be something (*a*) that we'd never experienced; and (*b*) that we knew absolutely nothing about at all, because we knew how you fought a war, and we knew how you fought a peace, but we didn't know how you did anything in between.

That was the view from the top. The view from the bottom was identical. Major M. Kelleher, a 3/1 Gurkha company commander, said that none of the officers wished to see their troops suffer casualties, especially since the war was over.[18] The British were there to keep order and ship the Japanese home — all the rest concerned only the French and Vietnamese, and the sooner the French took over, the sooner the British/Indian forces could leave. This attitude was an important factor in assessing British-French cooperation throughout the whole of the *coup* operations. And no one was more loath to accept needless casualties than Douglas Gracey — something for which he is still remembered. He wrote his own description of the *coup* just twelve months after the event.[19]

18. Major M. Kelleher, personal interview, Jan. 1978.
19. Gracey Papers, Correspondence with SEAC Recorder, 3 Oct. 1946:
   "9. By secret and very skilfully executed arrangements, a proportion of the best of the French prisoners of war were armed, and in spite of the fact that the fly-in of 80 Brigade had been much delayed by bad weather, and only half the expected number of troops had arrived, on the orders of the Allied Commander the French government was installed in Saigon, on September 23rd, and the puppet government evicted.
   "This revolution was noisy but there were no fatal casualties to the Annamite puppet government, or to their evicted police, though some rough handling and a few unnecessary reprisals by the French forces took place; this was natural under the circumstances, but was over-emphasized by various Press correspondents, who had the first chance, after being unmuzzled by censorship since 1939, of free and unfettered expression. It would be as well to state here that considering all the circumstances, the Press correspondents, having collected in large numbers in the

He felt revulsion and anger when reports of French excesses were brought to him by indignant British officers. A few hours after the *coup* he was in a "great rage", and sent for Cédile, who had been up all night with the principals in the *coup*. Gracey summoned all of them to his office and "addressed them like pickpockets". "*Never*", he said, "have I been so let down in my life!" He ended by saying that the whole lot would be disarmed. Cédile, who had been let down to a greater extent than Gracey, said how genuinely sorry he was, to which Gracey retorted that this "wasn't the slightest good, and he was not to reappear again until he could give an assurance that those who should have been disarmed *were* disarmed, those who had committed excesses were to be punished, and what it [the punishment] was, and there was nothing more to be said!"[20] Cédile left, a "shaken man". And echoing a universally-shared opinion, Maunsell said, "When Gracey signalled Mountbatten that it was on his orders the *coup* began, it was typical of Gracey to take full responsibility for the plan, once having been convinced of its merits."

Mountbatten passed the information to the Chiefs of Staff, drawing their attention to the fact that "Leclerc has rejected as impracticable the solution of parallel and independent British and French commands." Whereas Gracey had authorized the *coup*, and indeed had based all his assumptions on the anticipated arrival of his complete division, Mountbatten was now (on 24 September) suggesting the following to the Chiefs: "The first essential seems to me to avoid building up our forces in FIC, for the stronger we are the more the French will feel they can take provocative action against Annamites relying on presence of powerful British forces who may then be brought into conflict with indigenous population." This was why he had recommended the removal of southern Indochina from his theater as soon as possible. He wrote that when he suggested the British buildup should be stopped, Leclerc was "quite horrified" and stated that this proposed weak position "would be the surest way to invite civil strife and bloodshed." Slim agreed that the British were not strong enough to prevent a native uprising outside the key areas as Leclerc insisted; "since we were responsible for FIC south of 16 degrees under Tokyo surrender terms we could not evade our

---

initial stages of the occupation of FIC, were most fair on the whole in their reports and comments, with the exception of those few, mostly of a poor calibre, who were representatives of papers whose policy was anti-British, anti-French and in fact anti-anything which was sound policy."

20. Maunsell interview, 20 April 1977.

responsibilities and leave European population at the mercy of a native rising." Mountbatten added that he did not press the issue with Leclerc, "as I feel that it is essential for me to maintain friendly relations with my Allied Commanders-in-Chief." Furthermore, Gracey's proclamation "has in fact stabilized southern part of FIC," and Mountbatten now "strongly" recommended that it should not be cancelled. Mountbatten thought that if he stopped the British buildup now, the French strength would exceed British strength in Indochina by 20 October, but Leclerc might still not consider his forces strong enough to take over. In that case he should be ordered to do so by his government if the British were not to stay there indefinitely. Meanwhile, the Japanese could be used to maintain order.

The final paragraph was most significant, for this was apparently Gracey's first indication that he was to confine himself to key areas: "I have re-affirmed orders to Gracey that he is not to employ British forces outside key areas unless called upon by French in which case matter is to be referred through me to H. M. G." (A similar directive went simultaneously to Major-General Evans in Bangkok.)

On 24 September SEAC headquarters received a message sent the day before by the Control Commission. It said that the gathering of intelligence was increasing with the build-up of Allied troops. Admiral Chudo had been taken into custody and evacuated on 23 September, in spite of faking an illness. The Japanese had destroyed all their naval codes and ciphers. The Viet Minh boycott was continuing, and Dutch ex-POWs had volunteered to keep the hotels and other services going. The general opinion was that most of the local population were being terrorized by the Viet Minh.

On 23 September, 20 Indian Division Operational Order no. 15 had been published in confirmation of verbal instructions of 21 September. This order dealt with the proposed establishment of headquarters in Phnom Penh and Cam Ranh Bay, to be commanded respectively by Brigadier Hirst, Royal Artillery, and Lieutenant-Colonel Murray of 4/10 GR, representing 100 Brigade. It was a modest effort, involving but thirty-one officers and men, including Signals personnel, to Phnom Penh, and forty-one men to Cam Ranh Bay.

Headquarters ALFSEA now directed Gracey that in view of the attitude of the Labour Government he was to restrict the use of British troops to the absolute minimum; therefore his plan to send troops to Cam Ranh Bay was cancelled. He was advised to send French troops instead and tell Terauchi to instruct the Japanese there to obey the

French. This was easier said than done, for the Japanese would under no circumstances cooperate directly with the French at that time. Gracey replied that in view of his experience with French troops during what should have been a simple operation on the 23rd he could not agree to dispatch French forces to Cam Ranh; they were insufficiently trained and disciplined to be "landing in [a] very tricky situation". On the 23rd the French had been "unnecessarily provocative and undisciplined".

Headquarters SACSEA was worried about adverse publicity over the coup and asked Gracey about the "lurid" account by the *Daily Herald* correspondent. Some of the press reporting was as politically slanted then as it was to be thirty years later. Harold Isaacs wrote later in a book that "Viet Minh sentries were shot down."[21] He reported no French deaths, yet there were two Frenchman and no Vietnamese killed during the *coup*. One of the 1/1 Gurkha Rifles officers expressed the generally felt bitterness towards some of the hostile press reporting. The Gurkhas commented on the "fantastic" inaccuracies of the press, "always excluding the *Times*. One learns at last, the hard way, the bitter truth that there is no truth." A press conference, described by Maunsell as "ghastly", was held shortly after the *coup*. Gracey was attacked by the American and Australian reporters, and "given hell" for rearming the Japanese following MacArthur's statement that the Japanese were disarmed: why was he not following MacArthur's orders? The reporters appeared unaware of Allied policy regarding Japanese responsibility for keeping order, and no one know at that time that Mansergh was doing the same thing in the Netherlands East Indies. Gracey grew angry and said that the reporters did not understand the East. Maunsell, over thirty years later, laughed as he described what followed. An American replied: "The East is as unscrutable today as it was yesterday, and following this press conference is even more inscrutable." This "*really* set Gracey off," and about that time the Viet Minh attacked the power station and the lights went off. The conference continued in flickering candlelight, with sporadic bursts of gunfire and bullets whistling outside. The Viet Minh had reacted as if by reflex, and two platoons of Jarvis's Gurkhas were sent to help the small Hybad detachment in driving off an attack on the power station. The Viet Minh managed to set fire to part of it before being repelled with the loss of two dead and several wounded.

At 1600 hours Major Charles Blascheck, a veteran of some of the heaviest Burma combat, temporarily brought his D Company from 3/1

21. Harold Isaacs, *No Peace for Asia* (New York: Macmillan, 1947), p. 153.

GR to reinforce 1/1 GR and was in action almost immediately. As soon as night fell the electric power failed; the station had just been taken over by the 20th Division's engineers after the Vietnamese workers had fled. This was "the first of a succession of irritations and nightly failures for some weeks". The trouble prevented 100 Brigade's advance party from moving out of Saigon, and they were now given responsibility (under Lieutenant-Colonel Murray) for the city's North Sector, Saigon having been divided into two for more effective control immediately after the *coup*. Under North Sector were 1/1 GR, some French forces and two Japanese regiments. The area was bounded in the north by the Arroyo de l'Avalanche, and in the south by the Rue Verdun.

South Sector was commanded by Lieutenant-Colonel Purcell, commanding 3/1 Gurkha Rifles; under him were his own battalion less Blascheck's company, 1/19 Hybad, elements of 4 Dogra, some French police and a Japanese regiment. Purcell's battalion had just arrived in the afternoon of the 24th, and had driven through a French/Viet Minh firefight en route from Tan Son Nhut to Saigon. Major E. Gopsill later recalled that the battalion was driven from the airfield to Saigon by Japanese drivers. A few minutes after leaving Tan Son Nhut, they could see raging ahead of them a fierce gun battle between French soldiers and Viet Minh partisans. Dead and wounded men lay alongside the road, and the battalion passed a busy Viet Minh first aid post. The Gurkhas, rifles and Sten guns at the ready, passed through without incident. The 3/1 Gurkha Rifles were met at their barracks, a school, by their commander Lieutenant-Colonel Purcell, who told them, "You're going into Cholon." The Gurkhas were directed to establish a base area as quickly as possible. This they did and were immediately fired on by the Viet Minh; this was the start of several days of heavy street fighting for 3/1 GR. Throughout the nights following the *coup*, a series of small battles took place throughout Saigon, and several French, British, and Viet Minh soldiers were killed and wounded.[22]

22. Of these events the Commander of 1/1 Gurkha Rifles later wrote: "What occurred now affected me more than anything else in these operations; this was the death of a sentry of 1 Hybad, with whom we had been brigaded . . . it struck me how tragic it was that he should have survived a whole 'real' war, and then have lost his life in a country and for a cause in which he had only the remotest interest. That was the first casualty that hit me personally; it was unexpected, and there were of course more to come which affected me more closely but not so deeply, because by that time we had changed gear back into a war-time frame of mind. I think that the sepoy himself and his companions would simply regard it as the will of God: after all they were simply volunteer/professional/mercenary soldiers (as one happens to look at it)." (Lt.-Col.

Gracey was never to waver in his belief that the *coup* had been absolutely necessary, and that no alternative course existed at that time. In this he was reinforced, thirteen years after his death, by a former member of the Force 136 intelligence team sent to Saigon with the Control Commission, Hugh Astor: "When the British arrived in Saigon the intention was to try and work with the Viet Minh." But there was no such thing as a "Viet Minh": "British Intelligence soon discovered that the [Viet Minh] guards on the buildings, etcetera, were a façade, and that any agreement entered into with the Viet Minh could easily be abrogated by some other equally strong group, such as the Trotskyites and others, which often disagreed with them. It was a hopeless situation with no foreseeable chances of improvement, so the *coup* was decided on."[23] This implies a condition of anarchy which would eventually reach a flash point and explode; Viet Minh leaflets had stated ·clearly that they meant to launch an attack at some time in the future. Gracey lanced the abcess by acting decisively at a time of his own choosing.[24] By 24 September, when the Viet Minh was gathering its forces to launch a series of attacks on the city, British/Indian forces in Saigon comprised about three infantry battalions, plus one company, in addition to the Control Commission.

On 24/25 September 1945, the Viet Minh began their long war. Truong Chinh wrote not long after those events:

People's power had scarcely been founded in Viet Nam when the British forces . . . landed in Indo-China . . . On September 23, armed and protected by the British forces, the French colonialists launched their attack and occupied Saigon.

---

Cyril E. Jarvis, Commander 1/1 Gurkha Rifles, letter to author, "Note on Events in Vietnam, 1945–1946", 1975, and personal interviews and correspondence, 1977.)

23.  Hon. Hugh Astor, personal interview, 26 June 1977.

24.  Gracey's official report on the *coup*, as distinct from his personal feelings, said the following:
      "The promises given to General Gracey by the leaders of the French, both civil and military, that minimum force and iron discipline would be assured during the coup d'état proved a false assurance; by their instability and indiscipline, by their emotional behaviour and unnecessary violence the French soldiers, their police and civilians, invited active counter-measures as soon as the Annamites could gather themselves together.
      "It has always been a matter of great doubt whether the Annamite people would understand, let alone believe, in the rebirth of France; the excesses of the 23rd September, 1945, ensured that this difficulty would be even greater."
      (Gracey Papers, "Saigon Control Commission; Political Report," n.d.).

Our people replied by force of arms, and from that moment, our heroic resistance began.[25]

On the night of 24/25 September there occurred an incident so horrific that it colored events in Saigon for some time. In a north-central section of Saigon, the Cité Heyraud district, a screaming horde of Vietnamese appeared and entered the houses; they murdered about 150 French civilians, many of them women and children. An equal number were taken away, and many were later tortured, mutilated and killed. The area was guarded by Japanese troops, who stood by and allowed the mob to pass through. This occurrence, possibly more than any other, may have convinced Gracey that the Vietnamese population was beyond the control of any responsible organization. The Viet Minh and their sympathizers later blamed the Binh Xuyen gang for the slaughter, but this allegation is disputed by those who had contact with it. The Binh Xuyen was a brigand group which seldom engaged in any activity which did not return it profit, and the Cité Heyraud massacre was totally different in character from all their normal activity. Colonel Marcel Mingant, of French Intelligence, stated that subsequent investigation revealed the massacre to be the work of the Trotskyists,[26] and he independently confirmed Astor's assertion that at that time and in that area the Viet Minh "was not an identity".

The momentum of violence carried over to the 25th, when a large fire was started among disused *bashas* — native huts — about 800 yards south of 80 Brigade Headquarters. The central market was attacked by the Viet Minh and set on fire, the flames quickly spreading since the Viet Minh had stolen the fire engines three days before. Two more French civilians were kidnapped during the riot. One Viet Minh partisan was shot near a commissariat in Cholon. Small clearing operations took place all over Saigon, with heavy action occurring along the Boulevard Gallieni, in the south sector. Here the Viet Minh opened fire with light machine-guns, rifles and pistols. "A" Company, 1/1 GR, searched the north Saigon area enclosed by Rue Legrand de la Liraye, Rue Paul Blanchy and Arroyo de l'Avalanche; they found no firearms but removed daggers from a number of Vietnamese and, more important, found thirty-one French women and children, probably survivors of the Cité Heyraud bloodbath, locked up in a house on the outskirts of Saigon. The Viet Minh guards fled on sight of the Gurkhas.

25. Truong Chinh, *Primer for Revolt* (New York: Praeger, 1963), p. 17.
26. Col. Marcel Mingant, personal interview, 26 Oct. 1977.

The fighting along Boulevard Gallieni involved 3/1 Gurkha Rifles. They were conducting a sweep of the large area between Rue de Verdun and the Quai Belgiane (in the south, on the Arroyo Chinois). Boulevard Gallieni ran northeast-southwest, about three blocks from and paralleling the Arroyo Chinois. The battalion found the road heavily blocked, with the entrenched Viet Minh freely using automatic weapons and grenade dischargers. In the words of the 3/1 GR historian, ''A tedious battle of street fighting ensued.'' As soon as the Gurkhas saw what they were up against, they brought out their small 2-inch mortars and grenades and quickly cleared one block after another. The 3/1 Gurkha writer noted, ''Probably our greatest impression was the magnificent system of evacuation of casualties by the Annamites. Red Cross squads were always waiting on the scene of a battle and they got their casualties away remarkably quickly.'' Because of this, ''It was impossible to assess the number of casualties we gave the Annamites by nightfall, when the search was completed, but we had none ourselves, despite a vast number of 'near misses'.''[27] The confusion of the 24th was illustrated by the report of two Vietnamese groups attacking each other, which resulted in ten casualties.

The 24th may also have been the beginning of a change of heart towards the Japanese. The 1/1 GR recorder had written about the battalion's attitude on arriving in Saigon: ''The sight of Japanese sentries and armed piquets and the sensation of being driven by the Japanese chauffeurs were at first ludicrous in their unexpectedness since we had all entered Indo-China with the idea of suppressing the Japs completely and kicking them around as hard as we could.'' After the 24th, there was little talk of suppressing the Japanese or kicking them around, since ''it soon became obvious that with the small number of troops at the disposal of the Mission, it was essential to make the fullest possible use of the Japanese while maintaining our own forces as a reserve.'' On returning from helping out 1/19 Hybad at the power station, the two platoons of 1/1 GR (who were driven there by Japanese soldiers in Japanese trucks) found the road back to the barracks blocked by felled trees. As it was getting dark, the Gurkhas dismounted and the Japanese were told to make their way back with their trucks as best they could; the Gurkhas

---

27. Gracey Papers, 3/1 GR Newsletter. This efficient Viet Minh system of casualty evacuation was for thirty years a feature of the wars in Vietnam. It was necessary because of the Vietnamese views on death and proper burial, and without this efficient system for recovering their dead the Communists would not have been able to recruit and hold their soldiers. US troops were later to note the same efficiency.

would return to their area on foot. The Gurkha historian wrote: "They had not gone far however before the Japs, who had discovered a way round, rejoined and drove them back the rest of the way. This was the first of a series of incidents that showed a remarkable cooperation on their part in carrying out the terms of the treaty."

Although Gracey, on the 24th, had again asked ALFSEA to send him the rest of his division, as late as 26 September 100 Brigade was alerted for a move directly to Borneo. The next day (the 25th), Terauchi was summoned to Gracey's office, of which more will be said later.

Of the Cité Heyraud massacre itself, Cédile later strongly hinted at possible Vietnamese-Japanese cooperation, since a company of Japanese troops had allowed the Viet Minh to pass through. He verified Maunsell's account of Gracey's reaction to French behavior. The *coup* was carried out by

. . . . French civilians, with the help of a few released POWs and British troops, and they together, who had suffered under the Viet Minh, who were their enemy (a very nasty enemy) . . . turned against the Viet Minh, and General Gracey was very angry about this. He was angry with good reason and he ordered the POWs to be returned to barracks.

He wasn't well equipped and . . . the whole Japanese Army was still armed. The Japanese had only just begun to be disarmed, and he, like us, had very little information. General Gracey was saying to himself, "Well, if things start going badly, what should we do? There are hardly any planes, we're a long way from help in Singapore and Rangoon." When he saw the fact of the French civilians and rearmed troops composed of prisoners-of-war, that their maneuvers were not going well, he wanted me to return all the French troops to their barracks.

I had to obey him — he had his reasons at the time. But during the night there was this incident at the Cité Heyraud, and also one could see the Viet Minh revolutionaries, quite a lot of them, around in the streets shooting with their revolvers, and quite a lot of French were killed.

So [after the massacre] I had to go and see him. This meeting was quite dramatic. I told him, "General, . . . I have the responsibility for the French civil population. I can't allow women and children to be shot and killed, so please help us by allowing us to bring back the rearmed POWs into the street." At first he said no, but then kindly agreed with me and said, in fact, "All right, my dear boy, you are right," and very soon after that we had the French troops back in the streets.[28]

The period was reminiscent of the Boxer Rebellion, with British, Indian, Japanese, French, Australian and Dutch contingents patrolling

28. Cédile interview, 25 Oct. 1977.

the streets of Saigon; on this occasion, however, the Americans were on the other side. The Viet Minh repaid American moral support by immediately murdering the senior American officer.


# APPENDIX

The order was prefaced as follows (The references are to the Saigon Street Plan, 2nd edn, 1945):

1. On the night of 22/23 Sep the French Army and Administration are seizing the Police Stations, Post Office and Treasury from the Viet Minh who are at present controlling them. Z hr will be 0400 hrs Saigon time. The following objectives will be taken by French tps under the comd of Lt-Col Rivier:-

(a) Z-5 mins Post Office and Telephone Exchange (35) 22055410 — One Coy.

(b) Z-5 mins Surete (45) 22055395, one coy.

(c) Z hr Commissariat de Arrondissement (93) 21705250 — one coy.

(d) Z hr Commissariat Central (not marked) 20455160 — one coy.

(e) Z hr Commissariat 1er Arrondissement (77) 22805340 — one coy. (Navy)

(f) Z hr Commissariat du Port (99) 22705250

(g) Z hr Commissariat 6e      ) one coy.
Arrondissement                ) (Navy)

2. Later on 23 Sept French tps will also take over the Central Jail from 1/1 GR. *All Viet Minh* found at these objectives will be disarmed and interned by the French Administration until their credentials have been checked, when those considered harmless will be released.

3. Lt-Col Rivier's HQ will be located at the French Barracks in the Boulevard Norodon [*sic*] (10) 212547 till 0400 hrs when it will move to the Post Office.


## INTENTION.

4. 80 Ind Inf Bde will cooperate with the French Forces in their plan and will take one further objective:-
Garde Civile barracks (not marked) 19405380.


## METHOD.

5. (a) Two pls 1 Hybad comd by a BO will take the Garde Civile barracks at 0400 hrs 23 Sep.

(b) M. le Commandant Besson will accompany them as interpreter.

(c) *All Viet Minh* personnel will be disarmed, searched and detained under gd until such time as the French administration take them over on 23 Sep.

(d) As soon as the take over has been completed a report will be submitted to this HQ by jeep DR. Report will incl. casualties, prisoners, incidents, etc.

6. (a) The Jap gd at the Post Office and Telephone Exchange (35) 22055410 will be relieved by 1/1 GR (str 1 BO and two secs) at 1400 hrs 22 Sep.

(b) Sentries will be posted outside the building with a gd room inside in order that ingress may be effected at any time.

(c) On arrival of the French Coy at 0400 hrs 23 Sep they will permit them to enter the buildings to take over the Post Office and Telephone Exchange and will give any assistance required.

(d) The French will be responsible for any Viet Minh found on the premises.

(e) 1/1 GR gd will be relieved by the French Coy and will be dismissed after daylight.

7. (a) The 1/1 GR gd will permit French prison officials to enter the Central jail at 0700 hrs 23 Sep and will assist them to take over from the Viet Minh warders.

(b) The gd will be relieved by French tps on 23 Sep (time to be notified later).

AIM.

8. *Tpt* [Transport]

(a) Maj R. A. Harris REME [Royal Electrical and Mechanical Engineers] will detail 4 cars to be collected by French drivers at 1500 hrs 22 Sep. They will be returned by the French to this HQ by 1800 hrs 23 Sep.

(b) The Japs are being ordered to provide 10 lorries (formerly property of the French Army) to report to this HQ at 1400 hrs 22 Sep. These will also be collected by French drivers at 1500 hrs 22 Sep.

(c) One jeep of HQ 80 Bde will report to 1 Hybad at 2000 hrs 22 Sep for use by DR reporting completion of task.

9. *Arms*

(a) Pl weapons less 2" mtrs will be carried.

(b) Pistols Signalling will be carried by all dets.

INTERCOMN.

10. All reports to HQ 80 Ind Inf Bde Officers' Mess . . .

A postscript was added:

### AFTER ORDER

Ref para 1 (c) and (e).

Gds on these buildings were taken over by 1 Hybad night 21/22 Sep. French tps will take over from 1 Hybad at time laid down in original plan. [80 Ind Inf Bde O.O. No. 13, 22 September 1945].

The War Diary of 80 Brigade recorded the events of 23 September:

0345 — Coup de'état during night successfully accomplished and following its present position, Commissariats 227534, 216525 and Treasury 226532 hand over to French tps.

0530 — Post Office handed over to French tps. Yokohama Bank and Banque Indochine surrounded and taken over by 1 Hybad. French tps guarding brs over Arroyo de Lalanch [sic] at 203556–215557–217557–228555–231550 and some firing reported. French cas 1 killed.

1700–1900 — four fires started by Annamites at rly sta 214528, Market 216519 and warehouse 218518 other was Race Course area 197537.

# 9

# THE FIRST AMERICAN CASUALTY

When reports of the *coup* and the Viet Minh counterattacks reached SEAC headquarters it was decided to dispatch a senior officer to survey the situation in Saigon personally. Brigadier Myers, with his unique SOE experience as Head of Mission to the Greek Resistance, was summoned to Mountbatten's office by Major-General Penney, SEAC's Director of Intelligence, and briefed by Mountbatten in Slim's presence. Myers was told to get to the bottom of the problems in Saigon and to find out how the British could achieve their military objective of disarming the Japanese without becoming involved in the Franco-Vietnamese troubles, which were deemed to be none of Britain's business. As has been pointed out, memories of Scobie's experience in Athens were fresh at SEAC headquarters.

Myers was ordered to report to Slim's office before he left. Slim satisfied himself as to Myers' terms of reference after reminding him that he was operating in his (Slim's) own territory. Myers then took off for Saigon via Bangkok in a Mosquito aircraft. The weather en route to Saigon was atrocious, with zero visibility in heavy monsoon rain. At times they were flying close to the treetops when they got lost and eventually ran out of fuel. They were fortunate to find a small field which Myers spotted by chance, about 30 or 40 miles out of Saigon, where they crashlanded their Mosquito, fuel tanks dry, in the midst of a party of surprised Japanese, who were meeting the Allies for the first time.[1]

On 25 September Gracey telegraphed Mountbatten that Myers had finally arrived, and after initial discussions with him Gracey decided he should send a message to SEAC, reiterating what he considered his primary tasks. Gracey added that the "self-styled Viet Nam Southern Republic" government constituted a menace to law and order through its lack of control. Furthermore, the Viet Minh government was set up "under Japanese connivance", and no administrative services were operating in Saigon, although the "essential public services" did still function. Gracey also knew where the real power lay: "Main control Viet Minh party exercised from Hanoi was definitely vested in this provi-

1. Brig. E. C. J. Myers, personal interview, 6 Nov. 1977.

sional govt. for all southern areas of FIC'' (current OSS reporting confirmed this). Gracey then said simply why he could not recognize the Viet Minh: ''My brief contained instr[uction]s not to get involved politically. It was therefore impossible to have any dealings with the Viet Minh Govt. Reestablishment of French was therefore urgently essential to enable introduction proper adm[inistrative] services.''

Gracey was stating that the city had been at a standstill — and great cities cannot remain in such a state for long before a process of dissolution begins. His report continued by saying that the progressive disarmament of the Viet Minh police had begun on 16 September, but ''Insufficiency of [British] tps made it impossible for me to complete disarmament in this way.'' Cédile and Rivier then assured Gracey of the efficiency with which the French troops would finish the job, and ''Although actual take over achieved success, indiscipline of French troops and provocative acts of French civilians ensured later counter action by Annamese, who regard all French as Vichy and despise them.'' Gracey's assessment was correct. There was a potential for trouble in Annam and Cochinchina; Laos had been infiltrated by the Viet Minh and could be a problem, but Cambodia was still relatively trouble-free. He then briefly traced the history of the Vietnamese resistance, mentioning the risings of 1930 and 1940. His report concluded by saying that the Viet Minh strength had greatly increased since 9 March, that the Japanese did not regard themselves as defeated by France, and that the French had no prestige in the eyes of the Japanese. The appearance of French troops was producing a ''violent reaction by militant Annamites in their present mood''. Japanese headquarters was unexpectedly disorganized, and Japanese disarmament carried out by the French alone would bring about serious problems. Gracey's recommendations to Mountbatten were to speed up the movement of 20 Division, evacuate Japanese forces before the British departure, ship in experienced French troops, and work out a smooth transfer of power from the British to the French.

On 25 September Colonel C. R. Price, at the War Office, received a letter from the Foreign Office concerning ''certain disquieting developments in Indo-China'', where ''In the view of the Foreign Office the situation is one in which we shall have to proceed with great caution.'' But the British objective ''can only be attained if law and order are maintained,'' despite the War Office's insistence on diluting the law and order section of the draft Civil Affairs agreement with the French. Although Mountbatten could call upon the Japanese forces, ''he cannot thereby divest himself of the final responsibility for ensuring law and order throughout the territories embraced in his command. . . ."[2] Price's attention was drawn to the invidious position of the British forces: "If the British forces endeavour to suppress anti-French activities on the part of the Vietnam party or other groups, we shall open ourselves to attacks from American anti-Imperialist opinion and no doubt from the Chinese, whereas a policy of complete non-intervention in domestic affairs would no doubt be interpreted by the French as a further step towards our alleged long-term objective of pushing them out of their colonial territories." In view of this the Chiefs of Staff were asked to speed up the transfer of French troops to Indochina. The British could not state publicly that they were in French Indochina only to secure and disarm the Japanese and to repatriate the prisoners-of-war and internees. No matter how tempted they may have been to do so, "the danger is that it might be interpreted as an indication of our intention to wash our hands of all internal developments in Indo-China and as indicating that we do not accept any responsibility for the maintenance of law and order." The revolutionary elements would be encouraged by such an announcement, and the French would have their "worst suspicions" confirmed. The Foreign Office said that if Mountbatten felt compelled to make a statement on the situation, it would like him to state that while he did not wish to intervene in internal affairs, he could not tolerate a breakdown in law and order since this would impede his primary tasks. Mountbatten asked the Cabinet in London that the move of the 9th DIC to Indochina should be treated as an "over-riding priority", and that it should be as close behind Massu's Combat Command of the 2nd Armored Division (the *"Groupement Massu"*) as possible.

Exactly when Harry Brain reached Saigon is uncertain, but he submitted his first political report to Dening, his superior, on 25 September. This complemented Gracey's report, and suggested that the Viet Minh leaders be brought, under British protection, to talks with Cédile and the French. Should the talks break down they "would then be exfiltrated from Saigon and British protection." He thought that "such an action would not lay us open to blame politically and will demonstrate our impartiality." On 25 September a Viet Minh broadcast from Hanoi radio blasted Gracey's actions in Saigon.

In a message to the Foreign Office, Dening referred to the recent meeting at which Leclerc's comments had produced heated discussion. Dening had pointed out to Mountbatten that there were political move-

2. PRO, FO 371/46304, 25 Sept. 1945 [F 7161].

ments in all the countries of Southeast Asia which were political matters and not a concern for SEAC. But Leclerc claimed that the situation in Indochina amounted to banditry, and implied that SEAC forces should suppress what seemed to be political movements as part of their task of maintaining order. The next paragraph was a dreary reminder that the Mountbatten-Wedemeyer dispute continued to the end. Virulent propaganda was still pouring from Hanoi radio, and messages about it from Mountbatten to Wedemeyer had produced no results. Dening's concern, and perhaps despair, is evident in his conclusion: "The clouds are rolling up in the Far East and I think that there is a very serious danger of the west being regarded as aligning itself against the east, with incalculable consequences for the future. . . . If we are to avoid trouble full sovereignty should be resumed in French Indo-China and the Netherlands East Indies as soon as possible. In the meantime French Commanders in these areas are faced with an extremely difficult and delicate problem. . . ."

On 26 September Gracey, having received the pertinent messages from Mountbatten to the Cabinet, Mountbatten telegraphed: "Very much regret that Proclamation was not according to policy, but I much appreciate your very kind action to support me. I assure you I had no intention of deploying my forces outside Saigon-Cholon key area and will not do so. I fully understand your instructions. . . ."[3] Gracey said that he had ordered Terauchi to report to Commission headquarters because of the Japanese laxity in keeping the peace (and especially their behavior during the Cité Heyraud massacre). Gracey reported that during the previous twenty-four hours there had been a "considerable increase" in the abduction and murder of French men and women. There was "considerable evidence" of the reluctance of the Japanese to intervene, and they had been caught "red-handed" in refusing to fire on the Viet Minh; this was why he had called in Terauchi. Roadblocks were being set up all around Saigon and Cholon to a distance of 30 km., and bridges were being sabotaged. Mob violence had decreased in Saigon and Cholon "where rough treatment of two mobs and infliction [of] casualties estimated at 60 killed, unknown wounded, by 80 Brigade produced less keenness." There was, not unnaturally, an "increase in hostility to British Indian Gurkha troops".

Gracey stated that the strain appeared to be too much for Cédile, who "may collapse. His task is beyond him. Should this occur, his successor

3. PRO, WO 203/4349, COS 30, Gracey to Mountbatten, 26 Sept. 1945.

must be a man of resolution and high standing. This matter is urgent.''
Gracey's plans now were to open the approaches to the city, if necessary
by "ruthlessly enforcing" his orders, to reopen the market and encourage trading, and to urge the French to project a liberal policy in broadcasts over Saigon radio. French troops would be used "very sparingly"
during these operations, and Gracey concluded by again asking that his
20th Division be allowed to sail as their ships were loaded. He also
wanted to accelerate the arrival of "*good, well*-commanded French
troops". He had instructed Brain to forward a copy of this message to
local French officials, "who were useless and should immediately be
removed.'' Gracey, as Brain later noted, did not mince words with
Terauchi. During the meeting on the 26th, he opened by saying that he
wished "to reiterate and emphasise certain of the facts on the present
situation here and to give you certain definite orders.'' He said: "The
matter of the future government of French Indo-China has always been
one for the French Government,'' and the local uprisings were not helping them to implement their liberal policy. The Japanese Emperor had
recognized France as one of the Allied nations, and "The whole situation
in French Indo-China and its potential dangers are well known to you.''
Had the Japanese kept to the terms of the Rangoon agreement "the present Annamite rising would not have occurred or would have been very
greatly reduced and quickly stopped. Practically every case of murder of
Allied nationals, arson, pillage and looting has occurred in sectors
allotted to the Japanese troops in which to keep law and order.'' Japanese
troops, including officers, had stood by and watched the perpetration of
outrages, including the incident in the Dakao sector (Cité Heyraud).
Japanese guards on important positions were usually under strength and
had no reserves.

Gracey told Terauchi, "You will be as angry over such slipshod
methods as I am.'' Japanese troops were often allowed to pass roadblocks while the Allies were fired on or detained. In noting Numata's
earlier statement to Taunton that the Japanese troops were tired, Gracey
said that if this was the case then the commanding general was not doing
his job properly. Furthermore, it appeared that Terauchi did not know
what was going on in Saigon. In view of all this, Terauchi was ordered to
keep Japanese efficiency up and to correct the deficiencies mentioned. He
was also ordered to clear Thu Dau Mot and Bien Hoa of Viet Minh, and
to increase the guard over Admiral Decoux in Loc Ninh. Gracey concluded, "I wish to point out to you that the very unpleasant side of
unconditional surrender for those who have been compelled to do so is

fully realised." Furthermore, said Gracey, from what he had seen of the determination of Japanese troops in combat, they were sufficiently well armed to do the tasks they were now given.

Mountbatten had been most considerate to Terauchi personally, and the Japanese were fully aware of the imminent Viet Minh uprising at the time of the Rangoon agreement. Gracey said he knew that a speedy return to Japan was uppermost in the minds of the Japanese, but unless they cooperated they would stay where they were for the foreseeable future. Terauchi was then ordered to move to the Japanese headquarters until further notice, "sending for your kit immediately".[4] Terauchi bowed and left, determined to clamp down on his forces if only to avoid the shame of undergoing another humiliation like this. Gracey later wrote that without specific instructions from Mountbatten he had summoned and told Terauchi categorically that Japanese troops "must obey the spirit as well as the letter of orders, and specific cases of disobedience or partial compliance were [spelt out] to him." Gracey recalled that Terauchi's "anger at this state of affairs was genuine," and after his orders had been passed on, the situation improved dramatically, and the behavior of Japanese troops remained "exemplary" until after the British departed from Indochina. In addition, "the safety of the French nationals outside Saigon, and the security of all essential installations was therefore secured . . ."[5]

On the 26th the British and Japanese forces cleared roadblocks all over Saigon, and shots were fired by snipers scattered throughout the city. Large fires were started in several places, especially in the north, and some of them blazed through the night. A company of 3/1 Gurkha Rifles (Blascheck's company) swept the banks of the Arroyo de l'Avalanche from east to west in the disturbed northern part of the city and ran into opposition in the Dakao area. They captured a minor Viet Minh headquarters and four suspects. Three Gurkhas were wounded in the skirmish around the house. A little later the Gurkhas, continuing their sweep, rescued six French women and children from a locked pagoda, the children saying that their parents had been murdered before their eyes that morning.[6] The company returned to barracks at about 1300 hours, but as soon as they had sat down to a well-deserved lunch

4. Terauchi was in fact allowed to remain living in his house; a Japanese Liaison Officer moved in his place. (Brigadier Maunsell, interview 20 April 1977).
5. Gracey papers, Correspondence with SEAC Recorder, 3 Oct. 1946.
6. PRO, WO 172/7769, War Diary 1/1 Gurkha Rifles, 26 Sept. 1945.

they were called out by a report that the American detachment in the north of Saigon was under siege by the Viet Minh. The tired troops scrambled out of their barracks and set off for the OSS headquarters. The "scramble" order to Blascheck brought the news that Lieutenant-Colonel Peter Dewey had been ambushed and killed, making him, as it has often since been said, the first American casualty in Vietnam. (This of course is not correct, as Americans, both POWs and aircrew, had died in Vietnam during the war.)

The OSS account of this has often been cited, but the Allied Control Commission's version has seldom, if ever, been reported. Some published materials even hold the French responsible for Dewey's death, and almost everything in print blames someone other than Dewey himself, whose curious activities away from the available protection exposed him constantly to unnecessary danger. The OSS Major Small's affidavit, for example, blamed Gracey for everything that was wrong with Saigon, including indirect responsibility for Dewey's death; it made the ridiculous assertion that Gracey had underestimated the dangers (which would have been news to the British, who had continually but fruitlessly alerted the OSS to the precariousness of their position). In almost the next sentence Small wrote that the Viet Minh leaders were unable to control their men.

Dewey was Chief of the "Embankment" group, whose advance party of four arrived in Saigon on 2 September; he and four others arrived on the 4th, followed on the 5th by Captain Frank White (who later became a distinguished journalist) and two other officers. They arrived with eight US aircraft which evacuated 214 American POWs on the 6th, thus removing one of the two reasons for the OSS presence in Saigon. The OSS now officially had only to look after the modest amount of American property in the Saigon area and Cochinchina. But although they were charged to steer clear of political involvement, they promptly plunged into Saigon's political vortex and became involved with, among others, the Viet Minh.[7] It has been established with certainty that Dewey was ambushed by Vietnamese at a roadblock while *en route* for Tan Son Nhut airfield whence he was to fly out. The affidavits signed by Majors Bluechel (who was riding with Dewey when the ambush occurred), Small and Varner, and Captain White make no mention of the reason for

---

7. In December 1945, Lt. J. R. Withrow told the State Department that "Colonel Dewey had a plan to get Dr Thach to Washington incognito and that this plan may have played a role in causing Colonel Dewey's death." [NA, RG 59, Box 6177.]

Dewey's departure, other than that it had been planned. By the tone of their previous reporting and their attitude to Gracey, it seems likely that had Gracey ordered Dewey out (as was later charged) it would have been mentioned prominently in all their reports.

Dewey's aircraft was late in arriving at Tan Son Nhut, so he returned to his headquarters. There were numerous roadblocks all over the suburbs, usually manned by unarmed Vietnamese. The fatal block, between Tan Son Nhut and Gia Dinh, had been in existence since 23 September, and passed dozens of times by OSS personnel. On this day, at about 1230, Dewey and Bluechel approached it; Dewey, ironically, was deploring the Viet Minh attack on another American, Captain Coolidge, when a light machine-gun opened up at point-blank range. Dewey, who had seen his attackers and was said to have shouted "*Je suis Américain*",[8] was hit and died instantly. The jeep, slowed to 8 miles per hour to traverse the S-shaped road block, turned on its side; Dewey's body was trapped and remained hanging at the wheel. Bluechel made his way to OSS headquarters, where a defense was organized (the nine Japanese guards assigned to the villa showed little interest). When the Vietnamese mob attacked the house (over which a US flag flew in plain view) the correspondents Downs and McGlinty, of whom more will be said, were already inside, having arrived with an OSS officer.

The OSS books by Smith and, more recently, Patti seem to have relied on immediately recognizable secondary source material for the events surrounding Dewey's death, in addition to an account by a lower-ranking member of the OSS team. (Official OSS reports have since been declassified and will be reviewed here.) A number of inaccuracies mar these accounts, one being that the French *at that time* were in American uniforms; they were not, because the French were then outfitted by the British, as contemporary photos show. The question of the American flag has already been discussed, and Leclerc, despite Smith's assertion, had not yet arrived in Saigon, nor had the Viet Minh been running an effective government. The OSS, consistent in their anti-French and anti-British sympathies and reporting at that time, accused their Allies of having "embarked on a program of massacre and brutality against the generally defenseless Annamese population . . .,"[9] charges which were

8. It has been said, but not made part of the official record, that Dewey cursed the Vietnamese, who then killed him. It could explain why the Vietnamese shot him at this particular time, for no apparent reason, after allowing him to pass unmolested many times before.
9. R. Harris Smith, *OSS* (Berkeley: University of California Press, 1972), p. 341.

to come back and haunt the Americans two decades later. This wild charge closely resembled, both in content and language, those emanating from the Politburo of the Indochina Communist Party in Hanoi. According to Smith, who was apparently told this by an ex-OSS man, Gracey had ordered Dewey to leave Saigon, and Dewey was on his way out when ambushed. This is highly questionable, and is not corroborated by any of the available evidence, including official OSS reports of the incident, which clearly state that Dewey departed in accordance with arrangements "previously made".[10] Interviews with senior British and French officials, plus exhaustive searches through the archives at the Public Record Office and the National Archives in Washington, have failed to reveal the slightest indication that Gracey ordered Dewey to leave Saigon. There would have been no reason for such an order, for the OSS were more of nuisance than a threat to the Allied command, and their movements were well known. The OSS were a cause for concern only insofar as their safety could not be assured, and Dewey's death made the Americans aware of conditions in Saigon in a way that no amount of British or French argument had been able to accomplish.

On learning of Dewey's death Gracey sent the following message to Mountbatten: "Very much regret to report that Lt Col Dewey US Army OSS was shot dead by Annamite rebels this afternoon. . . . All officers of or attached to Mission had been warned by me previously not to move without escort or in dangerous places. He was trusting to Americans being inviolate. . . .[11] Please convey the deepest regrets of myself and all the Allies in Saigon to his father."

10. *Causes, Origins, and Lessons of the Vietnam War.* Hearings before the Senate Committee on Foreign Relations, 9–11 May 1972, p. 286.
11. This appeared to be a peculiar characteristic of some OSS personnel. Admiral Miles, USN, wrote: "The Washington office of the OSS appeared to have a queer, ostrich-like fixation. It was almost as if they thought their men wore invisible cloaks. . . ." (p. 160). Miles, not noted for his liking of the British, was referring to China operations in this case. He continued, "Before we had the wit to recognize it, we had tied the hands of our friends and turned over quantities of arms to their enemy and ours" (Miles, *A Different Kind of War*, p. 491).

Major Bluechel's affidavit illustrated this point. Even after Dewey's murder he still could not believe that the Viet Minh knowingly fired on him or that they knew what they were doing when they attacked the US mission. Although Dr Thach headed the violent Advanced Guard Youth, and had told the OSS that he was hoping his mass demonstration would provoke Anglo-French fire and produce some Viet Minh martyrs, OSS reports described him as a peaceful man who disdained violence.

Gracey was distressed by Dewey's death, for it should never have happened. The next day, on 27 September, he telegraphed SEAC headquarters:

Complete examination circumstances Dewey death action shows following:
(*a*) Dewey killed by planned ambush whilst driving jeep.
(*b*) Attack shows all signs of premeditation and planned attack direct OSS.
(*c*) OSS House flew American flag throughout.[12]
(*d*) Annamite party approx strength armed men 20 arrived and left in MT [motor transport].
(*e*) Locals stated American flag over this building was no security owing public visits various Frenchmen observed by Annamites.
(*f*) Other incidents prove that flags or other means of easy identification Allied Nationals do not afford any protection if position is met which is held by organized band determined execute planned raid or hold up.[13]

Neither Dewey's killers nor his body were ever found. The British almost had both in their hands, but two American news reporters placed themselves between the British assault force and Dewey's killers, permitting the latter to escape with the body. The reporters — Bill Downs, employed by CBS (the Columbia Broadcasting System), and Jim McGlinty — were termed "highly excitable" by the Gurkha company commander involved.[14]

Downs dispatched the following story as a CBS "eye-witness account of the pitched battle at the US HQ in Saigon on Wednesday . . . after the attack on the HQ, where a US Major requested British HQ to send Gurkha troops to go to relief of the US HQ." The title was, not surprisingly, "British Have 'Bungled Job Badly' ".

There was another sticky moment and it was just at this point that the firing started again. For by this time the British Gurkhas were marching to the relief of the US HQ, which had already in effect been relieved. Negotiations between us and Annamese ceased immediately. It didn't look good for us. [McGlinty?] and I said we thought we could stop the shooting . . . We walked down the road towards the Gurkhas waving our hats and our arms. The white flag was up. Even so the British troops let off a couple of shots at us that sent us to the ditch.

We got out again and started walking towards the Gurkhas. They held their fire, and out in front of them was a British major. He kept marching up the

12. This contradicts Smith's account; however, the flag was clearly seen by British troops who rescued the Americans, and was mentioned in Bluechel's affidavit.
13. PRO WO 203/4273, COS 32, 27 Sept. 1945. Noyes Thomas, war correspondent of *The Times of India*, wrote the most balanced account of the incident.
14. Lt.-Col. Charles U. Blascheck, personal interview, 3/4 Dec. 1977.

road. We begged him to stop shooting, to stop his troops. He told us to shut up, that he was commanding the party. He threatened us with arrest. We told him that we would walk ahead of his troops, if only they would not fire, and that the only thing ahead of him were women and children. The major got furious and another major came up from the rear ranks and got mad at us too. We never did get a chance to tell the British leader that there were four US officers virtually in hostage and that their lives were at stake: . . .[15]

Not surprisingly, the Gurkha War Diary differs from the reporter. After logging an account of 3/1 GR's morning sweep of the Arroyo de l'Avalanche, the fighting, the capture of Viet Minh suspects, the rescue of French civilians and the wounding of two Gurkha soldiers, it continued:

The [Company] returned for lunch. At about 1400 hrs it was reported that an American Col had been murdered and that a USA HQ was being besieged by the mob on the Rue Macmahon Prolongée. 3/1 Coy again went out to relieve the Americans, recover the Colonel's body and disperse the mob. Reaching the USA HQ they found no siege in progress but an irresolute mob whom they dispersed with fire wounding about 10; and further up the road USA press correspondents [Downs and McGlinty] negotiating with armed and uniformed Annamite leaders for the return of the body. It would have been simple to capture the hostile leaders had not the press correspondents interfered, stood between our own troops and the Annamites, and argued that the recovery of the Colonel's body was a matter of great political importance as some relation of his was a notorious politician in the States. Meanwhile, the Annamite leaders, promising to produce the body forthwith, slipped off, jumped into a truck and disappeared: not, of course, to return.[16]

The company left the OSS villa and continued the sweep; they met another Viet Minh armed mob and fire was exchanged, resulting in the deaths of twelve Annamites and the capture of five with rifles. The advance continued, but Dewey's body was not found, and the Gurkhas wrote that the news reporting of the incident "bordered on the fantastic".[17]

The 1/1 Gurkha Rifles Newsletter also described the incident:

On 26 Sep Charles Blascheck was frustrated by American journalists in his quest for Colonel Dewey's body. The Colonel had been ambushed by Vitamins [Gurkha slang for Viet Minh] and Blascheck was sent out to recover his remains.

15. PRO, FO 371/46398, 28 Sept. 1945 [F 7765].
16. PRO, WO 172/7769, War Diary 1/1 GR, 26 Sept. 1945.
17. *Ibid.*

He found the body at the scene of the crime surrounded by the killers, and was about to recapture it by force, when the journalists intervened and attempted to use appeasement. As a result the body disappeared and has not been seen since. The Colonel was some relative of the Republican candidate for the Presidency of the USA.[18]

In the picture that emerges from the Gurkha official and unofficial diaries, two American reporters appeared to be more interested in the publicity surrounding the recovery of Dewey's body than in capturing his killers or rescuing the Americans in the villa, and this is why the two British majors were "furious". Blascheck himself, wounded seriously in Burma, wounded again in Saigon, and to participate in another assault on the Viet Minh the next day, had this to say: "The American correspondents wanted to 'negotiate' with the Viet Minh, saying that they 'understood' the Annamites. I replied that Dewey was dead and was not so important now — the important thing was that several live Americans were still in the villa, but the idiotic correspondents kept saying that they were friends of the Viet Minh and that Dewey was important."[19]

Blascheck said he was perfectly aware that Dewey had important political connections in the United States. He had received a report that the Americans were in trouble, and had taken out his full company of Gurkhas, with instructions to get the Americans out to a safe place. He arrived to find a confused scene at the US headquarters, made more so by the two correspondents who kept getting in the way and who finally were dressed down by Blascheck.

Blascheck clearly remembered seeing some Viet Minh in the house which he believed to be the OSS headquarters.[20] While he was sizing up the situation he saw a body thrown from a window. Although he could not see the face, the body was in a US uniform. It was thrown into a large monsoon storm drainage ditch, and as it was still the rainy season the drains were filled with fast-flowing water and presumably the body was washed away.

In recently released OSS reports, it turns out that Captain Frank White had the same problems with Downs and McGlinty as did Charles Blascheck a little later. White went out as soon as possible after the battle

18. Gracey Papers, 1/1 Gurkha Rifles Newsletter, n.d.
19. Charles Blascheck, interview, 3/4 Dec. 1977.
20. From recently released archival material, an OSS diagram of the immediate area suggests that the house Blascheck described from memory was a large house adjacent to the OSS villa; this house was occupied by the Viet Minh.

to seek the return of Dewey's body, but his own negotiations were "hindered" and "complicated" by the two, who were "apparently . . . unfamiliar with the disposition of Gurkha troops during combat." White wrote that the correspondents "demanded that the Gurkhas retire;" they also charged the Gurkha company commander (Blascheck) with being a "murderer if he continued".[21]

Major-General Pyman, Slim's Chief of Staff, further rebutted the OSS claim that Gracey's ban on junior officers flying flags contributed to Dewey's death. He reported that only the General Officer Commanding (Gracey), Brigadiers and the senior Royal Navy and Royal Air Force officers were authorized to fly national flags on their staff cars. He also provided some information which the OSS omitted in their report: first, that *all* cars, including OSS vehicles, were issued with paper flags, to be stuck to the windshields; and secondly, that the OSS in Saigon had agreed not to fly flags on cars, but said that they would paint the Stars and Stripes on the hoods and doors.[22] Thus, had they carried out their intention the US flag would have been clearly visible from all angles to Dewey's killers. The OSS report was thus deliberately misleading or, like so much of their work in Asia, badly done.

Since the OSS appeared to be less than open in their report of the circumstances surrounding Dewey's death, Mountbatten had to fill in many blanks in this report which reached the hands of Brigadier-General Timberman, the senior US officer at SEAC headquarters. The OSS had not mentioned that Dewey had been called in by Gracey and warned about his subversive dealings with known Viet Minh, and that Gracey had forcefully warned Dewey against travelling without an escort, which was available to him at any time he required it. It was repeated that Gracey withheld from Dewey the privilege of flying a flag at the car's pennant solely because of his junior rank, which was standard international practice (and is still standard practice in the US armed forces today), but had urged him to fasten it across the radiator so that it could be seen from the front (from a roadblock). It was emphasized that in any case a small fluttering flag would probably not be distinguishable until too late. Mountbatten, who was on less than friendly terms with Gracey at the time, told Timberman he was satisfied that Gracey had done all he could to prevent the incident.[23]

---

21. *Causes, Origins, and Lessons of the Vietnam War*, p. 295.
22. PRO, WO 203/5644, Pyman to SACSEA, 29 Sept. 1945.
23. PRO, WO 203/5023, Mountbatten to Timberman, 30 Sept. 1945.

On 26 September, the day Dewey was killed, a disturbing report was received at SEAC headquarters on OSS activity in Indochina. Force 136 agents had now confirmed the extent of the evidently coordinated American efforts to subvert the French and British. The report described the anti-Allied efforts and the spreading of anti-French propaganda by the OSS "through all channels". Force 136 was so alarmed at the long-term implications of the American operations that it recommended that a series of outposts be established by the Allies along the entire 16th parallel. They had a more immediate cause for concern in that, as they reported, the Americans were refusing to allow Force 136 to evacuate French women and children to safety in Vientiane. The Force 136 telegram ended by independently confirming Sainteny's later assertions; the Americans were taking advantage of Viet Minh attacks "to discredit French and declaring that French administration will not repetition not be permitted in Chinese zone."[24]

The mentality of some of the OSS in the region was well illustrated in an incident which occurred as a small party had crossed the Mekong from Nakon Phanom into Laos, in the US area north of the 16th parallel. A British Force 136 captain and a French officer named Klotz were in Laos, accompanying an OSS officer and a band of Viet Minh.[25] The Viet Minh turned on the Frenchman, but the Force 136 officer, arms outstretched, immediately leaped between the Viet Minh assassins and the French officer in a desperate attempt to save his life. But two or three of the Viet Minh party slipped around the officer and shot the hapless Frenchman from the side. The American officer had watched all this, for when the attack was made he stood aside with the words, "I guess I am now a neutral." Mountbatten was so disgusted by the report that he complained to Wedemeyer about it.[26]

24. PRO, WO 203/5644, Force 136 to SACSEA, [I. 5304], 26 Sept. 1945.
25. The British officer, who now lives in London, was attempting to introduce Klotz to the Viet Minh in order to ensure his safety. The American, who is named in the appropriate archives, became an early US Army Special Forces commander, and is apparently ranked in their pantheon of founding members.
26. Many years later, Cédile spoke of Dewey's activities: "Well, you know there are always people who think they can do things better than others, who think they have a great talent for reconciliation and who want to put things into order — people who are a bit more liberal than those who are in command and who have to be more careful and who have to be much more restrained . . . But he was a dilettante, I think. He could say whatever he wanted, he had nothing to risk [politically], nothing to lose; no one could accuse him of anything . . . I remember feeling very annoyed. Well, Dewey was involved in his little adventure. I heard that an

Colonel Mingant, French Army, added a postscript to the affair. He remembered that Dewey, perhaps for the purpose of cover, was known in Saigon as "Mister" Dewey. Mingant had warned him that the Vietnamese were not under a strong central control but Dewey told Mingant not to worry, and that he had nothing to fear. Mingant and the French had known the Viet Minh long before Dewey arrived, and said that if Dewey had wanted to meet any of them he had only to ask and the French would have brought the Viet Minh to him. Mingant said that Dewey could well have had some influence with the Viet Minh, but it was unfortunate that he did not use it to promote a settlement, but rather backed the Viet Minh blindly. Mingant was later told by the Viet Minh that they had killed Dewey: "I heard a long time after from the Viet Minh. They said, 'We did a wrong thing. Mr Dewey had been killed, and this is no good for us.' "[27] Mingant, then a captain, said that Dewey was "a little shot [not important], just like me. I don't think he was mistaken for a French officer, but you know the Viet Minh at that time had no chief exactly, not yet." Dewey had told Mingant that he had plenty of questions to ask him, but was killed before they met again.

Not much was heard from the OSS after that, except for two other incidents which occurred at about the same time. On one occasion a platoon of Gurkhas was fired on when approaching the Viet Minh head-quarters in Saigon, with bows and arrows among other weapons. One of the Gurkhas received an arrow in the arm and the snipers were chased down and captured. The Viet Minh building was flying several flags, including the British, American and French. Captain Peter Prentice took them down and piled them into his jeep, and as he drove away an OSS jeep came up and an altercation followed. It seems that the Americans were incensed at having their flag removed from the Communist building. Prentice said, "Well, all right, if you want it flying from there I'll take it back and put it up again."[28] That was indeed what the OSS wanted and the Stars and Stripes remained the only Allied flag flying over the Viet Minh headquarters. Prentice never knew exactly what the OSS were doing, except that "one had the feeling that they were dashing about with big radio sets."

American mission [led by Dewey's brother] came to find out what happened, and after I left Saigon I even heard a body was found and identified as Dewey's by the teeth, but I don't know." (Personal interview, 26 Oct. 1977.)

27. Colonel Marcel Mingant, personal interview, 26 Oct. 1977.

28. Major Peter Prentice, personal interview, 19 Aug. 1977.

The other notable incident occurred earlier when OSS Captain Coolidge was wounded in another Viet Minh ambush the day before Dewey's death. He was cared for in the British hospital and, according to the "Medical History, Allied Land Forces, French Indo-China",

The Americans flew a special Skymaster hospital plane complete with Lt.-Col. Surgical specialist, Major Medical specialist and Capt. Pathologist to remove a wounded American officer from our care, and also an appendicitis case from Hôpital Grall. This dramatic incident was accompanied by much clicking of cameras, and one had the impression that our Allies were convinced they had saved two of their colleagues from a terrible fate.[29]

It would be difficult to disagree with Harris Smith's sentiment, expressed in his book on this period, that it was "a confused team of seven OSS men"[30] (there were actually twelve men) who went to Saigon, although he was again wrong in stating that it was the "first and only Allied force to reach Saigon during the week of 2 September." Dewey's death was indeed tragic, despite the repeated warnings he had been given of the possible consequences of his actions, because it was the Viet Minh's reward to him for his support.

29. Gracey Papers, "Medical History, Allied Land Forces, French Indo-China, Sept. 1945-Feb. 1946", n.d.
30. Smith, *OSS*, p. 337.

# 10

## PRELUDE TO WAR

In reporting that rioters were now showing "less keenness" as a result of 80 Brigade's response to the rioting, Gracey outlined for Mountbatten his future course of action. As telegraphed to SACSEA, it was in five parts: keep clear the northern approaches to Saigon, using Japanese troops with orders to use ruthless force if necessary; do the same with Saigon, using British/Indian troops and avoiding the use of French troops if possible; immediately reopen the markets and encourage an increase in trading in the city; reopen Saigon Radio and urge the French to broadcast a liberal policy, which they had prepared; and clear the southern approaches to Saigon when troops became available. He also sent Mountbatten a list of "useless" French colonial officials who should immediately be removed. Finally he asked for the rest of his Division and for good, well-commanded French troops.

On the 27th, with an increase in fighting likely, Numata requested a meeting with Maunsell; Brain sat in on this meeting between the two Chiefs of Staff. The Cité Heyraud massacre was evidently much on Numata's mind, for in an emotional statement he said that "in forty years of service he had acquired a reputation for absolute honesty if not wisdom," and begged General Gracey to trust him to carry out faithfully the orders given him.[1] But Brain thought that local Japanese policy was to leave a legacy of friction, and there was a "definite but unobtrusive output being given to the Annamites". The extreme compartmentalization of the Japanese headquarters ("of which we have had startling demonstrations") facilitated this; it was quite possible that Numata did not know what was happening. Only where the British could keep an eye on them could the Japanese be relied on to keep law and order.[2]

---

1. Brigadier Maunsell was impressed by Numata: "He [Numata] was a charming man. He was the kind of man that when I used to have him up to tell him that once again the Japanese had failed to do everything they said, he used to suck in his breath and hiss, and put his head down and say, 'I know I'm a stupid old man,' and I used to say, 'Yes, you are a very stupid old man and you'll be removed from your position if we could find anybody who was less stupid and more efficient.' And he could say, 'I will do my best'." (Brig. M. S. K. Maunsell, personal interview, 20 Apr. 1977.)
2. PRO, WO 203/5023 and WO 172/1785, Brain to Dening, 28 Sept. 1945.

On 27 September SEAC warned the Foreign Office Political Warfare Department, Calcutta, of impending trouble in Saigon. Further involvement by Gracey was anticipated because "restoration of French police almost certainly necessary and gradually French will take over control other public services, if necessary supported by force. Absence of guidance from Foreign Office regretted greatly."[3] A 12th Army report to SEAC headquarters described the French police as "trigger-happy"; also, "drastic action called for since French population near panic. Continental Palace Hotel besieged." French civilians, fearing for their lives, had fled the troubled areas of Saigon to seek refuge in the hotel, where men, women and children choked the corridors as stray bullets whistled across the square outside. The Vietnamese staff had departed, and Dutch ex-POWs, who had volunteered to keep the hotel going, were serving hot soup and stew to the refugees. The telegraphed report ended by saying that "As no light except few candles scene with crashing rain outside was ghostly and rather dramatic."

Under these conditions Gracey had ordered trucks loaded with Indian, Gurkha and Japanese soldiers to patrol the city and to disperse mobs, eliminate snipers, and dismantle any roadblocks they found. In the northern sector, under Lieutenant-Colonel E. D. Murray, Commander 4/10 GR, the French were on the right (east), Gurkhas in the middle and Japanese on the left. There were more problems in the southern sector, where Purcell of 3/1 GR was in command and where the vital power station was located. Japanese were seen leading many of the mobs, and one incident came to light in which a Frenchman was besieged in his shop by a hundred armed Viet Minh. He managed to reach a nearby Japanese military post, but the Japanese told him that he could expect no help from them. He made a miraculous escape under a hail of bullets. Gracey had reported that his single brigade was getting worn out with skirmishing and guard duties; his troops, he said, had fought continuously for three years and were tired. He again appealed for the rest of his Division, if only to enforce obedience from the Japanese.

On 27 September a number of Viet Minh were killed by the Japanese while attempting a water crossing to the north of Saigon in the Dakao area. Just west of that area, Blascheck again took out his company, this time to relieve two platoons of 1/1 GR who were pinned down by a strong Viet Minh force. There were no reserve troops available, so the Gurkhas spent the night in the area, "disturbed only by constant and

3. PRO, WO 172/1785, Hq. SEAC War Diary, 27 Sept. 1945.

unfounded alarums from the French''. At 0630 on the 27th, Blascheck's company from 3/1 GR crossed the bridge on Rue Paul Blanchy, turned left and attacked the Viet Minh from the rear, which cleared the area between the Canal de Ceinture and River Nhieu Loc. Six Viet Minh were killed and twenty-four wounded, and nearby houses harboring Viet Minh were burned. Blascheck's company then withdrew through the French.

The 3/1 Gurkha Rifles Newsletter captured the atmosphere of the days following the Viet Minh rising. "During the whole of this period, bazaars, factories and godowns were burnt nightly. French women, children and irregular troops were murdered and altogether the French community lived indoors in terror for their lives. The Bn was roughly disposed to keep open B. de Gallieni, the streets up to the Arroyo Chinois, and to protect vital points such as the fire station, leaving a small mobile force which was used exhaustively, dashing from the scene of one place of lawlessness to another.''[4] There were daily calls to rescue abducted French civilians — who, according to Charles Blascheck, were frequently locked up in pagodas — and Indian civilians living in Saigon were now being attacked by the Viet Minh because of the actions of the Indian troops; six Indian civilians were killed in a short period, and the 80 Brigade historian now noted: "The men have accepted the necessity of fighting the Annamites. At first their attitude was merely disinterested, but since casualties have been incurred and they have seen and heard of atrocities committed by the Annamites against the French women and children, feelings against the Annamites has risen. They now consider the Annamites as '*Dushman*' ['enemy' in Urdu, the *lingua franca* of the old Indian Army].'' Furthermore, "The Annamites have distributed propaganda in the form of leaflets among the men. The general trend of these leaflets is to compare the situation in FIC and the Annamite struggle for independence with that of India. These leaflets have had *no* effect on morale. Few VCOs or IORs have been bothered to read them . . . ''[5]

As Brain noted in his report of 27 September, the Japanese participation was extremely important to the Viet Minh during this period. When Indian troops were fired on from a house in the middle of Saigon, they attacked and found six Japanese with a radio set, with which they had apparently been in contact with Viet Minh headquarters. On 27

4. Gracey Papers, 3/1 Gurkha Rifles Newsletter.
5. PRO, WO 172/7128, War Diary 80 Indian Infantry Brigade, Sept.–Oct. 1945.

September Brain, as political adviser to Gracey, sent a fairly comprehensive report to SEAC. Since his arrival, when he "was welcomed with anticipatory sighs of relief," he had "been consulted at every point on matters of policy, and signals and reports to SACSEA have taken full account of my views." He spoke well of Numata, but General Manaki, the Saigon garrison commander and Commander, 2nd Division, gave the "impression of being dull-witted and rather bewildered with the situation in which he finds himself." Brain thought that Manaki "probably intends to carry out his instructions but is incapable of doing so expeditiously and efficiently." Wrote Brain:

Unfortunately the road which is paved with such good intentions leads to a hell made up of known inefficiency and strongly suspected sabotage. Preliminary examinations of the organisation of the headquarters of the Southern Army have shown it to be disjointed, ill-coordinated and badly administered. At a conference at which six Japanese staff officers were present, reference was made by us to the 'Planning Board' which was shown in the outline of their organisation . . . It may sound incredible but is true that only one of the officers present knew of the existence of this department and he was only able to identify it after being given a list of the officers comprising it.[6]

Brain was so struck with the Japanese organization, or lack of it, that he expanded on the subject: "It will be no news to you that the Japanese tend to work in watertight compartments and that the right hand frequently does not know what the left hand is doing, but here the hand does not appear to know what the fingers are doing. In every case it was found that an officer knew little of his department beyond the officers immediately subordinate to him and a GSO 1 had to send for a G2 in order to know the number of G3s under his own command." That said, Brain added that this disorganization, bad as it was, did not account for all the problems with the Japanese. He wrote that there was "no doubt" that there existed "some kind of Japanese organization whose object it is to make things as difficult as possible for the restoration of law and order and for the peaceful turnover of the country to Allied control." There was evidence that arms had been handed over or sold to the Viet Minh, that Japanese civilians and soldiers in plain clothes were involved in violent acts, and that Japanese troops had failed to intervene to prevent beatings, killings and abduction of the French population. "The system of watertight compartments would of course facilitate the working of such an independent organisation." The Japanese admitted that

6. PRO, FO 371/46309 (No. 1/FO), Brain to Dening, 27 Sept. 1945.

deserting Japanese troops might have been helping the Viet Minh, but "such an explanation could give excellent cover for what was in fact a planned activity."

Terauchi appeared to have been genuinely in ignorance of the situation regarding his forces. During the recent meeting with Gracey, he "took immediate action to have [Gracey's orders] transmitted in translation to all officers down to platoon commanders (an exceptional action which he himself suggested), that in areas for which they were responsible Japanese forces were to take firm military action to deal with any armed Annamites encountered and to give assistance when called upon by Allied personnel." While Terauchi's actions had improved Japanese overt cooperation, "It cannot be relied on of course to have any effect whatever on the undercover activities mentioned above, and we can expect the surreptitious supply of arms and encouragement to the Annamites to go on wherever this can be done without observation by Allied forces." Only the presence of a greater number of Allied troops would stop this.

Brain also discussed the three courses open to the British regarding Japanese disarmament. The Japanese could be concentrated, leaving most of the country to the Viet Minh; the British could replace the Japanese as the latter were concentrated; or the French could be left to deal with the Japanese. The first and third courses were impractical because of opposition from, respectively, the French and the Viet Minh. Furthermore, the Japanese would not stand for Course Three, either. Their attitude to the French was one of "veiled contempt", for "they have had to deal with no serious resistance from the French, and they know of them only as a defeated nation; they have no knowledge of the exploits of the French in Europe." To make matters worse, the French population were in a state of low morale and tended to panic. The only course open was the second: to replace the Japanese as they were disarmed, "however much we may wish to avoid the political implications of handing Indo-China back to French rule." As Brain noted, "The points that, with the limited forces available to us, we were able to take over ourselves were secured without difficulty and without a shot being fired."

Brain drew particular attention to the state of the French population: "As I have said their morale is low. They combine an almost hysterical fear of the Annamites (which to my mind denotes a guilty conscience) with an intense hatred and desire for revenge. These people will constitute one of the greatest obstacles to the institution by the French of a liberal policy and its acceptance by the Annamites. If at all possible I think that these people should be evacuated from Indo-China at the earliest possible moment.''[7] Brain said that Cédile, the ''Governor-General designate of Cochin China'', was a ''well-meaning and liberal man who appeared to be unfitted'' for his task. He was said to ''command neither the respect of the French population nor the trust of the Annamites,'' and appeared to be ''on the verge of a complete breakdown''. The French thought he was too tender-hearted while the Viet Minh held him responsible for rearming the French.

On 28 September the fighting flared up again as Gracey gave priority to the security of Tan Son Nhut airport. Patrols from 1/1 GR continually swept the road to the airfield without incident, but a 3/1 GR company on reconnaissance in the north met an entrenched force of Viet Minh at the bridge at Ap Dong Ni, east of Go Vap. The Viet Minh were heavily armed with rifles and machine-guns, and battle was joined. The Gurkhas had by now suffered their first casualties, and this company was from one of the most battle-hardened battalions, which had walked through Burma from Imphal. When the smoke and din had subsided, seven Viet Minh corpses lay on the ground. The surviving Viet Minh broke and scrambled away, suffering possibly fifty-three more killed in the flight as the Gurkhas grimly pursued them; in all three of their number were wounded in the whole action.

The Gurkhas were beginning to make a name for themselves in Vietnam, and the memories of these days were to last for decades. One of their convoys from Lai Thieu, a town on the river about 10 miles north of Saigon, did not fare so well. Again a platoon of 3/1 Gurkha Rifles was involved, and they suffered their worst casualties of their whole stay in Indochina. Eighteen Gurkhas, plus a detachment of Japanese and a handful of Dutch soldiers [an *ad hoc* force thrown together under Captain P.G. Malins, RIASC], had accompanied a convoy of thirteen vehicles which had been dispatched to evacuate a Japanese arms and ammunition dump in Lai Thieu. The Gurkhas earned their pay on this day, for they were ambushed six times on the return journey, when the trucks were filled with ammunition and unmaneuverable. When the convoy finally reached the British perimeter, five trucks had been lost; six Gurkhas had been killed (including two missing, believed killed) and three wounded. The loss of the Gurkhas was deeply felt by the battalion: ''This was a sad blow as we lost some first-class NCOs in this ambush.'' The Japanese had opted out of the fight: ''There is little doubt that the Japanese knew

---

7. *Ibid.* This was also a continuing argument among the French.

all about this ambush and they fired not a shot to defend the convoy.'' Of
the Dutch, one officer was killed and three soldiers wounded. Later in
the day four of the five trucks lost in the ambushed convoy made their
way to Saigon.

Mountbatten now summoned Gracey, Cédile and Brain to Singapore,
where in a meeting attended by Mr J. J. Lawson, a former miner and
union official now Secretary of State for War, the Indochina situation
was discussed. Again, Mountbatten's report of this conference (to the
Chiefs of Staff) was a bland recapitulation of the meeting with the three
officers but, as will be seen, Gracey directly confronted the Supreme
Allied Commander on the withholding of the rest of the 20th Division.
At this meeting (on 28 September) Mountbatten asked Gracey to explain
his proclamation; Gracey replied without hesitation that he had interpreted his instructions as meaning that he was confined to using British
forces in key areas around Saigon, but this did not absolve him from his
responsibility for ensuring law and order throughout French Indochina
south of the 16th parallel, in the whole of which area he was forced to
rely on the Japanese for security duties. Gracey said that merely to direct
the Japanese to maintain order was not enough; it was essential that the
Vietnamese behind the disorders should themselves know that he had
instructed the Japanese to maintain public security and that those who
persisted in provoking disturbances would be punished. A proclamation
was thought to be the best way of publicizing his message to the people
and indeed had he not taken this step many French lives would have been
lost. He was strongly backed in his action by Slim who, as will be seen,
was becoming somewhat disenchanted with Mountbatten's style of
command. Since Slim, Browning, Leclerc and practically everyone else
present approved of Gracey's action, Mountbatten accepted the explanation. When Gracey returned from Singapore, according to a source close
to him, he reported that Mountbatten had decided to relieve him of his
command; however, Slim had intervened by telling the SAC that ''if he
[Gracey] goes, I go!''

Gracey further reported that the Japanese were involved in most of the
disorders and he was compiling a list of the names of the responsible
Japanese commanders for later trial; he was of the opinion that they
should be shot, and Mountbatten agreed. Mountbatten allowed Gracey
to continue his efforts to bring the French and Viet Minh together for
discussions, but stipulated that he ''could only be the vehicle through
which such contact was established. He [Gracey] must not in any way

enter into discussions or negotiations with the Viet Minh.''[8] Mountbatten then expounded his own view of the situation. He said that His Majesty's Government was determined not to repeat the Greek experience, and the British forces must not incur casualties by becoming involved in local affairs. Law and order should be a French problem (but due to political delays there were insufficient French troops for this task). Cédile said that there were many French civilians throughout Indochina now dependent on the Japanese for their lives. Mountbatten then asked if they could all be brought into Saigon, but Gracey replied that Saigon was already overcrowded, that it would be difficult to find transportation and that each move would entail a military operation. Mountbatten told the Chiefs that he had ''persuaded'' Cédile to meet the Viet Minh, and Gracey was trying to get them all together. That was not exactly how Gracey remembered it. He wrote that he had not needed Mountbatten to remind him to try to effect a reconciliation between the French and the Viet Minh: ''From 25th September onwards, efforts had been made by Colonel Cédile, after full agreement with the Allied commander, to get in touch with the members of the late Annamite government, and these were eventually successful. Again, there was no question of waiting for orders from SEAC to do this.[9] Mountbatten said that Gracey agreed with following his Course B (see pages 176–7, above) ''but has pointed out that it will not be possible to limit his resources to the Brigade which is now in, since Saigon covers such an enormous area that he considers that the full 20th Indian Division, which is due to complete its build-up in Saigon by mid-October, will be required.''[10]

That is not exactly how Cédile remembered it. There were several generals (including Slim) at the meeting, besides Mountbatten. Cédile said that Gracey went to Singapore to ask for reinforcements:

Well, whatever you may say, that's what we went to ask for, especially air support, because we didn't have very much of that. I don't know why but they didn't give us much air support . . . I remember when I asked for reinforcements and they weren't forthcoming. I saw that Gracey was not very pleased, and Mountbatten said ''no reinforcements''. And General Gracey said to him — he used these very words — he said, ''Saigon is much bigger and much

---

8. PRO, WO 203/5068, 28 Sept. 1945.
9. Gracey Papers, correspondence with SEAC Recorder, 3 Oct. 1946.
10. PRO, WO 203/4349 (SEAC 421), 28 Sept. 1945, repeated as SEACOS 494, 29 Sept. 1945.

more important than Liverpool, and how would you expect to defend a town the size of Liverpool with just a few battalions of Gurkhas and Dogras?''[11]

Cédile appreciated Gracey's courage, for ''Gracey always said what he thought.'' All Cédile could do was to rely on Gracey's help, and he asked Leclerc to try and get Mountbatten to speed up the arrival of French troops. Leclerc intervened to support Gracey in his efforts to get French troops into Indochina. It was evident that Gracey had received solid support from all the senior officers present, with the possible exception of Mountbatten who wrote: ''Slim has investigated this matter personally and is strongly of the opinion that not less than one Division is required merely to comply with course (B). . . .'' Mountbatten now professed fear that unless there was a strong British force in Saigon ''I am of the opinion that it will become increasingly difficult to control the Japanese'' — which Gracey had been saying for two weeks. The Japanese had already violated Allied instructions by arming the Viet Minh. ''On Gracey making strong representation to Terauchi, he has promised to do his best to prevent this, but I feel is himself embarrassed at our lack of force.'' Gracey had restated his position of holding the Japanese responsible for the safety of Allied nationals outside his key areas until the French were strong enough to take over; ''Only then will these Japanese Forces be marched to the concentration area near Saigon for disarmament by British Forces.'' Mountbatten concluded by saying that Gracey's entire division would be needed for both Courses A and B: ''I have instructed Slim not to hold up the move of the rest of 20th Indian Div. I must point out that the need to get the 9th French Colonial Infantry Div into Indo China at the earliest moment has become more important than ever.''[12] Cédile had a final comment on the issue of Gracey's badly-needed reinforcements: ''When we went to Singapore he [Browning] supported Gracey — Slim also. There was much discussion because Gracey had a lot of support among the generals on Lord Mountbatten's staff, and he was obviously friendly enough to write to them, and so we got our reinforcements. We then achieved our

11. Jean Cédile, personal interview, 26 Oct. 1977.
12. PRO, WO 203/4349, SEACOS 494, 29 Sept. 1945. It was difficult to see how Gracey could have guaranteed the safety of Allied civilians in the key areas only while disclaiming responsibility for them in outlying areas. Apart from humanitarian grounds, all of French Indochina south of the 16th parallel was Mountbatten's responsibility, yet all the senior officers but Mountbatten appeared to have strongly supported Gracey. It was said that both Slim and Leclerc intervened forcefully to prevent Gracey's dismissal.

mission. . . . No Frenchman could say that he was not fully supported by the British."[13]

On 30 September, in London, the Joint Planning Staff (Chiefs of Staff Committee) prepared a report for the Chiefs titled "French Indo-China — Measures for Responsibility for Internal Security by SACSEA."[14] The JPS agreed that Mountbatten's Course B was the correct one to follow, and that Leclerc had been right to refuse to assume responsibility until the arrival of the 9th DIC. They also agreed that it would be unwise to revoke Gracey's proclamation, since that would further incite revolutionary activity. The report continued, "We are, therefore, perforce left in a situation in which we must remain legally responsible for law and order throughout South Indo-China until the French take over . . ." The Joint Planning Staff agreed with Gracey in recommending that the build-up of his Division should continue "in the light of the situation which has developed". As for "Policy for Employment of British Forces", the JPS said that "we must clearly gain and retain complete control of the Saigon area since this is required by our military object." The rest of the country must be left to the French due to the small size of the British forces available. But "Saigon is the most important centre of population in the country and control of this area may be sufficient to allow small forces to establish law and order throughout the rest of the country." The Joint Planning Staff then made a far-reaching recommendation which freed Gracey from a large measure of his restriction and authorized him to maneuver outside Saigon: "We should, however, be prepared to assist these [small French] forces to the limit of our ability provided that, in the judgment of the local commander, this can be done without prejudicing the local security of Saigon." It then recommended that "the following interim policy should be given to SACSEA: (*a*) His primary responsibility is control of the Saigon area, (*b*) He is authorised to assist the French in the interior of the country as far as he can without prejudice to (*a*)." The report concluded with the recommendation that the theater boundary remain unchanged until the French could assume responsibility for all Indochina.

In Saigon itself, repeated attacks by the Viet Minh on the power station underscored the importance for Saigon of that installation; the city depended for its water on the artesian wells, and it could not be

13. Cédile, interview, 26 Oct. 1977.
14. PRO, FO 371/46308 (JP(45) 258 (Final)), 30 Sept. 1945.

drawn from these without electric power to drive the pumps. But although the power house was successfully defended, its condition gave cause for concern. Before they departed the Vietnamese laborers had sabotaged the fuel elevator to the furnaces, the electric motors which drove the water injectors for the boilers, and more. A labor force of 200 Japanese soldiers was employed, working in shifts, carrying coal in sacks from barges in the canal to the furnaces. The resourceful electrical and mechanical engineer, an Australian, rewound some of the injector motors himself, and some Japanese marine engineers finished the job for him.[15] But having control of the power station, such as it was, had its tactical advantages: "There was always a curfew at night, and no street lights. If a unit got attacked at night, it could ask for the street lights in its area to be put on, which was a nasty surprise for the attackers who were caught in the open."

Brigadier Myers was moving about under these precarious conditions, conducting his own investigation into the explosive situation, and as he was leaving Saigon it was announced that General Gracey had managed to bring the French and the Viet Minh together for face-to-face discussions. Myers, an officer with an unusual depth of experience in clandestine operations, had no doubt as to what the major problem was: "My mission, given to me personally by Mountbatten, in Slim's presence, was a fact-finding one, basically to find out how we could achieve our military task in FIC, viz. accepting the surrender of the Japanese, without becoming involved in an internal war between the Annamites and the French, which was none of our business."[16] Myers then briefly described Scobie's experience in Athens, and continued: "To sum up, I reported that if we continued to support the re-establishment of the French Government in FIC, we couldn't avoid becoming involved in war with the indigenous population. The French were largely discredited. The Annamites had been promised independence when Japan had won the war. They had no intention of reverting back to the 1940 *status quo*." During his stay in Saigon, Myers spoke to a number of educated Vietnamese, few of whom had anything good to say about the French colonial government. All pleaded with Myers to tell Mountbatten that France must conduct a liberal policy "if bloodshed was to be avoided and FIC was not to be driven towards Communism." On the evidence available to him, Myers wrote that the Vietnamese nationalists

15. Major J. H. Clark, "Sappers and Miners in Saigon", *The Royal Engineers Journal*, vol. LXIV, no. 3, Sept. 1950, p. 281.
16. Brigadier E. C. W. Myers, letters to author, 19 Jan. 1976 and 24 March 1977.

were generally not Communist, and he shared Gracey's view that the problem was largely due to French intransigence.[17] The French, said Myers, could not go on ignoring the changes wrought by the Japanese occupation. The Vietnamese said that they did not wish to involve the British, but in their view there was no way that this could be avoided. The French insisted on "returning to square one", and the Communists would take advantage of this. Regarding the Vietnamese, "The last thing they wanted was to become 'second-class' French colonial citizens once again,"[18] and the Communists would know how to turn the nationalistic outburst to their advantage after liberation. Wrote Myers, "The French . . . couldn't understand what had hit them, any more than we did. Moreover, they blamed nearly all their troubles on the Communists and, initially, this only deepened the Annamite anti-French feelings and increased the troubles for the French — and ourselves." Like Brain, he had no use for the *colons* generally, and thought that a new class of Frenchmen should come out from the metropole.

Myers, who later went to Burma on a similar investigation into Aun Sang and his Burma National Army, interviewed Chinese and Frenchmen also, and personally shared Roosevelt's view of colonial France. But as the British Government was committed to the unequivocal return of Indochina to French sovereignty, and especially after having been ordered by Mountbatten to avoid entering into discussions with the Viet Minh, Gracey was left with no room for maneuver. And now that the Chiefs of Staff were about to free him from the confines of Saigon, war appeared unavoidable.

17. Myers, personal interview, 6 Nov. 1977.
18. Myers, letters to author, 1976, 1977.

# 11

# TRUCE

As September 1945 drew to a close, the military situation was visibly worsening. This meant that the possibility of employing the RAF Spitfires in some role other than reconnaissance and shows of force had to be considered. Some of the roadblocks were too well fortified to be attacked by small patrols, though Gracey believed that the decision about the use of Spitfires would have to be made by Mountbatten. He also (unsuccessfully) sought authority from Mountbatten to fly Terauchi's Assistant Chief of Staff to Hanoi to consult the Viet Minh leadership about the worsening political situation in the south and to provide Gracey with information about conditions in the north.

As a result of information received from Saigon, Mountbatten cabled the British Military Attaché in Washington that as of 30 September Lieutenant-Colonel Dewey's body had still not been recovered, and was unlikely to be in the future. He regretted, as did Gracey, being unable to comply with the wishes of Dewey's father, but promised that the Allies would continue looking. (Many leads were followed up and bodies exhumed both in Saigon and in the surrounding countryside, but to no avail.)

The RAF element in the Control Commission was fully extended in controlling Japanese air resources, the troop and supply airlift, and a host of similar duties; the shortage of aircraft throughout the South East Asia area was acute. The press at this point demanded that Mountbatten supply a plane for their exclusive use, to provide a regular airlift of their dispatches and materials to Rangoon, and Air Commodore Cheshire, in recommending that ACSEA (Air Chief Marshal Sir Keith Park) turn down the request, noted that the reporters "are unable or unwilling to understand" the severe operational shortages.

On 30 September Gracey asked Mountbatten directly, "Am I now empowered to use Spitfire aircraft to attack hostile targets? Am already employing Spitfire TAC/recce sorties. I wish to employ in attacking role against hostile concentrations, road blocks, etc. Grateful earliest reply as I am still not clear."[1] On 1 October Mountbatten replied: "As from

---

1. PRO, WO 203/5644, Gracey to Browning, 39 Sept. 1945. The confused scene was described years later by Air Commodore (later Air Chief Marshal Sir Walter)

daylight 3rd October you are empowered to use Spitfire aircraft to attack hostile targets if for over-riding operational reasons you require to clear road blocks or bunkers to ensure the safe movement of your troops for any vital task. In particular you may use Spitfires to keep open your lines of communication between your airfield and your key area in Saigon.'' But Mountbatten told Gracey to refrain from using the fighters on road blocks which did not interfere with his operations, or on ''concentrations of Annamites from which large casualties might result.'' Furthermore, in the manner of operations on the North West Frontier of India, leaflets must be dropped on the intended target at least two hours before any Spitfire attack; Gracey was then directed ''to report at once each case of using aircraft offensively together with reasons which made this imperative and telegraph the text of the leaflet that was dropped beforehand.'' But this was not North West India, and the two-hour restriction had to be rescinded a few days later. Mountbatten explained that these restrictions were necessary ''to counter the anti-British propaganda which is certain to be put out after each attack by the Vietnam-controlled Radio Station in Hanoi which General Wedemeyer, in spite of my repeated requests, appears unable to control.''

The Supreme Allied Commander had now received the instructions from the Chiefs of Staff concerning the relaxation of restrictions on Gracey, and he permitted Gracey to make a public announcement that while he did not wish to interfere in Indochina's internal politics, there would be no tolerance of activities which impeded the orderly administration of his major tasks and which were detrimental to internal security. It was no more than Gracey had said all along.

The situation on 1 October was described in the Saigon Control Commission's ''Political Report'', which stated that the second phase, from 23 September to 1 October, was ''one of rioting and bloodshed''. These actions were ''typical of those of all savages; murder, outrages, interference and molestation and murder with outrage of French women, atrocities on women and children . . .'' Without British intervention now, this phase could not end without ''the use of maximum force and its inevitable bloodbath''. The Viet Minh leaders were thus contacted, and on 1 October the first meeting took place between them

---

Cheshire: ''When Air Command Headquarters at Kandy detailed me for this appointment they were extremely vague about the duties and responsibilities involved, and this lack of positive instructions was further emphasised when the Staff invited me to write my own directive.''

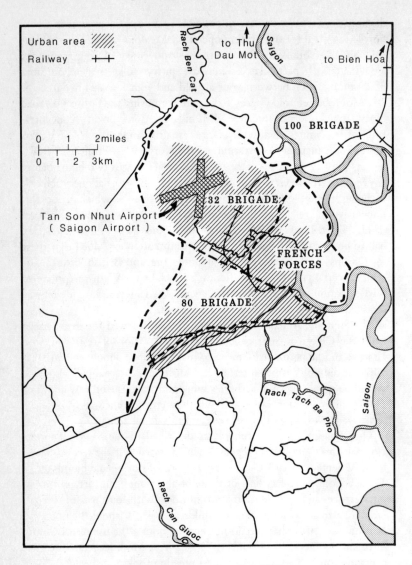

Situation map, October 1945.

and Gracey.[2] The report stated that "The object of this meeting was twofold: (*a*) To make the Annamites understand the senselessness of further bloodshed and to stress the immediate necessity of a truce; (*b*) To arrange further meetings . . . between the French representatives and the Annamite leaders, with a British representative present."

At 1630 the first meeting between the British and Viet Minh was opened by Harry Brain, Gracey's political adviser. Brain stated that he was present in two capacities, representing both the British Foreign Office and General Gracey who had been sent to Saigon by the Supreme Allied Commander to disarm and remove the Japanese. As Foreign Office representative, Brain stated that it was "not the intention of His Majesty's Government that British Forces should be used for any political purposes whatsoever." The fact that they were at that time actually fighting the Vietnamese did not mean that their object was the reinstatement of the French Administration by force. Said Brain, "Politically HM Government are neutral but they together with other members of the United Nations have decided that they will not recognize any change of sovereignty of any territory which has taken place by force during the war." At the same time, one of the aims of the UN was the "full and steady development of Colonial peoples all over the world and an increasing measure of self-government to them." As Gracey's representative Brain said that the present situation caused the General "the greatest distress and concern". The common victims of Japanese aggression were "at each other's throats" while the "real culprits — the Japanese themselves — stand by and smile."

Brain then addressed the spirit of Gracey's proclamation: "For the proper disposal of the Japanese, General Gracey must and will have law and order. But quite apart from the Japanese he is also grieved that such a spirit of animosity and distrust, which he feels is mainly due to misunderstanding, should persist between the French and Annamites here." Brain then announced that he was the bearer of a letter from General Gracey, at whose request he would now read it. Gracey stated in the letter that he was sure the Viet Minh deplored the lawlessness and loss of Vietnamese, French, British and American lives as much as he did, and this behavior would lose them "the sympathy of civilized people". The new French leaders were not bent on vengeance, and with their authority he asked the Viet Minh to meet them under his personal

---

2. Gracey Papers, "Saigon Control Commission, Political Report, 13th September 1945, to 9th Oct. 1945."

guarantee of their safety. Brain concluded by saying that General Gracey was in the building, and it was his desire to see and talk to those present about the situation if they were willing to hear what he had to say. But Brain emphasized the true purpose of the meeting, which was to bring the Viet Minh and the French together.

Gracey then entered and — in view of Mountbatten's order to avoid political discussions with the Viet Minh — began by saying, "This is no discussion of policy." He then said that the local situation was entirely a matter for the French and Vietnamese, and "my task here is to get the Japanese forces out of the country." But, apart from the needless suffering of the civil population, "the disarming and extradition of the Japanese forces is being delayed by the necessity of employing British and Japanese forces to stop attacks on Allied nationals and to keep the life of [the] Saigon-Cholon area going." Gracey said that his whole Division, "with tanks, guns and the finest infantry in the world", would arrive shortly, and "the sooner the Annamites return to normal peaceful conditions and behave themselves, the sooner can my task be completed of disarming the Japanese and getting them away out of French Indo-China." Continued Gracey, "But there is no intention of British forces leaving the Saigon-Cholon area for some time, and they will be here as guarantors that impartiality is shown in dealing with crime and disorders." But, he said, in order that he could carry out his main tasks, it was essential that the Viet Minh should take certain steps. First, Gracey wanted to know, could these Viet Minh representatives control their armed elements? He then listed the steps the Viet Minh should take regarding law and order "to ensure that I can carry out my task". Among other things, they were to return all hostages and Dewey's body (for "Christian burial"), "stop molesting Allied nationals", cease armed activities, order villagers and townspeople to return to their homes, remove all road and waterway blocks, return all stolen machinery parts (including railway engines), and "give full information as regards sabotage of the water supply."

In reply the Viet Minh said that they had welcomed the British troops as they thought they had come to liberate the Vietnamese from both the Japanese and the French. Most of the French were Vichyist and their past behaviour had "infuriated" the Vietnamese. The only way that "confidence could be regained" would be by restoring the Viet Minh to power. They would be prepared to meet the French "provided that the British acted as arbitrators and would protect their nationals against French aggression". Gracey replied that it was his duty to restore law and order and arrange a meeting between the French and Vietnamese. Neither he nor his officers or men would "meddle or interfere" in local politics. The Viet Minh would "lose the sympathy of the whole world" if they refused to meet the French for face-to-face talks, and law and order had to be "completely restored as a first essential". Gracey said that he would not permit the Japanese to take part in present or future discussions, and reminded the Viet Minh leaders that he "well knew that their forces had been aided and armed by the Japanese and that they still had a number of Japanese deserters and others assisting them." Gracey finally assured the Viet Minh that he would nominate a representative to attend their meeting with the French, "and that in my capacity as Commander Allied Forces I would deal severely with all acts of provocation irrespective of the nationality of the offender." On leaving, Gracey assured the Viet Minh once more that they would not again get such an opportunity to discuss the situation. Staff talks continued after his departure from the room, and the following agreements were reached. The Viet Minh agreed to a ceasefire taking effect from 1800 hours on 2 October — posters announcing this would be put up in Saigon and Cholon after 1200 hours on 2 October, with the Allies guaranteeing the safety of the billposters — and a meeting was scheduled for 1100 hours on 3 October between the Viet Minh and the French, at which Brain would represent Gracey.

The French senior representatives, Cédile and Repiton-Preneuf, Leclerc's Chief of Staff, were then informed of the results; but, telegraphed Gracey, "From their attitude [I] cannot be optimistic." He told Mountbatten, "I cannot stress too highly the importance of Leclerc's arrival here earliest possible, both for law and order as well as politically. Whether these Annamite representatives are really able to control their unruly bands only time can tell." Brain was assigned the specific task of seeing whether Gracey's demands were being carried out.

On 2 October Mountbatten wrote to the Chiefs of Staff, acknowledging the new instructions contained in COSSEA 366, authorizing Gracey to move out of Saigon. He reported that Leclerc was "horrified" at the delayed departure of the 9th DIC, and had "expressed his protest in the most emphatic terms." Leclerc had declared that he would not now be able to take over in Indochina until the end of the year. Delays in transferring the 9th DIC to Saigon would increase the danger of further involvement by British/Indian troops. Mountbatten pointed out that "the lift available within SEAC is already below that required for planned movements so that in the event of serious disturbances in FIC and the failure of the French forces to arrive, the greatest difficulty would be experienced in sending additional British support to FIC." Mountbatten then emphasized the major role played in Indochina by the Japanese, saying that the only way he could avoid involving British/Indian forces was to continue using the Japanese to maintain law and order. He could therefore not begin disarming them for another three months, by which time all the Allied POWs and internees would have returned home. Since it was obvious that the Japanese could be disarmed before the end of December, there would be little excuse for retaining British/Indian troops in Indochina. Wrote Mountbatten, "In fact we shall find it hard to counter the accusations that our forces are remaining in the country solely in order to hold the Viet Minh Independence Movement in check."[3] He went on to say that he had received a message from the Viceroy of India (Lord Wavell), stating that "Indian opinion is most sensitive about the use of Indian troops to suppress disturbances in other Eastern countries." Protests had already been made against the use of Indian troops in French Indochina and Java. He concluded by re-emphasizing the need to move the 9th DIC rapidly to Saigon, and added, "Meanwhile my task is not being made easier by persistent attacks against the British being broadcast by Hanoi radio which is presumably under China Theater's control. I have protested about these broadcasts but so far without result."

Gracey's meeting with the Viet Minh leaders produced the desired effect, and at 1100 hours on 3 October the French and Viet Minh met for discussions. Gracey opened the meeting with a short introductory address and then departed, leaving Brain to remain as his observer at the talks. These lasted for two hours, and at first the atmosphere was stiff and formal. However, as the talks progressed they gradually became more cordial. Gracey's report stated that "Tea and biscuits and cigarettes helped and at one point both sides were laughing together. At end of meeting both sides shook hands warmly." It was emphasized that the return of all hostages and of Colonel Dewey's body, together with an exchange of prisoners, was a prerequisite to satisfactory discussions. The Viet Minh "strongly deplored taking of hostages by extreme element not under their orders and undertook to do their utmost in next two days to find and return those who still live and also Colonel Dewey's body." The next Franco-Viet Minh meeting was set for 1100 hours on 6 October, when both sides were to produce written statements. But after

3. PRO, FO 371/46309, SEACOS 500 [F 7789], 2 Oct. 1945.

the meeting the leading Viet Minh negotiator, Dr Thach, asked Brain for a private interview the same day; after this private talk Brain told Gracey that he was not optimistic about the future, mainly because the wild men with the guns were in a position to dominate the Viet Minh political negotiators.

Brain's meeting with Dr Thach lasted two hours; they spoke in French and no one else was present. Thach repeated his statement that the Allies had been welcomed ''as liberators to free the Annamites of the French yoke''. Brain replied that if this was so, the Viet Minh were ''greatly mistaken''; Dr Thach must remember that the French had fought beside Britain, and were her closest neighbors in Europe. Said Brain, who emphasized that he was giving his personal view and not that of His Majesty's Government, ''As liberating forces our task was to free Southern Indochina from the Japanese who had usurped power from the French and not to interfere in the internal politics of the country.'' Dr Thach responded that the Viet Minh Government had thought that the British would support them as the ''*de facto* government with democratic principles which had shown itself capable of administration and which represented the aspiration of 99 percent of the Annamites''. Brain replied that to British and perhaps American eyes the facts appeared very different. ''In the first place they had been enabled to establish themselves in power solely as a result of the Japanese aggression against their country'' (thus turning on the Communists their own favorite description of their opponents, namely puppets — a term continually used by Gracey to describe the Viet Minh in Saigon at this time). Japan and Britain were enemies, and ''we could not recognize a change of sovereignty which had taken place through the action of our enemies at the expense of our allies. Furthermore Annam was bound to France by treaties signed by the Emperor. The Emperor had abdicated but the treaties he had signed were signed in the name of Annam.'' Only negotiations with France could bring about ''alterations and abrogations'' of existing treaties. The Viet Minh would lose sympathy, and perhaps the fight, should they attempt to secure their goals by force. As for Thach's claim that the Viet Minh was ''a democratic and effective administration'', Brain said, ''I pointed out that it had not been the result of a popular election and that its inability to control its followers was demonstrated to the world by the abduction of women and young children, the commission of outrages, and the murder of Col. Dewey, followed by an attack on a house flying the American flag.''

Dr Thach was ''greatly depressed'' by Brain's argument, ''but he recognized the force of it from the practical point of view." He then asked Brain what he would do if their positions were reversed. Brain replied that he would persuade the Party to drop its demand for immediate and unconditional independence, which would result in deadlock, but "try to secure some promise of eventual self-government, if possible with a fixed date." Thach said that had the Viet Minh been negotiating with the British and not the French, they would probably have been promised immediate independence. Brain disagreed, saying that in British areas it was necessary to include a transition period under British tutelage before the granting of independence. As an example he pointed to Burma, where the independent government had fought against the Japanese, but they had recognized the need for a transition period "before they could hope to be able to cope with the difficulties that face a state in modern times." It would be better for Vietnam to look temporarily to the French, "whose language they spoke and with whom, as he [Thach] admitted, they had close cultural ties." Thach "admitted sadly the wisdom of this advice," but said that the Party would immediately reject a transition period lasting more than a few months. "If he [Thach] and his colleagues accepted such a proposal they would be the first to be killed by their supporters." Brain wrote that "The interview took place in an atmosphere of frankness and friendliness," and he told Thach that his sincere advice had been given on the presumption that in the long run the Viet Minh "really had the interests of the Annamite people at heart."

While this was going on, there was trouble in Dalat, where on 3 October the Viet Minh occupied the public buildings. The Japanese reacted on 6 October, and a bloody battle accompanied the ouster of the Viet Minh; the Japanese lost eleven killed, seventeen wounded and two missing, while Viet Minh casualties were eighty killed and 160 wounded. On 5 October Leclerc finally arrived in Saigon where he was met as he alighted from his Dakota by Gracey and other senior officers. A platoon from D Company, 4/17 Dogra, and a platoon of Frenchmen formed a guard of honour. A French proclamation was issued to coincide with Leclerc's arrival, and leaflets bearing the message were scattered all over Saigon from the air. Leclerc stated that he was preceding Admiral d'Argenlieu, and carried the greetings of General de Gaulle and the French people. France, like Indochina, had known the sufferings of war, and the sudden collapse of Japan had not given France time to fight in this theater, but by taking part in crushing Germany she had taken part in Indochina's liberation. Japan had taken advantage of the delay in the return of the Allies to start disturbances and engage in propaganda, but as soon as Leclerc assumed command he would put a stop to this work of the enemy. The French Government had decided on a plan to bring prosperity to Indochina, and "Together we will feed those of you who are hungry, clothe your wives and children, build on your ruins, work for the wellbeing and the prosperity of your families whose great traditions are the best guarantees of peace and prosperity; this can only be achieved if order reigns . . . Until further notice the army of Great Britain, our ally, holds military authority."

In a letter to the Foreign Office, Dening wrote that the "basic evil" in Indochina was the Vichy French; they were despised by everyone, including the Gaullists, who unfortunately were "too few and far between, and not so remarkable at that". Said Dening, "I do not gain the impression that the independence movement of Indo-China is an insoluble problem. But there is little doubt that the Japanese are still fostering it covertly, and the badness — I can find no other word — of the Chinese and the Americans north of 16° is likely to make life difficult for some time to come." Dening wrote that the draft of the manifesto which Leclerc proposed to issue was irreproachable, and he concluded:

These independence movements in Asia must be treated with sympathy and understanding. Otherwise they will become really serious. As I have indicated, they are half-baked, and treated in the proper way they should not be very terrifying. But treated the wrong way they may well, in the end, spell the end of Europe in Asia. I think we should be leaders in handling the situation in the right way. After all, it is our forces who are liberating these areas and it is the British taxpayer who is paying. Let us, therefore, stand no nonsense from the Dutch or the French. In the end, they may well have cause to be grateful to us — though gratitude is not a very marked feature of international relations.

Throughout the history of this period the figure of General Slim grows ever larger, his brilliant military mind, combined with a keen understanding of human nature and political insight, being largely responsible for the British success in the East. Slim, in response to a request by the Chief of the Imperial General Staff, Field-Marshal Sir Alan Brooke, wrote Brooke a letter in which he summarized the situation in South East Asia. He reported that "we have got one [problem] now in French Indo-China, and in the Netherlands East Indies. I call it one problem because . . . the situation that faces us in each is in broad essentials the same."[4] Slim had a firm idea of the immediate problems

4. PRO, FO 371/46309, Slim to Alanbrooke, 6 Oct. 1945.

facing his land forces, and this accounted in some measure for the vital support he gave to his commanders on the spot like Douglas Gracey who, according to General Kimmins[5] (SACSEA Assistant Chief of Staff), were "pitchforked" into their respective turbulent areas.

Slim's letter presented an excellent comprehensive overview of the political situation in both FIC and NEI. In his opinion the main factors were (in each country) a large colony captured by the Japanese after "a very poor effort at defence by the responsible European power", which resulted in the collapse of especially French and Dutch prestige — and in Indochina "a very poor type [of colonial administration] which cooperated with the Japanese; a pre-war national independence movement which, fostered by the Japanese, "has increased in militant strength immeasurably in the war years and which now in both FIC and NEI can with reason claim to be the only *de facto* government"; well-armed but at best "partially trained nationalist forces"; "a lack of realisation" on the part of the French and Dutch civil populations of "the changed world attitude towards Colonial Nationalism and an ignorance of the great local changes in FIC and NEI"; large undefeated Japanese forces not yet disarmed; thousands of French and Dutch ex-POWs and civilians who were in real danger of massacre and who in many places were saved by the presence of Japanese forces; a Chinese occupation of northern Indochina which, with American encouragement, was "violently hostile" to France; no French or Dutch forces "of any real value" available; the enormous areas of British responsibility; and the shortage of shipping.

Slim stated that it had not been possible to disarm the Japanese because they were needed "for the protection of Europeans, to keep open communications, and to maintain a modicum of order outside the small areas we occupy. Our forces are small." Referring to Gracey's difficult situation in Saigon, he wrote that in Indochina "British forces have been compelled, in order to prevent the massacre of French civilians, to maintain essential services and, to secure themselves, to use force against armed Annamites." Several hundred Vietnamese had been killed, more wounded, and British, Indians, Dutch, French and Americans killed and wounded. "There is now an uneasy truce which will not, I think, last long." It was unfortunate that "the only troops with which we can make any attempt to maintain order outside the very small areas we can occupy ourselves, are the Japanese. Thus even in Saigon-Cholon, the greater part of the internal security duties are carried out by the

5. Personal interview, 26 Jan. 1978.

Japanese.'' Slim pointed out the disadvantages of this policy. First, as already mentioned the Allies could not disarm the Japanese, either then or in the immediate future, even if they were willing (as Slim thought they were) to disarm themselves — the Japanese did not want to go on keeping public order. The actual control they could exercise was, in any event, limited to a few vital points and communications, and there was, in their areas of responsibility, ''little security for life or property and, of course, no law. We earn the opprobrium of the local inhabitants and to some extent of our Allies for employing the Japanese . . .'' Slim then drew attention to a problem which appeared to be generally overlooked, and which was ''real and more likely the longer the present situation continues''. This was that ''through some provocative action by irresponsible French or Dutch elements there may be a large-scale native rising against Europeans.'' If that were to happen the small British garrison would be hard pressed ''even to maintain themselves'', and would not be able to prevent the massacre of French or Dutch civilians. There would also be great difficulty in finding reinforcements or shipping to help the garrison should this nightmare occur.

Slim then told Brooke that SEAC had been receiving directions from various sources, which ''seems to me to have been somewhat involved and at times contradictory.'' The British were originally to have disarmed the Japanese and repatriated Allied POWs and internees without in any way ''getting involved''. At the same time the British were to work ''in the closest possible accord with Dutch and French authorities'', who were to be responsible for ''general internal security''. Slim said these tasks were to be done by using British forces in key areas only, and Allied forces outside the key areas. But ''The difficulty of this is that up to the present [6 October] the British forces have not been large enough to hold even the key areas and there have been practically no Allied forces to hold outside them.'' Thus the Japanese had to be used ''even in key areas and wholly outside''. If the French or Dutch were used to extend the key areas, real trouble would follow ''unless the political situation improves immensely.'' When these clashes occurred, even if British troops do not have to help the Allies (as had happened), the Allied forces were under the command of the local British Force Commander, ''under my higher command, and the SAC's Supreme Command. As long as we retain this command we cannot divorce ourselves from the responsibility for their actions.'' Slim thought it likely that the British would soon be charged with internal security in the Netherlands East Indies. He made it clear to Brooke ''that this means either that we co-operate with the only existing government, the Indonesia Republic, *or we overthrow it and replace it*.[6] In fact we cannot take over security of anything except the smallest areas or put back the Dutch outside those areas without armed conflict with the Nationalist movement. The same applies in Indo-China until the arrival of effective and considerable French forces, at least the 9 DIC.'' Because of the actions the British were forced to take, "we have become unpopular with Annamites and Indonesians because we are regarded as re-imposing on them French and Dutch rule [which] they had already shaken off." To Slim, the only answer to these problems lay in an early handover to the French and Dutch governments. But this could not occur until "reasonable" French and Dutch forces had arrived "unless we are prepared to contemplate large scale massacres." At the moment, "it appears that for a variety of reasons their [adequate French and Dutch forces] arrival is being more and more delayed. I consider this most dangerous."

If the British were to continue to keep the situation under control till the arrival of adequate French and Dutch forces, "every means should be used to impress on the, I fear, somewhat unrealistic Governments of France and Holland, the need for conciliation and for the honest offer of a reasonable measure of Self-Government." This to Slim was as important as the early arrival of (in the case of FIC) French forces; also, in his opinion, "the more diehard officers and [colonial] officials should be transferred to some other sphere of activity." Slim's recommendations were that British forces should remain confined to key areas while securing, with Japanese forces, the safety of European civilians outside these areas (this was exactly Gracey's view), and that (depending on the speed of arrival of French and Dutch forces), FIC and NEI be removed from SEAC and made the responsibility of their own governments. Regarding the removal of Japanese forces, FIC and NEI should have priority over Malaya and Burma. Slim concluded, by saying, "Forgive me for writing at such length, but I am sure you agree that the present rather confused situation is fraught with great danger."

The Control Commission reported from Saigon that their work had been somewhat curtailed due to the necessity of having to move under escort since the "outbreaks of rioting, sabotage, looting, and murder which occurred on 2 Sept 45". For this reason "it has been difficult to

---

6. Author's italics. This is significant in view of Slim's visit to Gracey in Saigon just one week before the French coup.

obtain authoritative reports on the situation within the remainder of FIC south of 16° parallel.'' The scrutiny of documents submitted by Japanese headquarters had continued, but ''the accuracy of these documents is increasingly open to doubt.''[7] It had been impossible to examine Japanese headquarters ''and at the same time expect it to carry out the orders issued regarding the maintenance of law and order.'' But with a ''change in the internal situation an advance is now being made and the examination of the headquarters will be completed within the next week.'' The Mission had through force of circumstances become involved in tasks not originally assigned to it; this was due to the late arrival of the headquarters, 20th Indian Division, and included the necessary political liaison between the French and the Viet Minh, the initiation of proclamations in cooperation with the French government, law and order outside areas actually occupied by 20 Indian Division troops, and the control of all intelligence organizations and coordination of all reports for all areas outside the Saigon-Cholon area. The heavy workload was caused by a number of factors beyond the control of the Mission. Perhaps the major contributory factor to the problem had been MacArthur's ban on the Allies setting foot in Japanese-held territory before the formal surrender in Tokyo on 2 September.

On 6 October a further meeting took place between the French and the Viet Minh. The French were represented by Colonels Cédile and Repiton-Preneuf and Major Paul Mus; the Viet Minh team consisted of Pham Van Bach, Dr Pham Ngoc Thach and Hoang Quoc Viet. Harry Brain was again present as Gracey's observer. Cédile opened with ''a few words about the arrival of General Leclerc, describing his background and character and his good intentions towards the native peoples of Indochina, and making it clear at the same time that he was determined to ensure law and order.'' Dr Thach responded with a fairly lengthy statement, prepared by himself and Pham Van Bach, in which he traced the course of events in South Vietnam before and after the British arrival and the resumption of French administration. The Viet Minh disclaimed responsibility for the ensuing disturbances which, they claimed, ''expressed the anger of the people''. Dr Thach turned the Allied charges around and declared that a ''large number of Annamite men, women and children had been the victims of atrocities by the other side and that since Sept 23rd the houses of Viet Nam citizens had been systematically pillaged and women molested by Frenchmen and Indians.'' The Viet

7. See Louis Allen's comments, page 349, fn. 4.

Minh were ready to help in the search for kidnapped French civilians "and restore them to the French against a similar number of Annamites". The Viet Minh further denied all knowledge of hostages taken by Annamites "and declared with regret that attempts to discover Colonel Dewey's body had failed." Dr Thach concluded his statement with four demands, which, if complied with, "would guarantee a cessation of the disorders and safety for all French people" (a statement which seem to contradict the disclaimer of responsibility the Viet Minh had just made). These demands were the restoration of the Viet Minh government and return of essential services to Viet Minh control, the rearming of Viet Minh police and the return of police stations to them, the disarming of French forces, and the liberation of all Annamites, including Hoang Don Van (a member of the Viet Minh government). Not unnaturally, Cédile was unhappy with this statement and asked if the Viet Minh "had nothing further to say about the hostages", but the latter replied that their "careful enquiries had failed to produce any evidence of any abductions whatever. They suggested that the persons in question had been killed in the fighting." Cédile pointed out that Annamites had been seen leading the hostages away, and their corpses had not been found. "Did they seriously expect people to believe that over 100 French people, including women and children, could be led through the streets without a single person having seen or heard of them?" Dr Thach reiterated that no evidence of hostages had been discovered, at which point Brain intervened to suggest that the Viet Minh should make a fresh effort, for "the negative answer they had just given would prove to the world that their claims to be an efficient administration were not worth much." Dr Thach then said that further efforts would be made. Brain returned to Thach's original statement by demanding full details of all charges against British/Indian forces, for "Without full documentation such charges were meaningless and would be ignored."

Repiton-Preneuf then raised the key issue by saying that the French delegation present were not empowered to negotiate the question of sovereignty, so the Viet Minh were leaving little scope for discussion. "It was a legal question which was a matter for the French Government." But the French had nevertheless made "very liberal and practical offers; to install Annamites in positions of authority in the civil administration, police, etc. These were concrete steps which could be dealt with immediately. Had the Annamite leaders nothing to propose of that nature?" Dr Thach then raised the other key issue: that the Viet Minh would not consider anything except "the restoration of sovereignty to the Viet Nam government". Here was the insoluble problem: the Viet Minh wanted full sovereignty and the French delegates could not negotiate it. Repiton-Preneuf was not put off by the inflexibility of the Viet Minh and continued to urge some sort of compromise. Thach replied that the arrival of French troops (the 5th RIC aboard French warships) had come as a surprise, and warned "that if they disembarked it would be considered a hostile act for the results of which the Viet Nam government refused to accept any responsibility." Cédile interjected by pointing out that "these forces had left ports for Indochina before any question of conversations had arisen. Their movements had not been kept secret, and their purpose was not to fight the Annamites but to maintain law and order in Indochina and assist in disarming the Japanese." Pham Van Bach then said, like the French, that his delegation could not negotiate political questions, which would have to be referred to the central Viet Nam government in Hanoi. Here was the other problem. Both sides were stuck — neither was empowered to negotiate without instructions. Cédile seized this statement to illustrate the French position, saying that their "purpose in talking to Viet Nam leaders was to settle the local problem." The French at this point suggested a further meeting, but the Viet Minh representatives hesitated, saying that they were "already meeting with disapproval for imposing restraints on the people and getting no visible concessions in return, so they were not sure they could guarantee the maintenance of the truce." (In fact, they were proved right, for they were unable to control some of their own elements and the truce was eventually broken.) The meeting of the French and Viet Minh was finally scheduled for 1100 hours on 8 October.

Gracey reported the results of this meeting to Mountbatten and Slim, saying that the "fact that conversations have not yet broken down had gained us further time." Substantial British reinforcements were expected the following day, and Gracey ended by saying that while the attitude of the French was "irreproachable", the Viet Minh were not helpful and appeared to be controlled by the extremists. The only new feature was the additional emphasis by the Viet Minh on British responsibility in assisting the French.

On 6 October Leclerc received his orders appointing him Acting Commander-in-Chief, French Forces in the Far East, directly responsible to Mountbatten as Supreme Allied Commander. However, the British force commander (Gracey) would continue to be in command of all Allied forces, including the French, until the departure of British troops and the assumption of control by the French. To this already complex situation was added, on 7 October, yet another difficulty, and its source was General Auchinleck, Commander-in-Chief India, who was understandably concerned with developments in South East Asia, being under intense pressure from Indian politicians over the use of Indian troops for reoccupation duties. He therefore opposed the speed-up of the 9th DIC, arguing that due to loss of shipping spaces this would "result in retention in India for an extra six weeks at least of anything up to 18,000 British troops due for Python [return home to the United Kingdom]." There would also be delay in returning Indian troops from the Mediterranean and in the arrival of new British drafts from home. Auchinleck stated flatly, "I am not prepared to accept this delay in Python programme," particularly as the Secretary of War, Mr Lawson, had just personally promised British troops that he would do all he could to get them home. Furthermore, "Indian troops used for political reasons [must] be withdrawn from FIC."

The Control Commission's political report of the 1–8 October period stated that General Gracey had little confidence in the Viet Minh's ability to maintain law and order,[8] which he must have in order to carry out his main tasks. A truce was in effect, and would be broken only if the Viet Minh "themselves recommenced attacks" (this was exactly how the truce was broken). Meanwhile, the Viet Minh were trying to strangle the city. A third, unproductive meeting had occurred between them and the French. The report reiterated that the Viet Minh could not produce Dewey's body or any of the dozens of kidnapped French civilians, and both sides agreed that "there was no useful purpose to be served in continuing the conversations, but it was decided to refer the question to a meeting, if possible, between French representatives and the Viet Nam Central Government at Hanoi." The document concluded, resignedly, "It is still fervently hoped — but it is a forlorn hope — that sense will prevail. Then, in a peaceful atmosphere, the Japanese will be disarmed and the Annamites will be able to bring their case to a French government which will, we trust, examine it with a sympathy and fairness worthy of the cause for which they and we have fought for five years."

On 9 October Gracey sent Lieutenant-Colonel Murray, who had been commanding 4/10 GR in Burma, to Phnom Penh. Murray, who assumed the acting rank of Brigadier and, as Commander Allied Land

---

8. In Gracey's writings, this was a major factor in his decision to evict the Viet Minh by the *coup* of 23 September.

Forces in Cambodia, represented Gracey, was directed to take command of all Japanese forces in the area, and specifically charged with maintaining law and order in the Phnom Penh area, safeguarding all Allied nationals, ensuring the stability of the Cambodian government in accordance with Leclerc's directive, and disarming all Vietnamese (including the Viet Minh police).[9] Also on 9 October, a meeting was arranged between the British and the Viet Minh. Gracey was planning to move into Gia Dinh and Go Vap and so informed the Viet Minh at this time. The meeting, which appears to have been fairly short, was opened by Gracey's representative, Brigadier Hirst, who reiterated that British forces were in Indochina to disarm and repatriate the Japanese, and to maintain law and order while they were doing so. Hirst stated that all this was set out in Proclamation no. 1 issued by General Gracey, and that "the British troops are impartial, and after six years of war, fought to relieve *you* of Japanese domination, are anxious only to complete their tasks and then return to their own country. The British have no interest in the politics of this country as between you and the French. The Viet Minh should also let the population 'resume their normal work'. . . ."

Having wasted no time in setting down the British conditions, Hirst reminded the Viet Minh that a truce had been in force while the talks between the French and the Viet Minh were taking place; however, the talks had failed, and the problem was being addressed at a higher level. Hirst then asked if the Viet Minh were prepared to comply with the requirements of Proclamation no.1, lay down their arms, stop shooting and obstructing Allied forces, and allow the city to return to normal. If not, the British would use whatever force was necessary to accomplish these, saying that all available weapons — "armed cars, guns [artillery], mortars, aircraft, and so on" — would be used against "people of whatever nationality" who resisted the proclamation. Hirst declared, "The British Forces here are the finest trained troops in the world today — what chance have your half-trained levies against them? You are fools if you think your troops can oppose them successfully. The only result will be a lot of needless and useless bloodshed — the outcome of the struggle will not be in doubt." He then appealed to the Viet Minh "to be sensible about this"; this was a last offer, and their last chance. They would have twenty-four hours from midnight to pass orders to their leaders — after than he would "move my troops as I desire." Hirst then reassured the Viet Minh representatives that only British troops

9. Gracey Papers, ALFFIC Operation Instruction No. 2, 9 Oct. 1945.

would be used in disarming the Japanese. The Viet Minh expressed their satisfaction at this information and said that "it would have a big effect on their followers." They went even further by saying that "not only would they give the British all assistance possible but would even arrange civic receptions for our [British] troops." Hirst again warned them that they had until midnight on the 10/11 October to transmit their orders to their military leaders, after which he would move his troops at his pleasure — "and he expected them to be received peacefully." The Viet Minh were then told that British troops would initially occupy Gia Dinh and Go Vap, the northern suburbs of Saigon to the east of Tan Son Nhut. Maunsell reported the results of this meeting in a message to 12th Army, adding that during the conference "News [was] then received that action against airfield by Annamites was in progress. Annamite leader considerably taken aback. They expressed their regret and left at once to issue necessary orders to stop action."[10] He, Hirst, and Brain met with Repiton-Preneuf following the hasty Viet Minh departure, and the Frenchman agreed that no French troops should be used in the operation planned for 11 October north of the Arroyo de l'Avalanche (this operation affected only the key area). Two French companies were, however, still scheduled to fly to Cambodia within forty-eight hours.

While Hirst was warning the Viet Minh representatives to stop their disruptive activities, Gracey, Leclerc and Cédile were in Rangoon for another meeting with Mountbatten. The Viet Minh representatives had given Leclerc exactly the same information as they had given Cédile during the more publicized meetings, namely that they had lost control of their followers and could not produce any of the hostages taken or Dewey's body. Leclerc then added the puzzling news that a radio message from Hanoi to the Viet Minh in Saigon had been intercepted, ordering the Viet Minh to prolong negotiations with the French as long as possible. "He [Leclerc] was at a loss to understand what reasons could have prompted such an order, in view of the fact that the prolongation of negotiations was more in the interests of the French than of the Annamites." Gracey affirmed that he had been told the same thing by the Viet Minh, and that he had asked to see the man who controlled the guns. Gracey also told Mountbatten that he had issued a solemn warning to the Viet Minh not to impede the British task of disarming the Japanese. Douglas Gracey was one of a select few divisional commanders described by General Kimmins[11] (who attended this meeting) as "powerful", and

10. PRO, WO 203/4349, Sgn 181, COS47, 9 Oct. 1945.
11. Personal interview, 26 Jan. 1978.

he now spoke plainly to Mountbatten. Gracey said that "he had prepared plans, which he intended putting into action on 11th October, to move his troops into certain areas commanding Saigon and Cholon and between Saigon and the airfield. He considered this essential in order to ensure his communications against the action of the Annamites, and he would use force if necessary."[12] He then made it clear that "he was not prepared to accept indefinite casualties to his soldiers from sniping in the vicinity of Saigon." Mountbatten said that "although it was essential to continue further negotiations with the Annamite leaders they were unlikely to produce concrete results if the leaders had no control over their irregulars." But he again emphasized that the British were in a "preventive" role, and stipulated that his Political Warfare and Public Relations departments be informed before any action took place. Gracey replied that he fully understood these limitations, and in fact had already prepared a statement on the current political situation. Cédile told Mountbatten that the Viet Minh had now added "a fourth condition to any agreement with the French — namely, the re-establishment of Viet Minh control in the civil administration of Saigon, in fact a return to the situation which had prevailed during the later period of Japanese occupation." Gracey then outlined the current position: ". . . Saigon was run by French police, with the assistance of British/Indian troops in certain of the main utility services, and of Japanese troops in the provision of labour. The Annamite citizens did not take their usual part in the administration of the city, because of their complete intimidation by the Viet Minh." He said that "the establishment of Allied control in the area immediately around Saigon" would solve many problems and would induce the Vietnamese to return to their normal labors.

.Gracey and Cédile differed in their assessments of Saigon's food problem. Cédile reported that Saigon had only four days' supply left, and although there was an abundance of food a few miles from the city, the Vietnamese would not bring their produce into Saigon without armed protection. Gracey did not consider the problem quite as bad as that, serious though it undoubtedly was. He had set up a committee which "had the position in hand and under review."[13] While British/Indian troops, for political reasons, would not be used to clear and protect the food markets in the environs of Saigon, and French troops would not be

---

12. PRO, WO 172/1787, SAC's 33rd (Misc) Meeting, 9 Oct. 1945.
13. Under Lt.-Col. D. C. McLeod and Major P. G. Malins of the RIASC. I am indebted to Major Malins for his account of the Civil Food Control Organisation (CFCO) and their success in combatting the Viet Minh food blockade of Saigon.

available for this purpose for several days more, Gracey had ordered the Japanese "to give all possible assistance in this matter". While the food situation was tight in Saigon, it bordered on the catastrophic in the north. In response to desperate appeals from the Americans in Hanoi, Gracey's Civil Food Control Organization (CFCO) managed to scrape together 2,000 tons of food for shipment to the north.

In the south a serious problem was posed by the French Navy, which appeared to be conducting its own operations independent of any Allied command. Leclerc added that he was embarrassed at unauthorized naval actions, which included the use of landing parties, and the occasional refusal of naval commanders to obey him. Mountbatten made it clear that the French Navy was to respond to the wishes of Gracey and Leclerc, and invited Admiral Graziani — French Naval Commander-designate, Saigon — to visit Ceylon "so that his position should be cleared up." The meeting ended after Mountbatten had repeated his order that none of his commanders was to grant interviews to the press. This reflected instructions from the Chiefs of Staff "following gross misquotations in the press of an interview given by Lieutenant-General Christison" (Christison was also grappling with a difficult situation in the Netherlands East Indies).

These two weeks were a period of intense shipping activity in Saigon. Between 8 and 11 October substantial British/Indian reinforcements arrived,[14] but on 10 October occurred the incident which marked the turning point in the history of the British occupation. The extremist elements of the Viet Minh broke the truce by attacking a British engineer reconnaissance party near Tan Son Nhut, and the British force began hostilities in earnest. Gracey had warned the Viet Minh of the possible consequences of their hostile actions, and they were now to discover that he was a man of his word.

14. Nine ships arrived in two days, carrying an infantry brigade plus supporting troops and vehicles (including armored cars). These reinforcements were in addition to the 7,150 troops and 507 vehicles which had arrived by sea between 6 and 9 October.

# 12

# WAR

The 10 October entry in the War Diary of 20 Indian Division contains the following cryptic entry: "Annamites broke truce by ambush Engineer Recce Party, killing RE Adjutant, 1 VCO and 2 IORs of his escort and wounding remainder. ALFFIC Op Instr No. 3 issued." Mountbatten, in his official report to the Combined Chiefs of Staff, stated that during his meeting with Gracey and Leclerc news was received that the Viet Minh had broken the truce. He wrote: ". . . As it seemed clear that the Viet Minh spokesmen were incapable of ensuring that agreements into which they had entered would be honoured, I ordered that strong action should be taken by the British/Indian forces to secure further key-points, and to widen and consolidate the perimeter of these areas. At the same time I insisted that further attempts to negotiate must continue."[1]

The unofficial 9/14 and 2/8 Punjab Newsletters gave a more detailed account of the incident which sparked off an enlargement of the British military role ("As far as the Bn was concerned the shooting season for Annamites had opened"). A Section (i.e. about eight men) from B Company 2/8 Punjab, under Subedar Ladhu Ram, had escorted the engineer party and 9/14 Punjab drivers. They were returning from inspecting water lines between Saigon and Tan Son Nhut when they were stopped

---

1. Vice-Adm. the Earl Mountbatten of Burma, *Post Surrender Tasks*, Section E of the Report to the Combined Chiefs of Staff (London: HMSO, 1969), p. 282. Gracey later queried Mountbatten's frequent use of the pronoun "I", noting that most of the actions supposedly ordered by Mountbatten had already been carried out by himself (Gracey).

   Maj.-Gen. Harold Pyman, Slim's Chief of Staff at ALFSEA, was in Saigon on 8 and 9 October. His personal diary recorded his pessimism regarding a peaceful settlement in Indochina. He wrote that "nobody will believe a French guarantee," and if the Viet Minh were unable to maintain order they would suffer casualties at British hands, despite Gracey's having used minimum force up to now. Thus, "we can only hope that the French Government will be fair to the Annamites," and although it would be a "great tragedy" if the Viet Minh decided to fight, a "major rebellion" would probably break out if the [French-Viet Minh] talks failed. But if so, "We and the French — for what they are worth — are in a strong position to meet them." (Pyman Papers, Liddell Hart Centre for Military Archives, King's College, University of London.)

near the golf course by a large group of Vietnamese. The Subedar ordered his men to take up defensive positions in a nearby ditch. When things quieted down the Royal Engineers officer, Captain Rollason, got the men back in the trucks for the return to Saigon. As they remounted the Viet Minh opened fire, killing Ladhu Ram and wounding Captain Rollason. His car wrecked, Rollason boarded a truck and they went on, but they soon ran into another ambush. The officer, in the front seat, was hit again, some of the Punjabs were killed, and the truck was damaged. While dismounting Rollason was shot yet again and died, and the six survivors, mostly wounded, formed a small defensive perimeter, their arms consisting of rifles and one Bren gun. The defense was led by two Naiks, Tunda Ram from 2/8 Punjab and Punnu Khan of 9/14 Punjab (who had been shot in the elbow). It was now dusk, and they were surrounded by about 100 Vietnamese. Tunda Ram was killed during the night as a succession of attacks were desperately beaten off. At dawn Punnu Khan shouted to the Viet Minh ''that unless they fall in on the road he would knock hell out of them as he had a hundred men just coming up.'' While the Vietnamese were pondering this, Khan told the remaining men to ''hang on at all costs'' as he slipped out to try and reach the 3/8 Gurkhas a mile away. Although fired on, he was successful and returned with Gurkhas and Japanese troops. The Viet Minh withdrew, leaving behind thirty-five bodies; the survivors were down to a total of ten rounds of small arms ammunition when help arrived.[2] The *20th Indian Division's History* reported that the attacking Viet Minh force, which had been held off for twenty-four hours by less than a dozen wounded Punjabis and Gujaratis, had numbered 500. It was reminiscent of the Zulu attack on Rorke's Drift in an earlier, more colorful era of imperial history. The 20 Division historian wrote of the incident: ''Events of the 10th October . . . established beyond any doubt that the Viet Minh political leaders were in fact unable to control their armed forces. . . . The futility of negotiating with the Viet Minh had been demonstrated and our troops were ordered to take offensive action against Viet Minh forces where necessary.''

The ambush of the engineer reconnaissance party and the simultaneous attack on the Gurkhas at Tan Son Nhut, which was repulsed by Gurkha mortars with six Viet Minh known to have been killed, were not the only incidents of the day; 3/1 GR reported a fire at 2300 hours

---

2. Gracey Papers, 9/14 Punjab Newsletter. Punnu Khan and a 3/8th sepoy were awarded the Military Medal.

behind the soda factory on Knanh Hoi island, bridges were attacked and Gurkhas fired on, incendiary grenades were thrown at warehouses, and road blocks sprang up on main streets in their area. These reports suggest that the ambush of the engineer party was not an isolated incident but part of a deliberate series of actions designed to invite retaliation. The RAF at Tan Son Nhut received a warning from 20 Division that another Viet Minh attack was expected and troops of the RAF Regiment, only a small number at this time, immediately undertook preparations to defend the vital airfield. A local Japanese armory was found and Japanese and French weapons, in addition to the RAF's own guns, were distributed. Japanese machine-guns were mounted on the balcony of the control tower, with fields of fire down the runways and taxiways. The headquarters and Flying Control building became something like a small fortress, and all the Spitfires and C-47s were taxied up to the building. The aircrews were ordered to sleep in their cockpits and while awake to watch the tower for flare signals. Newly-arrived RAF Regiment troops, who had flown in at twenty-four hours' notice, were immediately deployed to the north to augment the small Japanese and Indian detachments there; some were placed in the headquarters building with a platoon of Dogras. That evening a violent tropical storm burst over Saigon and continued till 11 o'clock. Whether the heavy rains or defensive preparations deterred the Viet Minh is unknown, but there was no attack and the defensive arrangements were continued the next day. (The assault, a ferocious one, did come two days later.)

On 11 October Gracey reported that the Viet Minh had "attacked my troops", and listed the casualties: one British officer, one subedar and two Indian soldiers killed, and seven wounded. He pointed out that this "definite aggression" was in spite of recent assurances given by Viet Minh leaders, and he was "now proceeding to take necessary strong action against armed resistance. [I] have consulted Leclerc and we are in complete agreement." Gracey wrote that they would now take "strong action against armed men or bands who in any way resist disarmament or commit hostile acts or sabotage," but that there would be no provocative use of force — they would try to cause the minimum of disturbance "to all law-abiding citizens". Gracey then stated that he was now proceeding with his plan to occupy progressively the key areas of Bien Hoa, Laithieu and Thu Dau Mot. Responsibility for casualties must now rest with the Viet Minh, and Gracey thought that it should be made known that on 8 October he had personally warned the Viet Minh leaders, and on 9 October Hirst had told them of the consequences of their breaking the truce. Said Gracey, "I further stressed that this would entail the use of all weapons of war at our disposal." Mountbatten informed the Chiefs of Staff on 11 October that he had authorized Gracey to issue an announcement saying that the SAC had instructed Gracey "to tolerate no activity which might be inconvenient to the orderly administration" of his tasks of controlling and disarming the Japanese and evacuating the Allied POWs and internees.[3]

Brigadier Woodford's 32 Brigade was charged with investing Gia Dinh, the first move of the expanding British involvement in Vietnam. His orders directed him to secure Gia Dinh and the Thanh My Tay area; "D-Day" was set for 0800 hours on 11 October. The intelligence provided to Woodford was somewhat sketchy. It was difficult to estimate the numbers of Viet Minh in the Gia Dinh area, but intelligence personnel were reasonably sure that Gia Dinh and Go Vap were Viet Minh assembly points. Although a figure of 3,000 armed Viet Minh was suggested, Woodford was told that he was unlikely to encounter many of them. Since at the 9 October conference the Viet Minh had stated their intention to accept the British entry into Gia Dinh, and their violent opposition to the French, the latter were omitted from the operation. Three Japanese units (Yoshida, Sato and Yamagishi *butais*) were to come under Woodford's command for the Gia Dinh operation, and one troop each from 16 Cavalry and 114 Field Regiment (Royal Artillery), plus air support within the established guidlines, were to be available to him. Personnel from 604 Field Security would follow his forces into Gia Dinh and conduct their specialized intelligence and interrogation activities; arrested Vietnamese would be placed in the temporary custody of 20 Division Provost Company for transfer to the French.

At 0630 on 11 October the operation began. 9/14 Punjab, under Lieutenant-Colonel J. B. Hobbs, moved to a bridge on the southern extremity of Gia Dinh, north of Dakao, and at 0800 took command of one squadron of 16 Cavalry. At 0930 Gia Dinh was occupied without incident and posts were established at a bridge and road junction at the eastern edge of the town. By noon Battalion headquarters was established in Gia Dinh, and the Japanese forces were relieved of security duties. By 1315 an armored car troop, with a company of infantry, had made a reconnaissance of a major road running through Gia Dinh, stopping at an intersection between Binh Hoa and Go Vap, and reported the presence of half a dozen armed Viet Minh. Now occurred the first

3. PRO, CAB 105/162; also WO 203/4744, SEACOS 410, 11 Oct. 1945.

serious incident, which again proved (if further proof was still necessary) that the Viet Minh extremists were out of control, since Viet Minh negotiators had earlier agreed peacefully to accept the British occupation of Gia Dinh. Number 9 Platoon of 9/14 Punjab dismounted to cover the Viet Minh who were called on to surrender, and as the Viet Minh moved forward with their hands raised, another group of about thirty opened fire at short range from their positions in scrub just west of the intersection. The platoon havildar Ahmed Khan was killed, at which time "considerable prophylactic fire" was put down by the 37mm and Besa machine-guns of the armored cars. Four Viet Minh were killed, many were wounded, and three of the originally surrendered Viet Minh were hauled with their weapons from their prepared foxholes and handed over to the Field Security Section for interrogation. The rest of the Viet Minh were pinned down by Besa bursts, and at this point the troops withdrew. The withdrawal itself was a tricky operation involving the maneuvering and turning of armored cars and vehicles in the narrow road. So ended the first day of the occupation of Gia Dinh and Go Vap.

After a relatively quiet night at 9/14 Punjab headquarters, the Go Vap operation continued on 12 October. At 0600 two French liaison officers reported to the battalion; one squadron of armored cars from 16 Cavalry rumbled up at 0945, and at 1000 the occupation of Go Vap resumed when nearly five infantry companies, supported by the armored cars, searched about 200 houses on either side of the main road into the town. No contact was made with the Viet Minh, although a few shots were fired by snipers at a cross-roads. At noon the sweep was widened and there was sporadic action, resulting in some Vietnamese being killed and one Indian soldier wounded; the house from which his assailants fired was destroyed by armored car 37mm fire. At 1230 the Punjabis captured a Viet Minh officer in uniform, who was handed over to the Field Security Section detachment accompanying the battalion. A final Viet Minh attempt at defending Go Vap was broken up by armored car fire, and the occupation of the town was complete. The second objective was to patrol the road and tram-lines northwest of Go Vap and join up with 3/8 GR; in the course of these operations twenty French civilian captives of the Viet Minh were released and two roadblocks removed.

Viet Minh activity was noticeably increasing. The Spitfire pilots returning from their daily reconnaissance flights reported about 150 Viet Minh, in military formation, between Gia Dinh and Hoc Mon, and 500 Vietnamese were reported to be assembled in Thu Dau Mot. More disturbing was the report of six field-guns in Viet Minh hands, and the road from Cholon to Duc Hoa was completely trenched across. Trees had been felled across a number of other roads, and in Thu Duc the Viet Minh had held mass meetings and requisitioned all cars to transport their troops for an attack on Allied forces. The French 5th RIC and Marines played a part in the 9/14 Punjab operation of 11 October, as they secured the Thanh My Tay area to the Saigon river. On 11 October Hirst ordered the Japanese to reinforce the garrison in Phnom Penh by 140 men, who were to be armed with twenty light machine-guns and personal weapons. They were to be drawn from the three Japanese *butais* (battalions) attached to Woodford's 32 Brigade. The Japanese were now beginning to cooperate to the extent that the same orders drew attention to a Japanese soldier who, as driver for the RE Commander, was commended for "his devotion to duty on 10 October 1945 when a British officer and a small force of British troops were subjected to an unprovoked attack by a large band of Annamites . . . You will ensure that Lance-Corporal Niko Inouye's superior officers are acquainted with this fact."

At about this time a letter addressed to "The General Commander of English Army at Gia-Dinh" (presumably Woodford) was received at 9/14 Punjab Headquarters and passed on to Woodford and Gracey in Saigon. The letterhead bore the title, "Eastern Defending Committee; Head Office: Bien Hoa", and was datelined "Eastern Zone, 11th October 1945". It said that the Vietnamese only wanted to help the British in disarming the Japanese, and their sole purpose was to restrict the French people and soldiers to the Saigon area. The British were asked not to use French troops in their operations and to notify the Viet Minh of the time and place of their operations. The letter was signed by Hoang Cao Nha in his capacity as "Commander-in-Chief of [the] Vietnamese Army in the Eastern Zone". Adopting this style, a reply was sent back to the Commander-in-Chief, Vietnamese Army in the Eastern Zone, Eastern Defending Committee, Bien Hoa, by Lieutenant-Colonel Ritchie, 20 Division's Chief of Staff, saying that General Gracey was willing to receive a Viet Minh representative "to hear any statement or explanation or suggestion on the subject of law and order which you may wish to express; the representative will be sent as your personal representative."[4] Continued Ritchie, "You will remember both now and in the future that General D. D. Gracey speaks as the Commander of the Allied Land Forces in French Indo China south of 16 Parallel; I would draw

4. Gracey Papers, Ritchie to Viet Minh Commander, 14 Oct. 1945.

your attention to the word 'Allied'; the Allied nations include the French nation.'' It is not known whether the Viet Minh responded to Gracey's invitation to parley; it is likely that they lost interest when they were unable to split the British and French forces over reoccupation policy.

In a remarkably blunt report, the SEAC Assistant Director of Intelligence summed up the problems in South Indochina. He prefaced it with the statement that the document expressed his personal opinion, and should be treated as such. He commented that General Gracey was not permitted any contact with the Viet Minh, and the small number of French with him were not enough to take over administrative control. It was also hard to explain to the Vietnamese how large numbers of Vichy French were back in positions held during the war; ''Throughout the handling of the situation, the French appear to lack every vestige of imagination.'' He went on to say that there was conclusive evidence that Japanese intelligence organizations were behind the Viet Minh and the revolt ''to the hilt''. As far back as April 1945 Vietnamese officers were established in the same building as the headquarters of Minoda, the Japanese military governor of FIC, and high Kempei Tei officers were often seen with Caodists and other groups. The Brazzaville declaration (the loosely defined statement by France concerning greater autonomy, short of independence, for the colonies) was not enough, and the Japanese had publicized it to the Vietnamese as noncommital and worthless. Like most of the British participants, including Gracey, he had no doubt as to the root cause of the troubles: ''Provided the French are prepared to deal with the Annamites as human beings and not as chattels for exploitation as in the past, there is every reason to believe that the leading Annamites will not only listen to them, but will help them. . . .''

On the 12th, the night fighting in Saigon was intense, with delayed action mines continually exploding, large fires ringing the city, and the crackle of small arms fire and banging of artillery audible throughout the night.[5] The 3/1 Gurkhas again reported heavy activity as they swept Khanh Hoi Island; that night they beat back several reckless charges of the ''*banzai*'' type at the docks and their positions. To the north, in the early morning darkness of the 13th, a Viet Minh force had approached Tan Son Nhut from the southwest and fired on 16 Cavalry positions 600 yards from the airfield. The Viet Minh then fanned out and assaulted Tan Son Nhut from three directions. The situation looked desperate for

---

5. On the 12th, also, advance elements of 684 Squadron arrived; this was a Mosquito photo-reconnaissance squadron.

about twenty minutes when the Viet Minh stormed Tan Son Nhut in a major effort to destroy the aircraft and transmitters there, but the attackers were slowly driven back by 16 Cavalry. They did, however, reach the doors of the radio station and were within 300 yards of the control tower when they were stopped; the fight for the airfield then turned into a grim struggle as its loss would have cut Saigon off from the rest of the world. The RAF Regiment defense force, positioned east and southeast of the field, did not participate in this fire fight, but took part, with the Japanese, in the counter-attack which forced the Viet Minh back a distance of two miles. In Saigon, the 9th Frontier Force Rifles had a few pleasant days following their arrival but, as their historian wrote, ". . . every day some unit has an 'incident' with the rebel Annamites, but we had escaped so far. Grenades were thrown at some of our transport and the Jawans replied with a vengeance. Unfortunately one man was killed and several wounded by grenades a few days later and then the gloves were off."

Mountbatten, who a few weeks earlier had considered withholding Gracey's full division from him, was now gravely concerned over the worsening situation in Saigon and concluded his report to London by emphasizing the need to speed French reinforcements.

On 13 October Brigadier Hirst sent a stiff letter to General Manaki, Commander of the Japanese 2nd Division (responsible for the Saigon area). He related that while the British had been engaged in operations in Go Vap, they had discovered some thirty Japanese soldiers in various houses in the town. While saying that "Their attitude to the British soldiers was correct," he implied a collaboration between those Japanese troops and the Viet Minh, and demanded "to know what they were doing there and to which unit they belong". Hirst then charged that "During the French operations at Thanh My Tay I am practically certain that opposition was encountered from formed bodies of Japanese. These parties were dressed in proper uniform, which appeared to be Japanese, and were operating in conjunction with the Annamites, and were equipped and armed like proper soldiers. I know for *certain* that there were certain Japanese troops taking part with the Annamites." Hirst demanded to know who those troops were and what action Manaki was going to take to eliminate them.

Hirst then turned to the letter received by Lieutenant-Colonel Hobbs, 9/14 Punjab, from the Viet Minh army in the Eastern Zone, saying that General Gracey wanted to know why such a Viet Minh office still existed in Bien Hoa, a supposedly cleared town; Gracey had "grave doubts as to

General Manaki's sincerity . . .'' The response of Manaki (described by Brigadier Taunton of 80 Brigade as ''dull-witted'') is not known, but Hirst's charges added weight to the argument that the Japanese were actively assisting the Viet Minh. A number of other incidents had occurred throughout the Saigon area on the morning of 13 October, during which the French, who had lost six killed, captured two Japanese Air Force officers who had been with the Viet Minh; both were executed on the spot.

At Commission headquarters, Mr Meiklereid, Brain's successor as Gracey's political advisor, now wrote his first summary of the situation in Saigon. In a letter to Dening he, like Brain, was highly critical of the French population. He reported the breakdown in negotiations between the French and the Viet Minh (''as was to be expected''), but implied that the fault lay with the Viet Minh for demanding immediate and full autonomy. He also reiterated the very clear warnings personally given to Viet Minh leaders by both Gracey and Hirst, but the Viet Minh had inferred that ''we were acting as a screen for the building up of the French Forces.'' With the 10 October ambush of the British section near Tan Son Nhut, ''General Gracey was left with no other course but to implement his threat.'' Meiklereid echoed Slim's fear as he continued: ''There is little doubt that we shall now be accused of backing French Imperialism, but I frankly consider that no other course was possible if the Allied troops were to carry out their task, and enable us to hand over to the French as soon as possible and let them tackle their own problem — it is no small one!'' As for the immediate future, Meiklereid said that while it was still early, the strength of the Viet Minh opposition ''may not be inconsiderable.'' As for the Vietnamese, ''they must realise that it is now or never for them.'' The French could be expected to be ruthless in putting down the ''revolt'', and the Viet Minh here had ''little or no hold on their followers''. A guerrilla war was to be expected, ''with arms supplied by the Japanese''. Gracey agreed with Meiklereid's text, ''except to say that the Annamites are doing everything in their power to separate British and French forces, and thus to pave the way for a public declaration that British impartiality is a myth, and that the British never had any other intention than backing French imperialism. . . .''

Shortly after he wrote this report, Meiklereid received a copy of the Viet Minh reply to Hirst's questions of 9 October; ''It completely bears out General Gracey's point that their main object is to 'separate British-French forces'.'' Gracey's opinion was expressed in a message to

Mountbatten in which he described his recent correspondence with the "self-styled C-in-C Vietnam army of [the] Eastern Zone". In reporting Meiklereid's receipt of a letter on 13 October from the Committee for the South, and the continuing rigidity of the Viet Minh position, Gracey wrote:

I consider that Viet Minh Central Policy if such a thing exists is to attempt by every means of conciliation with British to split British and French. I have no doubt that they will accuse British through radio and all other means of coming to FIC with statement that they had no interest in politics but in fact providing shield for reinstatement of French. In fact it has now become inevitable for the proper execution of my tasks that I should act hand in hand with Leclerc policy as to key areas only. By doing so I inevitably provide very considerable assistance to political aims of French in this area.

Having been beaten back in frontal assaults the Viet Minh now intensified their attempts to strangle Saigon. RAF reconnaissance "indicated that the Viet Minh were determined to cut off the city from the outside world, and that extensive demolitions and roadblocks were visible on all roads leading out of the city. Large concentrations of Annamites seen in the area N. E. of Saigon (Thu Dau Mot/Thu Duc/Bien Hoa area) confirmed reports of a large Viet Minh build-up in this area." The situation grew ever more ugly, and any hopes of reaching a peaceful settlement had by now vanished. (On 1 October Gracey had written that unless the French promised *some* form of autonomy to the Vietnamese, the fighting was inevitable.) The French were determined to regain their position — and their prestige — by force of arms, the Viet Minh had despaired of gaining immediate independence, the British were intent on securing their key areas, and the Japanese, who had surrendered two months earlier, must have wondered by what means they could be allowed to lay down their arms again and go home. The important part played by the Japanese troops at this stage cannot be over-emphasized. They were doing most of the dirty work in clearing road blocks, patrolling, and investigating and rounding up wanted Vietnamese. After a slow start they were now taking a more active role in anti-Viet Minh operations, but their distaste for this activity remained undiminished. Their position was unenviable, but they were reaping where they had sown.

On 14 October, 32 Brigade continued to run into strong opposition as it consolidated its positions and gradually moved the Viet Minh out of their suburban stronghold in the north. The primary objectives of Woodford's Gurkhas and Punjabis were the river bridges north of

Saigon. The Gurkhas had to charge one bridge and use armored cars to secure another. More than five Japanese were seen with Viet Minh forces in the course of stiff fighting which left twenty-four Viet Minh and one Gurkha dead. Despite this, the north bank was still in Viet Minh hands and early in the battle the Gurkhas of 4/2 GR were forced to abandon a truck and a jeep which were captured by the Viet Minh. Most of Indochina was now tense, and in the Saigon area both sides rested from the fighting of the previous day. Pro-French individuals were being arrested and shot in southern Laos, while the coastal areas north and east of Saigon were nests of Viet Minh activity.

Mountbatten was informed by the Chiefs of Staff that action was being taken to accelerate the transfer of the 9th DIC to Saigon. He immediately wrote to Gracey, asking him to ''Please inform Leclerc and tell him how glad I am that our repeated attacks have borne fruit at last.'' General Leclerc flew to Phnom Penh on the 15th and arrested the Cambodian Prime Minister — which Gracey's representative in Phnom Penh, acting Brigadier Murray, had recommended because of the Prime Minister's pro-Japanese conduct. It was said that Lieutenant-Colonel Huard, commanding the 5th RIC (in Phnom Penh as acting High Commissioner for Cambodia), was supposed to carry out the arrest, but lacked the confidence to do so. Leclerc made the arrest by a simple nod of the head — not a word was said, and he and his captive flew back to Saigon the same afternoon. After their departure, Huard rounded up the remaining known extremists in Phnom Penh and the situation returned to normal. To avoid the unpleasantness the King of Cambodia had embarked on a pilgrimage before Leclerc arrived and returned the day after the arrest. As ALFFIC headquarters reported to ALFSEA, ''Altogether a very satisfactory coup d'état by the French with strong flavour of Ruritania.'' But there was no flavor of Ruritania in the Saigon area as there now occurred a number of small, sharp fights between the British/Indian troops and the Viet Minh, with all battalions (plus some Japanese units) reporting actions.

The British Military Attaché in Washington wrote to Mountbatten that the father of the assassinated Lieutenant-Colonel Dewey had offered to increase the reward for the return of his son's body from the current 5,000 piasters.[6] However, he agreed to withdraw the offer when he

---

6. The OSS were still involved in their anti-French (and now anti-British), pro-Communist activities, and at this time the full story of the murder in Laos of the French officer Klotz became known. An OSS officer (whom we shall here refer to as Major ''B'') and party had parachuted into French Indochina from Kunming in late

realized that it offered an incentive for the murder of other officers in the future.

Gracey's headquarters now divided the Saigon/Cholon area and suburbs into four sectors — known as 32 Brigade, French, 80 Brigade, and Royal Artillery. In the 80 Brigade sector, 4/17 Dogra were experiencing the frustrations associated with guerrilla warfare. Their unit War Diary stated that many sweeps were fruitless as weapons "are obviously hidden with great care, probably under floors and other such places, and unless the search is 100% thorough it is useless. With the troops available only very small areas can be tackled." As the 9/14 Punjab Newsletter stated, "It is an unpleasant type of war, the enemy wear no uniform and one seldom sees them carrying arms, but there is always the odd sniper and the apparently harmless bystander who throws a grenade and ducks for cover. It looks as though the French have a tricky time ahead of them." On the night of 15/16 October the Viet Minh assaulted a 3/8 Gurkha position at a bridge, and 400 desperate attackers, some armed with bows and arrows, were beaten back. The Viet Minh used a form of tear gas in the attack (apparently from Japanese stocks in Tonkin), and analysis of the arrowheads revealed sublethal traces of strychnine. One Gurkha was killed, and in this and other attacks sixteen more Viet Minh were shot dead. Giap himself later wrote: "After the triumph of the [August] revolution . . . many units of the Vietnam Liberation Army got ready to go south. These were not merely platoons of some dozens as before but thousands of young patriots from every locality who, responding to the appeal of the revolution, resolutely went south to fight the aggressors."[7] Truong Chinh described the main

---

September and crossed into Northeastern Thailand, where they carried out their activities on behalf of the Communists. Astonishingly, Major "B" announced that he was going to use the Nakon Phanom airstrip for his own purposes (although he had not bothered to ask the Thai authorities); this was ironic in that it was usually Wedemeyer's China Command who complained that Allied agents operated in their area without express permission, and Thailand fell within SEAC. The US general at SEAC, Timberman, sent a stiff note to China Command, and Major "B" and party were promptly ejected back whence they had come, but not before they had managed to cause some mischief. According to Force 136, Major "B" later reported that Captain Klotz's Viet Minh murderers had arrived on the scene at OSS request and later "escaped". Mackenzie, head of Force 136, wrote to Dening about this extraordinary action and was not surprised at the Viet Minh escape, which happened "as we foresaw".

7. Vo Nguyen Giap *The Military Art of People's War* (New York: Monthly Review Press, 1970), p. 76.

enemy as the reactionary French colonialists, "formerly the most zealous lackeys of the Japanese".[8]

The buildup of 20 Indian Division was completed on the 17th, when Gracey's third brigade arrived in Saigon. (This was 100 Brigade, commanded by the larger-than-life Brigadier C. H. B. Rodham, and consisting of 4,486 troops and 370 vehicles of 14/13 FFR, 4/10 GR, and 23 Mountain Regiment.) Allied intelligence estimated that the main Viet Minh strength lay in the Thu Duc/Bien Hoa/Thu Dau Mot area north and northeast of Saigon; it was here that General Gracey had decided to position the newly-arrived 100 Brigade. Gracey discussed at this time with General Leclerc the unauthorized burning by French troops of a village south of Rue Verdun. Leclerc said he would make sure that Colonel Rivier's forces did not repeat the act.

Gracey now asked Browning for permission to send a permanent British representative to the Chinese headquarters in Hanoi. This resulted from the exasperating discussions at Tourane (Danang) following the seizure there of eight Japanese aircraft under British control which were carrying food. As Gracey said in his telegram, "During discussions at Tourane to facilitate release of our aircraft it became evident Chinese consider exact position 16 degrees parallel as considerably south of position as demarcated by this Commission." The negotiations were complicated by Chinese annoyance that Terauchi was still in command of Japanese troops in Tourane; Gracey foresaw similar problems at other areas along the common border. His means of communicating with Hanoi were limited indeed; he could only go through SACSEA and General Carton de Wiart in Chungking. The Chinese themselves thought that Gracey should send a representative to Hanoi, but because of the Chinese attitude to the French, Gracey felt it would be wiser at this time to omit any French representation on the proposed liaison mission. He thought that, in addition to normal liaison duties, the mission would provide him with valuable intelligence on the political situation in the north. As it was, a British mission went to Hanoi in November.

As numerous small-unit actions continued throughout the key areas, the hapless General Manaki received another stern letter from Brigadier Hirst, demanding investigation into reports that Japanese forces had welcomed a large Viet Minh force in Thu Dau Mot. It was evident that

---

8. Truong Chinh, *Primer for Revolt: the August Revolution* (New York: Praeger, 1963), p. 17.

the only way the Thu Du Mot/Thu Duc/Bien Hoa assembly areas
would be denied to the Viet Minh was be by their being occupied, and
this the British would soon do. With the announcement of Operation
"Moussac" on 20 October, the figure of Jacques Massu first enters the
history of Indochina. The newly-arrived Lieutenant-Colonel, Commander of the *Groupement de Marche* of the 2nd *Division Blindée* (Armored
Division), was to be in charge of the operation.[9] It was the first French
thrust out of Saigon and the first step in the French effort to reconquer
Indochina. The operation to seize Mytho was planned for 24 October. It
was to be a French-British-Japanese affair, for the Royal Navy, the RAF,
a British Army liaison officer and the Japanese Army were involved in
supporting the French. Brigadier Taunton was assigned to provide a
Major from 80 Brigade to act as liaison for the transmission of orders to
the Japanese, who would still not accept orders from the French. The
French were authorized to receive air support "in case of grave
emergency",[10] and the British Royal Engineers' report on the Saigon-
Mytho road was delivered to Leclerc. Although the French troops
showed *élan* in quickly capturing Mytho, they got a taste of the
frustrating kind of war to come in the form of destroyed bridges and cut
roads along the way to their objective.

The Japanese were informed of the impending major British operation
when "Order no. 1" was issued by Brigadier Rodham to General
Manaki. Manaki was told that 100 Brigade would be occupying Thu
Duc, Bien Hoa and Thu Dau Mot on 23, 24 and 25 October respectively.
Wrote Rodham, "Having occupied these areas I will then assume
responsibility for the maintenance of law and order in the area." Manaki
was ordered to facilitate the move of 100 Brigade by taking the following
actions: (1) continue disarming all Vietnamese (including police) and
search for weapons in the Thu Duc/Thu Dau Mot/Bien Hoa area; (2)
keep the Route Coloniale open between those towns (Viet Minh dug in
at road blocks would be dealt with by Rodham's tanks and armored
cars); and (3) "thoroughly clear" a 3-mile radius around those three
towns. Steps were taken to minimize the possibility of the Viet Minh
fomenting trouble between British and Japanese troops by firing on

---

9. Massu had reached Saigon on 19 October after a circuitous air journey from Ceylon.
   For his own account of the raising of the *Groupement de Marche de la 2° DB* and its
   subsequent operations in Indochina, see his book *Sept Ans avec Leclerc* (Paris: Plon,
   1974).
10. Massu said that he never asked for, or received, air support from the British. (Per-
    sonal interview, Paris, 1977.)

Rodham's troops as they approached the Japanese. Therefore, Japanese troops in Thu Duc, Bien Hoa and Thu Dau Mot would come under the command of Major Mullaly (4/10 GR), Lieutenant-Colonel Pickard (14/13 FFR) and Lieutenant-Colonel Jarvis (1/1 GR) respectively.

The Viet Minh, in generally switching to a guerrilla role, had temporarily abandoned direct assaults on Gracey's forces. However, the sniping and grenading of the Allied troops continued. Word now arrived that on 10 October a Japanese patrol from Phanrang to Dalat had been attacked by the Viet Minh, and only one man had survived to reach safety. The Japanese further reported that the Viet Minh were training soldiers in the Xuan Loc area, about 55 km east of Bien Hoa. The population was also now treated to the hitherto unlikely spectacle of Japanese infantry units carrying out the occupations of Cho Ballom and Bin Dien (about 20 miles southwest of Saigon) and being supported in their minor clashes with the Viet Minh by 16 Cavalry armored cars. A "grade A" report from French sources identified the overall Viet Minh commander of the Bien Hoa district as Hoang Minh Chau, recently arrived from Hanoi. It was also reported to Allied intelligence that "1,000 Tonkinese troops", armed with rifles and one light machine-gun per eight men, had arrived in the Xuan Loc area on 15 October; they were said to be commanded by a dozen Japanese officers including Lieutenant Sakamoto, the ex-Kempei Tei chief at Cap St Jacques. More ominous was the report that the Japanese had handed over 200 tons of ammunition to the Viet Minh from dumps in Bien Hoa, Mytho, Binh Long, and Tanan.

In Kandy, Mountbatten dined with the French naval commander, Admiral Graziani, on the 22nd; Graziani carried a letter from d'Argenlieu to SACSEA. Mountbatten stated that d'Argenlieu should have been as delighted as he was himself "that the continued pressure which I have applied to the Chiefs of Staff has succeeded in advancing the date of the arrival of the 9th DIC from the end of December to November." He denied rumors that he was displeased with d'Argenlieu's impending arrival in Kandy and added: "My own hope is that General Gracey and his Division will be able to prove of real service to you within the limitations which, as you know, my Government have placed upon their activities."[11] (Someone on the Control Commission staff penciled two large exclamation marks beside the last statement. Actually, the Chiefs of Staff had overruled Mountbatten in freeing Gracey from the

11. Gracey Papers, Mountbatten to d'Argenlieu, 23 Oct. 1945.

unrealistic limitations SACSEA had imposed upon him.)

Japanese intelligence reporting was somewhat patchy, and the Control Commission intelligence officers had worked out their method of evaluating reports: "The principle adopted in considering these low-grade reports is (a) where Japanese and local sources disagree, to disregard the Japs and accept that a proportion of the figure suggested by the local source (usually 10%) is actually in the area as stated; (b) where Japanese and local source reports agree, to accept a rather higher percentage figure for the area." The intelligence staff also pointed out that the main support for the Viet Minh came from the Tonkinese coolies on the plantations, "so that any trained bodies of these already in the area may be the occasion" for reports of trainloads of Tonkinese arriving from the north. These rumors "would, of course, greatly encourage the wavering Annamites of Cochin-China, who have never been as active as those from the North." In conclusion, the Control Commission's intelligence summary stated that the consensus of reports — from both Japanese and local sources — was that the main Viet Minh strength was in the Thu Duc/Bien Hoa/Thu Dau Mot area. It remained to be confirmed that these Viet Minh were being reinforced from Hanoi, but better-disciplined Vietnamese were expected to arrive there.

Since Gracey intended to concentrate the bulk of the surrendered Japanese forces in the Thu Duc/Bien Hoa/Thu Dau Mot area, he would first have to occupy these towns and clear the area of Viet Minh. That task fell to Rodham's newly-arrived 100 Brigade.

# 13

# EXPANSION

With the arrival of 100 Brigade, Gracey could now implement his plan to secure and pacify the Thu Duc/Thu Dau Mot/Bien Hoa triangle, in which the bulk of the Japanese were to be concentrated before their transfer to Cap St Jacques for embarkation to Japan. As early as 19 October, 1/1 GR were alerted for their move to Thu Dau Mot. Certainly, Gracey wasted no time in pushing his third brigade out, for among other things Bien Hoa was developing into a major Viet Minh center. He therefore ordered Rodham to "(a) Establish forces at Bien Hoa and Thu Dau Mot; (b) Control the area and keep open the L of C [line of communication] to Saigon north and east of 32 Brigade's present boundary; (c) Concentrate and disarm the Japanese forces."[1]

Brigadier Woodford's 32 Brigade was tasked by Rodham to establish bridgeheads and secure crossroads leading out of Saigon, and the Japanese had been ordered to disarm the Viet Minh throughout the area. Also, "The day before the arrival of the Bde at Thu Duc — Bien Hoa and Thu Dau Mot, the Japanese have been ordered thoroughly to comb the area within three miles radius of each place for armed Annamites and hidden arms." To preclude the possibility of the Viet Minh firing on Rodham's troops from behind Japanese positions, and thereby forcing a British-Japanese fight, the Japanese were told to keep clear of the roads during the brigade's actual movement.

The operation itself was to be carried out in three phases consisting of the securing, successively, of Thu Duc, Bien Hoa and Thu Dau Mot. Spitfire reconnaissance had reported all "*Route Coloniale*" roads in good condition, but the road north of Saigon (to Thu Duc) was blocked at intervals with trees and trestles. Additional cavalry, artillery, machine-guns and supporting troops were to come under Rodham's command from 0800 hours on the day before D-day (23 October 1945). The whole force was divided into four groups, A, B, C and D, the first three being built around the three infantry battalions (4/10 and 1/1 Gurkhas and 14/13 FFR). It was a well-planned and well-executed operation, as the force moved counterclockwise in a triangle, dropping off groups on suc-

1. Gracey Papers, "ALFFIC Operation Instruction No. 7," 21 Oct. 1945. Thu Duc was omitted from this order, but inserted in 100 Brigade's "Op. Instr. No. 52".

cessive days along the way. The operation began under the command of Lieutenant-Colonel Chaudhuri, the Indian commander of 16 Cavalry.

At 0730 hours on 23 October, the operation began as the first battalion, the 4/10 Gurkha Rifles, moved out, marching out of Saigon carrying full packs and equipment. Five hours later the battalion entered Thu Duc, weary but unhindered. According to 1/1 GR, the first day's operation had gone well, with "no hindrance except for the Military Police in Saigon who were alleged to be directing traffic". The force moved out of Thu Duc early on 24 October arriving in Bien Hoa at 0845. There was no sign of the Tonkinese Viet Minh troops, numbering between four and eight thousand, reported in a previous low-grade estimate, but "reliable reports state that all armed Annamites, approx 2,000, evacuated the town on 22.10.45." The unit commanders were met by Colonel Miyake, the senior Japanese officer in the area, and the town was immediately "searched and found to be clear". The 14/13 FFR and ancillary units set up camp in the area of Bien Hoa jail, and at 1100 hours the Union Jack was "hoisted with ceremony" over the main entrance to the jail. For 1/1 GR, the afternoon was spent relaxing and bathing in the river, although their staging area had formerly been the Viet Minh headquarters, and quantities of Viet Minh documents were discovered there.

On 25 October, as the remaining group prepared to depart for Thu Dau Mot, the 14/13 FFR took up a new headquarters at the old French administration building. The group under Lieutenant-Colonel Cyril Jarvis, commanding the 1/1 Gurkhas, reached Thu Dau Mot at 1100 hours on 25 October, "after a peaceful journey along a road lined with Japanese troops". As the group entered Thu Dau Mot, six Spitfires took off from Tan Son Nhut "to do a show of force over Bien Hoa and Thu Dau Mot. This was a general beat-up of the place to keep the Annamites quiet while the Army went in. Bad visibility prevented a really good show." The British/Indian units were surprised by the absence of opposition, since Tonkinese troops (described as "well armed and disciplined") had arrived by the trainload to join the local Viet Minh reported in the area. The main Viet Minh bodies had cleared out of the three towns less than twenty-four hours earlier, but guerrilla elements left behind continued to harass 100 Brigade, and to have swept the whole area thoroughly "would have required many more troops than could be spared at this time."

The French now reported that the Viet Minh had attacked at Nha Trang, and the battleship *Richelieu* had been sent to back up the cruiser

*Triomphant* there; both had permission to use their guns if necessary. A small group of Vietnamese were said to be marching east out of Bien Hoa, and the Japanese report of 500 Viet Minh arrivals from Tonkin was accepted as fairly accurate. The Japanese estimated that 200 more Viet Minh were now northwest of Xuan Loc, and that 300 were in Trang Bom. ALFFIC headquarters stated that "Hostile activities of the Annamites have, to a large extent, receded from our expanding perimeter within and on the edge of which they have now confined themselves to minor guerrilla tactics." The 20th Division was to "commence systematic patrolling beyond the present perimeter . . . The object of these patrols is to show the flag, reconnoitre and open up the roads, rid the area of malcontents and reassure the peaceful inhabitants, so that they will recommence their normal trading." The patrols were not to fight unless attacked, and would clear undefended roadblocks.

The Japanese again protested at the French attitude towards them. The minutes of the 24 October conference held by Hirst state, "The Japanese complained of the lack of appreciation by certain elements of the local French population, and, more especially, the local press, of the work performed by the Japanese forces working side by side with the Allied forces in the suppression of disorder."

On 25 October, as far as can be ascertained, came the only evidence of direct Soviet involvement in South Vietnam. As there had earlier been "the first American casualty", now there was the first Russian casualty. The Japanese reported that in their sweep and disarming of the Viet Minh which immediately preceded the arrival of the 1st Gurkhas in Thu Dau Mot, their forces had found a Russian among the Viet Minh. The minutes of the 25 October British-Japanese conference said of him, "Being a subject of an Allied nation, he had been placed in protective custody. He was, however, reported to be the leader of the local Viet Minh party and is said to have come from China originally." The Japanese were ordered to hand the man over to 100 Brigade. The 1/1 GR War Diary reported the incident as follows: "At 1600 hrs a Russian claiming to be a French subject and a rubber planter was brought in by the Japanese: an exotic red-bearded figure by Kipling out of Conrad, he freely admitted having worked for the Viet Minh for two days before his detection. The papers he carried showed him to be a scientist of some learning. He was sent to Bde for detailed interrogation."[2]

2. PRO, WO 172/7769, War Diary 1/1 GR, 25 Oct. 1945. Lt.-Col. Jarvis remembered the incident well. Since he knew some rudimentary Russian he attempted to

In Thu Dau Mot, the 1st Gurkhas said of the Japanese, "Their intelligence information was to prove invariably accurate: it was always clearly illustrated by quite excellent maps."[3] The Japanese remained largely responsible for the maintenance of public order, as the Gurkhas "provided a mobile column to take action against irreconcilables who sniped and ambushed us and the Jap sentries, impartially, and made raids on warehouses and installations." However, "it meant, literally, death to go outside unescorted."

Lieutenant-Colonel Clark provided an insight into previous Japanese-Viet Minh cooperation in the area:

On the score of Jap support for the Viet Minh it may be of interest that when the 'Colons' took over the old French Residency in Thu Dau Mot they discovered that the evening before our arrival in the town the Japanese commander had given a banquet for the Viet Minh! They found the full list of guests and the menu. Unfortunately there was no list of Japanese officers against whom we could take action but I did warn the Jap commander of the area that I would have a Military Police investigation if I had an further cause to suspect collaboration. The interpreter used the term 'Kempei Tei' and you should have seen the Admiral's face. He was obviously really scared that our RMP [Royal Military Police] would use Kempei Tei methods![4]

Fires now blazed all over Saigon and Cholon as Viet Minh arsonists attempted, among other things, to burn down the power station. Japanese firefighters came under heavy sniping, and 4/2 GR killed three snipers north of Tan Son Nhut.

---

get the prisoner to talk, but to no avail. The Russian was wearing a regular Viet Minh uniform, with gold stars on the lapels of his jacket. He was handed over to the *Sûreté* and disappeared completely. (Lt.-Col. Cyril Jarvis, personal interview, 13 May 1977.) Jean Cédile also remembered him, but said that he had no direct knowledge of his fate (personal interview, 26 Oct. 1977).

Although King Chen (*Vietnam and China, 1938-1954*, p. 113), quoting Charles B. McClane, states that Moscow had no part in the insurrection, old *Sûreté* hands may be able to tell us what part, however small, it really did play during or immediately after the uprising. Because he was never heard of again, it is likely that the captured Russian was quietly executed.

3. This was probably because Lt.-Col. Cyril Jarvis developed a closer relationship with the local Japanese commander, Major Takahashi, than the other battalion commanders. Many years later, Jarvis returned Takahashi's sword to him, to discover that Takahashi had died. However, Jarvis received a photograph from the family, which showed Takahashi's widow holding the sword, surrounded by the immediate family.

4. Lt.-Col. R. W. Clark, former Commander 1/1 GR, letter to author, 1977.

The French under Massu had startling success in their first operation, the recapture of Mytho. One of Massu's officers had reconnoitered the area from the air in a Japanese Zero fighter, and although the mechanized column had rough going due to the numerous road cuts and blown bridges (destroyed by a Vietnamese graduate of the Ecole Polytechnique),[5] the commando group under the naval parachutist Ponchardier, supported by the sloops *Gazelle* and *Annamite*, seized the town in a lightning waterborne assault.

Reports that sizeable bodies of well-armed Viet Minh were slipping back into Go Vap seemed confirmed when the Viet Minh, using Japanese grenade-launchers, mounted a strong attack on 9/14 Punjab on the night of the 25th. At the same time Naik Ajmer Singh, of the 92nd Indian Field Company (Indian Engineers), who was guarding one of five wells in Cholon operated by the Bombay Sappers and Miners Company, was shot dead from a nearby house. In describing the incident and its aftermath, Major J. H. Clark of the Royal Engineers wrote that the only effective retaliatory measure against an ambush was to burn down the hut from which the shots came.[6] The wells were continually being sniped at by night. It was infuriating for the sappers, who had strict orders never to fire unless they had a target, "and of course they never did." The Naik's death triggered a reaction, an account of which is given here because of wild charges by some writers that the British deliberately burnt Saigon.

The murdered Naik's commander got angry and received permission to destroy the houses near the wells. The Sikh platoon had difficulty in burning the eight houses near the dead sapper's post due to their strong teak construction and the absence of any wind. In the afternoon the com-

5. Jacques Massu, *Sept Ans avec Leclerc* (Paris: Plon, 1974), p. 245. The Vietnamese, Nguyen Ngoc Bich, was later betrayed to the French by the Viet Minh.

6. J. H. Clark, "Sappers and Miners in Saigon", *The Royal Engineers Journal*, vol. LXIV, no. 3, 1950, pp. 284–5. All of this, however, was but more fuel for those writers who thirsted for news of Allied transgressions, and on 25 October Browning had written a prophetic letter to Penney: "I am absolutely convinced that the healing of our sick and weary world is going to be more complicated by the fact that a free, third rate and irresponsible Press are at large in the world today. They have consistently misquoted our statements and in fact done everything to embarrass the situation rather than help it. If you can only do something to persuade the people at home that 50% of our problems now have been due (and will be in the future) to the world Press, you will have done a most important thing." (Papers of Maj.-Gen. W. R. C. Penney, Letter from Lt.-Gen. Browning, 25 Oct. 1945. Liddell Hart Centre for Military Archives, King's College, University of London.)

mander picked another group of huts near a well "at the corner of a huge Chinese-Annamite slum, but separated from it by roads which would act as firebreaks." At 1500 hours an anxious phone call brought the commander back to the scene, over which a black pall of smoke had risen which could be seen for miles around. The Sikh Subadar had actually only burnt one hut, but a strong wind had caused the whole block, made of dry thatch, to go up, and a fire half a mile long by a quarter of a mile wide was now raging. The panic-stricken inhabitants had fled, and all of Cholon was threatened since there was no time to make a firebreak. The problem was exacerbated since the Viet Minh, as part of their arson strategy, had earlier stolen most of Saigon's fire trucks. While frantic efforts were being made to control the fire, "the unhappy OC [Officer Commanding] turned over in his mind what he was going to say at his court martial." However, the wind suddenly dropped and some light rain fell. The fire slowly died out. "The Sikh Naik had certainly been given a worthy funeral pyre," and "An anxious OC sat down and wrote his report, and had a worrying time waiting. . . . But his luck was in; for the Chinese had been making trouble for some time. . . ." When the Chinese complained, accusing the Indian troops of "committing all sorts of other offences against them", they were told that they had done nothing but obstruct the Allies in their duties, cheat the troops, run places of evil repute, spread diseases, shelter terrorists, and profit from both sides. Furthermore, if they didn't straighten out in the future, there would be another Fire of Cholon. There was little further trouble in Cholon until the French arrived.[7] News of this fire most probably caused Mountbatten to write a critical letter to Gracey, which is discussed later.

By the 26th the balance of 20 Indian Division (3,000 men) had arrived, completing the build-up of Gracey's own forces to a final strength of 22,190 men.[8] (French forces at this time totalled 4,575, including 2,150

7. *Ibid.* This may have been what R. Harris Smith was referring to in his book, *OSS* (Berkeley: University of California Press, 1972, p. 346), when he wrote that "the British had deliberately burned down great sections of the native quarter of Saigon." He probably meant Cholon, since nothing comparable happened in Saigon. With that curious selectivity which permeated the writings on this area in the 1960s and early 1970s, Smith fails to mention the Viet Minh fire compaign of September (to increase its effectiveness, they had carefully managed to remove Saigon's fire trucks beforehand), and the fact that arson and incendiarism were a major part of their strategy. A great deal of South Vietnam's property — warehouses, rubber dumps, etc. — was daily put to the torch by the Viet Minh as a matter of policy.

8. Meanwhile, in London, a political report was received at the Foreign Office on 26

personnel of the Combat Command, 2nd Armored Division — *Groupement Massu*.) The Division now informed 100 Brigade that Sato *butai* was soon to arrive in Bien Hoa. This Japanese battalion was 500 strong, and would come under the command of 100 Brigade in order to carry out the following tasks. Rodham was ordered to seize the Xuan Loc area and break up any Viet Minh force found there, establish a strong base at Xuan Loc while patrolling "vigorously" towards Baria, east on the Nha Trang road and north towards Dalat, and operate offensively at all times while maintaining control of communications in the Xuan Loc

October; it was the report sent earlier by Dening to Mountbatten, in which Brain recapitulated the reason for the 23 September *coup*, noting that pure hooligans and bandits had been flourishing "under the banner of the fight for independence". Wrote Brain, "Because these activities went on under the authority of the so-called Viet Nam government the latter could not be dealt with as an administration capable of maintaining order. It was for this reason that Gen Gracey arranged for the civil administration to be taken over by the French using rearmed French prisoners of war. This was done on 22 and 23 Sept in the form of a coup d'état."

It has not been possible up till now to find any evidence that Brain or Dening ever disapproved of the *coup*, and Brain was even-handed in his report, which severely criticized the French. He went straight to the heart of the matter:

All the French people I have met have assured me that the great majority of the Annamites want nothing more than to live in peace and carry on their work under French rule . . . But they are shutting their eyes to the fact that Annamite independence movements have existed for some 80 years and have broken out in violent forms more than once, only to be driven underground by the use of the harshest measures of suppression . . . There is not the slightest doubt that the Japanese backed the Annamites, but the flames were there before the fuel was added. The fact that resistance did not immediately collapse when the first heavy casualties began to be inflicted by our forces is alone sufficient proof of this. . . . It is difficult to place any reliance on the views of the French regarding the political importance of the demand for independence. They do not realise that in the eyes of the natives the French are no longer the superior beings that their domination and their force of arms made them appear in the past. The Annamites have seen the French dictated to, humiliated, and finally disarmed and kicked out of authority by an Oriental race, and, perhaps equally important, they have tasted power and known for a short time the pride of being a *de facto* government.

Brain emphasized that the Viet Minh leaders he had met "were no mere puppets of the Japanese, but educated and intelligent men with a strong determination to be free from, as they put it, the French yoke." He went on to say that he "also gained the impression that they were not entirely in control of the forces which threatened us, and this impression was confirmed by a private interview which I had on 3rd October with Dr Pham Ngoc Thach, who is the member of the local administration responsible for foreign affairs and at the same time a representative of the central Viet-Nam government in Hanoi."

area. Rodham was to nominate a British officer to command the force and to assign armored car and artillery support from his resources as he saw fit; the British officer and the supporting units would be withdrawn after they had established a block and issued orders for further Japanese operations in the Xuan Loc area. Rodham selected Major L. D. Gates of the 14/13 Frontier Force Rifles to command the force, to be called Gateforce. He was informed that Viet Minh headquarters, together with 2,000 troops, had been reported to have fled to the Xuan Loc area. Gates's infantry would consist of Sato *butai*, supported by a squadron of 16 Cavalry armored cars, a company of 14/13 FFR infantry and a 42 Indian Field Ambulance detachment; he would also have a platoon of 9 Jat machine-gunners, a section of 3-inch mortars from 14/13 FFR, and a Royal Engineers detachment. Gates was ordered to establish his patrol base at Xuan Loc on 29 October, patrol aggressively from 30 October to 1 November, and then return to Bien Hoa on 2 November with the whole force. While the British/Indian units were to take a seven-day food supply, the Japanese would be responsible for their own maintenance. The armored cars were to carry sufficient fuel for 500 miles. Gates was cautioned not to use half-measures if he met with opposition; Rodham thought that a strong show of force would disperse Viet Minh concentrations.

The operation itself was to be carried out in phases: the establishment of a patrol base in Xuan Loc on 29 October, patrolling the Baria road on 1 November, and the return to Bien Hoa on 2 November. Gates was ordered to use "maximum force" against enemy opposition, and all armed Vietnamese were to be disarmed. Further, "Any opposition from a village will be answered by complete destruction of the village." These were draconian instructions indeed, but the message to the Viet Minh and the population was brutally direct: there would be no safe haven for Viet Minh engaged in warfare, and villages should not shelter Viet Minh units. At 2100 on 28 October, Sato *butai* had still not arrived in Bien Hoa, and the Gateforce starting time was moved back to 0900 the next day. By 0800 on the 29th it was learned that Sato *butai* had been issued with incorrect orders by the Japanese staff and had turned up in Trang Bom, about 15 miles east of Bien Hoa. So at 0925 Gateforce left Bien Hoa and picked up Sato *butai* on the way. Shortly after, Gracey and Hirst arrived in Bien Hoa from Saigon to look over the area and discuss the battalion's operational role with Pickard.

While Gracey was in Bien Hoa, rumblings of discontent became audible at the highest levels of command in South East Asia. At the request of General Slim, Major-General Pyman, ALFSEA Chief of Staff, wrote an extremely blunt letter to General Sir Miles Dempsey, Commander of the 14th Army. The reason for the letter, and for its timing, was Dempsey's visit to Delhi to confer with the Chief of the Imperial General Staff, Sir Alan Brooke. So long as the war was being fought, Slim and the senior Army commanders had concealed their very considerable discontent and loyally supported the Supreme Allied Commander, Lord Louis Mountbatten, presenting the world with a façade of unruffled harmony. But with the massive post-war problems to be confronted, compounded by a home government for whom supporting the senior commanders in the troubled areas was not a high priority, officers like Slim could contain themselves no longer. Wrote Pyman:

As you know, the situation here is continuously complicated by the dynamic energy of SAC. He loves to dabble in matters which are not his concern and, when called to order, justifies his interference on the ground of the political aspect. He insists upon centralising all political matters entirely at his own HQ. Partly because practically every military matter out here has a political aspect, and partly because of his tremendous charm of manner, it is extremely difficult to establish a cast-iron case where he has really been naughty . . .

It would be wrong to say that the machinery of command in Kandy is really efficient. These interferences are taking place constantly and have always been a source of worry to the C-in-C [Slim].

As I once said to you before, SAC tries more and more to run these HQs as a Combined Operations Headquarters. He seems to find it particularly tempting to deal with military matters, but that I think is largely because the RAF have now practically nothing to do, and he knows better than to upset the Royal Navy.[9]

The planning procedure "in particular has been a source of irritation to the C-in-C." The Joint Planners had a dual allegiance to SAC and the Commanders-in-Chief, but the latter were prevented from doing their own staff planning. It was "contrary to the normal method of planning", and Browning had been approached several times, but neither he nor Slim could change Mountbatten's ideas. Continued Pyman, "This system has become particularly obnoxious of late because the Joint Planning Committee have tended to deal more and more with executive plans, and less with more distant projects."[10] Slim's disen-

9. Mountbatten's substantive naval rank was Captain (Colonel equivalent); as SACSEA he was acting Vice-Admiral.
10. Papers of Maj.-Gen. Harold Pyman, 29 Oct. 1945 (Liddell Hart Centre, King's College).

chantment extended to Mountbatten's reorganization of SEAC in Singapore. So if Gracey was less than happy with Mountbatten, he was not alone.

With Gracey on his way back to Saigon, Gateforce arrived in Trang Bom at 1300 hours, and local patrols discovered no Viet Minh activity. However, Gates reported that a body of 300 Viet Minh had left Trang Bom the day before, armed with 140 rifles, thirty light machine-guns, pistols and spears. In view of this information, which turned out to be accurate, Gates encamped west of Xuan Loc as darkness approached, and at 2000 hours radioed Bien Hoa for a company to come out and establish a base in Trang Bom. Meanwhile, Sato *butai* had moved ahead to reconnoiter and attempt to make contact with the Viet Minh. At 0600 hours on 30 October, A Company left Bien Hoa for Trang Bom while a section of artillery from 23 Mountain Regiment remained on alert to move out and support Gateforce if needed. At 1330 Gates radioed Lieutenant-Colonel Pickard, commander of the 14/13 FFR, that Gateforce had been fired on by the Viet Minh at first light, and his force had attacked at 0700. The Viet Minh withdrew to the northeast, pursued by a company of Sato *butai*. There were no British casualties, and the Japanese suffered three wounded. Unconfirmed Viet Minh casualties in this initial skirmish were three wounded, and twenty-seven prisoners were released from Viet Minh captivity; these were French and mixed French-Vietnamese whom the Viet Minh were to have executed. Over sixty Viet Minh were captured, including a number of North Vietnamese. Gateforce finally entered Xuan Loc and the armored cars immediately began patrolling the town.

The initial casualty estimates radioed by Gates to Bien Hoa were drastically revised when the battle was over, for a major encounter had taken place, with the Japanese bearing the brunt of it. Somewhere between 100 (100 Brigade report) and 130 (16 Cavalry report) Viet Minh had been killed, most by Sato *butai* in two engagements and the rest by the British force in one attack and in support of Sato *butai*. The 14/13 FFR now had a man killed. Several road blocks were removed and a quantity of arms recovered as many of the Viet Minh discarded their weapons as they retreated. Unarmed Viet Minh searched the battle area at night for wounded, but were driven off by Japanese looking for arms. A Viet Minh prisoner stated that the "Xuan Loc force was the largest in FIC."

At the end of the month the Japanese were authorized to draw down their garrisons in Qui Nhon, Tuy Hoa and Thach Ban, and to bring those troops plus the European populations to Nha Trang.

Earlier, at the 29 October British-Japanese conference, Brigadier Hirst angrily castigated the Japanese over the loss from the Phu Tho rubber plantation of a large quantity of ammunition amounting to several truck-loads. Hirst charged that this "can only be due to gross neglect of duty on the part of the commanding officer and the troops responsible for its protection, if not to actual cooperation with the Annamites." He demanded a full investigation, and was dissatisfied with what he considered inadequate punishment meted out to the officers commanding the guard. The Japanese were also asked to explain why the Allies had not previously been informed of the existence of a dump of this size, to which they could only answer lamely that it was an Air Force depot and as such not under Colonel Suzuki, Chief of Ordnance at Headquarters Southern Army. However, when asked which officer was ultimately responsible to General Manaki for all ordnance in Indochina, the Japanese admitted it was Suzuki. The specter of Japanese/Viet Minh collusion was very great in this and a number of other notable instances. The Japanese made known their anxiety about their small garrison at Phan Thiet, for the Viet Minh were being driven to that area. They were informed that Gateforce would soon be patrolling the road to Phan Thiet, and that the Royal Navy would supply landing craft if reinforcements were necessary.

On the 31st an emergency message from Gateforce advised Pickard that a potentially serious situation was in the making, for part of it was still in Trang Bom and the Viet Minh were now attempting to destroy a key bridge between Trang Bom and Xuan Loc, having set fire to it. However, Gates radioed back that the bridge could be repaired with his own resources, and the relief column remained in Bien Hoa. At this time Gates, no longer in danger of being cut off from Trang Bom and Bien Hoa, launched a three-pronged attack on Viet Minh forces in a plantation area near Xuan Loc. There followed a sharp, bloody fight until the Viet Minh retreated, leaving sixty-two bodies on the field; twenty-eight of their number were captured. Thus in two days the heart had been shot out of the Viet Minh main force unit in that area, as they had suffered between 162 and 192 killed and dozens of wounded and captured. To make things worse for them, the Japanese had surprised yet another Viet Minh party, numbering about fifty, during a physical training session and shot almost the whole group; only a few escaped.

Even as Gateforce was in action, Mountbatten, perhaps fearful of adverse publicity, wrote a letter to Gracey, who was stung into making a detailed reply. Mountbatten began by asking for Gracey's advice about

Terauchi's surrender ceremony, and wanted the fact that one of the Field-Marshal's swords was to be given to the King to be kept "completely secret". The niceties over, Mountbatten (who did not take Gracey's advice about Terauchi's surrender) now criticized his conduct of operations in Vietnam. It was, he wrote, "most indiscreet" for a British commander to go on record with air-dropped pamphlets saying that " 'tanks, ships, aircraft and guns' are massed against virtually unarmed people." These sorts of pamphlets must be signed by the French, for the British Government must not be embarrassed by appearing to have its forces "threatening the Independence Movement".[11] There was a handwritten postscript: "I was most distressed to see you had been burning down houses, in congested areas too! Cannot you give such unsavoury jobs (if they really are military necessities) to the French in future?"

Gracey replied that he had been glad to hear that the arrival date of the 9th DIC had been advanced. Since the sword was the symbol of Terauchi's authority, he suggested that Mountbatten receive the Field-Marshal's surrender in Singapore so that their authority would not be undermined in Saigon. In Singapore the Japanese were disarmed, while in Vietnam they were still operationally employed. Besides, the surrender ought to take place on British, not French, soil; Saigon, unlike Singapore, was "a place of no significance to the average person". Gracey was pleased to hear that Carton de Wiart had had some success with Chiang Kai-shek on behalf of the French in Hanoi, and the greatest difficulty appeared to be between the Chinese in Hanoi and those in Chungking: "There appears to be a singular lack of unanimity on the question of who commands who and why!"[12]

Gracey then turned his attention to "the two 'operational points' on which you take me to task", the wording of one of the leaflets, and the burning down of some houses in Cholon. Despite numerous British statements to the contrary, the Viet Minh had "vociferously" expressed the view that 20 Division was serving as a cover for the returning French, and was not impartial. They would actively resist the French everywhere, and it became "evident that they were going to find it impossible" to tell the difference between the British/Indian and French forces, "both of whom have been engaged in the maintenance of law and order and essential services in next door areas." Since the breakdown of

11. Gracey Papers, Letter from Mountbatten to Gracey, 31 Oct. 1945.
12. Gracey Papers, Letter from Gracey to Mountbatten, 9 Nov. 1945.

the truce, the Viet Minh no longer tried to tell the difference, and were "actively hostile to British forces". Thus in the execution of his own military tasks, such as the clearing of the key Japanese concentration areas, Gracey was forced to take offensive action; this was also to protect his troops from "needless casualties". Furthermore, he had to "maintain a proper standard of British prestige in the eyes of the French and Chinese, two very susceptible communities, with active uncensored press." Gracey then gave a list of casualties to date (about 9 November): nineteen men of all ranks of 20 Division killed, sixty-eight wounded, and four missing believed killed. The Japanese had lost fifty-four killed and seventy-nine wounded.[13] Most of his casualties were the result of "unprovoked attacks on my troops, *not* in affrays started by them". He was responsible for the security and safety of his own forces, and despite verbal and written warnings to "disturbers and likely disturbers of the peace", the revolutionaries had threatened his forces "infinitely more than I have threatened them".

The particular passage from a pamphlet to which Mountbatten had objected had been coordinated with the French around 1 October, "when we knew that few Annamites were really active extremists." Most were sitting on the fence and did not relish the thought of prolonged guerrilla warfare, loss of jobs and homes, and further misery. Gracey denied saying that "tanks, ships, aircraft and guns were massed against virtually unarmed people." What he did say was "that the Annamite extremists and irresponsible elements who were trying to continue the useless fight against the might of tanks, etc., were misleading their people." And it was not accurate for Mountbatten to refer to the Annamites as unarmed, since "they were and are well equipped with rifles, LMGs, medium machine-guns (in small quantities), grenades and

---

13. Casualty figures were now released by Allied Headquarters, as follows (as of 29 Oct.):

|  | Killed | Wounded | Missing |
|---|---|---|---|
| British/Indian | 18 | 51 | 3 |
| French | 17 | 34 | 2 |
| Japanese | 19 | 13 | 2 |
| Dutch | 1 | 3 | — |
| American | 1 | — | — |

An estimated 391 Viet Minh had been killed by British forces ("not for publication"), and 441 arrested. There were as yet no reliable figures for Vietnamese killed by French and Japanese forces, but certainly the total number of killed was far higher, especially in view of Gateforce's actions in the Xuan Loc area shortly thereafter.

grenade dischargers.'' He had dropped the pamphlet to save bloodshed, ''and as a warning not a threat''. Gracey said that he had been given the task of preserving law and order within key areas. He had told this to the Viet Minh and they agreed that he had to do it. But they had belittled to their followers the consequences of disobeying Gracey's orders, and he had warned them against forcing him ''to take action against their own people''. He could not agree to the French signing the pamphlet because they could not back it up except with British troops, which would have put the British government in a difficult position.

Gracey wrote that he had to clear certain areas to protect his troops when they moved ''on their lawful occasions''; these were areas ''which have shown themselves continually to harbour armed extremists''. The searching seldom produced results, and ''fresh sniping, grenade-throwing and further casualties'' were the usual result. However, when houses (''or as they really are, basha huts'') were burnt, it ''inevitably produced a series of resounding detonations giving ample proof of the presence of ammunition.'' In the key areas it was not wise to let the French do this, for the inhabitants knew Gracey was responsible for public safety; ''the actual effect of obtaining French assistance would result in the complete destruction of not 20 but 2,000 houses, and probably without warning to the occupants!'' In his area of responsibility he could not honestly ''risk such a travesty of justice''. Gracey emphasized that ''French measures in such cases know no such thing as minimum force.'' Gracey concluded by apologizing for having written at such length, ''because I felt from your letter that something must have been lacking from my reports as I had obviously failed to explain the background against which I have had to issue such pamphlets and demolish houses.''

October closed with a number of sharp engagements throughout the three brigade areas. The military action now assumed a fairly constant pattern, with few all-out battles but continual small-scale patrol engagements, yet the casualty rate continued to rise. Indicative of the high level of activity was a 20 Division order to cease all practice firing in order to conserve dwindling ammunition stocks.

Paddy field and jungle bore silent witness to this opening act of the bigger drama of years to come, as small groups of men fought one another in the half-light. Except for Gateforce there were, in this the first of the post-war counter-insurgency wars, few spectacular battles. It was more a matter of men falling silently and unrecorded into the thick undergrowth or beneath the languid brown surface of the swamps and canals. November appeared to offer little prospect of any change.

# 14

# CONSOLIDATION

November saw Gracey's forces fully committed to the immediate problem of pacifying the areas in which the Japanese were to be concentrated and disarmed. As the British achieved military success against the Viet Minh, and as substantial French forces began to arrive in Indochina, the emphasis gradually shifted to the primary task of preparing the Japanese armed forces for repatriation to Japan. The arrival of Mountbatten at the end of the month, when he received Terauchi's personal surrender, emphasized this. However, several more weeks were to elapse before British (and Japanese) units ceased fighting in Vietnam.

Although the counter-insurgency role was new to some of Gracey's troops, and although his individual battalions were greatly stretched, the 20 Division units had notable success in the campaign against Viet Minh forces. The most important reason for this was that the Division was well led; there were competent, seasoned British and Indian commanders, from Gracey down through brigade, battalion and company levels. Below that, the platoons and sections were also generally well led by Indian NCOs. The Division was also highly experienced in combat, having been committed to battle against the Japanese from the Imphal-Kohima days to the end of the war. The British were helped by the mutual antagonisms in the Viet Minh organization; the Tonkinese troops who came south to stiffen the local Viet Minh cadres were then, as now, to an extent strangers. Some of Gracey's professional soldiers also had experience in the task of pacification through their service on India's North West Frontier.

There were a number of recognizable features in the general pacification strategy. Disarming and concentrating the Japanese was part of Gracey's goal. By securing the important key area, he hoped to encourage the local population to return to their customary pursuits and restore the normal tempo of life and commerce to Saigon and the surrounding countryside. Much of this strategy appears to have been conceived by Rodham, for it was his brigade which remained to clear the Viet Minh on the departure of 32 and 80 Brigades (which had earlier borne the brunt of the street fighting in Saigon before Rodham's brigade arrived in Vietnam). By skillful employment of his limited resources, Rodham's tactics combined the use of mobile columns assigned to

specific objectives, surprise sweeps, static posts, and road-clearing operations which kept open his vital lines of communication and made his
troops highly visible to the local population — Rodham put a strong
emphasis on his soldiers keeping a "high profile" in their areas. British
responsibilities were further defined by the creation of Inner and Outer
Zones, of which more will be said.

As November opened, one of Rodham's special columns (Gateforce)
was proceeding down the Phan Thiet road to Gia Ray in its task of dispersing the Viet Minh main force and driving it further away from the
key areas. Gia Ray was found to be deserted, and the entire area of
Gateforce's operations was now believed to be cleared of Viet Minh main
units — which were now retreating east before the British/Japanese
advance. Despite reports of large boulders being poised on overhanging
cliffs, Gateforce returned uneventfully to base in Bien Hoa a day later,
leaving Sato *butai* in Xuan Loc as a garrison to keep the Viet Minh as far
from the key areas as possible. Perhaps encouraged by the success of
Gateforce in smashing the strong Viet Minh concentration in the Xuan
Loc area, Rodham, from his Thu Duc headquarters, noted that 20
Division's influence was now being extended beyond the Saigon
perimeter, and that 32 Brigade sweeps had been pushing up the Saigon
River's west bank, encountering small armed bands and snipers *en route*.
The evidence now showed that the Viet Minh had withdrawn to concentration areas around Ben Cat (northwest of Thu Dau Mot). Further
evidence indicated that Viet Minh were moving down from Loc Ninh to
Ben Cat, where there was a Japanese garrison of 300 artillerymen.
Rodham thought that a British advance to Ben Cat would meet opposition and roadblocks, but after a show of force during the "first brush,
this opposition will melt away and become confined to snipers and
saboteurs. There are certainly a number of diehards in the area."

An order to form another special mobile column was addressed to
Major R. W. Clark, second-in-command of 1/1 GR, and a number of
additional units were to come under his command at 1200 hours on 5
November. His force was to be known as "Clarkol", and his general
tasks were to break up any Viet Minh forces in the Ben Cat area, establish
a base in Ben Cat and "operate strong offensive patrols" on the roads
from the village while killing or capturing all armed Viet Minh. He was
further to assist and protect the Control Commission's financial adviser
in inspecting the Japanese printing press at Laikhe and collecting the
banknotes from the press, and to report by radio on the feasibility of
removing the press to Saigon. An amendment was later issued to Clark's

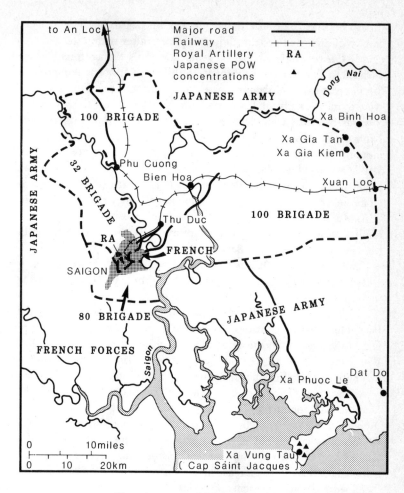

to An Loc

Major road
Railway
Royal Artillery    **RA**
Japanese POW
concentrations   ▲

**JAPANESE ARMY**

100 BRIGADE

*Dong Nai*

Xa Binh Hoa

Xa Gia Tan
Xa Gia Kiem

**JAPANESE ARMY**

*32 BRIGADE*

Phu Cuong
Bien Hoa

Xuan Loc

Thu Duc

**100 BRIGADE**

RA

**FRENCH**

SAIGON

80 BRIGADE

**JAPANESE ARMY**

**FRENCH FORCES**

*Saigon*

Xa Phuoc Le   Dat Do

0        10miles

0    10    20km

Xa Vung Tau
( Cap Saint Jacques )

Situation map, 3 November 1945.

orders, because "The operation of Clarkol is now part of a bigger operation to encircle and destroy all [armed] Annamites within the Ben Cat area." On the night of 7/8 November Massu's French force was to advance to Tay Ninh and occupy it, with French armor arriving on the 8th in order to establish a firm base there. The next day, French patrols were to move east from Tay Ninh in the hope of driving the Viet Minh towards Ben Cat, while Japanese forces were to move south from Loc Ninh and establish a block at Chon Thanh. In view of the enlarged plan, more firepower was added to Clarkol. The force's departure from Thu Dau Mot on 8 November coincided with the French drive east from Tay Ninh. It was to sweep the Ben Cat area in the north, and by 1015 was established in Ben Cat; a smaller mobile column was detached from Clarkol and drove to Long Thanh, but met no opposition. The operation resulted in several actions and the capture of 106 prisoners; Yamagishi *butai* remained to garrison Ben Cat.

Clark later wrote, "It was about this time that I was ordered out with Clarkforce to investigate the extent of Viet Minh activity towards the Cambodian border . . . My modus operandi was for the 1/1 GR Coy to ride on the armoured cars and, as soon as we hit trouble, to put in the Japs. This avoided casualties to our own men and, since the Japs supported the Viet Minh, the latter seldom continued the operation." The Viet Minh, while active, avoided contact with Clarkol, which returned to Thu Dau Mot after further wide-patrolling. Wrote Clark, "I remain convinced that Takahashi's Bn [Major Takahashi commanded the Japanese battalion in Thu Dau Mot] had throughout been giving active support to the Viet Minh but we couldn't prove anything and all orders to him were carried out with scrupulous correctness. He even shot a senior NCO through the thigh with his pistol, in my presence, because I complained that some task had not been completed."[1] Clark further described the initial French operations in the 1/1 GR area in a way commonly used by British officers: "The first French operation forces now began to arrive but we saw little of them as they only passed through our area to operate further North and towards the Cambodian border. They really were a band of pretty unruly cut-throats and it was subsequently no surprise to me that they were not accepted in the country by the Vietnamese." Describing French operational tactics Clark wrote: "Their method of 'pacifying' a village, without any provocation or indication that the place might be hostile, was to drive

---

1. Lt.-Col. R. W. Clark, letter to author, 1977.

through in American 3-ton trucks, .300 machine-guns on the cab, all
guns firing on alternate sides of the street at first floor level 'in case
someone might be about to snipe at the column.' They seldom hit
anyone but if that is the way friends arrive it is little wonder the
Vietnamese threw them out.''

Despite British suspicions concerning Japanese/Viet Minh collusion,
Yamagishi *butai* clashed with Viet Minh troops in the Ben Cat area on
the 9th, and suffered five wounded. The next day Clarkol fought a six-
hour battle with Viet Minh units armed with rifles and light machine-
guns. Five Viet Minh were known to have been killed, six wounded and
twenty captured. Two days later Clarkol split into two smaller columns;
one swept northwest from Ben Cat while the second reconnoitered the
road east to beyond Thanh Tay. The two mobile columns returned to
Ben Cat after a few hours, and then Clarkol returned to base at Thu Dau
Mot. In Thu Dau Mot itself, suspicions of Japanese/Viet Minh collusion
were strengthened when Viet Minh arsonists walked past Japanese
guarding 1,000 tons of rubber and set fire to the dump; incendiarism had
become part of Viet Minh strategy, and Gracey's troops were hard-
pressed to cope with fires throughout the key areas.

Although the emphasis was on military operations against the Viet
Minh, the first modest step towards disarming the Japanese was taken on
2 November, when the first of the many localized surrender ceremonies
took place. On this occasion the Saigon/Cholon Kempei Tei section
handed over their sidearms and swords, saluted the Union Jack and were
locked up. Following this surrender General Numata, in a paper titled
''Reorganisation of Japanese Forces in FIC'', was ordered to provide an
Army headquarters in Saigon which would command all Japanese Army
and Air Force units in South Indochina. The Army commander was to
be Lieutenant-General Nishioyada, because Field-Marshal Terauchi was
declining steadily and now spending much time convalescing at Cap St
Jacques. The Japanese 2nd Division, on being replaced in Saigon by the
5th Air Division, was to be relieved of all wider commitments and
moved to Lai Thieu to come under Brigadier Rodham to use as he
deemed necessary. At the daily staff meeting the Japanese were now
informed that they could reduce the size of their operational forces under
Brigadier Taunton of 80 Brigade. At the moment, 2,000 troops from the
Japanese 2nd Division were operating under Taunton; these were to be
reduced to 1,000 men.

The next day, 100 Brigade ''Jap Surrender Instr No. 1'' was issued to
provide guidance on forthcoming Japanese surrenders. Rodham wrote

that his brigade's operations were divided roughly into three phases. Phase I involved thoroughly combing the area "for elimination of hostiles and collection of rebel arms"; the reconnoitering and recording of Japanese arms, ammunition, explosives and other supplies before their evacuation to Saigon; and the clearance of roadblocks to facilitate these movements. In Phase II these supplies were to be collected or destroyed, and in Phase III the Japanese were to be disarmed. However, Rodham recognized that "We have not yet completed Phase I and this may yet take us a considerable time. Owing to extreme shortage of tpt the Div. Comd [Gracey] wishes us to start on Phase II in respect of dumps near firm bases." These instructions, however, referred to arms in dumps, as the Japanese were not yet to be fully disarmed. As for the Japanese themselves, the decision had now been made that on being disarmed they would be divided, except for war criminals, into two categories. In Category A would be "Those individuals and units which have scrupulously carried out orders and co-operated properly . . ."; in Category B were "The rest — non co-operators, the half-hearted undisciplined units, officers who have not carried out their orders to the best of their ability . . ." Category B individuals were to be returned last to Japan, and meanwhile given "all the menial and disagreeable jobs". This information, however, would not be passed to the Japanese until they were disarmed.

Gracey had been forced to turn his attention to the propaganda war being waged against him, which involved him in the loss of precious time. In a telegram to the Department of Public Relations in India he focused on the "sudden wholesale allegations by elements of Chinese Community and Chinese Press in Cholon district of Saigon against conduct and discipline of British Indian troops recently used as an excuse to strike, and non-cooperation movement by Chinese." Gracey had little doubt that this was because many of the opportunistic Chinese leaders, who had formerly collaborated with the Japanese, were now working with the Viet Minh to hinder the Allies. In fact, the President of the Chinese Chamber of Commerce had been arrested, and in his pocket was a letter stating his agreement to cooperate with the Viet Minh. Wrote Gracey, "His arrest and reason for it have had [a] salutary effect amongst those Chinese elements terrorizing their compatriots to acts against us."

Gracey was also worried by the possibility that Leclerc would gain control of British forces. With talk of his division leaving Vietnam, Gracey wrote to General Slim, ALFSEA Commander. He commented that the Commander-in-Chief had no doubt seen the recent critical letter from the Supreme Allied Commander (a copy of which he now attached), and wrote that when command of French forces passed to Leclerc he hoped he would not be placed under the French "for any purpose, even with the limitations placed on my activities by HMG". It was hard enough to resist some of Leclerc's "more extravagant demands" as it was. Furthermore, the Japanese would accept direction from the British but would do nothing for the French. Leclerc's troops had shown "great skill and speed (and . . . much unnecessary brutality)" in pacifying the area and would soon permit the British to work on concentrating the Japanese. Gracey wrote, "The French troops are leaving a pretty good trail of destruction behind them," which if continued would antagonize the Vietnamese and "result in guerrilla warfare, increased sabotage and arson as soon as we leave the country." It was Gracey's opinion that if Leclerc decided to rearm the Japanese, they would desert in large numbers with their arms. Finally, as 32 Brigade had experienced earlier, the Japanese had requested that all orders be passed to their forces by a British officer, and not by any Frenchman; they wrote that "we find it increasingly difficult to carry out the orders resulting from their schemeless plans." Gracey added that "The last is, alas, so true about the implementation of their [French] plans."[2]

While Gracey was exercised with the task of speeding up the concentration of the Japanese, and the likelihood that problems with the French would grow in relation to the size of their forces, the major activity during this period was the continuing difficult, grinding pursuit of the Viet Minh, both in the urban centers and in the countryside. Conditions had not yet reached the point where the Japanese could be completely disarmed and concentrated. With garrisons positioned in outlying districts, the security of vehicle convoys now became a matter of urgency. Likely ambush sites (and there was no shortage of these) were reconnoitered and the undergrowth was cut back as far as possible from the roads.

2. Gracey Papers, Letter from Gracey to Slim, 5 Nov. 1945. This tailpiece may have reflected a meeting between Brigadier Woodford and the senior Japanese officer in his area. The Japanese had requested the meeting shortly after a sizeable number of French troops had arrived in Saigon. When he entered Woodford's office, the Japanese officer said that he was speaking for all Japanese when he asked that they be excluded from having to operate with the French; in their eyes the French were a defeated nation and they did not wish to be humiliated by having to work with or for them. Woodford clearly recalled the word "schemeless". In other words, the French were indecisive and often changed their plans. (Brig. E.C.J. Woodford, personal interview, 23 Sept. 1973.)

Lieutenant-Colonel Clark, 1/1 GR, wrote that the Viet Minh were beginning to harass the twice-weekly ration convoy from Bien Hoa, despite the armored car escort and periodic Japanese guardposts. The Japanese were then "ordered to clear the jungle for 50 yards either side of the whole route. This they did, without batting an eyelid, within 3 days!" The Viet Minh then began to lob grenades by using bamboo ballistas, and the Japanese were told to cut the brush back several more yards along the route. The Japanese now complained, saying that the British had already removed all their tools. Wrote Clark, "My only reaction was to ask my Adjutant, Capt. Bob McMaster, how many officers' swords were in the surrendered weapons dump, intending to smash off the tips and reissue them as machetes. The Japanese reaction was immediate and before McMaster could answer, the interpreter agreed that they could do the job. They did so within a week." According to Clark, this was the only protest made by the Japanese at orders given at the daily Anglo-Japanese conferences.[3]

Rodham, noting that his area had been enlarged, now directed that a network of dozens of checkposts be established throughout 100 Brigade's area. The sentries at these posts were to search all vehicles other than British or Japanese ones for arms. The searching was to be done "politely and cheerfully and people themselves will *not* be searched."[4] He reiterated his main tasks of establishing "complete law and order", clearing lines of communication and ridding the area of hostile elements so that the Japanese could be disarmed and their arms dumps emptied. The Japanese were generally responsible for security in the Outer Zone, as British troops were restricted to operations in the Inner Zone unless used for specific tasks (such as the Gateforce and Clarkol operations). But even the Japanese were not present in sufficient strength to guard all vital points in the Outer Zone.

British/Indian troops increased the pressure on the Viet Minh during these first few days of November, and Brigadier Woodford, of 32 Brigade, now executed plans for a massive sweep in his sector, plans which involved all his battalions. This was a big operation which concentrated on an area of about one square mile, bordered by the road running northwest from the golf course, west of Go Vap and northeast of Tan Son Nhut. Two companies of 2/8 Punjab were detailed to search the area, while 4/2 GR and 3/8 GR blocked all exits from the area. All males

3. Lt.-Col. Clark, letter, 1977.
4. PRO, WO 172/7135, 100 Ind Inf Bde Op Instr no. 5, 5 Nov. 1945.

between eighteen and forty were detained, so that 2,000 men were held for questioning by the *Sûreté*; another 120 were arrested by Gurkhas at the exit blocks. French forces had now extended southwards into the Mekong delta, occupying Mytho, Cantho, Go Cong, Vinh Long and other towns.[5] They felt well enough established to assume complete control, and the Japanese forces were being withdrawn accordingly. However, it was still necessary to attach a British liaison officer to ensure Franco-Japanese cooperation.

Gracey now had a fairly firm plan for the proposed drawdown of Japanese forces and their subsequent concentration. He was hoping that by 20 November the Japanese, "less a certain number employed in operational roles and the staffs and guards of some Japanese Stores and Depots", would have moved to their concentration areas. He had heard news of the proposed departure of his Division from Indochina, and he forwarded to Leclerc a summary of the instructions received from ALFSEA concerning the withdrawal of 20 Division, asking for an estimate of when the French would be prepared to accept responsibility for the Japanese forces. He expressed the hope that the majority of the Japanese in the concentration areas could be disarmed by late November. Leclerc agreed that "It is of the greatest interest in view of the return to law and order that the Japanese should be embarked as a matter of first priority as was promised by SACSEA telegram 452 of 17 Aug. addressed SCAP." He further stated that in his view it was "indispensable" that after they had been disarmed, the Japanese should be transferred from their present concentration area in 100 Brigade's territory to some place where it would be "much more difficult to remain in contact with the civil population and desert, e.g. Baria/Cap St Jacques." Leclerc wrote that he accepted that the British were responsible for disarming the Japanese. "We have always respected this principle as even during the operations it is a British LO [liaison officer] who eventually transmits orders to the Japanese." For Leclerc and Massu, the sting from this procedure was difficult to conceal. Leclerc confirmed that it would not be possible for him to take over the task of disarming the Japanese until the 9th DIC and Corps support troops arrived, and until his own transportation situation improved.

5. A 3/1 Gurkha officer interviewed by the author stated that while he was on a mission to Mytho, local agents had passed him information of clandestine midnight flights in and out of the Mytho-Cantho area by US C-47 aircraft from Tonkin. These aircraft were said to be ferrying arms to the Viet Minh in the area, and the OSS were suspected of directing the operations.

Gracey agreed in part with Leclerc's arguments but disagreed over the requirement for the corps troops to be in place before 20 Division could depart; at the present shipping rate this could severely delay the departure of 20 Division. Although Leclerc wanted the British to disarm the Japanese garrisons in South Annam, Nha Trang, Delat, Phan Rang and Phan Thiet, Gracey thought that the French could do this by January as the total Japanese strength in those garrisons was only 3,500. Gracey recommended that the vehicles and troopships should arrive together, because the "time gap between the arrival of personnel and vehicle ships is most paralysing to the speed of French operations." He also recommended that the repatriation of the Japanese should begin immediately.

The SEAC Joint Planning Staff now laid down four conditions for the withdrawal of British forces. First, Japanese troops must be disarmed and isolated from any possible Viet Minh contact, and French troops must be in sufficient strength to ensure the isolation of the Japanese and the containment of the Viet Minh. Secondly, a civil administration should have been reestablished. Thirdly, the French and Chinese in the north should be negotiating. And finally, Terauchi's headquarters must have been moved to Malaya. The Planning Staff also stated that "in no circumstances should British forces be placed under French command or operational control in Indo-China." British forces remaining in Indochina after the resumption of French control should come directly under ALFSEA. The Planning Staff concluded that their four conditions would be met by early January 1946, so that the British troops could begin their withdrawal by mid-December. This proved an accurate assessment, but although the Planning Staff thought that "We should, therefore, be clear of Indo-China by Mid-January 1946", two battalions stayed on for a couple of extra months.

The French were gradually becoming more prominent in South Indochina, and on the 10th Brigadier Woodford and the newly-arrived French commander in Gia Dinh held a conference at which they agreed on the relief of certain 9/14 Punjab posts in Gia Dinh. At noon Woodford received a message from Division Headquarters, officially informing him that he and his brigade would be going to British North Borneo in mid-December. In the west, two French supply columns *en route* from Saigon to Massu's force in Tay Ninh were heavily attacked en route, and near Xuan Loc twenty Moi tribesmen led by a Viet Minh guerrilla struck a Japanese post, killing one Japanese soldier and wounding another. (The significance of this lowland Viet Minh's influence on the Moi was not lost on Allied Intelligence.) Roadblocks and trenches were still making travel on the roads from Saigon difficult. The increasing level of violence was reflected in the higher casualties now being suffered by Gracey's forces. "D" Company, 14/13 FFR, conducted what seemed a routine sweep of the village of Tan Tu (about 4 miles north of Bien Hoa). When the soldiers mounted their vehicles to leave the village, three grenades were suddenly hurled into the bed of one of the trucks. The explosions wounded twelve of the 14/13 FFR troops, three of whom died the following day. The rest of the column immediately jumped out of the trucks and again swept the village, killing six Viet Minh, capturing one and arresting four suspects. But casualties were not confined to the soldiers of the opposing sides, for on the morning of the 13th a patrol came across a shocking sight in Cholon — a Vietnamese woman tied to a tree and stabbed to death. She was the wife of an Indian merchant, and a note in Vietnamese, attached to her body, warned all traitors that they could expect a similar fate from the Viet Minh.

An example of the types and amounts of Japanese arms and ammunition collected from their scattered depots was the single convoy load arriving in Saigon at this time for storage and disposal — this included 18,000 grenades, 1,158 rifles and forty light machine-guns. At the same time the 4/2 GR War Diary reported collecting 50,000 mortar rounds, 111 rocket launchers, and other arms and ordnance too numerous to list (including rifles, machine-guns etc.) The problem was that many of these dumps were not discovered by, or were inaccessible to, Gracey's forces, and much undoubtedly ended up in Viet Minh hands to be shipped north.

The recent history of political and military activities was summed up in "ALFFIC Intelligence Summary no. 2". Part 1 dealt with events between 22 October and 14 November. It was stated by Gracey's Intelligence officers that the Viet Minh siege of Saigon was largely broken by 100 Brigade's operations to the north and by the French drive to Mytho and Can Tho. The Viet Minh main force units had been driven eastwards after the Xuan Loc battle and were now concentrated around Phan Thiet. However, in all previously occupied areas groups of Viet Minh were active, and their operations ranged from the throwing of grenades at passing vehicles to "well organized attacks on isolated posts and picquets". Gracey's battalions had kept up the offensive and carried out numerous sweeps in their areas, "but the ability of these guerrillas to hide themselves amongst the large native population in these areas renders the task of combing them out extremely difficult." This was to become a painfully familiar problem to French and American troops in the coming years.

In and around Nha Trang the Japanese had fought several engagements with the Viet Minh, who were finally cleared from the area around the town when French Marines arrived on the cruiser *Triomphant*. However, the report continued, "The whole east coast is a Viet Minh playground in which Viet Minh bands have complete freedom of movement including the use of the railway which the small isolated Japanese garrisons were powerless to prevent." The most serious opposition was expected when operations were to begin in the Dalat and Ban Me Thuot areas. An ominous statement reported that it was now "worth noting that the hill tribes of this area, the Mois, have become reconciled to Annamite control." The Vietnamese, plainsmen, previously had little contact with the Moi, who were often under the influence of individual Frenchmen. But the Viet Minh had gained "considerable influence over the Mois, in some case organizing parties of them within Viet Minh bands. This new familiarity permits the Annamites to take refuge in jungle areas, where pursuit will be difficult." While the Tay Ninh/Loc Ninh/Saigon triangle had largely been cleared by joint British-French action (Massu's drive on Tay Ninh and Clarkol's to Ben Cat and north), the Viet Minh continued to pose a problem in the Mytho-Cantho and Plaine des Joncs areas. Although Viet Minh main force units had retreated east and north, guerrilla activity was expected to continue in the British key areas. The interrogation of Nguyen Van Hai, former secretary to the senior Viet Minh commander in Cochinchina, revealed that the Viet Minh main force (totalling 5,000) had retreated to Phan Thiet the day before the arrival of Gateforce in Xuan Loc. What the British and Japanese fought were Viet Minh suicide units totalling 444 men. The main force had retreated because the Xuan Loc area was considered unsuitable for defense. In the suicide units, 100 had been killed and many wounded, although in the initial skirmishing the Japanese troops had intentionally fired high and inflicted no casualties.

Within the last week or so the emphasis in the British area of South Vietnam had, it seemed, swung suddenly from fighting the Viet Minh to concentrating and disarming the Japanese. On 16 November "100 Inf Bde Jap Surrender Instruction no. 3" was issued, which began by saying that orders had been received that the concentration and disarming of the Japanese must be speeded up. This was Phase III of the British operations in the area, and Rodham emphasized, "*We have got to get a move on.*"

Phase I had been "the elimination of hostiles from the area". But from now on the Japanese would not be used for offensive operations except for Yamagishi and Sato *butais* in Ben Cat and Xuan Loc respectively, which would remain armed for the time being. Phase II was the collection of all Japanese arms, ammunition and stores. This was now almost complete.

It was at French insistence that Gracey made arrangements for the Japanese to surrender all currency negotiable in South Indochina, beginning Sunday, 25 November, and continuing as fresh drafts of Japanese troops moved into the concentration areas. This matter of currency, to be discussed later, was potentially a problem of enormous importance, the full magnitude of which had only now become apparent to the Allies (especially the French). Hundreds of millions of piasters appeared to be held by the Japanese, and the French feared the disaster of inflation and the danger that this large amount of money might fall into Viet Minh hands.

Gracey also laid down some guidelines for the formal surrender ceremonies, which were to be kept as simple as possible while still bringing home to the Japanese the fact that they had lost the war. Downright humiliation of the Japanese was to be avoided, and "The essential point is that every man realises that he personally surrenders and pays an act of respect to the nation to which he surrenders, symbolised by the Union Jack." Before the surrender parade the Japanese unit was to hand in all arms except sidearms. The parade itself was to be conducted by an Indian VCO (Viceroy's Commissioned Officer). The Japanese units surrendered in dozens of scattered ceremonies.

The Chinese in the north appeared to be less than fully exercised with the task of concentrating and disarming the Japanese. The French reported that thirteen Chinese divisions were said to be in Tonkin, of which five were in transit to Formosa and Manchuria. At least 20,000 of these Chinese soldiers had left the army by permission of their commanders in order to settle as civilians in Tonkin. Except for the Red River delta, no attempt had been made to disarm the Japanese, of whom increasing numbers were deserting to the Viet Minh.

In Kandy, Mountbatten suggested to Browning that Terauchi should be moved to Singapore the day after the handover of responsibility for South Indochina to the French. Mountbatten was perturbed at reports that Terauchi had hoarded a two-year supply of stores and some gold bullion; he had thought that Terauchi was eating normal army rations. Although the Field-Marshal was no longer in effective control of

Japanese forces, he was, as Mountbatten acknowledged, the chief cover for the British presence in Vietnam and thus could not be moved before the British departure.[6] Mountbatten had also decided to spare him a trial for war crimes, saying, "I doubt the wisdom of trying a cripple of 67 unless it is known that he gave orders which render him guilty." Because of Terauchi's condition it was decided that he should have a deputy Supreme Commander, and General Itagaki was so designated, despite his "militaristic outlook".

On the 19th a special meeting was held between the British and Japanese senior staffs in Saigon. The British participants were Brigadiers Hirst and Maunsell and Air Commodore Cheshire; Japanese members present were Lieutenant-General Numata, Commander Kusumi and Lieutenant-Colonel Tomura (around whom, as Maunsell had earlier said, "everything revolved"). The Japanese were at the meeting to answer the charge of fomenting unrest in Java, where the fighting between British and Indonesian nationalist forces was particularly savage. Of the local situation, Numata said that he was disturbed at the idea that the Japanese were to be concentrated at Cap St Jacques (which British reconnaissance had shown to be the best place to concentrate them and sever their links with the Viet Minh). Numata protested, "It is a surprising fact that some of your forces are still harbouring the idea that the Japanese forces are assisting or cooperating with the Annamites, and I regret very much indeed that the present order to concentrate the Japanese forces in Cap St Jacques would seem to have been issued on this assumption. I certainly hope that you will review our hearty cooperation with the Allied forces since their arrival here and wipe out such an idea entirely." Numata then pointed out some of the problems associated with collecting all the Japanese at Cap St Jacques — the shortage of water, endemic malaria, shortage of building materials and food, and lack of transport. These were causing concern to the Japanese, for the area was damp and swampy. If it was indeed necessary for this to be the gathering point, Numata requested that the number be limited to 20,000. These would live in town, but if new barracks could be built the number could be raised to 40,000. The greatest problem was water. The present supply system could provide a maximum capacity of 1,000 tons per day, but large-scale repairs to the system were necessary to achieve this capacity.

6. Since Terauchi was the chief cover, he "should not blow the gaff by leaving long before we do" (SAC's personal minute, 16 November 1945).

Hirst replied firmly that the British knew all about this and the area would not have been selected had it not been capable of taking all the Japanese. Maunsell then made his own comment on the "hearty cooperation" of the Japanese, which, he said, was not substantiated by events at the weekend when British casualties had been inflicted by Japanese deserters working with the Annamites. They had been clearly recognizable by their uniforms and their superior military training and marksmanship. Furthermore, recent interrogation of Kempei Tei personnel had generated grave doubts of Japanese assertions that no officers had deserted from Headquarters Japanese Southern Regions; a list of such officers was in fact being drawn up. Despite this, however, good and efficient work by Japanese officers and men would be recorded. Maunsell closed by saying that he would not allow Numata to continue this statement which was a waste of time and undesirable — Brigadier Hirst was in charge of arrangements and needed no advice from Numata, and Japanese headquarters would be told in the future not to reproduce such statements.

In Kandy, the SEAC staff thought that it was now time to bring Headquarters Japanese Southern Regions to an end; in their view, the work required of it in fulfillment of the surrender terms had been completed. Furthermore, Terauchi was no longer in effective control, power having been almost completely decentralized to subordinate commanders. Breaking up the Japanese headquarters and the "Japanese war machine in South East Asia" would "bring home to the rank and file full realisation of their defeat". This assertion by the SEAC staff had a somewhat hollow ring, for they had been unable to do this until the survival of Gracey's forces had been assured — with Japanese help.

Now that their freedom to operate as formed units of the Imperial forces was drawing to a close, the Japanese were proving more effective, possibly because they wished to win the respect of the British victors before finally departing from Vietnam. (If this was indeed part of their motivation during the final weeks, then they achieved their objective. Or perhaps it was that they knew that the seeds they had planted in Vietnam, as elsewhere, were already germinating and could no longer be prevented from reaching full growth.) Thus, at Ben Cat, Yamagishi *butai* began aggressive sweeping operations and dislodged the Viet Minh from the area, killing and capturing dozens. They now reported Ben Cat cleared of Viet Minh to a radius of 5 km. Japanese patrols in Budop brought in thirty-three Viet Minh suspects and a number of weapons. There were, as in all armies, some problems with second echelon (non-frontline) troops: two patrols from a Japanese motor company claimed to have been "captured" by the Viet Minh 4 miles east of Saigon. The Japanese officer and eighteen men were released after handing over their weapons (a sword and eighteen rifles). This report was received with great skepticism at Control Commission headquarters. On the other hand, as these troops (described as "third-rate" by the Japanese Command) were cooperating with the Viet Minh, an infantry patrol lost an officer killed and five men wounded in a fight with the Viet Minh about 5 miles east of Gia Dinh.

Brigadier Rodham now ordered that the Japanese disarmament be accelerated, with one vital exception. Commanders responsible for the "All Red Route" (100 Brigade's lines of communication) were to maintain their Japanese guards for the time being. This route encompassed the road from Saigon to Thu Duc, and the main routes connecting the key areas with Lai Thieu, Thu Dau Mot, Ben Cat, Bien Hoa and Xuan Loc. All Japanese guards on other roads were to be dispensed with immediately, and the risk of having bridges blown would have to be accepted. Since some of these roads served Japanese supply dumps, it seems that they were being abandoned in order to concentrate the Japanese as quickly as possible. Ten per cent of the Japanese were to retain their arms for self-defense, for "In all fairness, we cannot allow these tps to march long distances completely unarmed at the mercy of any Annamite 'grenade-thrower'." Even as plans were being made to disarm the Japanese, their casualty rate was slowly rising. Japanese patrols clashed with the Viet Minh on three occasions in the always disputed area about 6 miles east of Saigon across the river, and lost one officer and three men killed and seven wounded. Another Japanese guard on a bridge was killed and two others wounded, and a Japanese patrol was said to have surrendered when cut off by a downed bridge east of the Saigon River.

The Joint Planning Staff recognized that SEAC would have to maintain the French forces (which totalled 22,000 by 10 December 1945) for some time to come. The Staff now suggested that Mountbatten should consider relinquishing responsibility for South Indochina on the departure of the last British troops, for "in the event of a deterioration in the political situation, resulting in widespread disorder and bloodshed, world opinion would attribute the blame to SEAC and British/Indian forces might again have to be employed to restore the situation." On the other hand, other areas in SEAC's sphere of responsibility needed Indochina's rice, and since SEAC had to maintain the French for the foreseeable future, it might be desirable to keep some measure of control over them. Also, the Japanese, though disarmed, might yet cause the French some trouble. Finally, ''The indefinite retention of even a reserve of operational control in FIC would materially assist the future problem of theatre defence strategy in the Far East.'' It was suggested that after consultation with the French, the question of the degree of control to be exercised in Indochina by Mountbatten should be referred to the British Chiefs of Staff.

Browning now informed Gracey that he could tell the Japanese that they were to be given first priority for repatriation from Southeast Asia to Japan. In SEAC's eyes this would be likely to cut down the number of Japanese desertions to the Viet Minh; Terauchi was to broadcast this to the Japanese in Vietnam (but not to Japanese in other areas). As for the future of the Control Commission, the SEAC staff had Gracey's letter on the subject under consideration. Gracey's proposals were that the Commission as now organized could be disbanded when Terauchi had been transferred to Singapore. There would be no need for a special agency to control Terauchi's headquarters in Singapore, but since reference was still to be made to Headquarters Southern Regions, some portion of the Commission should remain in Saigon.

The continuing fighting and unrest made it impractical for Gracey to concentrate the Japanese as quickly as he wished, for his battalions were still preoccupied with the Viet Minh. South of Saigon, villagers reported the presence of 300 armed Viet Minh and five Japanese deserters in a village about 10 miles south of Cholon. This force was engaged by artillery, after which they had reportedly split, one group heading for another village about 5 miles southwest of Long Kien, which turned out to be the site of a stiff fight between 3/1 Gurkhas and strong, dug-in Viet Minh troops. The Long Kien operation had been mounted because of intelligence that the Viet Minh were holding a number of French hostages in that village. Thus on 18 November a force of two platoons under Major E. W. MacDonald left the 3/1 GR base at Khanh Hoi for Long Kien. MacDonald was supported by a waterborne party of forty Gurkhas who approached Long Kien from the southeast. MacDonald's force had gone only a few hundred yards when they were engaged by a party of about thirty Viet Minh armed with rifles, and a thirty-minute firefight followed before the Vietnamese were dispersed. Only a mile further on, the party encountered another Viet Minh position defending a bridge over a river. The bridge was in a village, the north of which was ringed with well-sited Japanese-style bunkers occupied by about fifty

Viet Minh armed with machine-guns and rifles. This proved a formidable task for two Gurkha platoons, and Long Kien was not taken until
four days later. One of MacDonald's platoons attacked the defenses "in a
good old-fashioned charge" and broke through, dispersing the
defenders. That particular village, on the elbow bend of the Khanh
Hoi/Long Kien road, was cleared, but a destroyed bridge and more
entrenched Viet Minh along the road forced the platoon to turn back.
The whole force retired northwards to the south bank of the Canal de
Derivation (the battalion's south perimeter), under fire all the way back
from light machine-guns and rifles. Local reports stated that a force of
200 Viet Minh and twenty Japanese were in that area, and the day's
action resulted in the death of between twenty and thirty Viet Minh and
the capture of four. One Gurkha was wounded, and Lieutenant-Colonel
Purcell, the battalion commander, had to bring out reinforcements with
mortars to see the force safely back to battalion lines.

While MacDonald had slow going along the road, the waterborne
party under Major E. Gopsill travelled a circuitous route down a number
of connecting streams and canals, swinging an arc to the east and south
and approaching Long Kien from the east-southeast. As they approached
Long Kien, heavy firing from scattered Viet Minh positions forced the
landing craft to a halt; then followed a short withdrawal, when the party
discovered to their horror that the tide had come in and the landing craft
could not pass under the nearest bridges to enable them to withdraw to
safety. The two platoons of Gurkhas and Japanese sailors were now sta-
tionary targets for the Viet Minh, who soon observed their predicament.
Whether by design or by accident, the Japanese Navy had neglected to
tell the British about the tides.

Tactical reconnaissance flights had earlier reported downed bridges
and defended positions along the Long Kien road, and Gopsill himself
had reconnoitered the approach to Long Kien, so the fierce opposition
should have come as no surprise; thus the wisdom of assigning a total
force of eighty Gurkhas in two groups to such a heavily defended area
appears questionable.[7] During the withdrawal the Viet Minh attacked

7. Lt.-Col. Gopsill, talking of the Long Kien operation in a personal interview with
   the author on 12 December 1977, recalled that the Viet Minh fire was so intense that
   he thought that possibly 1,000 Viet Minh had opposed his two platoons. He contacted Lt.-Col. Purcell, the 3/1 Commander, by radio and said, "It's very difficult.
   I can push on if you like, but I think we'll be cut off." Purcell radioed back orders
   for Gopsillforce to hold in place and withdraw as soon as possible. Said Gopsill:
      I couldn't come out because the river had risen and I couldn't get under the

the group with machine-guns, grenades and an anti-tank gun. The retreat was in the nature of a blitz as "Gopsillforce" ran the gauntlet back to Saigon, firing its way through Viet Minh positions on both banks. By now both craft had been hit numerous times, and the anti-tank gun had blasted holes in both boats near the water line. Miraculously, no Gurkhas were killed in the operation, although two were wounded, along with a Japanese sailor. The boats had been so heavily shot up that Gopsill and his Gurkhas had to plug the holes with their clothes to keep them afloat long enough to reach safety. As Gopsill said of the anti-tank gunfire: "They had [the gun] firing just below the waterline at us; we could see and hear it hitting. God knows what would have happened had they aimed above the waterline because we were crowded on the boats. As we got out of the boats one sank, and the other sank during the night."

The first phase of the Long Kien operation ended with the 3/1 Gurkhas being heavily engaged but unable to reach their objective. The next attempt was to be made on 22 November. As it was, thirty to forty-five Viet Minh had been killed and a number of others wounded and put out of action at a cost of three wounded Gurkhas, one wounded Japanese and a lot of sweat and excitement. Two Japanese had been seen with the Viet Minh, who appeared to be exceptionally well trained and aggressive here, and it was thought that the Japanese were responsible for the more accurate sniping aimed especially at the British officers. The 20th Division History reported that the Vietnamese defenders at Long Kien were members of the Binh Xuyen gang, reinforced by some Japanese deserters.

On the 22nd the Gurkhas made a second attempt to oust the strong Viet Minh force from the area of Long Kien and to seize the village and rescue French hostages, if any were still left there. This time the British collected a large enough force to do the job. Two full companies, rather

---

bridges. We were stuck there. I said this to the men and they said, 'Never mind, Sahib, we'll be OK.' We were there for six hours. I got on the road bridge and dropped a plumb line to the approximate height of the boat, and reckoned when it swung we could get out. Eventually it swung free and we came out.

I've never forgotten it. I said to my senior Gurkha officer, 'Load your chaps, I'll wait here,' and he said, 'Oh, no, Sahib, you get out and *you* can lie in midstream and give me covering fire.' He was a wily old bugger — we were both laughing, and he got the MC [Military Cross] for that. Well, I got to midstream and we commenced fire while he got into the boat and we went downstream together.

than the two platoons used earlier, were tasked to lead the operation, and these were supported by a troop of guns from the 114th Field Regiment, Royal Artillery. The two companies (A and C) were relieved of their commitments in Khanh Hoi on the evening of the 21st by companies from the 14/17 Dogra and 9/12 FFR. Gopsill's company led the operation. The first objective was an old French fort about a mile south of the Canal de Derivation; the fort was to be seized at 0500 hours. On the way, not long after leaving the Khanh Hoi base area, Gopsill's company was attacked by a Viet Minh ambush party armed with grenades. Two of the grenade-throwers were captured and the Gurkhas continued their advance along the Long Kien road. Stiffer opposition was met soon after this first engagement, this time from dug-in Viet Minh defenders on the banks of a stream. The defenders were driven off and the gunners laid a few rounds into the midst of a group of about thirty Viet Minh retreating through the paddy fields. The next objective was the fort and the village of Ben Ho, which proved to be an important local Viet Minh headquarters and refuge for Japanese deserters. The assault on the "Beau Geste" fort and village was preceded by a short artillery bombardment, during which a Japanese deserter was killed. Another Japanese deserter was killed by a burst of Sten fire when the two sides closed. The clearing of the fort involved one of the few true *kukri* charges (if not the only one) of the campaign. Gopsill, who led the assault, said that the Viet Minh defenders in the fort opened fire as a Gurkha company approached. "We used rocket launchers to blow the doors down, and before I could say 'knife' the Gurkhas were across and in with the kukris and butchered everyone in it."[8] The immediate area was cleared and local patrols carried out, after which the rest of the force (including Major Mike Kelleher's A Company) passed through on the way to Long Kien. A large quantity of arms and a variety of ammunition, plus Japanese and Viet Minh documents, were captured by Gopsill's force.

It was now just past noon, and the heat was "unbelievable". Kelleher's force reached Long Kien about two hours later, but this time there was little opposition and the only Viet Minh visible were three wounded who were captured in the local hospital. However, driving out the Viet Minh was only half the objective; the French hostages were searched for after Long Kien was occupied, but to no avail. Information from local sources indicated that two of the French civilians had been executed the previous night, but the three remaining hostages had

8. Lt.-Col. E. Gopsill, personal interview, 12 Dec. 1977.

escaped. Since it seemed that the Viet Minh now held no French hostages, and that to leave the company overnight in Long Kien would serve no useful purpose, especially with strong Viet Minh forces known to be in the vicinity, withdrawal was decided upon. It was accomplished in "good NWFP [North West Frontier Province] style", with rearguards covering the exit by the main force. Two rearguard actions were fought as the company, returning to base, was engaged by fire from light machine-guns and rifles. Quick use of artillery and mortars silenced the Viet Minh pursuers. The 3/1 GR force finally returned to Khanh Hoi at about 1930 hours. No hostages were found, but some fifty Viet Minh had been killed and their forces dispersed and pushed out of the immediate area. It was estimated that about thirty Japanese were operating with the Viet Minh in the course of the operation and, as the Gurkhas later wrote, "the accurate sniping and encircling tactics indicated that they were well to the fore."[9] Leclerc was well satisfied with this operation, which enabled the French to occupy the area not long afterwards.

Mountbatten asked Gracey for his views on the SEAC staff's plans for closing down Japanese Southern Army headquarters. It was now proposed that Terauchi should move to Singapore (travelling in a Japanese ship so as not to be at the expense of British movements) as soon as possible after 1 December, the actual date to be fixed in conjunction with Gracey's handover of command to the French. Among other groups, an Intelligence (Reconnaissance) Checking Party was to be formed to verify Japanese information and study airfields, communications and port facilities in the south; members of this team were to be the last British casualties in Vietnam. Mountbatten and Gracey were in general agreement on the main issues.

As the British were thinking about drawing down, the French were meeting increasing resistance wherever they operated. In Nha Trang, the Viet Minh fiercely resisted French efforts to move inland from the town. The six French and ninety-five Viet Minh dead in that clash were indicative of the savagery of the fighting whenever French and Vietnamese met in battle. The *Richelieu* brought her guns to bear on the railway station west of Nha Trang, shelling a trainload of Viet Minh arrivals from Tonkin. The Japanese commander in Nha Trang admitted that a "large number"[10] of his troops had deserted to the Viet Minh,

---

9. Gracey Papers, 3/1 GR Newsletter.
10. PRO, 172/7008, War Diary 20 Indian Division, INTSUM no. 65, 22 Nov. 1945.

which could have accounted for the stiffening of Viet Minh defenses in the area.

Admiral d'Argenlieu held his first formal press conference as the 3/1 Gurkhas were returning to Long Kien. In reply to written questions he stated that the Viet Minh leaders were regarded not as war criminals but as individuals accused of criminal activities who would be dealt with by the courts. The press were suitably impressed with the Admiral's sincerity as he said that talks with the Viet Minh could go on. By now the French government had received assurances of Anglo-American support for France's sovereignty over Indochina. The dispatches of E. W. Meiklereid, Brain's successor as political adviser to Gracey, described life in Saigon during this period. With d'Argenlieu's arrival, Jean Cédile had reverted to the status of Governor of Cochinchina. Criticism was being voiced of the way the French were conducting the trials of captured Viet Minh (Meiklereid remarked that judges were human and were sometimes "touched by the hysteria of the moment"), and certain press correspondents were exacerbating the issue. Two in particular (one a well-known American left-wing figure) produced daily denunciations in vitriolic terms of "neocolonialism" and the "brutality" of the Anglo-French occupation. The Viet Minh were still described by the French administration as uncontrollable armed bands and criminal elements, with pillaging occurring in their operational areas. Leclerc's tactics and the behaviour of his troops had encouraged the French population to demand revenge and reprisals. Although life was slowly returning to normal, the general strike imposed by the Viet Minh continued. Essential services, such as water and electricity, were still being operated by the armed forces (largely British and Japanese engineers). The French came in for some harsh words in this regard. The French population, as yet unaccustomed to queueing, were inclined to do their buying on the black market rather than take their turns at the food distribution points. The French administration was gradually reimposing its authority. The Police, CID, Public Health, Information, Finance, Economic Affairs, Justice, Political Affairs, Post and Telegraph, Education and other major departments resumed their functions, in some cases despite lack of staff and office space. There were still few Vietnamese civil servants, for many who had earlier left their posts had not yet returned.

Cédile was reluctant to employ Vichy officials, but found himself forced to do so since most of the French in Indochina were tainted by collaboration with the Japanese. He took the precaution of stipulating that all appointments were provisional pending future enquiries. The judicial service was now being reorganized, but it restricted its activity for the time being to penal cases, since the Viet Minh had removed all case histories, books, dossiers and archives, and what little remained was in disorder. What part, if any, the Viet Minh played in manipulating French passions during this period of heightened tension in South Vietnam must remain a matter of speculation. In late November there was a violent reaction by the French civilian community to the murder and mutilation of two French children. The demand for reprisals, of which little had been heard for some time, now rose again. Stories of outrageous French behavior were supplied by Vietnamese propagandists to known left-wing foreign correspondents, who, to the mounting anger of French officials in Indochina, seized on them eagerly and despatched them to the world press.

On 23 November, as Meiklereid was sending an unflattering report of the French,[11] the first steps were taken to relieve the British of their commitments in Vietnam. Gracey issued orders dealing with the relief by the French of his forces in Cholon (9/12 FFR). All Japanese guards in Cholon and Saigon were to be relieved on the day before 9/12 FFR handed over to the French. Soon after, 9/14 Punjab was relieved in Gia Dinh by 9th DIC units. The 9/12 FFR was to move to Cap St Jacques in order to prepare to receive the great majority of the surrendered Japanese. The French assumption of control had an ominous beginning: an explosion and fire in their Cholon barracks. It seemed as if everyone in the French Army smoked cigarettes, and that a match or lighted

---

11. PRO, FO 371/53957, SITREP, Meiklereid to Dening, 30 Nov. 1945. "The primary foci of British complaints were the apparent lack of fire discipline of the French troops and the French attitude towards, and treatment of, the Vietnamese. . . ."

   A 20 Division Intelligence Summary GB, PRO, WO 172/7128, 20 Division Intelligence Summary, Appendix E, 22 Nov. 1945. had this to say: "The IORs have begun to distrust both the French troops and civil authorities. The shoddy turnout of French troops, their bad discipline and their habit of lounging about on street corners have caused the average sepoy to feel contempt for them." Nor were the leaders spared. On 29 October Gracey, who already criticised Cédile and Rivier, had harsh words for two other officials. Cédile's deputy, Lt.-Col. Anthonioz, was described as "small-minded, lacking in imagination and pigheaded", and Colonel Martin (head of the French mission to the Control Commission) "does little but waste the time of our overworked staff with minor details and cannot even speak English." However, Gracey complimented Leclerc's Chief of Staff, Repiton-Preneuf.

cigarette end had accidentally fallen into some petrol, which set off some nearby ammunition and added to the pyrotechnics of the evening, during which the Viet Minh started two other fires. To add to French problems, the news from Laos reflected the difficulty faced by their still weak positions in vital areas there. Two captured French soldiers were beheaded by the Viet Minh in Vientiane, and the severed heads were publicly exhibited. To facilitate Franco-Japanese cooperation in the coming battles to eliminate the Viet Minh around Nha Trang, where Viet Minh broadcasts stated that trainloads of their reinforcements were arriving, Lieutenant-Colonel Gopsill of 3/1 Gurkha Rifles (fresh from the Long Kien operations) was flown in by the RAF to act as the liaison between the French and Japanese. Gopsill stayed there for about six weeks, and was in the thick of the fighting in the Nha Trang area; he returned to Saigon in time to embark with his unit for Makassar (Celebes) in January. In the Inner Zone Rodham's brigade appeared to have heeded his exhortations to ''get a move on'', and despite the Viet Minh guerrilla war the 14/13 FFR disarmed five Japanese units totalling 1,380 men on the 23rd. This was at least a significant start to the disarming of the Japanese forces, and on the next day Rodham addressed the problem of relieving the Japanese of their money.

Even now, when the Financial Adviser to the Control Commission had not yet fully come to grips with the problem, there was growing unease over the extent of Japanese tampering with the local economy. Rodham stated, ''There is evidence that the Japanese have secreted vast sums of French Indo-China currency in cash. The amount may be in the region of 800 million piasters [more than $300 million].'' He went on to say that if indeed the Japanese had such sums under their control, they would quite likely seek to undermine the currencies of nearby British territories and build up commercial undertakings ''under bogus names''. It must be made economically impossible for the Japanese ever again to become a military power, and by stripping them of their cash the Division would be doing its part in this worthwhile enterprise. Terauchi had been notified of this policy in writing, and after the Japanese had been ''de-piastered'' they were to be handed back 2 million piasters for subsistence. Rodham had about eighty Japanese units with 35,000 troops' to disarm and de-piaster in his Inner and Outer Zones. As he recognized, ''The amount of work to be got through in this connection is colossal. . . .'' The Control Commission's Financial Adviser, Lieutenant-Colonel Sweeny, was to be in Bien Hoa on 26 November to lecture the 100 Brigade personnel directly involved in the operation.

Available officers were drafted in for this purpose and were directed to look for educated VCOs, NCOs and soldiers to help in the task.

On 25 November, a day on which Numata was personally reprimanded by Gracey for disobeying curfew orders, the French invalidated all 500-piaster notes as legal tender. This caused an uproar throughout Vietnam as not only were the hoarders (mainly Chinese) affected, but thousands of British troops would now be out of pocket as well. The notes had actually been declared invalid on the 18th, with an announcement that they must be paid in by the 25th. Of the total of 500-piaster notes, those issued before 9 March 1945 (the date of the Japanese *coup*) would have 70 per cent of their value credited to blocked accounts. The really bad news was that all 500-piaster notes issued after 9 March were declared invalid. This was done to deflate the economy and counter the effects of the Japanese having issued about 940 million piasters in notes between 9 March and 23 September 1945; the total of 500-piaster notes issued before March had been no more than 300 million piasters.[12] This move reduced note issue by a third, and made a large proportion of notes held by the Japanese and, presumably, the Viet Minh valueless.

The British Army's Financial Adviser to the Control Commission discovered extensive financial manipulations by the Japanese, showing that they had drawn 615 million piasters in excess of normal commitments in 1945, of which 369 million were drawn in the two weeks immediately preceding the Japanese surrender. Most of this appeared to have gone to support subversive activities, and considerable pressure was now being exerted on the Japanese to trace these funds. To look ahead for a moment, of 63,402,275 piasters in cash actually recovered from the Japanese forces, about one-third (22,391,000) was in 500-piaster notes. The full extent of Japanese currency manipulation is revealed by the fact that, between early 1943 and 9 March 1945, the Bank of Indochina printed 1,200 million piasters.

Operationally the Japanese continued to maintain their integrity, and when Yamagishi *butai* swept through a village near Ben Cat, fourteen Viet Minh were killed and five captured. These Japanese frontline infantry units, as opposed to the support troops, were giving a good account of themselves right up to the moment when they had to disarm. It was an extraordinary episode in the history of warfare.

Negotiations between the British and Chinese on the exchange of missions in Indochina had now been successfully concluded (perhaps due

12. PRO, FO 371/53957, F 1058, 30 Nov. 1945.

partly to the north's desperate need for southern rice), and Gracey had decided on the composition of the liaison team he was about to send to Hanoi. The officer he selected to represent him at Lu Han's headquarters, leading a mission of four men, was Lieutenant-Colonel A. G. Trevor-Wilson, a Secret Intelligence Service officer well suited for this delicate task. He was advised by Gracey that his tasks were "solely military and in no way concerned with politics or economics except in the rare cases in which they definitely affect your military tasks."[13] Trevor-Wilson became a valuable source of information through his weekly meetings with Ho Chi Minh.

In the south, although the emphasis was on Japanese disarmament, the end of November saw Gracey's battalions still busy coping with the Viet Minh guerrilla attacks. A unique situation developed down in Cap St Jacques when the 9/12 FFR advance party arrived and immediately held a meeting with the local Viet Minh chief, G. Wong. The British were willing to leave the Viet Minh alone to run essential services and markets, provided the latter did not interfere with the main task of concentrating the Japanese in the area. But unfortunately all the goodwill in the world could not get around the main sticking point, namely the problem of the returning French. Although the Viet Minh appeared able to sustain a steady level of violence, and in the south had a free hand outside the British key areas, the Allied emphasis at the end of November was on the disarming of the Japanese and their formal surrender ceremonies. Mountbatten's intended visit to Saigon on 30 November to receive Terauchi's personal surrender sharpened this emphasis as Gracey's staff made preparations for the big event.

There were now few big targets for Gracey's battalions to hit — fewer large groups for columns such as Gateforce to meet and destroy. But the level of violence, though locally lethal, was generally not such as to make life intolerable. The once-paralyzing Viet Minh blockade of Saigon had been broken and normality was slowly returning. The French were taking greater responsibility for affairs in South Vietnam, and the Gurkhas, Punjabis and Dogras were speculating on their next postings. On the 28th a large part of 32 Brigade's sector, north of Saigon, was handed over to the French as the 14th Army Commander, General Sir Miles Dempsey, landed at Tan Son Nhut on the eve of Mountbatten's arrival. The end of the beginning of the modern Vietnam wars was in sight.

13. Papers of Lt.-Col. A. G. Trevor-Wilson, 24 Nov. 1945, and personal interviews, 1977.

# 15

# DRAWDOWN

As November drew to a close, a 3/1 Gurkha writer wrote: "November closed fairly quietly after a similar beginning, but a stormy middle period." The arrival of the French in British key areas was viewed with mixed feelings. A 9/14 Punjab writer reported that since the arrival of the French "Our nights, previously quiet and peaceful, have resounded to the noise of musketry on all sides . . . The French maxim seems to be 'when in doubt discharge your weapon as rapidly as possible and in any direction'!"[1] This indiscipline resulted in Gurkhas being shot dead and, in at least one instance, of silent retaliation by the Gurkhas.

Gracey now had a direct link to Hanoi; Trevor-Wilson had announced on 28 November that the Saigon-Hanoi communications link was open. The same day, at 1700 hours, the main body of 9 FFR had arrived at Cap St Jacques by river and found the town almost deserted and most of the better bungalows looted. The Japanese helped the battalion to unload and move into their new home (the Grand Hotel) on the sea front. The Mayor's house became the officers' mess.

In Thu Duc, 4/10 GR now began their vitally important "Japanese Financial Disarmament", and four Gurkha officers collected more than $8\frac{1}{2}$ million piasters, gold bullion worth about £2 million sterling — and a "considerable quantity" of opium also handed in by the Japanese.[2] On the following day they collected about 3 million piasters in addition to jewelry, watches, cameras, and so on. Collecting these enormous amounts of money, gold and opium with a single battalion in two days was an extraordinary achievement. In addition, thousands of Japanese troops outside the British key areas had to travel to the key areas to be disarmed and to turn over their valuables. There was just no way to check on the amount of arms, ammunition and money which might have been turned over to the Viet Minh as these Japanese units were moving to the British area around Saigon.

On 29 November the Supremo himself arrived in Saigon. He had earlier visited Tavoy, on the Tennasserim coast, and at 1630 landed at

1. Gracey Papers, 9/14 Punjab Newsletter.
2. PRO, WO 172/7793, War Diary 4/10 Gurkha Rifles, 28 Nov. 1945. 9,500 kilos of opium worth £2,000,000 were backloaded.

313

Tan Son Nhut. In their discussions Gracey stated that Terauchi's health was getting rapidly worse and there was some doubt as to whether he "could stand the strain of a move to Singapore". Mountbatten agreed that the Field-Marshal should at least remain the titular head of Japanese forces to keep unbroken the chain of command from the Emperor on down; he was to remain in Saigon until Gracey departed, when it would be decided whether he would be moved to Singapore, stay in Saigon or be returned to Japan. Mountbatten reiterated that he was aware "Terauchi was a major war criminal but that in his present state of health he doubted that he would ever be brought to trial, and that he would inform the Chiefs of Staff accordingly."

At last, on 30 November, the moment came for Mountbatten to receive the personal surrender of his Japanese counterpart. The scene was the rear of Gracey's residence, where a red carpet was laid at the foot of the flight of steps leading down from the palace. Representatives from the various Indian, Gurkha and British units were represented and lined up on the steps down which Mountbatten was to descend. Waiting in the courtyard, off the carpet, were the old Field-Marshal and his aide, who was holding the box containing the two swords, specially flown in from Terauchi's home in Japan. After a suitable delay Mountbatten, in white, descended the steps and faced Terauchi; the time was 1000. The Supreme Allied Commander then stated: "I am now going to accept the swords of Field-Marshal Count Terauchi as a symbol of the final act of surrender of the Supreme Commander of the Japanese Expeditionary Forces of the Southern Regions to me as Supreme Allied Commander of the South East Asia Command." Terauchi then saluted and handed over the box. It was all over in a few minutes; for some reason Dempsey had not stayed for the ceremony, as he left Saigon at 0900. According to Gracey's papers, two British Army doctors also attended — they stood by with a syringe of morphine at the ready; Terauchi had been examined at Japanese headquarters by a board of three British doctors, and found "hemiplegic, and suffering from marked arteriosclerosis with cerebral degeneration". They advised that a private, rather than public, ceremony be conducted, and this was done.[3]

By 1030 Mountbatten was holding a meeting at Gracey's residence attended by the two senior French officials d'Argenlieu and Leclerc (plus their Chiefs of Staff), Gracey, Kimmins, Hirst, Scott-Bell (Royal Navy),

3. Gracey Papers, "Medical History, Allied Land Forces French Indo China, Sept 1945-Feb 1946".

Meiklereid, Clarac (d'Argenlieu's Political Adviser) and J. Rayner (Psychological Warfare). Coming straight to the point, Mountbatten said that it looked as if the first brigade of 20 Division (32 Brigade) would leave at the end of December, followed a month later by General Gracey, Division headquarters and the second brigade (80). He then asked the French if these proposals were acceptable, to which Leclerc replied that the departure of the first brigade posed no problem, but the movement of Gracey and the second brigade "should not be fixed firmly, as it depended on the arrival of the 9th DIC." Although Gracey and Leclerc had great respect for each other, Gracey now interjected to express his opinion that the second brigade could depart as planned, as it was not necessary to await the arrival of 9 DIC's equipment. The driving factors in this case were the intricate interlocking theater movements, one being the departure of 80 Brigade and its subsequent relief of the Australians in Celebes. Mountbatten said that the third brigade (100 Brigade) would also probably be used to relieve Australians, and that any undue delays would have to be negotiated with the Australian Prime Minister. Could General Leclerc give any indication of when 100 Brigade could be withdrawn?

Leclerc replied "that he could not possibly take the responsibility for guarding all the disarmed Japanese in French Indo-China until all the French forces which he was expecting had arrived from Europe." This, however, depended mainly on the shipment of equipment from Britain. However, it appeared that the third brigade could depart when 3 DIC had received its equipment. Mountbatten said that when he had been in Delhi, "the Viceroy had informed him that Indian agitators were making much capital out of the employment of Indian troops in French Indo-China and the Netherlands East Indies." The minutes of the meeting went on to record: "In these circumstances he [Mountbatten] regretted that at the request of the Government of India the original intention to place British/Indian troops under French command after the departure of General Gracey could not now be carried out. He regretted this decision, but the matter was out of his hands." It is doubtful whether all this handwashing was really necessary for a straightforward soldier like Leclerc, but both d'Argenlieu and Leclerc assured Mountbatten that they understood. Mountbatten then returned to this theme of avoiding potentially unfavorable publicity. He told the French that he would have no objection to Leclerc immediately taking over direct command of French forces, acting under d'Argenlieu instead of Gracey; Government approval would have to be sought for this, and "he did not wish to press it, but he put it forward from a desire to help the French as much as possible." It would also "ease the political criticisms being levelled in India and other parts of the world". The French again said that they understood, but Leclerc, in saying that he appreciated the offer, thought that "certain difficulties" might make it impossible to separate the commands at this time. In his opinion the proper time for that was the departure of General Gracey and the arrival of the remainder of 9 DIC.

After again turning down d'Argenlieu's request to transfer the disputed Cambodian area from General Evans in Bangkok to Gracey, Mountbatten turned to the subject of aircraft for the French. Leclerc had asked for a squadron of Spitfires, and Mountbatten wondered whether the French would accept Japanese fighters pending consideration of the request. Leclerc replied that he did not want to consider the proposal unless there was no hope of obtaining the Spitfires. Mountbatten again indicated his feelings concerning adverse criticism, explaining that "as an Allied Commander he had to follow the general principle of the United Nations in regard to the use of force against native populations." The Allied forces under Gracey had to conform to these principles and he "did not want to lay down definite guidelines which would restrict the French unduly". He left it to Gracey and Leclerc to sort out the separation of British and French commands in Vietnam. Mountbatten had to tread lightly over this issue, for the next item of discussion concerned the export of food from Cochinchina. Mountbatten needed the rice surpluses from Indo-China to alleviate the serious food shortages throughout the rest of his command. D'Argenlieu replied that his own situation was not good either, but he would do what he could to help "if his situation improved".

Saigon Radio was discussed next, and the British proposed that the French should take over immediately, subject to certain reservations. D'Argenlieu raised the question of SACSEA directives after Gracey's departure, for he felt that "one of the principal points of sovereignty was control of the radio. . . ." Mountbatten again replied that these directives "were not entirely his own product, but that they were based on directives received from the Foreign Office in London, and that he understood that they were issued under the auspices of the United Nations." The Supreme Allied Commander had now twice invoked the United Nations, giving the impression that he was so far down the chain of command as to be virtually powerless in this matter. At this point, d'Argenlieu pinned Mountbatten down by quietly asking if it might be confirmed that these directives were indeed issued under the authority of the United Nations; Mountbatten replied that he would have to check on this. D'Argenlieu then asked if Mountbatten had listened to Hanoi Radio, and suggested that the Chinese "might also be reminded of their obligations to the United Nations". But Mountbatten had been attempting for some time, without success, to get the Americans to intervene with the Chinese to control the vituperative and inflammatory Communist propaganda emanating from Hanoi.

Mountbatten departed for Singapore the next day. Terauchi, whose request to say a few words during his surrender ceremony had been curtly denied, was waiting at the airfield to speak to Mountbatten. The Supreme Allied Commander had granted Terauchi's request to deliver a note, provided the interview was brief (no more than ninety seconds). The old Field-Marshal, now a pathetic figure despite his status as a major war criminal, expressed his "heartfelt gratitude and deep emotion" at the consideration shown to him by Mountbatten during the surrender ceremony the previous day. On behalf of the officers and men of the Southern Army he thanked the Allied Commander for granting a special holiday on the occasion of the Meiji Festival on 3 November, and assured Mountbatten that Southern Army "will continue faithfully to carry out their duties in connection with the surrender". Terauchi said that he looked forward "with pleasure" to receiving Mountbatten's personal guidance, and concluded, "May I congratulate Your Excellency on your notable victory and express to you my warm appreciation for your having granted me a personal interview." Terauchi again burst into tears during this meeting. He remains an enigma, for an RAF witness wrote that the Field-Marshal and his senior officers appeared to be in good spirits when Mountbatten had departed.

Mountbatten, on leaving Saigon, noted in his diary that Leclerc had declared, "Your General Gracey has saved French Indo China!" The Supreme Allied Commander also wrote that Gracey was "doing a first-class job", a significant reversal of opinion, since he had been on the point of dismissing Gracey only a few weeks earlier (before the Chiefs of Staff had overruled his wish to restrict Gracey to the immediate vicinity of Saigon).

A few days later Mountbatten was joined in Singapore by the two senior Allied officers in Vietnam, as Gracey[4] and Leclerc arrived to attend

---

4. At about this time the Viet Minh announced that on 20 November at 1130 hours General Gracey had been assassinated by Indian soldiers in Saigon: ". . . Thus an

the Supreme Allied Commander's 300th Meeting, held in Government House on 6 December at 1730 hours. This was an unusually important occasion because the Chief of the Imperial General Staff, Field-Marshal Sir Alan Brooke, was present.[5] What his thoughts were at this time tempt speculation, for he had already received Major-General Pyman's letter informing him of the dissatisfaction with Mountbatten's leadership shared by a number of the most senior officers, and there is little doubt he had already discussed this matter with some of them.[6] Also present were Browning, Park (RAF), Dempsey (who was succeeding Slim as ALFSEA Commander-in-Chief), Major-General G. C. Evans (ALFSIAM), Major-General Denning (SEAC staff), Meiklereid (Gracey's Political Adviser) and other key staff officers. After a discussion of disputed territory between Siam and Cambodia, the rest of the meeting was devoted to Indochina.

The Supreme Allied Commander asked Leclerc to "give a brief summary of the situation as he saw it in French Indo-China". Leclerc began by saying that by comparison with what was happening in Java things were not too bad in Indochina. But he stressed that the reason the French had achieved success so far was because they had not over-extended themselves — they had done only what was possible. He also said that the part of Indochina under control was small compared to the remainder. In order to finish the task he needed the 3rd DIC and the Expeditionary Corps units — especially their equipment. In response to a question from Sir Alan Brooke, Major-General Denning stated that eleven ships with French troops had arrived in Saigon or were at sea between Singapore and Saigon; two more ships were expected in mid-December, which should complete the buildup of 9 DIC. The British had already supplied the French with 600 vehicles in Indochina, and

---

enemy who was dangerous and bloodthirsty has been annihilated." Why this propaganda came to light on 7 December is not clear — it was repeated in posters stuck to trees in 14/13 FFR's area on 12 December. (GB, PRO, WO 172/7135, War Diary 100 Brigade, INTSUM No. 8 1500 hours, 7 Dec. 1945.)

5. It was during this time that Brooke assured Gracey that the proclamation of 19/21 September, to which Mountbatten had violently objected, was correct in its form and timing.

6. These discussions may have influenced the decision of the Chiefs of Staff to disapprove Mountbatten's strong suggestion that a Supreme Commander, and associated command and staff structure, be retained after his departure and the disbandment of SEAC. The services, especially the Army and Navy, strongly opposed the retention of a Supreme Commander.

would hand over another 1,300 on the departure of 20 Indian Division. In response to another question from Brooke, Denning replied that 1,900 vehicles in India were earmarked for 3 DIC, of which 400 were to be shipped in December. Mountbatten then informed Leclerc of a recent report in the *Chicago Sun* newspaper that the crews of eight American ships (each of which had carried 2,000 French troops to Saigon) were "resentful of this task". These crews "had declared that they would have preferred to have been employed repatriating American troops from Europe." Leclerc then voiced his agreement with the proposed British drawdown in Indochina. He added that he wished to emphasize his overriding need for landing craft; most of the roads in Indochina were in bad shape or cut by rebels, but many places could be reached by river, canal, or the sea. The French had already suffered casualties at Nha Trang when they had been unable to land on the beach and so had had to enter the harbor in a light native junk. Sir Keith Park then said that the Air Ministry in London had authorized the transfer of twelve Mark VIII Spitfires to the French.

Meiklereid went on to discuss the tangled financial situation in Indochina, where on 18 November the first anti-inflationary measure (cancellation of the 500-piaster notes) had been introduced, adding that much of this money was in Viet Minh hands. The Chinese merchants, "who are not prone to the utilization of bank facilities," were hit hard. While the French were mounting "a considerable press campaign" to explain the necessity of such severe action, they were now wondering if "they may have been a trifle hasty in introducing these measures which may adversely affect the political situation." Meiklereid drew SEAC's attention to the recent report by Lt.-Col. Sweeny, Gracey's Financial Adviser, who had uncovered evidence of "extensive Japanese financial manipulations", and there was "little doubt that a considerable portion of these funds had gone to ground for subsequent use in subversive activities."

Mountbatten closed the meeting by announcing the appointment of Brigadier Maunsell as Head of the Inter-Service Mission which was to be established on Gracey's departure and the disbandment of the Control Commission, and Leclerc said that "he agreed that this was a most suitable appointment." Maunsell had been recommended for the job by Gracey.

In Indochina one pressing problem was the shortage of food. This was reflected in the amount of rice exported: 922,000 tons in 1943, 500,000 tons in 1944, and only 61,000 tons in 1945 (to the end of August). In a report to SEAC, Meiklereid wrote that the political turmoil had directly affected the situation, which was so bad in the north, in Tonkin, that the French had set aside the first 200,000 tons of the new crop for that part of the country. Although the rubber plantations were generally intact, machinery was badly damaged. Planters were now beginning to return to their plantations, where they were reorganizing their labor forces under the protection of armed guards.

On 9 December Brigadier Woodford held a conference at 32 Brigade headquarters to discuss plans for the brigade's last major operation in Vietnam: the assault on Han Phu island. Attending were the Commanders of 9/14 Punjab and 4/2 GR, and representatives from the Royal Navy and 114 Field Regiment (Royal Artillery). According to the 20th Division's History, Han Phu had developed into a major base for Viet Minh guerrillas driven out from Saigon. The operation was 32 Brigade's biggest undertaking since October, when it had spearheaded the expanding British role with the investment of Go Vap and Gia Dinh. Briefly, the plan called for 4/2 Gurkha Rifles to assault and sweep Han Phu, while 9/14 Punjab was to take up blocking positions to cover possible Viet Minh escape routes, to include the shooting of Viet Minh retreating across the river. The 9/14 Punjab were also to be prepared to cross the river in rubber boats or "country craft" if called on by the 4/2 Gurkhas. The Royal Navy was tasked to provide five craft in which to transport the Gurkha battalion to Han Phu; the departure point was to be the RN barracks in Saigon, and the time 0630 hours. One battery of artillery from 114 Field Regiment was to support the operation from its gun emplacement area on the golf course near Tan Son Nhut. The area to be bracketed was about 1 km. due north of Ben Cat and 2–3 km. northeast of Go Vap, in the pocket formed by the bifurcation of the river. The Han Phu area encompassed about 1 square km.

Unfortunately, the Viet Minh scored first, for on the eve of the operation three 9/14 Punjab soldiers were killed, and one was wounded, by Viet Minh snipers in Go Vap as the Punjab company was moving into position to support the Han Phu assault. On 15 December the 4/2 Gurkhas embarked as briefed at the Royal Navy area in Saigon, and at 0830 the 4/2 GR Mission Commander radioed that his landing had been unopposed. Brigadier Woodford observed the landing from the opposite bank of the river, and it appeared that the Viet Minh had not expected a waterborne approach. The two companies of 4/2 GR, plus a tactical headquarters, had disembarked from five landing craft without opposition ("but in great danger from our own guns") in the area between the

Cho and Saigon Rivers. They then turned west and south to drive the Viet Minh towards 9/14 Punjab lining the south and west banks of the river Cho. While most of the Viet Minh had fled, about 100 remained to oppose 4/2 GR. The Gurkhas lost one man killed and four wounded; the Viet Minh retreated, having lost thirty killed. A considerable booty was collected and destroyed by the Gurkhas; the Viet Minh headquarters was found gutted, and over 400 men were rounded up and sent to the *Sûreté* in Saigon for interrogation.[7]

The Gurkhas spent the night on the island, and after a thorough house-to-house search, in which they were joined by a company of 9/14 Punjab, the force reembarked and returned to Saigon. The 9/14 Punjab view of the Han Phu operation was as follows: "This party was a complete success. . . . Firstly, the area was cleaned up and secondly the unpleasant task of wading through the paddy was done by 4/2nd GR. . . ." On the return, 4/2 GR engaged in a potentially disastrous three-way firefight with the Viet Minh and the French. A French armored column of the 2nd Armored Division, returning from the north, was fired on by Viet Minh troops at a bridge near Hanh Thong Tay, about 5 km. straight north of Tan Son Nhut. The French troops, unaware that British troops were in the area, mistook the returning Gurkhas for Viet Minh and opened fire on them. A confused battle followed in which the Gurkhas fired on the Viet Minh, who were shooting at the French while the French shot up the Gurkhas. One French soldier was killed and three Gurkhas were slightly wounded in the face by flying brick splinters.

But even as 32 Brigade battalions were operating in the Han Phu area, ALFFIC orders addressed the relief of 32 Brigade by the French, and on 18 and 19 December it became the first British brigade to relinquish responsibility in Vietnam. Rodham's 100 Brigade remained in place, the Royal Artillery was to be responsible for the area due north of Cholon and west of Saigon (which included the artillery barracks and the race course), and Taunton's 80 Brigade held the area from Tan Son Nhi (about 3 km. southwest of Tan Son Nhut) to the eastern tip of Khanh Hoi island. This area included most of Cholon and was bordered in the

7. Gracey Papers, 4/2 GR Newsletter. According to the 20th Division History, Han Phu was "the last remaining Vietminh stronghold in the Saigon/Cholon area," and "The elimination of this hotbed of Vietminh activity had an immediate effect on the situation in the suburbs north of Saigon which rapidly improved from that date."

north by the main road which became known as Le Van Duyet. The French assumed complete responsibility for Saigon. They took over Go Vap from 9/14 Punjab on the 18th, according to plan; or, as a 9/14 Punjab writer put it, "on [the] 18th the French took over complete control, or as near control as they could get." The next day, 4/2 GR and 3/8 GR were relieved by French troops, and on the 20th the last of the Japanese Go Vap garrison — forty-two men — surrendered to 9/14 Punjab. Woodford's battalions were now in their final concentration areas and on the same day 32 Brigade was declared non-operational to permit all units to prepare for their impending move to British North Borneo. With 32 Brigade preparing for its departure and 80 Brigade fairly quiet, 100 Brigade was bearing the brunt of the Viet Minh guerrilla activity.

The fighting between the Japanese and the Viet Minh had increased in intensity. In mid-December a Japanese unit summarily executed two Viet Minh captured while attempting to poison it at a crossroads north-west of Tan Son Nhut. Seven Japanese were poisoned in another incident; all recovered, but two "went mad". During the next few days several sharp firefights occurred in several parts of South Vietnam between Japanese and Viet Minh troops, resulting in scores of Viet Minh dead. Nearer Saigon, there was trouble every day in Go Vap, where the Viet Minh were making things difficult for the French. Two Japanese soldiers were killed there on the 13th as the French and Japanese were continually engaged by guerrillas. Another Japanese was killed when one of their convoys was attacked in 1/1 GR's area. In the south, where 9/12 FFR was coexisting with the Viet Minh, two armed Viet Minh were arrested inside the 9/12th battalion area and sent under escort to Saigon for interrogation by the Field Security Section; at this time the local Viet Minh were "warned not to make trouble in Cap St Jacques." The next day, the local Viet Minh chief met the battalion commander and apologized for the incident, and arrangements were made with the Viet Minh to permit the battalion Medical Officer to give medical aid to the local inhabitants twice a week. The Japanese in Cap St Jacques were ordered to guard the water points, and the Vietnamese were requested to repair the water works and restore electricity. The Viet Minh replied that they were willing to cooperate with the British so long as no French returned to the area.

A meeting was held on 6 December between the 9/12 FFR Adjutant, representatives of the Japanese Army and local Vietnamese (presumably the Viet Minh, who controlled the area) to decide on a suitable concentration area for Japanese troops, 60,000 of whom were expected in Cap St Jacques by mid-January. The next day, the 9/12 FFR officers again met Viet Minh officials to discuss the evacuation of certain areas on the arrival of the Japanese Army units. Because the British and Viet Minh were conferring regularly here, there was little combat activity, and the 9/12th was reverting to peacetime training — something that most of the other battalions were not able to do.

Rodham reported that "Hostile activity on the 'All Red Route' is on the increase," but he maintained the offensive and kept the Viet Minh off balance by his adroit use of the troops at his disposal (relatively few given the area of his responsibility). Rodham specifically drew the attention of his commanders to previous experience: "The old North West Frontier rule 'of never doing the same thing twice the same way' applies equally to these mobile piquets and will bewilder the enemy." After suggesting courses of action regarding protection for convoys, he wrote that while he knew his units were under strength, "strenuous action" now would avoid casualties later. Rodham's stringent precautions were paying dividends, for an intercepted Viet Minh message to their headquarters stated that "the clearance of hedges and undergrowth from the road to a depth of 25 metres on either side was making their guerrilla warfare most difficult and that they were considering moving off further westwards." He was now using every available Japanese on these road-clearing operations, and authorized the issue to the Japanese of "extra cutting implements" for this purpose.

But the Viet Minh were not without their successes. In Thu Dau Mot a column of 1/1 Gurkhas and 9th Jat Regiment machine-gunners departed for Tan Thanh, about 4 miles to the east-northeast. They were to inspect a Japanese hospital there and collect medical supplies. The mobile column had barely cleared the outskirts of Thu Dau Mot when it was ambushed by the Viet Minh — this attack came just ninety minutes after a 4/10 company was ambushed. Two Jat soldiers were immediately killed by grenades and machine-gun fire. One of the most successful Viet Minh operations occurred four days later with the ambush of a British/Indian column of thirty-six vehicles. This column was transporting printing press machinery from Ben Cat to Thu Dau Mot. The Allied force was not weak, being composed of 1/1 Gurkhas with a mortar section and a Jat medium machine-gun section. The column was attacked by a Viet Minh force armed with light machine-guns, rifles and grenades, and in a skillfully executed ambush the Gurkhas and Jats suffered thirteen casualties. Two Gurkhas soldiers were killed and one

Gurkha officer and four soldiers wounded, while the Jats lost one soldier killed, and one VCO and three soldiers wounded; in addition, a transport driver was killed. Viet Minh casualties, if any, were not known. The column finally proceeded while two 14/13 FFR companies raced over from Bien Hoa and swept the area.

The Inner Zone remained divided into the three sub-areas of Thu Duc (4/10 GR), Bien Hoa (14/13 FFR) and Thu Dau Mot (1/1 GR). Since the decision had been made in November to make Cap St Jacques the final Japanese concentration area instead of the Thu Duc/Bien Hoa/Thu Dau Mot triangle, Rodham's Inner Zone became a holding pool through which the Japanese would pass *en route* to Cap St Jacques after having been disarmed and de-piastered by Rodham's forces. Two Dogra companies with their mortar sections came under 4/10 GR command on the 27th so as to implement this policy more fully. The main tasks of the Sub Area Commanders remained the ''Maint[enance] of law and order, the extermination of all hostile elements and arrest of all custodians of arms'' and the protection of a variety of vital points. Rodham also decided that his troops should become more visible to encourage a return to normality among the local Vietnamese, so ''100 Ind Inf Bde and att[ached] tps will est[ablish] permanent posts throughout the present Inner Zone with a view to restoring confidence amongst peaceful Annamites and thereby assist restoration of law and order and the disarmament and evac[uation] of the Japanese forces.''[8] But although the Viet Minh guerrilla activity showed no signs of abating, Gracey's forces were suffering attrition from the effects of the war's end. A representative comment was made by a 9/14 Punjab writer: ''We are still suffering acutely from a shortage of men. Although we have lost all our Sikhs, no Jats have yet arrived to replace them. The same applies to the Dogra Coy now that the Ahirs and Gujars have gone. Men who went off on 28 days leave in June have not yet returned. As a result we are working on three weak Coys . . . we hope that it will not be long before the Jat Coy is a full strength going concern . . . Repat[riation] is beginning to hit us. . . .''[9]

8. PRO, WO 172/7135, War Diary 100 Indian Infantry Brigade, 22 Dec. 1945. Gracey had now identified the three main Japanese concentration areas as Thu Dau Mot and Thu Duc, Phnom Penh and Cap St Jacques. The initial target dates for Japanese repatriation were as follows: up to 5,000 by 10 December, 10,000 more by 15 December, 10,000 by 25 December, and 20,000 by 1 January 1946. It was thus hoped that 45,000 Japanese could be repatriated by 1 January.
9. Gracey Papers, 9/14 Punjab Newsletter. If this was a widespread complaint, then Mountbatten's later assertions that he could have simultaneously secured the key

Against this background of sustained violence and constant contacts with Viet Minh guerrillas, Gracey wrote a letter to Leclerc, which implied a barely controlled exasperation with French demands on the overstretched British resources, their now superior attitude towards the Japanese, their apparent lack of appreciation of the current situation, and above all their attitude toward his non-white soldiers in 20 Division. Gracey began by referring to his recent conversation with Leclerc and wrote, "I think it would be of great value to publish the following figures to all French units." He proceeded to list the numbers and types of vehicles already turned over to the French, and the amount of vehicle maintenance he was providing to French forces. Furthermore, "French troops should know what it entails in the way of transport to concentrate the Japanese in the Cap St Jacques area."[10] The numbers of Japanese involved were 6,000 from Saigon-Cholon, 26,000 from Thu Dau Mot/Bien Hoa, 11,000 from Phnom Penh and 7,000 from outlying districts such as Loc Ninh, Budop, Tay Ninh, Nha Trang, etc. Also, more than 7,000 tons of stores and 7,000 sick would have to be transported by road and river.

Despite their genuine mutual respect, Gracey's angry letter was to the point:

They should learn of the road and bridge repairs, and the railway repairs being carried out by British and Japanese engineers, all requiring transport, and all greatly assisting the free movement of French forces.

It might be of value for them to realise that, had not the Japanese in most cases carried out my orders faithfully, there would have been a disaster of the first magnitude in Southern French Indo China with a massacre of thousands of French people, and the destruction of a vast amount of French property.

They should know I think, that I, and you, depend on the Japanese maintaining their discipline in order to ensure that they continue to carry out their orders faithfully, and that anything done to undermine their discipline will, in fact, react against your plans for the resettlement of French Indo China. . . .

Having placed the situation in perspective for the newly-arrived French forces, Gracey kept his sharpest point to the last:

The camaraderie which exists between officers of the Indian Army and their Gurkha and Indian soldiers must be explained to them. Our men, of whatever

---

areas of Tonkin (including Hanoi) may be questioned in that his forces were diminishing while his commitments were increasing.

10. Gracey Papers, "Personal and Confidential" letter from Gracey to Leclerc, 2110/G, 12 Dec. 1945.

colour, are our friends and not considered "black" men. They expect and deserve to be treated in every way as first-class soldiers, and their treatment should be, and is, exactly the same as that of white troops.

There is no more fruitful source of friction between Indian Army officers and their men on the one side, and French troops on the other, than when our Indian and Gurkha troops are regarded and treated as "black" by French officers and men. I mention this point particularly as cases have occurred in which it is obvious that our Indian Army traditions have not been understood.

Gracey said that, for his part, he had "fully explained to all my officers and men the magnitude of the task you have before you, and the steps you are taking to get your young soldiers into trim for their formidable task." He concluded by congratulating Leclerc on the "remarkable improvement shown in the last week".

Although the Army remained continually engaged against the Viet Minh guerrillas, the RAF had not yet been employed in a combat role. After weeks of flying tactical reconnaissance sorties, punctuated by an occasional leaflet drop, the Spitfire pilots were eager to become involved in attacking the Viet Minh forces; however, constraints on their use made this almost impossible. But at last, on 11 December, came the day for which the pilots of 273 Squadron had been waiting — the chance to expend ordnance on the enemy. Three Spitfires made a noteworthy feat of navigation to find a surrounded French force in the mountainous Ban Me Thuot area, where the cloud cover was 10/10 at 400 feet. They strafed according to the direction of pre-agreed panels on the ground, and did not fire on seeing a set of French panels which the pilots did not recognize. The sight of the Spitfires did cause a strong Viet Minh force to break off their attacks.[11] Despite what has been written elsewhere, this was the only action of the single Spitfire squadron in Indochina, and in this, their only attack, no bombs were dropped and no Vietnamese were even seen, let alone hit. Warning leaflets were dropped and most of the strafing was directed at empty ground as map coordinates only were attacked, and no free armed reconnaissance was conducted. Soon afterwards, the whole squadron was disbanded and the pilots left Indochina.

Headquarters ALFSEA now approved Gracey's proposal to hand over to the French the complete equipment of one troop of 114 Field Regiment, Royal Artillery. As the day of his departure approached, Gracey wrote to ALFSEA about the future of his Division, a formation which, as Brigadier Woodford wrote, was perhaps unique in that it was born,

11.  PRO, Air 27/1583, 273 Squadron Log, 11 Dec. 1945.

lived and eventually died under but one commander. Gracey knew that his Division, like proud battleships no longer needed, would eventually be broken up; but rather than being split up and fading away by degrees, "It is the wish of all Officers and Other Ranks in the formation", as Gracey wrote, "to keep the Division as such until it is finally disbanded." However, Major-General Pyman, Chief of Staff to the Commander-in-Chief, ALFSEA, was unable to reassure Gracey on this point.

The political situation as of 15 December was described by Meiklereid in his report to Esler Dening. He touched on the problems being created by the "very arrogant" behavior and indiscipline of the newly-arrived French troops, who were being increasingly criticized by the press for the way they had conducted their clearing operations. Leclerc was taking all possible steps to improve matters, and had instituted weekly press meetings to explain the military operations to Allied press correspondents. Friction existed between the new French arrivals and the colonial French population, and the Vietnamese in Saigon had adopted a policy of noncooperation with the administration. The news of the impending departure of British troops was being received "in some quarters with considerable perturbation, as it is felt that with the French troops disseminated throughout the territory the danger of acts of violence on the part of the Annamites is likely to increase." Older residents were pessimistic and desired to "cut their losses and get out", but strict censorship had been imposed to keep news of this sort from reaching France, where it would have a bad effect on recruitment for the Administrative Service and on commercial interests.

In Meiklereid's opinion the paddy situation was not as bad as had been anticipated, and the Viet Minh had actually been advancing cash (of which they should have had no shortage, in view of the massive financial assistance they had received from the Japanese) for the gathering of the crop in certain areas. They had taken over the mills in Soc Trang and Cantho and, contrary to good Marxist doctrine, were making a profit from the sale of their goods. In Laos, the situation was "still confused", and Prince Souphanouvong (the "Red Prince") had gone to Hanoi.

After describing the difficulties faced by the French due to the Chinese in Tonkin, Meiklereid wrote that the French there continually had to give in while realizing that pacifying the south would take longer than expected; it would be some time before the French were able to tackle the problem in the north. On the 28th a more comprehensive report from the perceptive Lieutenant-Colonel Trevor-Wilson, Gracey's representative in Hanoi, was received at Commission headquarters in Saigon. His assessment of the political situation is of more than passing interest as he was probably the most disinterested observer in Hanoi. After describing the differences between the Viet Minh and the elements comprising the Dong Minh Hoi, Trevor-Wilson wrote:

The actual Viet Minh Government is greatly criticised both in the native press and by means of street demonstrations and distribution of pamphlets. Since the Viet Minh took over power in August 1945, i.e. four months ago, there has been ample proof of its inability to administer the country. The administration was completely disorganised by the sudden removal of the Mandarin system, the Mandarins having been replaced by improvised committees. The public treasury has been completely emptied as a result of demagogic measures such as the cancellation of direct taxation. No remedy has been found to offset the great floods of 1945 as a result of which large parts of Tonkin are still under water; nothing has been done to keep the dykes in repair. Railways, roads and bridges are in a very bad state. Coal mines produce very small output. No measures have been taken to prevent outbreaks of cholera and above all to remedy the almost certain famine conditions which will ravage the country within a few months. Government has been carried on by terrorist tactics, e.g. arbitrary arrest, suppression of free press, etc.

Five Government ministers are communists, two of them extremist. . . .[12]

Although a military team of seven Russians (headed by a full colonel) was due to arrive at Hanoi in the near future, Trevor-Wilson wrote that "There is no evidence, however, that the Viet Minh is in contact with Moscow." He thought that a shift of power to the Dong Minh Hoi was possible "In view of the fact that the Viet Minh Government is so much discredited in the eyes of the mass of the native population . . ." However, "It is possible that the two sides will form a coalition before the withdrawal of the Chinese forces."

In the south, as Christmas drew near, 32 Brigade prepared to depart.

12. PRO, WO 203/5563, 28 Dec. 1945. Professor P. J. Honey later commented on Trevor-Wilson's report from Hanoi: "This letter made me think back, and I questioned two old Vietnamese friends about the time, one of whom lived in Hanoi and the other in Saigon. It was very much as Trevor reported, though I hadn't noticed this before, and these two friends confirmed it. In the north, where the people had had direct experience of the Viet Minh in power, the man in the street knew them as communists, as oppressors, as incompetents in administration, and he hated them. In the south they were less well known, identified in the minds of the people with the struggle for independence from colonial rule, and, for all their violence and coercion, they were regarded as noble, worth supporting, and idealists." (Letter to Author, November 1978.)

During this time the 4/2 Gurkhas threw a party. As Lieutenant-Colonel Kitson, their Commander, had written earlier of a successful cocktail party and dance they had held, it was "marred only by the fact that a couple of Frenchmen were murdered almost within sight of our house only an hour before the party started and some of us had to go and clear up the mess."

On Christmas Day the 3/8 Gurkha Rifles embarked on the MV *Highland Brigade*,[13] which set sail a day later for Labuan. The British withdrawal from Vietnam had begun, and the rest of the brigade was soon to follow. At Cap St Jacques several 9/12 Frontier Force Regiment officers and VCOs took to the water in landing craft to wave goodbye to their friends in 32 Brigade as the liner sailed slowly past them on the Saigon River and out to sea. These two battalions, which had gone through so much together, would not meet again owing to the breakup of 20 Indian Division. With the partition of India, the 9/12th Frontier Force Rifles went to Pakistan and the 8th Gurkha Regiment to India. Thus they later faced each other on opposite sides in war.

So 32 Brigade was *en route* to Borneo and 80 Brigade was gradually disengaging in Cholon. 100 Brigade was left to deal with the complex problems of maintaining internal security, neutralizing the Viet Minh, disarming, de-piastering and concentrating the Japanese and sorting out the numerous and varied Japanese supply dumps throughout their area. On the 26th there had been an air attack by the French on the railway station and sidings at Bien Hoa. Although the Viet Minh largely controlled the railways and had used them to transport a sizeable number of Tonkinese troops to Cochinchina, the station and rolling stock in Bien Hoa were in Allied hands. Five valuable engines were destroyed in the attack, and some rolling stock and the barracks of the Japanese guards were damaged. The Spitfires making the raid had just been handed over to the French, and French and RAF roundels and fin flashes were very similar. The Japanese reported the attack, and as the 14/13 FFR War Diary reported, "Incident unexplained."

13. On the 26th, as the *Highland Brigade* slipped her moorings in Saigon, 4/2 Gurkha Rifles and associated detachments embarked on the SS *Aronda*. As they were boarding, Brigadier Woodford and some of his headquarters staff left Saigon for Labuan on the destroyer HMS *Nith*. The next day, as the *Aronda* left Saigon for Jesselton, 9/14 Punjab embarked: "On the 28th we reluctantly said goodbye to our comfortable quarters at Giadinh and set out for the docks . . . The Bn. marched, with the Dhol and Surnai playing nobly, through the streets of Saigon and aboard the SS *Lake Charles Victory*. Our first and we hope our last experience of an American Victory ship."

December did not end quietly. Four French scout cars were ambushed *en route* to Lai Thieu. Return fire killed thirteen Viet Minh, and several houses in the immediate area were burned. A 4/10 GR patrol "bumped" a Viet Minh force of unknown strength just southwest of Thu Duc. One Gurkha and eight Viet Minh were killed. The patrol, two sections of 4/10 Gurkhas searching for snipers who had fired on the radio station, met "considerable resistance", and one Gurkha was wounded when shot by a pistol at a range of 6 feet. The 1/1 Gurkhas reported that "90% of rebels in the area are Tonkinese, who by force of arms have instituted a reign of terror." But while the Saigon area was quieting down as the new year approached, there was little relaxing in 100 Brigade's Inner Zone.

# 16

## CITOYEN D'HONNEUR

On New Year's Eve Rodham, closing the year on a sombre note, directed his battalions to mount a series of pre-emptive strikes against the Viet Minh, since "Information from very many different sources indicates that the rebels are planning some sort of co-ordinated offensive to take place between now and 10 Jan '46. The Viet Minh leader is reported to have said that this will be 'the last grand offensive before the British leave'." Rodham noted that "The sudden increase in rebel activity in the last three days . . . certainly does indicate . . . some foundation for these reports. . . . The Viet Minh bands in this area are now reported to have been placed under . . . one man." Intelligence placed the four main Viet Minh concentration areas as respectively between Thu Dau Mot and Ben Cat, west and southwest of Bung, around Ben Go, and northeast of Bien Hoa. One squadron of armored cars was to be placed under command of 100 Brigade from 1 to 5 January; as Rodham wrote, "The first essential is to strike at the rebel concentration areas and discourage them before they start."

The 1/1 Gurkhas were ordered to "destroy all hostiles in the Bung area on 2 Jan." Supporting the Commander, Lieutenant-Colonel Clark, were armored cars, a section of artillery, medium machine-guns and mortars. The Commander of 14/13 FFR was ordered to destroy all hostiles in the Ben Go area in operations set for 4 January; Ben Go was on the river, about 8 km. south of Bien Hoa. One company from 4/10 GR would travel to Bien Hoa and cover for 14/13 FFR while it swept Ben Go. The exact location of the third Viet Minh concentration northeast of Bien Hoa had not been pinpointed, and if the fighting patrols failed to make contact with the Viet Minh in Ben Go, they were to be prepared to switch their operations to the northeast of Bien Hoa, provided firm intelligence of that area was received. Regarding the fourth area, around Ben Cat, the French were planning an operation to clear out the Viet Minh up there. Rodham emphasized that "The above operations deal with specific enemy concentrations only." Commanders were told to strike as hard as they could during the next ten days at any reported enemy concentration within reach, as Rodham's information indicated that the locals were wearying of military operations and the Viet Minh were becoming discouraged; "If we can give him one or two good knocks *now* we will have every chance of discouraging him from worrying us in the future." Commanders were advised to regard "all locals anywhere near where a shot has been fired as enemies", for "The difficulty is to catch him, as immediately he has had his shot or thrown his grenade he pretends to be friendly." Commanders were also encouraged to bring in suspects from troublesome areas, for "Locals do *not* like a trip to the Sûreté in Saigon and this will encourage them in future to give us information before the enemy start any of their nonsense. . . ." In view of the increased Viet Minh activity, company and post commanders in out-lying areas "must have *no* compunction in clearing an adequate field of fire round their posts. Obstacles, wire, poonjis etc. must be placed far enough out to prevent the enemy getting within grenade throwing range." With the increasingly rapid drawdown of Japanese fighting units, the number of incidents increased to an almost intolerable level as the Viet Minh quickly moved to fill the gaps left by the withdrawal of Japanese forces. In the last three days of 1945 the French killed ninety-three Viet Minh and captured thirty-two for the loss of one Frenchman wounded.

At this time a remarkably successful patrol was undertaken by a small party of 14/13 FFR soldiers led by Havildar Bagh Bahar. The patrol, called "Sherforce", had been attached to a strong fighting column which on New Year's Day had left the main base at Bien Hoa to sweep Vinh Cuu. Sherforce slipped away as the main column departed Vinh Cuu for the return to Bien Hoa. The Havildar's orders were to observe Viet Minh activity in the Ben Go area (about 10 km. southeast of Bien Hoa); they were to return early on the 3rd. The eleven men, entirely on their own in Viet Minh territory, moved through very thick jungle and undergrowth, skirting road blocks and trenches discovered on the back trails and roads. They came upon twenty Viet Minh accompanied by two Japanese in uniform, all armed with rifles or submachine-guns. Continuing south they laid in wait on a road and ambushed and captured one man. The patrol then split into two groups. Five hours later one group returned to the starting point, having moved about from midnight to 0500 in the morning. They reported "constant movement on the roads of armed bands often including women and much noise in the houses". The other small force reported much the same thing — the roads at night swarming with armed bands and a great deal of activity in houses and, in this case, a Cao Dai temple. On one occasion barking dogs nearby gave them away, but the patrol avoided villages and came to a bridge over which a Viet Minh patrol was passing. The Viet Minh were joined by another party, at which time Havildar Bagh Bahar's squad moved on, crossing a creek — this was now at the northern loop of the Song Cai, just east of Bien Hoa. At this point they heard a group approaching from the west, and took up ambush positions. The party approached to within 5 yards of the Havildar's squad when they realized that they were being observed, at which time they shouted *"Japani!"* The patrol were not taken in and opened fire, killing at least fifteen Viet Minh — including their prisoner who tried to escape in the confusion. The rest of the Viet Minh force, including some women, ran to a nearby village, from which they fired a few shots, and the 14/13th patrol went on to Bien Hoa, reporting to the battalion at 0715.

This well-executed patrol revealed the extent to which the Viet Minh owned the countryside at night — armed bands everywhere and roaming at will. But during Sherforce's final night out in the bush the parent battalion, the 14/13 FFR, had come under heavy attack from a strong Viet Minh force of at least battalion size. The first assault had hit the northeast sector of the Bien Hoa perimeter, which was held by D Company under Major T. B. Hunter, plus Jat machine-guns. The attack was opened by a heavy machine-gun firing explosive bullets, and this was the signal for simultaneous assaults on C Company, 14/13 FFR, under Major J. L. Stewart (on the river bridges) and a post under Jemadar Karim Dad of D Company (across the river and west of the bridge). The main attack was on the battalion's perimeter, where the Viet Minh, using all available cover, were aided by heavy supporting fire. The attack was finally beaten off by concentrated machine-gun fire, assisted by heavy mortar concentrations on the Viet Minh rear. The two other attacks, on C Company and Post RP3, were also beaten off, as were two attacks on Japanese positions at the jail and railway station. It was four hours before the Viet Minh withdrew — and an hour later Havildar Bagh Bahar's squad entered the lines.

Although the Viet Minh were unsuccessful in breaking through the 14/13th perimeter they had displayed sound planning in mounting five simultaneous attacks in the area. At 0645 14/13 FFR patrols swept the area around their perimeter and found nineteen bodies of Viet Minh soldiers — mainly Tonkinese, and including one woman — though it is highly probable that the total number of killed was greater. Also recovered were several rifles, grenades, bayonets, Bren magazines and nine Japanese helmets. At 1045 Brigadier Hirst, acting Division Commander, drove up and congratulated the 14/13th Commander on his battalion's performance during the night. Known Viet Minh killed (during the big attack and by the Havildar's ambush) on this morning came to thirty-four, but the figure was subsequently found to be much higher — it turned out that the 14/13th and the Jats had almost annihilated the Viet Minh attackers. On 5 January the Japanese captured a Tonkinese in the act of throwing a grenade at the Bien Hoa mental hospital. He revealed that he had been a member of the force of 700 (including 183 Tonkinese) who had assaulted the Bien Hoa perimeter on the 3rd. Of this force, no less than eighty had been killed and 200 wounded. The North Vietnamese prisoner claimed that they had suffered such severe losses because only 10 percent of them had possessed firearms. Although supported by four machine-guns and two mortars, most of the attackers were armed with knives and swords — good planning, but bad judgement! The real killing was done when the Viet Minh were caught in a crossfire by the Jat machine-guns. There were no 14/13 FFR or Jat casualties. Headquarters 100 Brigade reported that 14/13 FFR officers considered the figure of eighty Viet Minh killed "substantially correct". Two remaining hours of darkness had permitted the Viet Minh to remove most of the bodies. The 100 Brigade report stated that "the attack recklessly carried out came straight in on the cross fire of two Sec[tion]s MMGs [medium machine-guns] and the whole area was spattered with blood." A remnant of this force had been ambushed by Havildar Bagh Bahar's patrol and fifteen more were killed. Whatever the military wisdom of the operation the courage of the Viet Minh soldiers was beyond question, as Brain and Meiklereid noted in their political reports.

Meanwhile, the search for Japanese arms dumps continued, and it is highly probable that the Allies recovered only a small proportion of the huge arsenal of arms, ammunition, bombs, grenades, and other ordnance stockpiled by the Japanese in Indochina. There was no way of adequately accounting for Japanese equipment, as a report dated 16 December 1945 made clear. For example, in one report the Japanese claimed to have turned in 27,177 rifles, 1,134 machine-guns, 276,000 grenades, 610 wireless sets and 60,535,000 rounds of small arms ammunition. The British reported receiving 3,707 rifles, 148 machine guns, 65,000 grenades, fourteen wireless sets and 7,046,000 rounds of ammunition.

At this time Colonel de Guillebon (Chief of Staff French Forces in the Far East) wrote to Brigadier Hirst that the French agreed with the withdrawal of 80 Brigade on or about 15 January, and in view of operations to the north and east of Saigon concurrently with the arrival of the Madagascar Brigade, Leclerc would soon be forwarding plans for the relief of

100 Brigade. Brigadier Taunton's 80 Brigade units were given definite news of their standdown; the brigade was to be relieved of all commitments by 2/8 Punjab, 9 Jat, and the French at 1600 hours on 11 January. Thus the Kumaons, 23 Mountain Regiment, 3/1 GR and the Dogras were to be relieved of their various guard commitments on vital points such as the central jail, the Yokahama Specie Bank, the Japanese transmitter, Phu Tho airfield, artesian wells, the power house and Gracey's residence. The brewery was to be taken over by the French.

Things appeared to be going well enough for the French also to talk about the relief of 100 Brigade. They announced that they should have one mechanized cavalry squadron each in Bien Hoa and Thu Dau Mot by 15 January, which would permit a "progressive evacuation" of those places by 100 Brigade units. By the 20th they hoped to have been able to relieve 100 Brigade everywhere except in Thu Duc itself. Gracey penned a short comment on de Guillebon's letter which called for the relief of the Japanese battalions in Xuan Loc and Ben Cat before 100 Brigade could draw down.

Rodham's methods were now bearing fruit, for when 4/10 GR swept Binh Phu, west of Thu Duc, some locals pointed out the houses of pro-Viet Minh inhabitants. The houses were "suitably dealt with" by the Gurkhas, and two Viet Minh flags and a number of documents were captured. In Khanh Hoi, the 3/1 Gurkhas engaged four boats carrying a party of Vietnamese attempting to land on the eastern tip of the island at night. One boat escaped, but the remaining three were captured and their twelve occupants killed in the water.

Gracey was now requested to issue a statement simultaneously with a similar one by Admiral d'Argenlieu. It said that France would henceforth assume the task of maintaining order in Southern French Indochina, except for certain defined zones containing Japanese armed forces, and that although British and Indian troops were withdrawing from the country some would remain to guard the disarmed Japanese.[1]

One-third of Gracey's Division left the parent body on 4 January when a terse message from ALFSEA to ALFFIC announced that at noon on the 5th, 32 Indian Infantry Brigade "ceases to be under command 20 Ind Div and comes under command HQ ALFSEA for all purposes."

In Vietnam, the tempo of military activity by the French quickened

---

1. See Mountbatten's Section E of the Report to the Combined Chiefs of Staff for the relevant information, pronouncements etc. on this period.

perceptibly. They killed fifty Viet Minh in operations just 2 km. north of Thu Dau Mot; Colonel Massu's column was slicing through the area southeast of Saigon, and thirty-one more Viet Minh were killed around Ban Me Thuot. There were heavy engagements in several other places, notably in Tay Ninh, Can Tho and Mytho. In the Travinh area of the Delta the French had the unusual experience of being petitioned by one group of rebels for protection against another group of rebels. Officers on the warship *Gazelle* were asked to help 3,000 Vietnamese being attacked by the Viet Minh. Ironically, the boat carrying the petitioners was flying a Viet Minh flag. This was probably a Hoa Hao group seeking assistance against communist attacks.

The French lost no time in integrating their new air support capability into their repacification operations. Rodham's 100 Brigade, in an operations plan, reported scheduled French Spitfire ground attack sorties as early as 7 January 1946. This particular order dealt with comprehensive French operations throughout the Inner Zone, with French Spitfires tasked to bomb and strafe a number of areas including An Hoa and up to the west bank of the Saigon River, and the hook of land formed by the Saigon River around An Loc Dong (1 km. north of Han Phu and about 4 km. north of Go Vap). The RAF had by now practically ceased all tactical operations, and even the daily Spitfire tactical reconnaissance sorties had been discontinued on 8 January 1946. Rodham's forces were to act as stops, but they were covering a large area — a line running from south of Lai Thieu to a bridge just west of Thu Dau Mot. French columns and naval craft were driving in to this area, including Lieutenant-Colonel Sizaire' force coming down Route Coloniale 13 from Ben Cat towards Thu Dau Mot. The Japanese were not given advance warning of the operations. A dawn sweep by the French through the western outskirts of Thu Duc resulted in two Viet Minh killed and twenty-five suspects detained. The French, apparently acting on solid intelligence, had picked up two known Viet Minh agents, the Viet Minh secretary for Thu Duc, two members of the force which had attacked Bien Hoa on 3 January, and a man known to have murdered several Frenchmen before the Viet Minh "uprising".

In French operations northwest of Thu Dau Mot during 6 to 8 January three columns had converged on Thanh Phu. They accounted for 150 Viet Minh killed and forty captured. In the past week the Viet Minh had suffered serious losses, and the outlook for them in the Inner Zone was grim as the French were rapidly gaining strength and becoming more familiar with the new type of warfare in Indochina. A 20

Indian Division historian wrote that the French were moving steadily southwards, and the road from Saigon to Phnom Penh had been opened. Ban Me Thuot, in the highlands, had been occupied and the surrounding Darlac plateau cleared. With the exception of the east coast, the disintegration of the Viet Minh armed forces appeared complete. Remnants of these forces had joined together in places to form guerrilla bands and would be likely to present a threat to law and order. The Viet Minh still remained active around Bien Hoa, despite the costly defeats they had recently suffered in the area, and "jitter parties" continued to probe the 14/13 FFR lines, firing submachine-guns and rifles, and throwing grenades.

Gracey now told Leclerc that while he generally agreed with the proposed schedule of relief for 100 Brigade, there were still two Japanese battalions under operational control of 100 Brigade: Sato *butai* of 500 men at Xuan Loc and Yamagishi *butai*, also of 500 men, at Ben Cat. He considered the early relief of these units "a matter of first priority" so that they could be concentrated at Cap St Jacques (Vungtau). They had performed well hitherto, but since the rest of the Japanese armed forces had been disarmed, it would not be wise to rely for long on their continued operational efficiency. Gracey then suggested that "the first troops which you may have available should be used for the relief of these Japanese, and that after that has been completed the relief of 100 Bde (except Thu Duc) should continue." Gracey also brought up the problem of the relief of Japanese guards on vital points. Over 100 VPs of all kinds were (as of 8 January) still being guarded by 3,224 Japanese soldiers, 2,490 of them armed. Gracey wanted to keep the Japanese guards on his lines of communication, for "The rebels are always attempting to destroy bridges on this road and guards on these VPs are essential until my troops are withdrawn."

In Bien Hoa, the Japanese units were evidently less than enthusiastic about their role as Anglo-French allies, and Colonel Miyake, their commander, was called in to talk to the 14/13th Commander, Lieutenant-Colonel Gates, because a recent inspection of Japanese posts on the important "All Red Route" by Major Wenham and a Japanese liaison Officer revealed "discipline slack and men untidy". Some posts were deserted, and the commanders of others were absent. Local purchase orders were being disobeyed, and post garrisons were sharing houses with Vietnamese, "a procedure to which the Comd strongly objected". Gates had further cause for complaint regarding "co-operation of Japanese forces with the Annamites". Sato *butai*, in Xuan Loc, had captured four important Viet Minh prisoners. However, "No report was given until an explanation was asked for by the Comd himself. By this time the prisoners had been released and a doubtful story was forwarded from Sato Butai that they had escaped."[2] Miyake was ordered to go out and inspect Japanese posts on the "All Red Route" and to censure Major Sato; but Gates was not yet finished. In the big night attack on 3 January, when the Japanese on Bien Hoa railway station were attacked, two of the Japanese light machine-guns had broken down. "Colonel Miyake was informed that these guns should *not* break down. In addition the Japanese garrison at the station only fired when they thought they were being attacked." The French had also complained of bridges being cut near Japanese posts. Gates told Miyake that poor Japanese units would be the last to be sent home to Japan; also that General Gracey would be informed that he was not cooperating fully and that the discipline of the Japanese Army in this area was poor. In order to strengthen Miyake's authority, the British handed his sword back to him.

For Gracey and his Division, their stay in Vietnam was thankless and unwelcome. His troops were not yet allowed — for political reasons — to receive the decorations which the French wanted to bestow on them, and Gracey wrote that the apparent apathy at Headquarters ALFSEA over the matter of French awards for 20 Division troops was producing a feeling of slight resentment in the ranks. He realized the difficulties, but d'Argenlieu and Leclerc wanted personally to present some decorations to Gracey's troops before their departure. He also expressed his disappointment at the decision to send 20 Division headquarters and troops to Malaya, saying that the splitting of the Division gave rise to "rumours of dissolution", which he wanted to suppress. If General Dempsey could outline 20 Division's future task in Malaya, with the possibility of regaining command of 32 and 80 Brigades, then Gracey could "quieten fears which I hope are quite unfounded."

Gracey's Division — his own creation — was slowly falling away form him, as on 10 January the 114th Field Regiment, Royal Artillery (the only British troops in Vietnam excepting the RAF and RN — the rest were Indian) left for Malaya. They were followed two days later by the 16th Light Cavalry (minus C Squadron) and their armored cars. So, except for 23 Mountain Regiment, Gracey now had no heavy firepower

2.   PRO, WO 172/10272, War Diary 14/13 FFR, Conference Minutes, 7 Jan. 1946.

left to him, and the loss of 16 Cavalry meant that Rodham was now effectively stripped of his ability to mount strong and fast preemptive sweeps through suspected Viet Minh areas. On the 11th, Taunton's advance party from 80 Brigade flew to Makassar (Celebes) as 80 Brigade itself was relieved of all commitments by the French and stood down. Responsibility for the shrinking British sector in the Saigon area itself was assumed by Brigadier Hendriks and 555 Sub Area, with forces composed of 2/8 Punjab and the Jat machine-gun battalion.

A week later Gracey received a response to his query about decorations for his soldiers; the philosophy was contained in a note from SACSEA to Browning. Mountbatten was against an Anglo-French parade at which French medals were to be given to the British. This "may well give the Hearst press[3] and the many pro-Annamite and pro-Indonesian journalists the chance to say that the French were publicly rewarding British soldiers for having put them back into FIC by force." It was hard to see how the handing out of a few medals (which could have been done quietly) to brave privates, corporals and sergeants would alter world opinion while senior officers, like Mountbatten himself, were being covered with foreign decorations.

Gracey accepted the premise that the French would not be able to relieve all Japanese troops before the departure of 100 Brigade, but he was standing firm on his insistence that the two remaining active Japanese infantry battalions (Sato and Yamagishi *butais*) be relieved concurrently with the standing down of 100 Brigade. Gracey now informed Dempsey of the proposed French relief of 100 Brigade units. Rodham's task would then be to command British troops in Indochina for a short time, until the Inter-Service Mission took over. In Saigon itself, 2/8 Punjab was charged with guarding the Mission and jail; one battalion (9/12 FFR) was in Cap St Jacques. The future of 20 Division was still uncertain, although only two weeks remained before Gracey was to leave Saigon, and a little over three weeks before 20 Division headquarters was due to depart. On the 12th Dempsey wrote to Gracey about "the future of your Division". He said that 20 Division would be concentrated in Malaya under Gracey, then would eventually return to India like the

---

3. Gracey Papers, 18 Jan. 1946. Mountbatten's criticism of the American press was well founded. The *Chicago Tribune,* for example, had described British retaliatory action against an Indonesian village, whose inhabitants had butchered British/Indian soldiers in a plane which had crash-landed nearby, as "another Lidice". American soldiers were later to suffer similar treatment from their own press reporting of the Vietnam war.

other Divisions. Meanwhile 100 Brigade would have to remain in Indo-china, 32 Brigade was in Borneo, and 80 Brigade would be in Makassar (under 15 Corps) for an undetermined length of time. He hoped that Gracey would not have to go to Makassar with a small headquarters.

Rodham now wrote that "The move of British Tps ex FIC has been speeded up," and "This entails a redistribution of 20 Div Tps in FIC." Furthermore, "The majority if not all of the Jap guards on rubber dumps, installations, VPs, bridges, etc. in Thu Dau Mot and Bien Hoa Sub-Areas are being abandoned and *not* taken over by the French," but Japanese guards in the new Thu Duc Sub-Area were to remain for the present. Rodham described the overall relief plan in an Operational Order to his units; in the Order he announced that the relief of 100 Brigade would be carried out in two phases. Phase I was the relief of Thu Dau Mot sub area "in conjunction with a combined British/French sweep through the whole of 100 Bde area between Saigon R and the Dong Nai R;" Phase II was the relief of the Bien Hoa Sub-Area and the move of Brigade headquarters to Saigon.

The exact date on which command of French forces was to pass to the French was now published: it was to be 28 January, the date of Gracey's departure from Vietnam. There were to be three phases for the with-drawal of 20 Division. Brigadier Hirst was to command all British troops in Vietnam from Gracey's departure until 7 February, when command would pass to Brigadier Maunsell, who would be directly under ALFSEA. Maunsell was to have under him a force not quite equivalent to a brigade in strength. So determined were the British to disengage that it was announced that all Japanese guards were to be withdrawn by 23 January "whether or *not* the French take over the gds." The French were heavily involved everywhere. In mid-January twenty Viet Minh were killed in Gia Dinh, which till recently had been relatively quiet under 9/14 Punjab. The extent of the Viet Minh hold on the countryside was noted in a 4/10 GR report which stated that in a number of villages only women, children and old men could be found.

It was now decided that Sato *butai* would go from Xuan Loc directly to Cap St Jacques, bypassing Thu Duc British Sector. The French, as they passed through Xuan Loc, were to hand Sato a written order from Brigadier Rodham to this effect. As planned earlier, Yamagishi *butai* was to come through Thu Duc for disarming, then proceed to Saigon, to raise the Japanese 2nd Division labor pool to 6,000. General Manaki was to remain in Thu Duc for the time being.

80 Brigade's departure from Vietnam was approaching. On 14

January it ceremonially handed over to the French at a parade commanded by Brigadier Taunton, the pipes and drums of 4/17 Dogra playing the General Salute for the brigade's march past Gracey and Leclerc. The first of the two RAF tactical squadrons left Vietnam at about this time, as the first two Mosquitoes were flown from Saigon to Bangkok on the 12th. A large proportion of 684 Squadron's supplies were flown out by the "Gremlin Task Force" (of which more will be said). In the Saigon-Cholon area itself the British zone shrank to an area encompassing the Colonial Artillery barracks and the race course, so that there were now three main British areas of responsibility in Vietnam: Thu Duc British Sector, the Saigon-Cholon area, and Cap St Jacques (Vungtau). Gracey wrote to Dempsey about the final departure plans. He mentioned that Leclerc had been given a promise that the last British brigade would leave Vietnam only on the arrival of the whole French Expeditionary Force. Gracey said that in view of this "he [Leclerc] will stick his toes in probably. I think I can come to a compromise with him whereby I leave approximately two battalions and some service troops here to carry out the spirit if not the letter of the agreement."[4] Dempsey agreed that the promise should be kept, and backed Gracey's plan, to which Leclerc agreed.

A report by Meiklereid described how a number of French soldiers were complaining that they had been brought to Indochina under false pretences. They claimed that they had been told that their purpose was to fight the Japanese, but instead they found themselves fighting Annamite *maquis*. Although a better type of French soldier was now arriving, indiscipline was still in evidence; the crime rate had soared and the courts were swamped.

By the end of January nearly 54,000 Japanese had been disarmed and concentrated. The British Foreign Secretary, in a parliamentary reply, stated that British casualties from the breach of the truce in mid-October to 13 January amounted to forty killed, 110 wounded and five missing. Vietnamese casualties came to 2,756 killed — 1,565 by French forces, 641 by the British and 550 by the Japanese.

The now-famous Dogra pipes and drums played before the citizens of Saigon for the last time on the 21st, as the Battalion and other 80 Brigade units marched from the Annamite barracks past the familiar red cathedral and down Rue Catinat (Tu-Do) to the waiting ship. On the 22nd the *Orduna*, bound for Makassar via Singapore, sailed slowly and majestically

4. Gracey Papers, Gracey to Dempsey, 22 Jan. 1946.

down the Saigon River — until it got about 10 miles downriver from Saigon, when it got stuck on a mudbank. The next morning, the *Orduna* was piped off the mudbank by the Dogra band, and passing Cap St Jacques a party of 9/12 FFR came alongside to wave farewell to the Brigade.

Gracey now wrote to Dempsey, saying that the 20 Division Engineers were "dithering over [the] handover of stores [to the French]'', due to "lack of direction from ALFSEA''. He had therefore told his Engineers to go ahead and hand over the stores immediately. At the same time he informed ALFSEA of the proposed order of battle of British forces remaining under Maunsell. On the 24th, the next day, ALFSEA issued orders for the departure of 20 Division's main headquarters, who were to leave on the *Sefton* no later than 28 January. Even at this late date there was no firm destination given for 20 Division, but it was now believed to be India.

While the role of the British was reduced, and the Viet Minh now appeared to leave them alone, the fighting between the Viet Minh and French was getting worse and casualties were heavy. Amazingly, the Japanese were still inflicting casualties on the Viet Minh: on the 19th a patrol from Thu Duc had surprised a Viet Minh party attempting to block the Thu Duc-Bien Hoa road. The Viet Minh were dispersed and suffered at least one killed.

Three days before Gracey's departure from Vietnam, he was informed by Mountbatten that the British Chiefs of Staff had now decided that the French could assume the task of guarding Japanese surrendered personnel in the southern half of Indochina. There was thus no official reason for any British troops to remain in Vietnam. Gracey was told to press the French to take over this responsibility as soon as possible and no later than the end of February. The Japanese were then to receive their orders directly from the French. Mountbatten wrote that his only remaining direct responsibility concerning the surrendered Japanese in Indochina was to supply what maintenance the French might initially be unable to provide, and to provide shipping for the repatriation of the Japanese to Japan.

On the 26th Gracey's neadquarters published the final plan for the withdrawal of 20 Division. Headquarters ALFFIC and Main Headquarters 20 Indian Division were to close at 0001 hours on 28 January, when command of all British troops in French Indochina would pass to Rear Headquarters 20 Division. Rear Headquarters was scheduled to close at 0001 on 7 February, when command of British forces would pass to Brigadier Maunsell and the Inter-Service Mission. A draft of Mount-batten's four-page directive to Maunsell was sent to London on 28 January. Maunsell's two infantry battalions were not to be used for fighting except in two eventualities: against mutinous Japanese or if British lives were in danger. Since the equipping of the French 3rd DIC was a British responsibility, Maunsell was directed to report twice monthly on its progress. The "SACSEA Inter-Service Mission" was to be officially formed on 28 January, the date of Gracey's departure from Saigon. Dempsey had recently denied Gracey's request to fly straight home to India from Saigon, saying that there were reasons "which make it desirable that you come to Singapore on 28 Jan as originally planned. You will stay a night or two here then go direct from Singapore to India."[5]

On the 28th, Gracey issued his final report, titled "Notes on Overall Situation in FIC". He stated that d'Argenlieu would have overall command of French forces from 28 January, the Army being com-manded by Leclerc, the Navy by Auboyneau, and the Air Force by Andrea (*sic*). Except for "odd bands of desperate characters", there was no organized resistance left in the south and southwest of Saigon. Japan-ese armed detachments remained in Dalat (three battalions) and Nha Trang (one and a half battalions) to safeguard the French, and these would soon be relieved by the French, so that except for a few rifles for local protection all Japanese forces in Southern Indochina would have then been disarmed. Although there were now three concentration areas for the Japanese (Navy in Thu Dau Mot, working parties and technicians in Saigon, all others at Cap St Jacques), all should be concentrated in Cap St Jacques by late February. Most important to Gracey was the fact that it was "Apparent that French policy is now being more clearly linked with French military action. General tendency to show by practical mea-sures that policy will be sincerely carried out." This was helped by "(*a*) Disgust of majority local Annamites at Viet-Minh army brutality and terrorism, (*b*) Better discipline of troops, (*c*) Better tactics used by French troops and (*d*) Steady establishment of French Administration and police." Under "How We Can Assist French", Gracey wrote "Start, even a trickle, repatriation of Japanese." The propaganda and psycho-logical warfare aspects should be emphasized, and "Brutalities com-mitted by Viet-Minh forces against their own people should be men-tioned whenever they occur." These measures "will greatly assist SEAC

5.  Gracey Papers, Cipher 2555, 23 Jan. 1946.

in my opinion, as the easier we make the French task in Northern FIC, the quicker will we be able to leave the French entirely to it." Gracey reported that the Japanese were "dreading" being taken over by the French; they expected the French to treat them very harshly and withhold their rations. Gracey had reassured the Japanese on these points. He closed his report by saying that he expected little or no trouble, but thought that Leclerc would put off as long as possible the assumption of control of the Japanese.

Before he left Saigon, the French accorded Gracey a singular honor. In a ceremony in the City Hall he was presented with a scroll and made a *Citoyen d'Honneur* of Saigon — equivalent to the freedom of the city. This was the first time in the eighty or so years that the municipal government of Saigon had existed that any man had been so honored. In a response to Gracey's inquiry, Mountbatten (reflecting the Foreign Office view) said that he had no objection to his receiving the title of *Citoyen d'Honneur* from the people of Saigon, but for obvious political reasons his directive must not be prejudiced in any way. In a message to Gracey, Browning wrote that "However distasteful it may be to you, you should stress, if asked by the press, that this is a mark of personal esteem for you on giving up your association with the French and should not be construed as a national gesture." Meiklereid, who had a high opinion of Gracey, had returned from Singapore on the 27th and impressed upon the French that it was necessary "for political reasons" to confine the ceremony to a personal tribute to General Gracey — nothing must transpire which "might in any way embarrass the General on the eve of his departure from Indo-China." The French agreed, and the *Préfet's* speech had to be rewritten at the last minute. Meiklereid told the Foreign Office that the French population "consider that they owe their personal safety to him [Gracey] and his troops," and spoke of the "great success achieved by General Gracey in carrying out the mission with which he was entrusted."[6]

Large crowds cheered Gracey, who was popular and highly regarded by almost everyone, as he entered the City Hall accompanied by his wife. He was greeted by Jean Cédile, and the Mayor spoke. "No one will ever forget the feeling of exuberance which greeted the arrival of the first Dakotas bringing the advance elements of the Allied Commission," he

6. PRO, FO 371/53959, Meiklereid to Foreign Office, 1 Feb. 1946. The Labour Government in London refused to authorise decorations for Gracey's troops who had been killed and wounded on this unpopular mission.

said; this arrival brought Saigon's four-year nightmare to an end, within a few months of the liberation of the mother country, and renewed relations with the "world of free men, amongst whom those of Free England are the most dear to the hearts of Frenchmen. . . ." Gracey replied in French, saying that he accepted the honor on behalf of the British, Indian and Gurkha troops he had the honor to command in French Indochina. He concluded, "I am pleased to take the opportunity of this occasion to thank all those who helped the British, Indian, and Allied POWs both before and after the unconditional surrender of the Japanese. Never shall we forget what you did for them, especially those of you who at the risk of your own lives gave shelter to our escaped comrades in danger."[7] (Not long after, Numata conveyed Terauchi's appreciation of the "fair and courteous manner" in which Gracey had conducted affairs in Indochina.) When Gracey left after the ceremony to shouts of "*Vive* Gracey!", the British involvement in Vietnam, for all practical purposes, came to an end.

The following day, in Singapore, Gracey attended Mountbatten's 311th Meeting, during which Indochina was the topic of discussion. Mountbatten "expressed his very high appreciation of the way in which Major-General Gracey had carried out a very difficult task as Head of the Control Commission in French Indochina. He wished to add his tribute to the gratitude which had already been expressed by Admiral d'Argenlieu and Lieutenant-General Leclerc." The Chiefs of Staff had agreed to SACSEA's proposal that French Indochina south of the 16th parallel should be withdrawn from SEAC on Gracey's departure (with the temporary exclusion of the Cap St Jacques area). Mountbatten thought that the US Chiefs of Staff would raise objections to his relinquishing command in Indochina to the French, and since at least six weeks had elapsed since he had suggested doing this, it was possible that the US Chiefs did indeed object. Mr Brain thought that "the only explanation . . . was that the Americans did not wish to associate themselves with the idea of handing over the Annamites to the control of the French."

7. Gracey had presented Japanese swords to dozens of French men and women who had helped Allied prisoners and escapees over the years. Three days before he left he held a ceremony, with 100 Brigade troops as a Guard of Honor, during which he presented Madame Bétaille with a check for a sizeable sum of money from a grateful British Government. Her husband had been executed by the Japanese for running an escape route which had saved a number of Allied lives (including American aircrews).

The British presence in Vietnam was still needed, apart from anything else, for the administration of the French 3rd Colonial Infantry Division. As the French had not officially made known their views on the necessity for the Inter-Service Mission, Mountbatten set forth his own ideas. He would not accept the idea of the British quietly folding their tents and slipping away from Saigon now that the area was secure. He directed Maunsell to tell the French as tactfully as possible that if they dismissed the Mission, the Supreme Allied Commander would withdraw their vital logistical support. Furthermore, as the British had ''cleared FIC for them by force of arms, . . . our Mission was not to be a 'hole and corner' affair or 'here on sufferance'.''

It was generally accepted that Anglo-French relations were at their best at this point, and would probably not be as good again. Although the French were anxious to reassert themselves as completely as possible, they were having difficulties in recruiting and keeping Vietnamese labor. They could not have kept vital installations like the docks and the power plant operating without British help, and were in the uncomfortable position of wanting the British to leave but not being able to afford to see them go. On the last day of January, what little role the RAF still had in Vietnam ended with the disbandment of 273 Squadron (Spitfire). As early as 7 December they had been sharing their ground support equipment, generators etc. with the French, whose own Spitfires had begun to arrive from France in mid-December. The French were now masters of their own destiny, at least in Southern Indochina.

# 17

# THE END OF THE BEGINNING

With Gracey gone, command of British troops in Vietnam passed to Brigadier Hirst. On 2 February a schedule was published which outlined the program of relief of British and Japanese Army troops by French and Japanese Naval units. For the British, the main points were the relief on 5 February of 4/10 GR (Thu Duc), one company 2/8 Punjab (Tan Son Nhut) and one company MG Jat (Phu Tho petrol depot). These units were to be relieved by the French Army, but all depended on the arrival of French troops on the *Cameronia*, due in on the 4th. Japanese troops at the Phu Tho petrol depot were to remain in place.

As for the rest of the Japanese Army, all detachments on guard duties in the Thu Dau Mot/Bien Hoa/Thu Duc area were to be withdrawn by noon on 4 February for movement to Cap St Jacques, where they were to be disarmed on the 5th. These Army units were to be replaced by Japanese Naval units under French Army command, and would receive their arms from the Army units they replaced. Of the two Japanese infantry battalions, Yamagishi *butai* (down to company strength in Ben Cat) was to be relieved by the Japanese Navy on the 7th while the stronger Sato *butai* would remain in Xuan Loc until the 15th. Both Japanese battalions were to make their own way to Cap St Jacques for disarming and de-piastering by 9/12 FFR. All Japanese in Cambodia were now ordered to proceed there immediately. The situation at Cap St Jacques was curious in that this was the one place where the British and Viet Minh were still getting along fairly well. Regular meetings were held between 9/12 FFR and the local Viet Minh leaders, at whose request the British had arranged to transport more salt to the area. However, as the 9/12th historian wrote, "a growing complication was the arrival of the French . . ."[1]

Mountbatten returned to Saigon a few days after Gracey's departure, and on 2 February held a meeting at Tan Son Nhut, attended by Maunsell, Meiklereid, and four other officers. Maunsell reported that the local situation reflected a change of policy coming from Paris: the French attitude was "Now that Gracey is gone, let us make it FIC and not

---

1. W. E. H. Condon, *The History of the Frontier Force Regiment* (Aldershot: Gale and Polden, 1962), p. 512.

Anglo-FIC.'' Mountbatten "said that his fear had always been that there would be incidents for which he would have been blamed.'' Maunsell drew Mountbatten's attention to the press, who were eagerly looking for evidence of French atrocities against the Vietnamese. The sooner the British got out, he thought, the better. To SACSEA's query, Maunsell reported that the "French advance by road was moving very quickly to the 16th parallel, which would be reached in two or three months, but he felt that an overall clearance of FIC would take up to three years.'' Again in reply to Mountbatten, Maunsell stated that French troops could not get to Hanoi before 1 March. The French wanted to take over responsibility for the Japanese on 20 or 25 February, "which will make the retention of all British forces, apart from the Mission, unnecessary.'' Mountbatten asked if the French still wanted the Mission, to which Maunsell replied that "they had not shown their hands yet . . . but that it would be necessary for the administration of the French 3rd Division.'' It was at this point that the Supreme Commander stated that the Mission would not be a "hole and corner affair''. Maunsell then said that there had been "a tremendous send-off for Major-General Gracey'', adding that "General Gracey had even been complimented by the Annamites.''

For the Mission, there were only small arms left in Vietnam on the 5th, since the last British guns had gone when the 23rd Mountain Regiment (Indian Artillery) sailed on the *Dunera* for Singapore. The *Dunera* passed the *Cameronia*, inbound with French reinforcements — their arrival meant that the third and last British brigade could depart. The *Cameronia* docked in Saigon on the 6th, with 3,391 French troops on board, and two days later Rodham's hard-working 100 Brigade headquarters embarked.[2] Their last week had been taken up with handing over paperwork to Maunsell's Mission. The next day, Rear Headquarters 20 Indian Division and Headquarters 100 Brigade sailed for India and disbandment, but not oblivion: they had left as a legacy a foundation of security on which the French now had to build.

In February the Foreign Office received a report on financial manipulations in Indochina by the Japanese; they had done the same throughout their areas of occupation. The report was compiled by Lieutenant-Colonel Sweeny, Gracey's Financial Adviser on the Control Commis-

---

2. In January 6,292 British/Indian troops left Vietnam, followed by 5,638 in February. Mountbatten's original plan had been to put 100 Brigade under French command, but had changed his mind when faced with the strenuous objections of General Auchinleck and the Viceroy of India, Lord Wavell.

sion. His had been an arduous and seemingly impossible task, hampered by falsified records and uncooperative witnesses, but his investigative work succeeded in clarifying the extent of these manipulations. In his summation Meiklereid told the Foreign Office that a "considerable sum, estimated at 200 million piasters in South FIC and 75 million piasters in North FIC, has gone to ground."[3] The Japanese "Economic Co-Operation Association" had met regularly in the former British consular residence in Saigon, and in fact had been in session when the building was bombed in February 1945 — the members were killed.

Regarding South Indochina, two of a list of thirteen areas of expenditure were "likely to prove dangerous" — these concerned items 5 (work on fortifications and supplies) and 13 (normal maintenance). Some firms had been passing "large sums" on to third parties before closing up business following the Japanese defeat. Up to 200 million piasters had "gone to ground" under these two items alone: "The money in the whole of FIC that may be available for undesirable use should not exceed 275,000,000 piasters. . . . It seems likely that a large number of the 500-piaster notes declared illegal recently have found their way from South FIC to Hanoi and may strengthen the forces opposing French reoccupation of North FIC."[4] Sweeny traced Japanese expenditures in Indochina from 1941 to 1945: 57,210,188 piasters in 1941, 85,607,019 in 1942, 119,227,320 in 1943, 359,836,910 in 1944, and 935,667,000 in 1945. The revised figures for the rise in fiduciary issue in French Indochina were as follows. In August 1939, notes in issue totalled 186,206,000 piasters. In November 1941, after the entry of the Japanese, they amounted to 338,865,000 piasters. On 9 March 1945, the day of the Japanese *coup*, the total had leaped to 1,548,287,000, and by 30 August 1945, when printing stopped, it was 2,349,543,000. It was thought that the French in Hanoi had smashed the printing plates at the time of the Japanese surrender. General Numata claimed that the greatly increased expenses in 1945 were due to the decision to turn Indochina into a strongly fortified zone and the supply base for Southeast Asia in a fight to the last. During the last nine months before the surrender, the Japanese had withdrawn nearly a billion piasters — 256,147,000 on 14 August

3. GB, PRO, FO 371/53959, 19 Jan. 1946; also FO 371/53459.
4. Louis Allen expressed reservations about Meiklereid's assertion that the Japanese passed on large sums of money to the Viet Minh, but wrote, "I agree there's more to be known about Japanese funding of Vietnamese organizations, and I sometimes suspect I may have let the evidence slip through my fingers in 1946 . . . but it isn't *very* likely . . ." See also Appendix to this chapter.

alone — of which a large sum had gone to Hanoi.

What the Japanese failed to tell Sweeny was that on 23 August 1945 they had advanced six months' pay to all ranks, amounting to some 16 million piasters, yet on 17 November Terauchi had requested the release of 41 million piasters to cover the pay of his troops from 15 October to 31 December 1945. As Sweeny mentioned, "The sum would have covered fourteen months' pay and they had already been paid up to February 14, 1946!" Among other things, the six months' advance caused a steep rise in black market prices during September.

It was not until almost the end of November that the British were in a position to get access to Japanese assets, the value of which came to just 58,930,573 piasters. As the Control Commission tightened its hold on Japanese accounts, so Japanese expenditure dropped. In September this had totalled 17,000,000, in October 15,000,000, and in November 13,000,000. The British had full control by December, when it plummeted to 4,500,000 piasters; it was forecast that it would be 3,500,000 in January and remain at 3,000,000 per month thereafter. Japanese firms in Indochina represented many different manufacturing industries and services. Over 100,000,000 piasters had been paid to these firms *after* the Japanese headquarters knew that Tokyo was asking for peace terms. Nearly all of this had passed to third parties and disappeared. There is more to Sweeny's report, but it seems clear that Ho Chi Minh and the Viet Minh may not have established the Democratic Republic of Vietnam as destitutes, despite their failure to seize the Bank of Indochina in Hanoi. As well as these not insignificant sums of money, they inherited a large quantity of Japanese arms and ordnance so that there can be little doubt that the Japanese left them in a moderately sound position — certainly, having been supported by both the Americans and the Japanese, they were more fortunate than some revolutionaries.

In Cochinchina, French Marines came to Cap St Jacques on the 10th, and presumably British/Viet Minh conferences ceased at this time. The Japanese High Command enforced a standard of discipline among their troops to the end. Senior Japanese officers constantly visited their forces, both in the concentration areas and in the field, where they were still armed. On 28 January, the day of Gracey's departure, Numata, who was on an inspection trip throughout the vast area of Japanese Southern Army, had a talk with Dempsey in Singapore. Dempsey asked him to be completely candid in describing Field-Marshal Terauchi's condition: was he really in charge or did he command in name only? Numata said that Terauchi now spent most of his time convalescing near the sea at Cap St

Jacques, and while his health had not improved, at least it was getting no worse. He suggested making General Itagaki the Deputy Supreme Commander under Terauchi, and, despite misgivings over Itagaki's militaristic past, this was done. Numata said that Itagaki's appointment to that position would be accepted by the Demobilization Ministry (formerly the War Ministry) in Tokyo. On Itagaki's elevation, Numata (whose specific statements were "off the record" and not included in the SEAC report) thought that Terauchi's headquarters could be moved to Singapore. He also said that it was Terauchi's wish to remain in the theater of war in which he had fought, and not return to Japan too soon.

On the 15th it was Air Commodore Cheshire's turn to hand over, as RAF headquarters, French Indochina, was disbanded — for the RAF only No. 2 Staging Post remained actively employed at Tan Son Nhut.[5] With the British presence reduced to just two battalions, Leclerc was beginning to show signs of the increased burdens which had now fallen on his shoulders. This was illustrated in a report from Meiklereid to the Foreign Office, in which he described Leclerc's reaction to an article by a minor new weekly periodical, *Justice*, organ of the "Section Socialists" of Saigon. It normally had only a small circulation except among party members, but on 12 February its front-page leader was titled "Pacification". This was a "violent criticism" of the French Army, which was called too brutal, undisciplined, and so on. The article at first caused little

5. Air Commodore Cheshire later provided an account of his employment of the Japanese Air Force — the "Gremlin Task Force" (GTF) referred to in the log of 684 Squadron. Wrote Cheshire at the start, "When Air Command Headquarters at Kandy detailed me for this appointment they were extremely vague about the duties and responsibilities involved, and this lack of positive instructions was further emphasized when the Staff invited me to write my own directive. . . ."

The Japanese Air Force Commander seemed pleased at being assigned an operational role, which was confined to "transport" and unarmed reconnaissance duties only. Cheshire noted, "Experience in operations showed that once their aircraft were offered a task, there were few technical failures."

The Gremlin Task Force with RAF markings undertook a variety of assignments, and their major role in moving 684 Squadron to Bangkok was their big operation: "In the short period of their existence they had successfully completed over 2,000 sorties. By the standard of later massive operations, such as the Berlin airlift, this was small beer, but it had usefully filled an unavoidable gap in our logistic operation, and did so at little cost to the British Treasury."

These Japanese aircraft had proved extremely useful to both British and French Army Commanders, for much of their pre-operations reconnaissance was done in GTF aircraft. (Air Chief Marshal Sir Walter G. Cheshire, letter to author, 16 Nov. 1977.)

comment, as the paper's political background was well known, but much to everyone's surprise Leclerc chose to respond to it. On the 14th he spoke to a large crowd outside the High Commissioner's palace (in d'Argenlieu's absence he was acting High Commissioner). He said that the reason for his address was attacks by the local press on his troops, and the Army were not going to let their flag be besmirched without replying. He went on to summarize French successes despite difficulties with the rebels and the type of war they had been fighting. Meiklereid thought it worth noting that his delivery — normally clear and precise, since Leclerc was an excellent extempore speaker — was now halting, and he constantly glanced at a sheaf of notes in his hand. A French businessman later said that the audience were embarrassed.

The United States, which had sided with the Communists in their bid for power in Vietnam, now expressed concern that the colonial powers — whom the Americans had sometimes treated as pariahs — were not comfortable in their role as scapegoat. The British Cabinet had had enough, and having (like the French) met US opposition in Southeast Asia, refused to consider an American request that Indochina remain in South East Asia Command: "We appreciate, however, that it is unlikely that we shall get the Americans to agree to our point of view now [that the French and Dutch take responsibility for their own territories], and as an interim measure we would agree to an arrangement whereby Admiral Mountbatten hands over to the French full responsibility for Southern French Indo-China. This arrangement would avoid the necessity of Leclerc dealing direct with SCAP."[6] Mountbatten affirmed that at midnight 4/5 March a public announcement was to be made to the effect that French Indochina would pass completely to French control, except for SACSEA's "continued responsibility as SCAP's representative for matters directly concerned with the repatriation of the Japanese".[7] The Japanese were concentrated in four general areas in the Cap St Jacques/Baria area, and 9 FFR divided its area of responsibility into five sectors: Baria North, Xa Bang, Baria East, Long Hai, and Cap St Jacques; companies were to "organize at least two patrols a week" in every sector except Cap St Jacques, which would be patrolled locally under battalion arrangements. In other words, the Japanese were left pretty much to themselves and their own officers. Brigadier Maunsell reported that the French (d'Argenlieu and Leclerc) were in complete

---

6. PRO, WO 203/5026, Cabinet to SACSEA, No. 873, 26 Feb. 1946.
7. See PRO, WO 203/5556, Comd 32, 3 Mar. 1946.

agreement with the proposed handover of responsibility.

The French assumed responsibility for Japanese administration on 15 March 1946. Leclerc travelled to Haiphong to facilitate the entry of French forces to Tonkin. He returned to Saigon on 25 March and saw Maunsell the next day. Although General Lu Han, the local Chinese commander in Haiphong, had been heavily bribed by the French (he had already been heavily bribed by Ho Chi Minh), he had apparently felt slighted; the resulting French-Chinese battle at Haiphong is well recorded elsewhere. But events in Tonkin are briefly touched on only in regard to the involvement of two British officers, Lieutenant-Colonel Trevor-Wilson in Hanoi and Commander Simpson-Jones in Haiphong, who — unknown to Gracey or, apparently, SEAC — had been sent to Haiphong by the British Pacific Fleet headquarters.

Maunsell's message to SACSEA was as follows:

> He [Leclerc] thanked me for Brit Military Mission in Hanoi and said "Cannot tell you what comradeship of Trevor-Wilson and Simpson-Jones [said to have gone out in a small boat and almost alone stopped the French-Chinese battle in Haiphong] meant to me nor can I imagine how we could have obtained Franco Chinese agreement without them."
>
> Behavior of Americans in Hanoi/Haiphong was apparently so pro-Chinese if not definitely anti-French that Leclerc has taken some, though not yet defined, action here. This has produced considerable consternation with Saigon American reps.
>
> From Leclerc staff and Hanoi it appears that arrival Trevor-Wilson and Simpson-Jones at official saluting base at Hanoi was greeted with "spontaneous and prolonged cheers from crowd".

The Americans were received in complete silence.

Both Trevor-Wilson and Simpson-Jones held regular meetings with Ho Chi Minh, and got to know him as well as anyone could. Apart from their official duties they did much humanitarian work, and in noticeable contrast to dozens of American officers in Hanoi, were responsible for providing relief (and in some cases release) for Frenchmen imprisoned by the Viet Minh. Trevor-Wilson wrote, "The extent of villainy of the Vietnamese [Viet Minh] police and army authorities was incredible. I was taken to see at the French police headquarters a number of French men and women who had been murdered in a vicious way. Many other people were chained together and marched off. . . ."

Of particular interest was Ho Chi Minh's assistance to Trevor-Wilson in the arrest of the Indian nationalist and Chandra Bose's deputy, Major-General A.C. Chatterjee. As Trevor-Wilson later wrote:

Another job I had to do, all alone, was to try to capture the members of the provisional government of India who were in residence in Hanoi. They were awaiting a plane to take them to Manchuria or Russia. The Foreign Minister, Major-General A.C. Chatterjee, had taken over the command of the provisional government of India at a time when the original commander, Chandra Bose, was killed in an aircraft accident . . .

In view of the fact that Ho Chi Minh appeared to be friendly towards me, I decided to consult him first. I told him that I had received a message from India (which was of course wrong) saying that the Indian Government would welcome the return of these people who would do better in India than in Hanoi.

Ho Chi Minh told me that he would place a cordon of his policemen around the 123 Rue Laloe if I went there. He gave me a whistle to blow if I had any disturbance, and then his policemen would come to my aid. In the airfield I had a Dakota with several Royal Air Force men aboard. I went to 123 Rue Laloe unarmed, as Ho Chi Minh had said, and asked to meet Chatterjee. He later appeared in full uniform, with a revolver at his waist . . . Somehow or another I managed to make him happy.[8]

Trevor-Wilson persuaded Chatterjee and his staff to spend the night at the British Mission, and the next day they all left for Saigon and Singapore. Trevor-Wilson went on to France with Ho Chi Minh, and returned to Hanoi as Consul; he remained in Indochina for several years. The reason for Ho's action over Chatterjee remains mysterious.

On 18 March there was a parade in Saigon "marking the termination of the stay of major British forces in FIC". This was also the date that Gracey nominated Mr Meiklereid for the 1946 King's Birthday Honors List. Mountbatten did not want to forward Meiklereid's name, because of his short period of service, but Gracey intervened strongly: "His tactful determination to steer the political ship out of what promised to be very troubled waters has succeeded beyond all expectations in seeing it safely in harbor." The nomination for the CMG was approved.

Terauchi had since been moved to Singapore, having sailed on the 13th on the *Kashima Maru* — two days before the French assumed responsibility for the Japanese. He took with him a staff of forty-three, six tons of baggage and equipment and one car — he had asked to take along gold bullion, and it is not clear how or why he still possessed wealth of this kind. As to the Field-Marshal's future, Dempsey agreed with Mountbatten that he should be spared the rigors of a War Crimes trial. Sir Keith Park disagreed, saying that Terauchi should be tried, "especially in con-

---

8.   Papers of Lt.-Col. A. G. Trevor-Wilson; also personal interviews and letters, 1977.

nection with his responsibility for the deaths which had occurred among those prisoners who had been forced to work on the Bangkok to Moulmein railway, unless he was actually certified insane." In the view of Mountbatten, expressed at his 297th Meeting, the real culprit was Tojo, and Terauchi was only an intermediary; Tojo, said the SAC, had ordered it built at all costs. In the event, Terauchi was not tried.

In mid-March, in Hanoi, the newly-arrived American Consul opened the US Consulate, and "expressed himself very dissatisfied with the results so far attained by the US Mission and expects to have them replaced shortly by Military, Naval and Air Advisors attached to his staff. He fully realises the unfavorable comparison made by the French between the Americans and ourselves, and is obviously going to do his utmost to improve the situation."[9] In fact, he was appalled at the political damage wrought by the OSS, not to mention their callous inhumanity to the French POWs, and had them unceremoniously removed with the utmost speed.

Mountbatten returned to Saigon in mid-March for a conference with d'Argenlieu and Maunsell. The French reported that there was still trouble in the south, and that Ho Chi Minh himself had earlier said he found it necessary to promote resistance there to provide him with political leverage.[10] It was now time for the last two British battalions to leave Vietnam, their responsibilities having been assumed by the French. For 2/8 Punjab, there had been a break in their routine when on the 11th an entire platoon in seventeen vehicles had to make the long journey to Siem Reap, Cambodia, to provide Mountbatten with a suitable reception for his visit to Angkor Wat. At 1030 on 29 March, 2/8 Punjab, less B Company (which remained to guard the Inter-Service Mission), embarked on the *Islami* and sailed slowly down the Saigon River to Cap St Jacques. At the Cap, 9/12 FFR had been reduced to a heavy schedule of cinemas, shooting competitions, football and swimming to keep busy — a favorite pastime was putting to sea in Japanese trawlers to watch their charges fishing. When the time came for 9 FFR to leave, the Japanese staged for the Battalion a farewell drama, which was well received. There can scarcely have been a more unusual relationship between victor and vanquished, as mutual respect and fraternization grew. When the *Islami*, with 2/8 Punjab aboard, moored at Cap St

9.  PRO, WO 203/5556, SACSEA to Cabinet, 17 Mar. 1946; also, FO 371/53961, Meiklereid to Foreign Office, 27 Mar. 1946.
10.  GB, PRO, CAB 122/512, Report on FIC by Colonel Chapman-Walker, 17–29 Dec. 1945.

Jacques and it was time for the 9/12 FFR to go, a large number of Japanese senior officers and men lined the Battalion's route of march from their barracks to the jetty. The 9th formed up and marched smartly to the docks, "From lines to the Naval jetty drums and surnais were played. Men shouted their religious cries." Another writer said of that moment, "It was a curious, if not pathetic, scene to find the very men who had fought against us so bitterly, now so manifestly sorry to bid the Battalion farewell."[11] In a poignant and starkly memorable scene the Japanese along the route bowed in a final act of respect to the Battalion as the last British/Indian soldiers marched away from Vietnam. Maunsell came aboard to wish the battalions goodbye, and at 1215 on the 30th the *Islami* slipped her moorings and sailed for India.

The British had been responsible for the support of the French and the Japanese Surrendered Personnel up to 31 March 1946. From 1 April onwards the French took over these obligations, and on 3 April the Combined Chiefs of Staff informed Mountbatten that he could hand over his responsibilities for the Japanese to the French. The French accepted this duty with the proviso that the Japanese should have gone before their eight- or nine-month stockpile of supplies (sold to the French by the British) was exhausted.[12]

On 8 April there was a terrific explosion in Saigon when the main French ammunition dump blew up. The ceilings in Maunsell's office — 2 km. away — collapsed, and Saigon Radio, located nearby, was blown off the air. The explosion was caused by a careless French soldier who overturned his speeding truck in the depot. It destroyed almost all French Army records, so that the screenings for war criminals, personnel files, records, dossiers, histories etc. were lost. (Destroyed also were the personal records and papers of Pierre Messmer, recently returned from Viet Minh captivity in Tonkin.)

Mountbatten wrote to the Cabinet on 4 May, informing the Government that as a result of discussions between the Mission in Saigon and the French, the latter had agreed to accept complete responsibility for all matters affecting Japanese disarming and repatriation as of midnight

11. W. E. H. Condon, *The History of the Frontier Force Regiment*, pp. 512, 513.
12. Towards the end of March M.E.Dening, in his capacity as Chief Political Adviser to SACSEA, submitted a brilliant final report to Ernest Bevin, the Foreign Secretary. With the recent appointment of Lord Killearn as a special commissioner in South East Asia, and the abolition on 15 March 1946 of the office of Chief Political Adviser to SACSEA, Dening's functions as political adviser to Mountbatten had come to an end.

(GMT), 13/14 May 1946. At 0001 on 14 May the Inter-Service Mission was disbanded; by 15 May all but 920 Japanese (retained by the French) had been repatriated. A reduced ALFSEA Liaison Detachment replaced the Inter-Service Mission, and Maunsell left Saigon to become Commandant of the Royal Military Academy at Woolwich. The last company of British troops, B Company of 2/8 Punjab, left Vietnam the next day. The Liaison Detachment personnel eventually became the military attachés, and they met regularly with the Consul, Mr Meiklereid. The RAF Staging Post, with a strength of 330, remained at Tan Son Nhut, which had become a major stopover point. From Hanoi Simpson-Jones told Meiklereid that during his frequent and lengthy visits with Ho Chi Minh — he met Ho at least three times a week, never for less than an hour and a half each visit — Ho had expressed the fear that the French would pull back into Cochinchina and cut Tonkin adrift; this was a current argument among the French as well.

On 10 June 1946 occurred the last British casualties of the First Vietnam War, when a "Check Recce Party" was involved in the ambush of a small French convoy of three vehicles near Baria. The British (a group of ten in one truck) were actually travelling in the opposite direction and, by the most unfortunate of coincidences, happened to be passing by the French convoy during the first seconds of the ambush, so that they were caught in it. The British party returned fire until their ammunition ran out; then the ambushers moved in for the kill. Six of the British were killed, — four Army, one RAF and one civilian interpreter — but miraculously four survived badly wounded; one man was missing. The attackers were thought to have been Japanese rather than Viet Minh.

By July 1946 Saigon was still not quiet and the French were continuing their mopping-up operations. At Meiklereid's 8th Staff Meeting with the British service representatives, it was noted that there were still about 200 Japanese with the Viet Minh; on 13 July a force of 150 Viet Minh, accompanied by twenty Japanese, had attacked and derailed the train from Saigon to Loc Ninh, but were driven off by the strong French escort. At Meiklereid's 24 July meeting it was reported that the Japanese Naval headquarters had finally been wound up, and the Japanese Naval personnel had returned to Japan. Of the Japanese only war criminals and witnesses remained together with a few officers detained by the French. On 28 August it was announced that thirty-five Japanese war criminals were being returned from Singapore to Indochina to stand trial for the Langson massacre.

On 11 September 1946 — exactly one year after the advance elements of 20 Indian Division had entered a tense and frightened Saigon — Meiklereid held his weekly staff meeting with the British military representatives. The most senior military officer present was a Lieutenant-Colonel, the Press Officer, who was about to be demo-bilized. There were also an Army Major, a Naval Lieutenant-Commander, and an RAF Flight-Lieutenant. On that date it was also announced that six Vietnamese had been found guilty of the Cité Heyraud massacres the previous year. They were executed.

## APPENDIX

Louis Allen kindly translated for the author a relevant portion of the Japanese official history of the war (produced by the Self Defense Force): fourth volume of Burma campaign, *Shittan: Mei-go Sakusen* ("Sittang, and the *coup de force* in Indo-China"), Asagumo Shimbunsha, Tokyo, 1970.

### MONEY
P. 683. "Restraints on inflation"
It was not only the three countries (Vietnam, Laos, Cambodia) which were poor, but the Japanese Army also . . . At that time, the Banque d'Indochine (the source of supply) was under Army control. However, Lt.-Gen. Tsuchihashi, the Army C-in-C, avoided as much as possible the release of currency, to prevent inflation. So no great inflation occurred. However, around July (1945), 500-piastre notes were issued, and used for military expenditure. These military notes did not command much confidence, and became ineffective after the end of the war. (*Source*: Post-war recollections of Tsuchihashi, and of Colonel Ogata, OC 38 Paymaster Department.)

### ARMS
P. 683 also refers to the period at the beginning of August when ammunition, bayonets, pistols and 10,000 rifles taken from the (French) Army of Indochina were collected and sent off to Hue for use by the new Vietnamese government, but on the way fell into the hands of the Viet Minh (*source*: Tsuchihashi). The arms and ammunition were not greater than this in quantity, because Southern Area Army had earlier ordered that all weapons &c taken from the French should be sent off to the Burma front.

### VIET MINH APPROACHES
P. 684. This page details approaches made to the Viet Minh by the Japanese Army, i.e. Tsuchihashi (whose diary, in Allen's words, is "one of *the* prime historical sources for the period" — letter to author, 1 Aug. 1977). This was

after the failure, in June 1945, of the punitive expedition in the North carried out by 21 Division. The proposed intermediaries were the Kam Sai, Ke Toai, and the mayor of Hanoi, Chan Ban Lai, who drew up a number of propositions describing what the Japanese wanted their relations with the Viet Minh to be, and asking Ho Chi Minh to send a representative for discussions. The end of the war intervened, so nothing seems to have come of this notion.

# 18

# EPILOGUE

In the vast, complex and bloody story of post-war Indochina, Gracey's relatively small band operated in a restricted area of Vietnam for a brief period of time. Yet their presence was of profound importance and had far-reaching consequences out of all proportion to their numbers and the length of their stay. Central to this history was the character of Douglas Gracey himself, and his accomplishments are the more impressive when viewed in the context of the conflicting pressures under which he was operating. He could hardly have found himself in a more complex situation. He performed his mission while squeezed on the one hand by the French and the Viet Minh, and on the other by an ambitious and politically sensitive Supreme Commander, a Labour government at home and the Viceroy and Commander-in-Chief, India — in an area full of tension, and with a small force amid a numerically superior and undefeated Japanese Army. An officer not possessing Gracey's professional competence, common sense and force of character might have proved unequal to the task. When he left Vietnam he had accomplished all he had been asked to do and had earned the respect of the French, the Japanese and, as we are told by official sources, the Vietnamese.

Germane to this history are passages from F. S. V. Donnison's official history, *British Military Administration in the Far East, 1943–1946.* Donnison pointed out that, the French were anxious to regain their position as a world power and to reestablish their prestige, and thus did not wish the occupying forces of SEAC to do more than the minimum necessary to establish the Saigon bridgehead. The French administration was to run the country, as before the war. The only problem was that there was no French administration in Saigon on Gracey's arrival. Wrote Donnison, "In all cases the Allied (but in fact British) Force Commander was required to conduct his dealings with the civilian population through the agency of the French Administration."[1] Furthermore, "the immediate paramountcy of military interests and the inability of the French Administration to function without the support of British

---

1. F. S. V. Donnison, *British Military Administration in the Far East, 1943–46* (London: HMSO, 1956), pp. 294, 295.

troops'' finally drove Gracey to issue the proclamation of 19 September 1945, announcing his intention to maintain order in his area of responsibility without proclaiming any law that could be enforced.

Nationalism, ever present but contained, had been given fresh impetus as the Europeans were humiliated and driven out by the Japanese. But the Japanese knew only how to take; they could not give, and soon — like the Germans in the Ukraine — they managed, by their brutality and arrogance, to alienate the peoples they freed. As Donnison pointed out, ''In fact all parties, friend and foe alike, were vigorously engaged in whipping up nationalist enthusiasm.'' The Allies did this to build resistance against the Japanese, the Japanese for their own purposes; thus ''Everywhere nationalist armies had been raised, whether to eject the Japanese or to resist the return of the Europeans, or both. . . . It is more difficult to answer fairly the question whether the movements were in fact representative of the majority of the people or not. . . .'' Since the Charter of the United Nations had just been promulgated, stressing fundamental human rights and the dignity of the individual, ''Britain could afford even less than most to disregard and so to stultify the organization for mutual security that she was helping to build and upon which she must expect increasingly to depend for protection against major aggression.''[2]

Addressing specifically the problems faced by officers like Gracey, Donnison noted that while no formal British military administrations were proclaimed in the foreign territories of Indochina and Indonesia, the complex political situations forced the British commanders to exercise considerable administrative and political responsibilities, not all of which could be foreseen and codified beforehand. Military commanders set up local administrations, and British military engineers revived essential public services. The laws of politics and physics being often strikingly similar, ''outside these limited areas of active administration, the vacuum left by the absence of any effective government tended always to suck the British military commanders into situations in which they found themselves driven to accept varying degrees of . . . responsibility.''[3] It was a ''sharp and distressing dilemma'', what today would be called a ''no-win situation''. The British commanders, as Donnison points out, had to balance their friendship towards their Dutch and French allies, and loyalty to the policies of the Atlantic

2. *Ibid.*, pp. 332, 333, 340.
3. *Ibid.*, p. 401.

Charter, against the restrictions imposed by commanding mainly Indian troops.

Dennis Duncanson has stated that the tasks of a wartime conference, such as that held at Potsdam, did not include the permanent disposal of territories; Potsdam was concerned with humanitarian problems including the care of Allied POWs, the return of Japanese troops, the state of the various urban populations, installations, and so on. "The contrary view, that conquest bestowed absolute rights of decision on the conqueror — implicit in current strictures on General Gracey — is supposed by writers on international law to have gone out with the eighteenth century."[4] Duncanson points out that not only was General Gracey charged with keeping public order, but that he could not have discharged his primary tasks in conditions of general anarchy and disorder. Even without his specific orders on the subject,

General Gracey was in fact, even though there had been no fighting, an occupying military power and liable to perform the duties falling to an occupying power under the laws and usages of war on land. The Hague Regulations were explicit, placing this duty before all others . . .

Even if a British Commander of an occupying force were not given explicit instructions on this point — and General Gracey was — he would still be bound by the British Manual of Military Law, which reproduces the Hague Regulation word for word and so makes its observance by British forces mandatory.

The British, as occupying power, were not required to set up a military administration; the local French administration was to resume functioning, and "the arrangements described were in full accord with the principles of international law and custom." Thus Gracey's remark that the question of government in Indochina was exclusively French was correct. In the last analysis, as Duncanson has pointed out, "No summary executions under General Gracey's proclamation were ever carried out, nor did he in practice exercise any jurisdiction outside the vicinity of Saigon."[5] Gracey personally was little concerned with who ran Vietnam, and it is plain from his character and conduct that he would have kept the French out had he been so ordered. Neither in any official documents, nor in the General's own papers, nor in interviews with his closest subordinates can any evidence be found that Gracey was at that

4. Dennis J. Duncanson, "General Gracey and the Viet Minh", *Royal Central Asian Society Journal*, vol. LV, Oct. 1968, part III, pp. 290–2.
5. *Ibid.*, pp. 294–5.

time particularly sympathetic to the return of the French to Indochina. As Dennis Duncanson has mentioned, he was simply reiterating his government's policy when he stated that the French were responsible for the administration of Indochina.

The implication in some well-known contemporary histories of this period is that Gracey was politically a bumbler who did not think much of the oriental's ability to manage. Yet some of Gracey's own unit commanders were Indian, and he had spent years in building up the Indian Army. Again, to say, as did Joseph Buttinger, that Gracey could not entertain the possibility of an Eastern country ceasing to be a colony cannot be correct, since he knew very well that India itself, paramount in the British Empire, was a long way down the road to independence. The entire discussion of Gracey very much underestimates the man who became the first Commander-in-Chief of the independent Pakistan Army and who, with the Indian Army Commander of that time (another Briton), personally averted a war between India and Pakistan over Kashmir in 1948 by talking their respective Governments out of it.

Jean-Michel Hertrich, a known Viet Minh sympathizer, was given a seat by Gracey on the first RAF aircraft to land in Saigon after the war. He is said to have praised Gracey for his patience in seeking a negotiated settlement, and reported that he was initially sympathetic to the Viet Minh, until the outrages began and until they told Gracey that they could no longer control their followers. On the extempore remarks made by Gracey in response to a lecture on 29 April 1953 at the Royal Central Asian Society in London, of which more will be said, Dennis Duncanson has noted that they were taken out of context by Bernard Fall (who was not critical of Gracey). They were recorded in the Royal Central Asian Society's *Journal*, probably without prior reference to Gracey, and "his critics, without exception, base their judgments — on what was a question of international law, not one of political favour — upon a very limited selection of the evidence available."

The Viet Minh spokesmen who attempted to meet Gracey at the airport themselves faded rapidly from sight, and Gracey could not "recognize the precarious authority which his virtually anonymous Communist contacts in Saigon were claiming, on the fragile evidence of messages being broadcast over Radio Hanoi in the name of the self-proclaimed Democratic Republic."[6] Added to this, Gracey's directives did not anticipate the complex situation in Saigon.

---

6. *Ibid.*, p. 290.

Gracey's extempore remarks deserve closer scrutiny, in context. The hitherto little-known lecture which prompted them was delivered by retired US Air Force Colonel Melvin Hall, and was entitled "Aspects of the Present Situation in Indo-China". Hall began by saying, "Indochina has been described as a 'basket of crabs.' If that gives you some idea of what the situation is, I can assure you that trying to trace out the movements and manifestations of a basketful of crabs is no more difficult than following events in Indo-China."[7] As soon as Hall had finished his talk Gracey, now retired from active service, rose and said the following:

". . . I was interested in what Colonel Hall said about Ho Chi Minh's resistance movement, because I am quite certain that it was leading up to such a result all the time and that anything he did was for himself and his party alone and not for the good of French Indo-China as a whole.

"I was welcomed on arrival by the Viet Minh, who said 'Welcome' and all that sort of thing. It was a very unpleasant situation, and I promptly kicked them out. They are obviously Communists, and I think, as does Colonel Hall, that it is a very dangerous situation and that unless we do everything in our power with all the determination we possibly can, the only hope for the independence of Indo-China is under Ho Chi Minh."[8]

Gracey stressed that the incompetence of the Communists was a factor in their long struggles in Indochina:

"When I was out there two years ago [1951] there was one question that the Vietnamese asked me. I think that that was the reason why the French asked me out there, so that I could give the answer. This is what they said: 'The French say that they cannot nationalize or give us an army in under fifteen or twenty years — without French assistance. How is it, first of all, that the Pakistan Army has been able to be reorganized in three years? And, secondly, how is it that the Viet Minh forces are able to find their officers? After all, they have not been going at it very much longer than we have.' The first part was easy to answer. I merely pointed out that we had been nationalizing the Indian Army, of which the Pakistan Army was only an offshoot, for thirty years. That was an easy one to answer, but the question of Ho Chi Minh and the Viet Minh officers was a very difficult one to answer. The only answer I could give to that was that if the Viet Minh had had decent officers, they would have had possession of French Indo-China long ago."

Duncanson wrote correctly: "Many years will pass perhaps before the last word is said about events in Vietnam in 1945." He suggests that, far

---

7. Colonel Melvin Hall, "Aspects of the Present Situation in Indo-China", *Royal Central Asian Society Journal*, vol. XL, parts III and IV, July-Oct. 1953, pp. 204–11.
8. *Ibid.*, pp. 213–14.

from departing from his instructions, Gracey "exercised under wartime conditions a forbearance in preserving law and order greater than is often shown in many countries in peacetime." Duncanson also noted "the prophetic words of Labour's Sir Stafford Cripps in the House of Commons in June 1945: 'We do not want to see in Burma, or in any other country, the rapid seizing of power by any particular group of people, in order to improvise some force of government.' "[9] Duncanson stressed what many of Gracey's officers have said: "The issue that faced him in Saigon was not that of colonial emancipation, but the ordinary decencies of life and the protection of individual people from terror, injury, and robbery — a duty falling to all persons thrust into positions of authority but often callously disregarded by revolutionaries."

From the volume of evidence now available — official documents, contemporary comment, interviews with the original participants etc. — several conclusions can be drawn about Gracey's role in Vietnam, which should be stated if only to rebut the often incorrect and apparently biased historical accounts of this period given by a number of writers. First, these writers (Ellen Hammer and Buttinger were two such, and there were many more influenced by them) were entirely wrong to assert that Gracey's tasks did not include the maintenance of public order. Gracey's own orders as Commander, Allied Land Forces French Indo China, have been quoted in this book. The US Government was undoubtedly aware of them, for a memorandum of 24 September 1945 by the Director of the Office of Far Eastern Affairs, Mr John Carter Vincent, records a meeting in Washington between Sir George Sansom of the British Embassy, Mr Vincent himself, and Mr Abbot Moffat, Chief of the Division of Southeast Asian Affairs. The following is an excerpt from that memo: "Mr Moffat inquired whether Sir George was familiar with the statement of General Slim, Commander of the SEAC land forces, that the British would be in Indochina to disarm Japanese and to maintain order until French troops could arrive."[10]

A second conclusion, requiring particular emphasis, is the reasoning which prompted Gracey to obey his government's decision to permit the French to assume responsibility for civil administration (on 23 September). The current literature depicts Gracey as an officer who went to Saigon impatient to conduct a *coup* and restore political power to the

9. Duncanson, p. 297, referring here to Donnison, op. cit., p. 370.
10. Foreign Relations of the United States, vol. VI (Washington: US Government Printing Office, 1969), p. 313.

French. This is incorrect and misleading, for Gracey was fully cognizant of his government's policy of minimal involvement while recognizing (with the United States) France's sole sovereignty in Indochina. Gracey was persuaded that the *coup* was necessary by the knowledge that, without it, anarchy would quickly have developed in Saigon, which would almost certainly have prevented him from carrying out his tasks and resulted in the massacre of the French population. The evidence which led him to this conclusion was there in the form of mounting personal atrocities against the French, and his Intelligence officers had warned him of impending disaster. Furthermore, Viet Minh officials admitted that they were incapable of controlling their armed groups. This, coupled with what the released Allied POWs had told him of the anarchy in Saigon before his arrival, convinced Gracey that, no matter what the personal consequences to him, he could afford to wait no longer. On 6 October 1945, General Slim informed the Chief of the Imperial General Staff that, in addition to everything else, a rising of the French civilian population had been a real possibility. But had Gracey's own Division not initially been withheld from him by Mountbatten it is conceivable that the *coup* would not have taken place, for Gracey would have disposed of enough force to guarantee public safety in Saigon without resorting to French help. But as Gracey later told Mountbatten, he had only few companies at his disposal at that time to accomplish his complex tasks in an area as big and important as Liverpool. Also, the Japanese (still mostly "on the fence" or sullenly hostile at the time) would not be impressed by the spectacle of the Allied Commander dancing to the Viet Minh tune.

On several occasions Gracey took the French to task for not according proper treatment and respect to the Asians — scarcely consistent with the colonialist bigotry that some historians have ascribed to him. During the four and a half months he was in Saigon, Gracey prevented the massacre of the French civil population, secured the Japanese Supreme Headquarters, kept the capital city alive through a Viet Minh siege, and was the instrument by which the Communist presence in Saigon was ejected. In other post-war *coups*, Communist power liquidated the existing administration. In South Vietnam occurred the only contemporary example of the Communists suffering a reverse, and it may be that because they suffered it at Gracey's hands, the political Left and their sympathizers have never forgiven him.

A further matter which needs to be clarified concerns the figure of 2,700 Viet Minh killed, cited in several histories. The total is correct, but what all accounts omit is the fact that while slightly more than 600 of them were killed by British/Indian troops, the remainder, more than 2,000, were killed by the French and Japanese who, outside key areas, were not under direct British supervision. Virtually every historian of the period has followed Isaacs in stating that Vietnamese sentries were "shot down" and killed during the 23 September *coup*. Yet it has been shown that this was not so, and that only Frenchmen were killed during the *coup*. If the French overreacted by behaving outrageously for a few hours before a furious Gracey disarmed them, it must be borne in mind that Viet Minh jailers had replaced Japanese guards on the French POW camps. The British did not kill 2,700 Vietnamese, and Gracey did not "take it upon himself" (Hammer) to restore the French to Indochina.

In 1971, according to Brigadier Maunsell, a journalist interviewed him for forty minutes (after stating that he wanted to give proper credit to General Gracey), "never took a note"[11] and subsequently attacked Gracey and the British in a book on Vietnam, some of which appeared in the London *Sunday Times*. The British Broadcasting Corporation commissioned the same journalist to write the script for a radio broadcast on the battle of Dien Bien Phu. The 1977 broadcast opened with the statement that Gracey singlehandedly caused the start of the Vietnam wars — the names of Ho Chi Minh, Giap, Tran Van Giau and other life-long fanatical Marxist revolutionaries were not mentioned. Most of the books dealing with Indochina that have appeared in the past fifteen years attack Gracey, besides containing many errors of fact relating to the 1945 action.

The British legacy in Vietnam was, for thirty years, the state of South Vietnam. Saigon was economically and politically crucial; even if the Viet Minh had captured 90 percent of the south without taking Saigon they would still have been regarded as rebels and not as a government, and conversely the occupiers of 10 percent of the country which included Saigon would be recognized as the government. The British drove the Viet Minh from Saigon and left it to the French. When the French returned to Indochina in strength they came first to Cochinchina and Saigon. The Viet Minh were thus never able to consolidate their position in the south. Had the Chinese in North Vietnam done similar favors for the French, it is not impossible that the Viet Minh would have been smothered before reaching full bloom.

Thus an obvious question arises from the earlier French suggestion

11. Brig. M. S. K. Maunsell, personal interview, 20 Apr. 1977.

that SEAC should be responsible for northern Indochina as well as the south. Lord Mountbatten opined, many years after he had completed his mission as Supreme Allied Commander, that the Vietnamese Communists would never have been able to take over the country had his Command been given responsibility for the north as well as the south. What he had in mind was a situation in which another commander would have been sent to Hanoi where, like Gracey in Saigon, he would have perceived the hollowness of the Viet Minh claim to speak and act for the whole of the Vietnamese people and refused to accept its pretensions to be the effective government. By maintaining law and order, ensuring essential supplies and services, and protecting the ordinary people from coercion and terror from armed political thugs, such a commander might have provided the period of respite necessary for the mass of the people to express, and perhaps even realize, its aspirations, which were certainly not for a Communist state. But perhaps this view is fundamentally unrealistic, and Ho Chi Minh's tiny Communist Party, with the backing of the OSS's material resources and no less political naiveté, would have been victorious anyway. Nevertheless, some explanation must be found for the fact that France suffered military defeat at the hands of the Communists in the north within a few years, but did not do so in the south, and for the resistance to Communist rule which has continued since the victory of 1975 with thousands of Vietnamese risking their lives in tiny craft on monsoon seas rather than live under it. It is at least possible that the cause of the great differences between the behavior of North and South Vietnam was the vastly different experiences of the two regions in 1945, when Gracey assumed responsibility for the south and General Lu Han with his Chinese forces did so for the north.

The official version of events in Saigon compiled by the SEAC Recorder on the instructions of Mountbatten was evidently regarded by Gracey as little better than propaganda and he took strong exception to it. Mention has been made of this document earlier, but it is necessary at this juncture to list the remainder of Gracey's corrections to it. The matters with which these corrections are concerned will be apparent to the reader:

The Japanese were inclined to regard the situation as one in which, by virtue of the fact that they had large armed forces, they held the whip hand. The proclamation [of 19 September] made it quite clear to them all, as it had been made clear to their senior officers in Rangoon, that the British commander was going to stand no nonsense from them, or anyone else, for that matter. . . .
The majority of the Annamite population was horror-stricken at the turn of

events, and at the barbaric and monstrous cruelties of the puppet forces. Though imbued with the thought of independence, without much idea as to what it meant, they were soon alienated from their so-called deliverers. As they were progressively released from the ruthlessly terroristic attention of the rebels, they resumed their work and opened their markets. The intelligentsia were mainly, and quite justifiably, concerned with removing the many discriminations in pay and status between them and the French.

As regards Laos, and the rest of FIC, I am not in a position to give a true picture. I doubt if anyone can . . . It was an unpleasant situation, outside the orbit of the forces under the SAC.[12]

Gracey remarked that the French would ''strongly dislike the statement that the Chinese pursued a strict policy of non-intervention in Laos''. He also drew the Recorder's attention to the notable omission of the relevant facts of his directive on keeping law and order; unless amended to show Slim's orders to him, it was ''most misleading and unfair to the Allied commander [i.e. Gracey himself].'' Furthermore, at the time of the proclamation of 19 September there was never any doubt that the whole of 20 Division was not going to Indochina. ''There was never any intention . . . to interfere in the internal affairs of a foreign country,'' wrote Gracey. ''The proclamation, followed by the eviction of the puppet government, saved a massacre!'' And since the SEAC Recorder had written of the British role in Indonesia that strong action in the beginning would have saved many lives, ''Why not apply this to FIC and state categorically that the strong action taken by the Allied commander, his staff and troops did that, and more?'' In a number of places Gracey posed the question, ''Why the 'I' [Mountbatten]? Why not the Allied commander [Gracey] who did it!''

Gracey had no known wish to be remembered in history, and his objections were not to occasional errors but to what appeared to him to be a deliberately and grossly distorted record of what had actually happened in his sphere of operations. He also took full and public responsibility for what he knew would be controversial decisions, such as that which brought about the *coup*, but at all times he was guided by what he considered necessary for the common good, regardless of personal risk to himself. Brigadier Woodford observed that this characteristic had kept him as a Major-General when he had the capacity for higher rank and greater responsibilities. (However, after he had left Mountbattern's command he rose to four-star rank.)

In an earlier study the author wrote the following:

12. Gracey Papers, 3 Oct. 1946.

The rain clouds which had sprinkled Saigon were soon to burst open and unleash torrents throughout all Indochina. The last Englishman and Indian to sail away would eventually be joined by a last Frenchman, a last Australian, a last Korean, a last Thai, a last Filipino, a last New Zealander, and a last American. Who would next be the last out of Vietnam?

The answer to this question was unexpected. The last out of Vietnam were the common Vietnamese themselves, in numbers vastly exceeding their former colonizers and occupiers.

In the last years before 1975, few South Vietnamese knew of Douglas Gracey and how he had influenced their history. That was a pity — both deserved better.

# BIBLIOGRAPHY

## PRIMARY SOURCES

### Unpublished Documents

GREAT BRITAIN (Public Record Office)

*War Office Files* (includes War Diaries of all relevant units from Battalion through Theater Headquarters): WO 172 and 203 Series.
*Royal Air Force Files:* Air 20, 23, 24, 25, 26, 27, 28, 29, 40.
*Foreign Office Files:* FO 371 Series.
*Cabinet Files:* Cab. 79, 88, 96, 105, 106, 107, 119, 122.
*Prime Minister's Office Files:* Prem. 3, 4, 8.

Relevant charts and Saigon street plans from British Army Map Repository.
Contemporary photographs from Imperial War Museum, Gracey Papers, Lt.-Col. Trevor-Wilson; motion picture film from Lt.-Col. Blascheck.

THE UNITED STATES

US Army Operations Division, War Department' General Staff; ABC (American-British Conferences): all RG 165.
SWNCC (State-War-Navy Coordinating Committee): RG 165, 218.
Joint Chiefs of Staff Minutes: RG 218.
Department of State: RG 59.
National Security Agency/CSS Cryptographic Documents: RG 457.
National Security Council: RG 273.
Office of Strategic Services, reports and assessments: RG 226 (all above, National Archives).
Office of Air Force History, Histories and Operational Reports of 14th Air Force Units.

PRIVATE PAPERS

Gen. Sir Douglas D. Gracey (from Lady Gracey; papers now in King's College, London).
Gen. Lord Ismay (King's College, London).
Maj.-Gen. W. R. C. Penney (King's College, London).
Maj.-Gen. Harold E. Pyman (King's College, London).
Lt.-Col. A. G. Trevor-Wilson (from Lt.-Col. Trevor-Wilson).

## PRIVATE WRITTEN ACCOUNTS TO AUTHOR

Louis Allen, Letters.
Air Chief Marshal Sir Walter Cheshire, RAF, "The Gremlin Task Force".
Pierre Messmer, "Evasion — 1945".
Philip G. Malins, "The Operations of 20 Indian Division in French Indo China, September to December 1945.


## Published Official Documents

### GREAT BRITAIN

*Documents Relating to the British Involvement in the Indo-China Conflict, 1945–1965*, Cmnd 2834. London: HMSO, 1965.
Mountbatten of Burma, Earl, *Report to the Combined Chiefs of Staff by the Supreme Commander, South-East Asia, 1943–1946*. London: HMSO, 1951.
_____, *Supplement to Report to the Combined Chefs of Staff by the Supreme Allied Commander South-East Asia* [n.p., n.d.].
_____, *Post Surrender Tasks; Section E of the Report to the Combined Chiefs of Staff by the Supreme Allied Commander South-East Asia, 1943–1945*. London: HMSO, 1969.
Naval Intelligence Division, *Indochina*. Cambridge: HMSO, 1943.


### THE UNITED STATES

US Department of State, *Foreign Relations of the United States, Diplomatic Papers*, 1940 [hereafter *FRUS*], vol. IV: *The Far East*. Washington: Government Printing Office, 1955.
*FRUS*, 1941. vol. II: *Europe*. Washington, 1959.
*FRUS, The Conferences of Cairo and Tehran, 1943*. Washington, 1961.
*FRUS, The Conference of Berlin; The Potsdam Conference, 1945*. Washington, 1969.
*FRUS*, 1945, vol. VII: The Far East, China. Washington, 1969.
US Department of State, Office of Intelligence Research, Research and Analysis Branch; OIR Report 3369, "Programs of Japanese in Indo-China". 10 Aug. 1945.
US Government, *The United States and Vietnam: 1944–1947,* Study no. 2 (Staff Study for Senate Committee on Foreign Relations).
*Causes, Origins, and Lessons of the Vietnam War*. Hearings before the Senate Committee on Foreign Relations, 9–11 May 1972.
*The History of the Joint Chiefs of Staff: The Joint Chiefs of Staff and the War in Vietnam; History of the Indochina Incident, 1940–1954.*
US Army Forces Far East, Japanese Monograph no. 25: *French Indo-China Area Operations Record* (1940–5).

DEMOCRATIC REPUBLIC OF VIETNAM

*An Outline History of the Vietnam Workers' Party (1930–1970).* Hanoi: Foreign Languages Publishing House (FLPH), 1970.
*Thirty Years Struggle of the Party.* Hanoi: FLPH, 1960.
*History of the August Revolution.* Hanoi: FLPH, 1972.


FRANCE

*French Army, Lessons of the War in Indochina*, vol. 2, transl. V. J. Croizat. Santa Monica, Calif.: Rand Corp., 1967.
*Revue des Troupes Coloniales*, no. 275, March 1946. Paris: Service Historique de l'Armée (Bibliothèque).


## Journals, Articles, Reports, Pamphlets

*A Happy Family*, n.p., n.d. (from Gracey Papers, hereafter GP) — abbreviated history of 20 Indian Division.
Allen, Louis, "Studies in the Japanese Occupation of South-East Asia (II)", *Durham University Journal*, vol. LXIV (New Series, vol. XXXIII), March 1972.
*Buildup of 80 Ind Inf Bde at Saigon.* (GP)
Charlton, Michael, "Many Reasons Why", *The Listener* (London), vol. 98, no. 2527, 22 Sept. 1977; and vol. 98, no. 2528, 29 Sept. 1977.
Clark, Major J. H., "Sappers and Miners in Saigon", *The Royal Engineers Journal*, vol. LXIV, no. 3, Sept. 1950.
Duncanson, Dennis, "General Gracey and the Viet Minh", *Journal of the Royal Central Asian Society*, vol. LV, part III, Oct. 1968.
Gracey, Lt.-Gen. Sir Douglas D., Reply to Report by the *SEAC Recorder*, 3 Oct. 1946. (GP)
Hall, Melvin, "Aspects of the Present Situation in Indo-China", *Journal of the Royal Central Asian Society*, vol. XL, pts III and IV, July–Oct. 1953.
La Feber, Walter, "Roosevelt, Churchill and Indochina: 1942–45", *American Historical Review*, vol. 80, 1975.
Langlade, François de, "Résistance en Indochine", *Historia*, No. 334, Sept. 1974.
Marshall, Jonathan, "Southeast Asia and US-Japan Relations: 1940–1941", *Pacific Research and World Telegram*, vol. IV, no. 3, Mar.–Apr. 1973.
*Medical History, Allied Land Forces French Indo-China, September 1945–February 1946.* (GP)
Newsletters of the following Battalions: 1/1 Gurkha Rifles, 3/1 Gurkha Rifles, 4/2 Gurkha Rifles, 4/10 Gurkha Rifles, 2/8 Punjab, 9/14 Punjab, 9 (MG) Jat, 4/17 Dogra. (GP)

Park, Air Chief Marshal Sir K. R., Supplement to the *London Gazette*, 19 Apr. 1951.

Political Report of Saigon Control Commission, 13 Sept.–9 Oct. 1945. (GP)

"Saigon Youth in the 1945 Insurrection", *Vietnam Youth*, no. 122, Mar. 1976.

*Short History of 20th Indian Division.* (GP)

*The Frontier Force Regimental Magazine*, vol. III, no. 1, Feb. 1946.

20th Indian Division; pamphlet printed by 7 Rep. Sec., RE, Apr. 1946. (GP)

Welfare in F. I.C. (GP)

Japanese Report of 9 March Incident. (GP)

## Press

Various files of *The Times* and *The Daily Telegraph*, 1945–6 (British Museum Newspaper Library, Colindale, London).

*Times of Saigon.* (GP)

*Peace News.*

## Documents, Personal Accounts, Memoirs

Catroux, Georges, *Deux Actes du Drame Indochinoise*. Paris: Plon, 1959.

Cao Van Luan, *Ben Giong Lich Su 1940–1965* (excerpts translated by P. J. Honey). Saigon: Tri Dung, 1972.

De Gaulle, Charles, *The Complete War Memoirs*. New York: Simon and Schuster, 1964.

Hull, Cordell, *The Memoirs of Cordell Hull*, vols. 1 and 2. Macmillan, 1948.

Le Duan, *On the Socialist Revolution in Vietnam,* vol. 1. Hanoi: FLPH, 1967.

———, *Forward Under the Glorious Banner of the October Revolution*. Hanoi 1967.

Lenin, V., *Lenin on the National and Colonial Questions*. Peking: Foreign Languages Press, 1967.

Massu, Jacques, *Sept Ans avec Leclerc*. Paris: Plon, 1974.

Miles, M. E., *A Different Kind of War*. Garden City, NY: Doubleday, 1967.

Rathauskey, R. (ed.), *Documents of the August 1945 Revolution in Vietnam* (transl. C. Kiriloff). Canberra: Research School of Pacific Studies, Australian National University, 1963.

Sainteny, Jean. *Histoire d'une Paix Manquée: Indochine 1945–1947*. Paris: Amiot, Dumont, 1953.

Salan, Raoul, *Mémoires, Fin d'une Empire*. Paris: Presses de la Cité, 1970.

Slim, Field-Marshal Sir William, *Defeat into Victory*. London: Cassell, 1956.

Truong Chinh, *Primer for Revolt: the August Revolution*. New York: Praeger, 1963.

Van der Post, Laurens, *The Night of the New Moon*. London: Hogarth Press, 1970.

Vo Nguyen Giap, *To Arm the Revolutionary Masses to Build the People's Army*. Hanoi: FLPH, 1975.

_____, *People's War, People's Army*. New York: Praeger, 1962.

_____, *The Military Art of People's War*. New York: Monthly Review Press, 1970.

_____, *Unforgettable Days*. Hanoi, 1975.

## Personal Interviews

**C** = Correspondence only; **T** = Telephone conversation. Contemporary position/unit in brackets.

Louis Allen, Author/Linguist/Professor, Durham University, England (CSDIC [Combined Services Detailed Interrogation Centre] Team, Saigon).

The Hon. Hugh Astor (Major, Force 136, Saigon).

P. C. Bastit (mining engineer, French Indochina).

Maj.-Gen. Maurice Belleaux, French Army (later Chief of Military Intelligence, French Expeditionary Forces, Indochina).

Lt.-Col. Charles U. Blascheck (Company Commander, 3/1 Gurkha Rifles).

Sir Norman H. Brain (Foreign Office, Political Adviser to General Gracey, Saigon).

Jean Cédile (French Commissioner-designate, Cochinchina; Governor of Cochinchina).

Air Chief Marshal Sir Walter G. Cheshire (Head of RAF Element, Saigon Control Commission; Commander RAF Forces, Indochina). **C**.

Lt.-Col. Robert W. Clark (Battalion Commander, 1/1 Gurkha Rifles).

Brig. E. J. Gibbons (Chief, Civil Affairs Staff, Headquarters South East Asia Command). **T**.

Lt.-Col. E. Gopsill (Company Commander, 3/1 Gurkha Rifles).

Lady Gracey.

P. J. Honey, Author/Linguist/Reader in Vietnamese Studies and Head of South-East Asia Department, School of Oriental and African Studies, University of London (Commander, Royal Navy).

Lt.-Col. Cyril E. Jarvis (Battalion Commander, 1/1 Gurkha Rifles).

Major M. Kelleher (Company Commander, 3/1 Gurkha Rifles).

Lt.-Gen. Sir Brian Kimmins (Assistant Chief of Staff, Headquarters South East Asia Command).

François de Langlade (Major, Force 136/DGER; Adviser to General de Gaulle on French Indochina).

Major P. G. Malins (RIASC/Civil Feed Control Organisation). **C**.

Gen. Jacques Massu, French Army (*Groupement Massu*, French Indochina).

Brig. M. S. K. Maunsell (Chief of Staff, Saigon Control Commission).

Pierre Messmer (Commissioner-designate, Tonkin; later Prime Minister of France).

Col. Marcel Mingant (French Colonial Army Intelligence, Indochina).

Brig. E. C. W. Myers (Chief of Counter-Intelligence, Headquarters South East Asia Command).

Nguyen De (businessman, Financial Adviser to Ho Chi Minh, *Chef de Cabinet* to Emperor Bao Dai).

Major Richard Ogden (Intelligence Officer, 20 Indian Division, Burma).

Major Peter Prentice (Company Commander, 1/1 Gurkha Rifles).

Gen. Raoul Salan, French Army (Commander, French Forces, Tonkin; later Commander-in-Chief, French Expeditionary Corps).

Brig. D. E. Taunton (Commander, 80 Infantry Brigade).

Lt.-Col. A. G. Trevor-Wilson (SIS; Saigon Control Commission Liaison in Hanoi).

H. Vallat (Governor of Annam; Head of Association of Indochina Resistance Network). **C.**

Gen. A. C. Wedemeyer (Commander, China Theater).

Brig. E. C. J. Woodford (Commander, 32 Infantry Brigade).

## SECONDARY SOURCES

### Books

Allen, Louis, *The End of the War in Asia*. London: Hart-Davis MacGibbon, 1976.

Bain, Chester, *Vietnam: The Roots of Conflict*. Englewood Cliffs, NJ: Prentice-Hall, 1969.

Barrow, John, *A Voyage to Cochinchina*. Kuala Lumpur: Oxford University Press, 1975.

Bellers, E. V. R., *The 1st King George V's Own Gurkha Rifles (the Malaun Regiment)*, vol. 2: 1920–1947. Aldershot, England: Gale & Polden, 1956.

Bergamini, David, *Japan's Imperial Conspiracy*. New York: Morrow, 1971.

Brimmell, J. H., *Communism in South East Asia: A Political Analysis*. Oxford University Press, 1959.

Buttinger, Joseph, *A Dragon Defiant*. Newton Abbot, Devon: David & Charles, 1972.

_____, *Vietnam: a Political History*, vol. I. New York: Praeger, 1963.

_____, *The Smaller Dragon*. New York: Praeger, 1958.

Cady, John F., *Southeast Asia: Its Historical Development*. New York: McGraw-Hill, 1964.

_____, *The Roots of French Imperialism in Eastern Asia*. Ithaca, NY: Cornell University Press, 1967.

Cameron, Allan W., *Viet-Nam Crisis: A Documentary History*, vol. 1.: 1940–1956. Ithaca, NY: Cornell University Press, 1971.

Chen, King C., *Vietnam and China, 1938–1954*. Princeton University Press, 1969.

Chesneaux, Jean, *Contribution à l'Histoire de la Nation Vietnamienne*. Paris: Editions Sociales, 1955.

Coedès, George, *The Making of Southeast Asia*. London: Routledge & Kegan Paul, 1966.

Cole, Allan B. (ed.), *Conflict in Indo-China and International Repercussions: a Documentary History, 1945–1955*. Ithaca, NY: Cornell University Press, 1956.

Condon, W. E. H., *The History of the Frontier Force Regiment*. Aldershot: Gale & Polden, 1962.

Dening, Esler, *Japan*. London: Benn, 1960.

Deutscher, Isaac, *Stalin*. Harmondsworth: Pelican Books, 1966.

Devillers, Philippe, *Histoire du Vietnam de 1940 à 1952*. Paris: Eds du Seuil, 1952.

Divine, Robert A., *Roosevelt and World War II*. Baltimore, Md.: Johns Hopkins University Press, 1969.

Donnison, F. S. W., *British Military Administration in the Far East, 1943–1946*. London: HMSO, 1956.

Drachman, Edward R., *United States Policy toward Vietnam, 1940–1945*. Cranbury, NJ: Associated University Pres, 1970.

Duiker, William J., "Building the United Front: The Rise of Communism in Vietnam" in J. J. Zasloff and M. Brown (eds), *Communism in Indochina*. Lexington, Mass.: Lexington Books, 1975.

_____, *The Rise of Nationalism in Vietnam, 1900–1941*. Ithaca, NY: Cornell University Press, 1976.

Duncanson, Dennis J., *Government and Revolution in Vietnam*. Oxford University Press, 1968.

Elsbree, Willard H., *Japan's Role in Southeast Asian Nationalist Movements, 1940 to 1945*. New York: Russell & Russell, 1970.

Fairburn, Geoffrey, *Revolutionary Guerilla Warfare*. Harmondsworth: Penguin Books, 1974.

_____, *Revolutionary Warfare and Communist Strategy: The Threat to South-East Asia*. London: Faber & Faber, 1968.

Fall, Bernard B., *Street Without Joy*. Harrisburg, Pa.: Stackpole Co., 1961.

_____, *The Two Vietnams*. New York: Praeger, 1967.

_____, *The Viet-Minh Regime*. New York: Institute of Pacific Relations, 1956.

_____ (ed.), *Ho Chi Minh on Revolution*. New York: Signet Books, 1968.

Fenn, Charles, *Ho Chi Minh*. London: Studio Vista, 1973.

Girling, J. L. S., *People's War*. London: George Allen & Unwin, 1969.

Greene, Graham, *The Quiet American*. New York: Viking Press, 1956.

Grew, Joseph G., *Ten Years in Japan*. New York: Simon and Schuster, 1943.

Halberstam, David, *Ho*. New York: Random House, 1971.

Hall, D. G. E., *A History of South-East Asia*. New York: Macmillan, 1968.

Hammer, Ellen, *The Struggle for Indochina, 1940-1955*. Stanford University Press, 1955.

*Histoire et Epopée des Troupes Coloniales*. Paris: Les Presses Modernes, 1956.

Hoang Van Chi, *From Colonialism to Communism*. London: Pall Mall Press, 1964.

Honey, P. J., *Communism in North Vietnam*. Cambridge, Mass.: MIT Press, 1963.

_____, *Genesis of a Tragedy: The Historical Background to the Vietnam War*. London: Benn, 1968.

_____, *North Vietnam Today*. New York: Praeger, 1962.

Ike, Nobutaka (transl./ed.), *Japan's Decision for War*. Stanford University Press, 1967.

Irving, R. E. M., *The First Indochina War*. London: Croom-Helm, 1975.

Isaacs, Harold, *No Peace for Asia*. New York: Macmillan, 1947.

Johnson, Chalmers, *An Instance of Treason: Ozaki Hatsumi and the Sorge Spy Ring*. Stanford University Press, 1970.

_____, *Peasant Nationalism and Communist Power*. Stanford University Press, 1970.

Jones, F. C., *Japan's New Order in East Asia: Its Rise and Fall, 1937-1945*. London: Oxford University Press, 1954.

Jumper, Roy, *Bibliography on the Political and Adminstrative History of Vietnam*. Michigan State University Vietnam Advisory Group (n.d.).

Kirby, S. Woodburn, *et al. The War Against Japan*, vol. 5. London: HMSO, 1969.

Lacouture, Jean, *Ho Chi Minh* (transl. Peter Wiles). Harmondsworth: Penguin Books, 1968.

Lancaster, Donald, *The Emancipation of French Indochina*. Oxford University Press, 1961.

Langlois, Walter G., *André Malraux: the Indochina Adventure*. London: Pall Mall Press, 1966.

Lensen, G. A. and L. H. Kutakov, *Japanese Foreign Policy on the Eve of the Pacific War: A Soviet View*. Tallahassee, Fla.: Diplomatic Press, 1971.

Marr, David G., *Vietnamese Anticolonialism, 1885-1925*. Berkeley: University of California Press, 1971.

McAleavy, Henry, *Black Flags in Vietnam*. London: George Allen & Unwin, 1968.

McAlister, John T., Jr., *Vietnam: The Origins of Revolution*. New York: Knopf, 1969.

McLane, Charles B., *Soviet Strategies in Southeast Asia*. Princeton University Press, 1966.

Mullaly, B. R., *Bugle and Kukri: The Story of the 10th Princess Mary's Own Gurkha Rifles*. Edinburgh: Wm. Blackwood & Sons, 1957.

Nguyen Phut Tan, *A Modern History of Vietnam, 1802-1954*. Saigon: Khai-Tré, 1964.

Norman, C. B., *Tonkin, or France in the Far East*. London: Chapman and Hall, 1884.

O'Ballance, Edgar, *The Indo-China War (1945–1954)*. London: Faber & Faber, 1964.

Osborne, Edgar, *The French Presence in Cochinchina and Cambodia: Rule and Response, 1859–1905*. Ithaca, NY: Cornell University Press, 1969.

Pallat, Claude, *Dossier Secret de l'Indochine*. Paris: Presses de la Cité, 1964.

Patti, Archimedes, *Why Vietnam?* Berkeley: University of California Press, 1981.

Prasad, B. (ed.), *Official History of the Indian Armed Forces in the Second World War, 1939–1945: Post-War Occupation Forces, Japan and South East Asia*. Orient Longmans, 1958.

Rolph, Hammond, *Vietnamese Communism and the Protracted War*. American Bar Association, 1971.

Rosie, George, *The British in Vietnam*. London: Panther Books, 1970.

Sacks, Milton, "Marxism in Vietnam" in Frank N. Trager (ed.), *Marxism in Southeast Asia: A Study of Four Countries*. Stanford University Press, 1959.

Shaplen, Robert, *The Lost Revolution: Vietnam 1945–1965*. London: André Deutsch, 1966.

Smith, R. Harris, *OSS*, Berkeley: University of California Press, 1972.

Stevens, G. R., *History of the 2nd King Edward's Own Gurkhas*, vol. III: *1921–1948*. Aldershot: Gale & Polden, 1952.

Swearingen, Rodger, and Hammond Rolph, *Communism in Vietnam*. Chicago: American Bar Association, 1967.

Tarling, Nicholas, *Imperial Britain in South-East Asia*. Kuala Lumpur: Oxford University Press, 1975.

*The Times, Far East Crisis*. London: The Times Publishing Co., 1941.

Thompson, Virginia, *French Indo-China*. New York: Macmillan, 1942.

Trager, Frank N., *Why Vietnam?* New York: Praeger, 1966.

Tran Van Giau, *The South Viet Nam Liberation National Front*. Hanoi: FLPH, 1962.

Truong Chinh, *Forward along the Path charted by K. Marx*. Hanoi: FLPH, 1969.

Trotsky, Leon (ed. Naomi Allen and George Breitman), *Writings of Leon Trotsky (1939–40)*. New York: Pathfinder Press, 1969.

Turner, Robert F., *Vietnamese Communism: Its Origins and Development*. Stanford, Calif.: Hoover Institution Press, 1975.

Warbey, William, *Ho Chi Minh*. London: Merlin Press, 1972.

Wedemeyer, Albert C., *Wedemeyer Reports*, New York: Nevin-Adair, 1958.

Werth, Alexander, *De Gaulle*. Harmondsworth: Penguin Books, 1965.

Whitfield, Danny J., *Historical and Cultural Dictionary of Vietnam*. Metuchen, NJ: Scarecrow Press, 1976.

Woodward, Llewellyn, *British Foreign Policy in the Second World War*. London: HMSO, 1962.

Zasloff, J. J., and M. Brown (ed.), *Communism in Indochina*. Lexington, Mass.: D.C. Heath, 1975.

## Unpublished papers

Nguyen Duc Minh, "A Study of the Literature of Political Persuasion in North Vietnam". Unpubl. Ph.D. dissertation, School of Oriental and African Studies, University of London, 1973.

# INDEX

*Note.* Army and Air Force formations are listed according to the appropriate numeral — e.g. '14th Army' under 'F'.